Strategies of Deviance

THEORIES OF REPRESENTATION
AND DIFFERENCE
Teresa de Lauretis, *General Editor*

STRATEGIES OF DEVIANCE

Studies in Gay Male Representation

Earl Jackson, Jr.

Indiana University Press

Bloomington and Indianapolis

The paper used in this publication meets the minimum
requirements of American National Standard for Information
Sciences—Permanence of Paper for Printed
Library Materials, ANSI Z39.48-1984.

Manufactured in the United States of America

Library of Congress Cataloging-in-Publication Data

Jackson, Earl, date
Strategies of deviance : studies in gay male
representation / Earl Jackson.
p. cm.—(Theories of representation and difference)
Includes bibliographical references and index.
ISBN 0-253-33115-3 (cloth : alk. paper).—ISBN 0-253-20950-1
(pbk. : alk. paper)
1. Homosexuality, Male—Psychological aspects.
2. Homosexuality in literature. 3. Homosexuality in motion
pictures. 4. Gays—Identity. 5. Gay men—Psychology.
I. Title. II. Series.
HQ76.J3   1995
306.76'62—dc20
94-38370

1 2 3 4 5 00 99 98 97 96 95

To Bo Huston,
who should be here.

Contents

Acknowledgments

THERE HAVE BEEN two occasions when reading a book has literally changed my life. In 1972 I was expelled from high school as "a detriment to the morale of the school." In other words, I was unapologetically effeminate, very possibly "homosexual," and chose to skip school for weeks at a time to avoid the beatings and other abuse I regularly experienced at the hands of the students (often in the presence of "indulgent" teachers) because of my (sexual) differences. I took a part-time job cleaning a bakery at night, and continued to live in my parents' house in a lower-middle-class, inner-city neighborhood of Buffalo, New York. My biological family was a merger of two lunatic fringe Christian sects, Pentecostal and Seventh-Day Adventist. I was raised strictly observant of the latter, although I also had to attend "Sunday" services in deference to the former. My anger and frustration over my situation were expressed in a kind of vengeful glamour. In order to get through dinner, I would take mescaline or LSD, and descend from my bedroom into the kitchen in high drag: Liz Taylor–as–Cleopatra-inspired eye makeup, Eva Gabor wigs, stiletto heels, and ridiculously long cigarette holders. One afternoon in 1973, while getting ready to go to an Alice Cooper concert, I began reading Thomas Hardy's *Jude the Obscure*. Before I was finished with the first chapter I knew I had to focus all my energies into getting into college. That night I threw away the psychedelics, put away the Maybelline, and never looked back.

The second time a book changed my life was in the autumn of 1989, when, one afternoon, while taking a break from reorganizing the salvageable portions of my dissertation on Japanese Symbolist poetry, I opened Robert Glück's novel *Jack the Modernist*. Before I had finished the first chapter, I knew I had to write a book other than the one I was working on. I threw away my Association of Asian Studies membership renewal form, put away the dissertation, and never looked back. My entry into higher education proved a far more rewarding experience for me than that of the Hardy character who inspired it. How successful the book that Glück's novel inspired, however, awaits the determination of those who venture beyond these pages.

My research and writing have been supported by two grants from the University of California at Santa Cruz Faculty Senate, and by a Humanities Research Grant from the Dean of the Humanities Division, University of California, Santa Cruz, for which I am deeply grateful.

I would also like to thank the many people who have helped me in numerous ways to realize this project. In particular I thank:

• Kurt Gering, who appeared, appropriately enough, at the end of my last Minnesota winter. Our two-month romance was ephemeral—as ephemeral as the lightning whose flash not only illuminates the otherwise unimaginable fantasy landscape in which one lives, but etches an afterimage of that landscape so indelibly in the mind's eye that it can serve as a map long after the darkness has reclaimed the vision. The thrill of the passion Kurt reawakened in me still informs and sustains my political, intellectual, and emotional commitments—as well as my libidinal investments—in the sexually deviant countercultures and countercultural practices that constitute the focus of this book.

• Gilberto Martínez, whose love, endurance, support, humor, and courage made up much of the best of my life for so long. If I had been smart enough to confront and deal with the workaholism and obsessive-compulsiveness that contaminated my writing regimen for the present project before Gilberto was smart enough to give up, this book would have contained the following lines: "And finally, I wish to express my astonished joy and loving gratitude to Gilberto Martínez for his insistent love, his courage, his imagination, for what he taught me and teaches me, and for the daily privilege of our shared life together—for this and so much more this book is dedicated to him." On the dedication page it would read: "To Gilberto Martínez, in lieu of a cup of tea I promised him one March evening but never managed to brew."

• the writers whom I have met in doing the research for this book: Dodie Bellamy, Bruce Boone, Dennis Cooper, Samuel R. Delany, Robert Glück, and Kevin Killian. They have been unbelievably magnanimous with their time, their archives, and their interest in my speculations. Their candor, their bibliographic generosity, and their conversations about their own work—and each other's— have added depth and richness to the present work that I could never have approximated on my own in the library.

• Teresa de Lauretis and David M. Halperin, without whose work this book would have been literally inconceivable. Words cannot convey my indebtedness to them for the invaluable intellectual and editorial advice and support they have given me on innumerable occasions.

• the friends and colleagues who gave me critical comments on drafts of the chapters, or who arranged for me to present various portions of the book at conferences or other public fora—in particular, Harry Berger, Todd Baker, Julie H. Brower, William Burgwinkle, Judith Butler, Sue-Ellen Case, Kate Davy, Carolyn Dinshaw, Mark Driscoll, Michael Edwards, Carla Freccero, Marcella Greening, Travis Hamilton, Andrew Hewitt, Adam Klein, Liz Kotz, Judith Mayne, Susan McClary, Stephen D. Miller, Masao Miyoshi, Stephen Orgel, Joseph Parker, B. Ruby Rich, Danny Scheie, Juliana Schiesari, Daniel L. Selden, John Solt, Steve Snyder, Nancy Stoller, Jim Swan, Alex R. Textor, Gary

Thomas, Becky W. Thompson, Sangeeta Tyagi, Michael Warren, Alan Wolfe, and Magdalena Zschokke.

• my wonderful undergraduates at UCSC, whose intelligence, sense of adventure, and kindness have supported me throughout my writing this book and in all aspects of my professional life. Among those who directly aided this project are John Beacham, Jeanne Buffa, Damian Chadwick, Camilla Fojas, Daniel Getzoff, Lisa Guderjohn, Stacey Hamilton, Andy Hasse, Tamara Ja, Ryan Kaufman, Christopher Kelty, Min Kim, Sarah Manuel, Tristan Nathe, N. Bonnie Reese, James Robbins, Sandra Schwitzgebel, Lara Weitzman, Benjamin G. White, and Hillary Wilson.

• my extended family of choice: Eleanora Muntañola Thornburg, Trinidad Castro, Lourdes Martínez Echazabal, Sean McGuinness, David Jansen Mendoza, and my cats Jane, Gus, and Ron (and in loving memory, Ed).

• Steven Johnstone, who, after reading the first chapter of this book, asked me where love was in my theory, then proceeded to show me.

• Kenyon Brown for being a magician whose tricks don't include a vanishing act.

• Jaye Miller, one of my most valued colleagues at UCSC, whose loss is still deeply felt, but whose love, courage, and dancer's *chutzpah* continue to be a source of strength and inspiration for those of us fortunate enough to have known him.

• Gary Reynolds, the first student I have known to die of AIDS—a consummate activist, he would have hated this book (I can hear him saying, "Just say what you mean—we don't have time for this!"—and he may be right). He was loud, creative, committed, arrogant, annoying, surly, aggressive, beautiful, insightful, honest, offensive, loving, kooky, and absolutely fabulous.

• Bo Huston, who made me promise not to include his work in this book so that he could review it. I kept my promise, but unfortunately before I could finish the book, Bo finished everything he needed to do, and brought closure to his life with the clarity, honesty, and integrity with which he lived it. Although I do not write about it here, I recommend all of Bo's work—in particular his novel *The Dream Life*, and his final collection, *The Listener*—as some of the most important and miraculous writing of the late twentieth-century U.S.

• my Santa Cruz queer connections: Peter Brown, Wendy Chapkis, Bruce Lee, Gabriel Morte, Jim Schwenterley, Wilton Woods, and the Bulkhead Gallery.

• Pedro Almodóvar and his staff at El Deseo, Inc., for generously granting permission to use the image from *Law of Desire* for the cover photograph.

• Dave Kirk, Media and Reference, McHenry Library U. C. Santa Cruz, who was invaluable in locating copies of the pornographic films necessary for the development of my fundamental argument in chapter 4.

- Laura McClanathan, interlibrary loan, McHenry Library, U. C. Santa Cruz.
- the wonderful administrative staff of Kresge College, Betsy Wooten, Susan Nishiyama, and Barbara Lee.
- Jane Lyle, my copy editor at Indiana University Press, not only for her unerring precision, but also for her patience, humor, and sheer fortitude above and beyond the call of duty.
- Joan Catapano, Senior Sponsoring Editor, Indiana University Press, for her imaginative and empowering enthusiasm for this project from its formative stages to its culmination.
- the men of the sexual undergrounds of Tokyo, Boston, Minneapolis, New Orleans, Barcelona, Amsterdam, and especially San Francisco. And among these sodomitical brotherhoods: Thomas Avena; Michael Blue and Club Uranus; Kenyon Brown; Newton Butler; Paul Cameli; Danny at Image Leather; Vic St. Blaize, founding editor of *Whorezine*; the staff at Eros; the Fourteenth Street Tuesday Sex Potluck; Vince Fusco and Dave McDonald; Gay Male Nudists of California; David Groode; the boys at the Hancock Street House; Steve Johnstone; Matthew Kennedy; Andrew Martínez; Jerry Montana; William Roehl; the Solstice Sex Party; Richard Stearns.

A small portion of chapter 1 and an earlier version of a portion of chapter 5 appeared as "Scandalous Subjects: Robert Glück's Embodied Narratives," *differences* 3.2, in *Queer Theory: Lesbian and Gay Sexualities*, ed. Teresa de Lauretis (1991), pp. 112–134.

An earlier version of the portion of chapter 5 on Dennis Cooper appeared as "Death Drives across Pornotopia: Dennis Cooper on the Extremities of Being," *GLQ* 1.2 (1994): 143–161.

An earlier version of the section of chapter 4 on the films of Pedro Almodóvar appeared as "Graphic Specularity: Pornography, Almodóvar and the Gay Male Subject of Cinema," in *Transformations/Translations: Gender and Sexuality in Film and Literature*, ed. Cecelia Moore and Valerie Wayne (Honolulu: University of Hawaii Press, 1992), pp. 63–81.

I

Calling the Questions
Gay Male Subjectivity, Representation, and Agency

Specula ab omni parte opponerentur, ut ipse flagitiorum suorum spectator esset
et . . . secreta . . . non in os tantum sed in oculos suos ingereret.

—Seneca

Terms, Orientations, Agendas

IN MY READINGS of literary, paraliterary, and cinematic texts I am primarily concerned with the ways in which gay men assume representational agency to articulate deliberately "deviant" or contestatory subjectivities. I offer these essays, however, neither as a genealogy of a monolithic "gay male subject," nor as an archeological recovery of a "gay self" heretofore occluded within heterosexist intellectual history. Drawing upon several material analyses of culture, including linguistics, semiotics, Marxism, feminist theory, and psychoanalysis, I assume the subject to be not an origin but rather an effect of signification.[1] Although this subject is socially constructed and discursively realized, agency is nevertheless possible because neither the mechanisms of its constructions nor its discursive formations ever totalize or even fully stabilize the subject. It is within, among, and out of their indeterminacies, overdeterminations, contradictions, and signifying excesses and insufficiencies that agency emerges. I base the theoretical feasibility and political necessity of advancing the notion of "gay male subjects" and "gay male subjectivity" in large part upon a redefinition of "sexual difference" that includes but extends beyond sexual dimorphism. Because the terms of my definition—sex, gender, and sexuality—receive their standard meanings from, and circulate within, heteropatriarchy, my reschematizations of their relations within alternative sexual identities will necessarily develop out of a sustained critique of normative heterosexuality.

I conceive of "gay male subjectivity" as a range of subject positions dynamically constituted by irreducible contradictions between hegemonically val-

orized gender identity and a marginalized sexuality (both of which are further
determined by racial and class formations). White gay men, especially, have had
a purchase on power unique to otherwise disenfranchised individuals.[2] Male
homosexuality, moreover, is not simply condemned by the dominant order, but
rather sublimated within the latter's own ambivalent mythographies of phallic
primacy. A truly subversive gay representational practice therefore must contest
not only the gay subject's experience of heterosexist persecution, but also his
experience of patriarchal privilege. It is in this dual antagonism that I locate a
shared oppositional commitment between many of the texts I read and the
critical apparatus through which I read them. In other words, I assume that
certain gay male cultural practices that transvalue deviance as a positive mode
of self-identification contain at least an implicit critique of the normative male
ideal (and the dominant heterosexual sex/gender system) from which the gay
male deviates. I will amplify these associations in my textual analyses, but I will
also incorporate these readings into a larger theoretical argument that I advance
as a deviant cultural intervention in its own right. Unlike its sociological predecessors, this critical discourse scruples to attain and even exacerbate the "deviance" of the objects of its investigation.

The trajectories of observation and participation in my deviant critical
strategies are most clearly discernible in the ways I deploy psychoanalysis: (1) I
use psychoanalysis as a diagnostic tool for a critical understanding of sexuality
and subjectivity; (2) I read psychoanalysis (its histories, internal logics, alle-
giances) as symptomatic of the phallocentric psychosocial structures it describes; (3) I enter into ironic or reappropriative dialogues with psychoanalytic
accounts of sexual difference and perversion.

Both diagnostic and symptomatological readings of the "master narrative"
of the Oedipus complex and the "universality" of castration anxiety are fundamental to distinguishing and disengaging gay male sexuality from the
monosexuality of phallocentric patriarchy. Even the latter symptomatological
readings of psychoanalysis, however, do not necessarily discredit the accuracy
of the statements, but often indict the social situations that make those statements accurate. My expositions of the Oedipus and castration anxiety in turn
will ground my reappropriative dialogues with Freud's "On Narcissism" and
other texts through which I develop opposing typologies of dominant heterosexual male and gay male subject formations.

I feel justified in recuperating psychoanalytic conceptions of "homosexuality" for a radical theory of gay male subjectivity, because gay male identity
has always had organic relations with the dominant modes of its delegitimization, as Michel Foucault's "reverse discourse" so concisely formulated it. Foucault's "reverse discourse" names a dynamic operation in the incipient consolidation of a "homosexual" subcultural identity, effected by appropriating the
vocabulary of the pathologizing and criminalizing discourses of the late nine-

teenth century, whereby "homosexuality began to speak in its own behalf, to demand that its legitimacy or 'naturality' be acknowledged, often in the same vocabulary, using the same categories by which it was medically disqualified" (Foucault, *History* I: 101). Moreover, since any sign or "identity" (itself a sign) is always conditioned by its meanings for the dominant order as much as by the innovative meanings held by dissenting minorities, gay male sexualities and their representations are typically self-contesting negotiations of oppressive and subversive, hegemonic and heterodox mythemes of the psychosexual and sociosexual possibilities of a gay male subject.

To foreground the political connections that inform gay male subject positions, I begin with a linear synopsis of emblematic moments of the assimilation of male homoerotic desire to dominant phallocentric ideologies, paying particular attention to how these reified associations figure within feminist critiques of patriarchies. I intervene in this history by introducing into its analysis my model of sexual difference, and through this model, characterize a gay male as a "sexually differenced subject" by virtue of several aspects derived from his interiority/exteriority to the dominant sex/gender system that distinguish him from the heterosexual male subject produced and valorized by that system. From there, I turn to the relations of representation to the marginal subject-in-process, and the shifting political valences of representational practices as they traverse heterogeneous discursive fields. Finally, I outline the imbrications of subjectivity, representation, and agency informing both the strategies and texts featured in the subsequent chapters as well as my examinations of them that constitute this book.

Male Homoeroticism and the Phallocratic Norm

Assimilation through Representation

The sexual activity between men sanctioned in classical Greece reflected the male dominance of the society, both in practice and in principle, the former in the hierarchization of partners into active and submissive, and the latter in the Platonic distinctions of heavenly (masculine) and earthly (female-directed) eros. After the rediscovery of antiquity in the Renaissance, scholars neutralized the overt expressions of male same-sex lust by interpreting them as metaphors for the spiritual communion possible only among men, envisioning women as irreducibly corporeal beings whose passions were exhausted in physical gratification, and bound to the animality of reproduction. This rationalization was aided by the first translator of Plato's dialogues, Marsilio Ficino (1433–1499), who developed the idea of "Platonic love" as an exclusively male desire transcending the tangible (female) world. Ficino's work became central to a revival of Neo-Platonism,[3] a principal theme in Renaissance thought that also informed the "masculine" and "feminine" polarizations of mind and matter in the rhetoric of Baconian science.[4]

The Neo-Platonic disavowal of "literal" homosexual desire, therefore, depended upon an axiomatic denigration of women. Although developed in response to the texts of antiquity, this hermeneutic was readily adapted to contemporary texts as well. The poet's desire for the male addressee of Shakespeare's *Sonnets* becomes nonsexual, "Platonic" (note the irony in this adjective's semantic fate) through this disciplined reading:

> A reader accustomed to the conventions of Renaissance poetry . . . can stress
> the coarse and fleshly sexuality of the poet's relation to the lady, and then
> contrast this with the thematically ideal, ascetic eroticism of the poet's rela-
> tion to the man. . . . Thus . . . the two subsequences [refer to] . . . the Neo-
> Platonic tradition of the double Venus, with the young man taken to be the
> image of spiritual and intellectual desire as opposed to the dark lady's em-
> bodiment of the material corporality of lust. (Fineman 57)

The desexualization of male eros, formalized in Neo-Platonism, enabled the ruling class to canonize the classics without compromising the proscriptions against "sodomy," but it also allowed clandestine expressions of less metaphysically motivated desire among men, as evidenced in the careers of Leonardo da Vinci and Michele Caravaggio, not to mention the poetry of Michelangelo. The euphemisms of moralistic classicists and the masquerades of the sodomites merge in a tacitly symbiotic tradition of nonrecognition of male homoeroticism; the classicists deny what they see, and the sodomites hide within those appearances that the cultural guardians had divested of referential liability.[5]

This tradition took on various forms in each period of European history. In the eighteenth century, Johannes Winckelmann invested his libidinal energies into the male nudes of Greek statuary, but he was so skillful in his public sublimation of his cathexis that his work essentially founded German neoclassicism and defined German Hellenic archeology for years to come.[6] In the nineteenth century, the British cult of Greece was fostered by emergent "homosexuals" who followed in this tradition. Walter Pater's studies of Greek athletes and Greek conceptions of beauty are erotic celebrations of the male body couched in the rhetoric of Winckelmannian passionate observation and Ficinian transcendence. His essays on Winckelmann, Michelangelo, and Leonardo were part of a tradition of encoded meditations on male homoerotic desire that maintained a "deniability" regarding their referent. Pater's double messages intimated an *empathetic* knowledge of and a retrospective, covert assertion of the physical consummation of same-sex desire that motivated his predecessors.[7] These strategies were extended by J. A. Symonds and Oscar Wilde, among others. Of course, such practices often reinforced the unholy alliance between male homoeroticism and misogyny, a conflation that took on new forms after the creation of the "homosexual" as a medical category at the turn of the century.

Since its conceptual origins, male homosexuality has been elaborated within the internal contradictions of male heterosexuality and the anxieties over sexual difference thematized in dominant constructions of the latter. In Freud's histories of the male sexual subject, it is often difficult to distinguish the heterosexual male from the homosexual: at times the traumatic discovery of the woman's "lack" of a penis is fundamental to the psychosexual constitution of the *heterosexual* male ("Some Psychical Consequences" 251–53); at other times, the same discovery is given as a leading cause for male *homosexuality* ("Some Neurotic Mechanisms" 224–26).

Fetishism, which Freud considered an exclusively male perversion, is a defensive reaction to the discovery of sexual difference, a "split belief" which allows the male subject to recognize the woman's "castration" and yet retain a fantasy of the existence of her penis ("Loss of Reality" 184; "Splitting of the Ego" 273). In every case of fetishism Freud encountered, analysis revealed the fetish to be "a penis-substitute . . . not . . . for any chance penis, but for a particular quite special penis . . . the woman's (mother's) phallus which the little boy once believed in and does not wish to forgo" ("Fetishism" 149–50). The fetish restores the mother's penis in the boy's fantasies, enabling him to disavow the threat sexual difference becomes (in phallocratic frameworks) at this stage in the boy's development. The fetish "also saves the fetishist from being a homosexual by endowing women with the attribute which makes them acceptable as sexual objects" (ibid. 151). Nevertheless, Freud still manages to diagnose male homosexuality as an excessive esteem for the "male organ" (Freud, "Analysis of a Phobia" 109–110).

Freud uses the Medusa symbol as an economic illustration of the horror experienced by heterosexual men at the sight of female genitalia, but he attributes the "insight" figured in this mythic emblem to the Greeks' "strongly homosexual" nature, stating that it "was inevitable that we should find among them a representation of woman as a being who frightens and repels because she is castrated" ("Medusa's Head" 273). Even if, for the sake of the argument, we were to accept the classification of homoerotic practices in ancient Greece as "homosexual" (a category that would have been unintelligible to them), it is puzzling that Freud would use a symbol of a sexually anomalous population to image the dynamics involved in the construction of "normal" male identity and "normal" male antagonistic insecurities in relation to those people (women) who are alleged to be the "mature" object of sexual desire. In previous centuries the sodomite slipped behind the facades of neoclassical "masculinity"; now the heterosexual male conceals the intensity of his gynophobia and his constitutional intolerance of sexual difference within the ideal homosexual male he conjures.

Male homosexuality continues to prove useful in contemporary heterosexual identity politics too. Claiming to have been inspired by feminist critical speculation on *écriture feminine*, Peter Schwenger attempted to extract a corresponding "masculine mode" from modern male texts. Contrary to his initial assertion that the "maleness of experience" requires "an infusion of a particular sense of the body into the attitudes and encounters of a life" (Schwenger 102)—which would imply both specificities and heterogeneities in texts and subjectivities irreducible to generalization—Schwenger often speaks for all men in his personal responses to the texts he examines. Schwenger considers Federico, the protagonist of Alberto Moravia's *Io et Lui*, exemplary of every man's relation to his genitalia, because of Federico's habit of talking to his penis, and referring to it constantly as "him." Schwenger explains:

> The penis has a quality of independence from the body; it has movements and moods, it sulks, it overbears, it overpowers. So it seems natural to find Federico having conversations and arguments with "him." . . . It seems the literary version of a normal psychological experience. It is then a shock and a challenge for the reader to find, halfway through the novel, that the narrator, with whom the reader has been identifying, is not normal. . . . Federico admits to a psychologist friend that he literally does hear a voice from his penis . . . [but] Federico resents [his own] admission . . . and ultimately ignores it. Curiously enough, the reader ignores it too and continues to identify with the narrator as before. Only an undercurrent of strangeness remains as implied comment on the normal male's relationship to his male organ. (107)

Schwenger's argument comprehends at least three counterempirical assumptions: (1) all readers are male; (2) all men read in the same way; (3) all men have the same bodily self-conceptions. The "reader" of Moravia's novel fulfills his sexed position by recognizing in Moravia's hero his own animistic fascination with his penis, the "naturalness" of which is paradoxically affirmed by a text that in fact questions that "naturalness." Schwenger's and his reader's beliefs are phantasmatically insulated from both extratextual reality and the implications of Schwenger's own arguments (not to mention the "feminist criticism" which he purports to be "applying"), at the moment in the novel when both Federico and Schwenger's compliant reader are confronted with the truth but choose to ignore it. This disavowal allows "the male reader" to maintain a symbiotic relation between "self" and "penis" while denying the fragmentation and contingencies of the identity so constituted. The penis becomes its own fetish, and a totemic point of identification requiring absolute denial of difference within and among men (not to mention the complete exclusion of women from consideration).

Schwenger's enthusiastic readings of male homosexual texts further collapse the differences among men and the specificities of sexuality that ostensibly inform the inquiry. In his admiration of Mishima Yukio, the ease with which Schwenger "identifies" with the "homosexual sensibility" as he perceives it (reminiscent of Freud's empathetic elucidation of the "Greek male homosexuals' " horror of female genitalia) underscores the need in gay male theory for rigorously rethinking sexual difference: "As a male who is himself fascinated and attracted by the nature of masculinity, the homosexual is fully capable of insight into that masculine nature. He may tend to see men in isolation from women and to define men's sexuality exclusively in its own terms. But in that he is no different from heterosexual writers. . . . Masculinity becomes reflexive, both perceiver and perceived" (109).[8] Schwenger's conclusion that such forms of homosexual male writing represent the logical extreme of "the masculine mode" essentially echoes Marilyn Frye's contention that "gay men . . . are in significant ways . . . more loyal to masculinity and male-supremacy than other men" (Frye 132), but for Schwenger this is not an indictment but grateful praise, delivered in the context of an allegedly feminist-sympathetic investigation of an "enlightened masculinity." Schwenger tautologically assumes an empathetic understanding of the "male homosexual's" relation to masculinity, because of what he learned in speaking for "them."[9]

Conflicts with Feminism

Schwenger's reading of Moravia's novel is an idiosyncratic (and therefore more easily recognized) instance of a general conflation between the monosexuality of phallocentric discourse and male homosexuality per se. More pervasive (and therefore more difficult to isolate) instances of this conflation include the castration anxiety Freud claims to be a common experience for boys and girls ("Dissolution" 178–79), particularly at the stage of sexual maturation which he first called, in the *Three Essays*, the "genital" phase, but which he redesignated in 1923 the "phallic phase," arguing that "for both sexes in childhood only one kind of genital organ comes into account—the male. The primacy reached is, therefore, not a primacy of the genital, but of the phallus" ("Infantile Genital Organization" 142). Lacan extends this primacy, while denying its masculine bias, in naming the "phallus" the "privileged signifier" of desire, around which heterosexual relations are organized, according to each person's biomorphological relation to that signifier's anatomical icon. The woman, "lacking" the penis, strives to be the phallus, "the signifer of the desire of the Other," because "it is for what she is not that she expects to be desired as well as loved." The man pretends to "have" the phallus, so that the woman "finds the signifier of her own desire in the body of the one to whom she addresses her demand for love" (Lacan, "Meaning" 84).

It is against such a monosexuality that Luce Irigaray writes of the foreclosure of female sexuality from representation: "All Western discourse presents a certain isomorphism with the masculine sex; the privilege of unity, form of the self, of the visible, of the specularisable, or the erection. . . . Now this morphologic does not correspond to the female sex: there is not 'a' sex. The 'no sex' that has been assigned to the woman can mean that she does not have 'a' sex and that her sex is not visible nor identifiable or representable in a definite form" (Irigaray, "Women's Exile" 64).

Some of Irigaray's other rhetorical interventions are more difficult to endorse. She describes patriarchal societies as "homosexual monopolies" among men, and homosexuality their "organizing principle." Overt male homosexual relations are prohibited simply because "they openly interpret the law according to which society operates" (Irigaray, *This Sex* 180–81, 192–93). For Andrea Dworkin, gay male pornography is evidence that gay men share the hatred of women underlying heterosexual male pornography (*Pornography* 35–37). Marilyn Frye has characterized gay men as "more like ardent priests [of phallocratic culture] than infidels," and the gay rights movement as "the fundamentalism of the global religion that is Patriarchy" (Frye 133). Given the problematic interiority of male homosexuality to male heterosexuality, and the effortless elision of differences between the two accomplished by male heterosexual writers, it should not be surprising that feminist theorists have at times further naturalized the associations. This tendency needs to be examined dialogically (not defensively), preliminary to any resituating of gay male cultural and sexual politics. While Irigaray and Frye have very valid points about dominant masculinity and sexual terrorism, these metaphoric identifications ultimately harm their argument by foreclosing from discussion some of the complex psychosocial dynamics of the very issues they seek to address. The "alliance" between gay men and heterosexual men figured in these texts is, first of all, counterempirical, given the tendency of this type of heterosexual man to harass, assault, and even kill gay men for being gay. Secondly, this rhetorical strategy not only elides the murderous rage the dominant heterosexual male expresses toward the gay male, but it obscures the intimate relation between this rage and a profound contempt for women.[10]

Marilyn Frye's essay requires a more nuanced engagement and response than similar passages in Irigaray, as Frye's theses stem from and are addressed to a specific moment in gay and lesbian political history in the late 1970s in the United States. Furthermore, Frye's criticism of "gay politics" contains neither the metaphoric ethereality of Irigaray nor the dogmatism of Dworkin.[11] Since Frye wrote the essay, the politics and the configurations of alliances between lesbians and gay men have also changed dramatically, partially as a result of internal divisions in feminist communities over sexuality and heterosexism, and because of the new coalitions among lesbians and gay men in response to the AIDS crisis.[12] While it is hoped that many of the political circumstances which had originally prompted Frye's essay have improved, Frye's analysis incisively abstracts certain patterns within dominant masculine identity paradigms that remain valuable in formulating the critical differences of deviant countercultures from the social inscriptions of power-based sexual hierarchies as gendered destinies (gender fate-alities)—in other words, heterosexuality itself.

Frye begins by enumerating six principles and values she perceives as common to "male supremacist society" and "gay male culture," three of which I will discuss below: "the presumption of male citizenship"; "the worship of the penis"; and "the presumption of general phallic access" (Frye 130). The first two are intrinsically related, first of all since the presence of the penis is what gives both gay and straight men their social status and privileges. Gay sexual desire obviously can be conflated with the socially installed overestimation of the penis-as-phallus. Heterosexual writers such as Peter Schwenger only aid in reifying such conflations.[13] Frye uses the third principle, "the presumption of general phallic access," to criticize gay male claims to sexual rights, identifying these claims with the heterosexual male's vouchsafed right to "fuck": "Men in general in this culture . . . in virtue of their genital maleness . . . have a right [of] access to whatever they want. . . . The translation of this cosmic male arrogance to the level of the individual male body is the individual's presumption of the almost universal right to fuck—to assert his individual male dominance over all that is not himself by using it for his phallic gratification or self-assertion at either a physical or a symbolic level" (141–42).

The parallels Frye draws between the heterosexual and the gay male in her analysis of "general phallic access" rest on an assumption that the "right" that gay men are demanding is the right of "ass-fucking"—in other words, she assumes that the point of real connection is a universalized demand and central perspective of gay male sexuality in terms of the "active" or "penetrative" partner of "fucking" (142–43). As such, her argument does not address those activists who fight for the right to "be fucked"—or for those without such specifically dichotomized sexual agendas in their civil rights struggles. Since the existence of those who fight for "ass-fucking" rights logically implies the existence of willing partners on the other end, Frye's exclusive focus on the "ass-fucking" activists connotes two subtextual assumptions that need to be excavated and examined: (1) these two desires occur in mutually exclusive categories of individuals (which recontains gay sexuality within heterosexual gender categories); (2) the desire to "be fucked" either precludes a political agency or is in itself theoretically unintelligible within the parameters of the analysis (which also recontains Frye's critique of male heterosexuality within the phallic values she contests).[14]

Such an insistently phallic conception of sexuality harks back to Hellenic norms. In both Frye's essay and "official" pronouncements of sexual propriety in classical Greek texts, "sex" is defined exclusively in terms of the penetrative partner; sexual activities other than penetrative intercourse are not considered. In ancient Greece, oral sexuality, for instance, was considered "unspeakable" and something to be avoided (Winkler 38; 223 n. 20)—perhaps because such practices do not admit clear distinctions between the "active" and "passive" roles. Sexual relations among males in Athens were condoned if they involved an adult male citizen as the insertive partner, and as a receptive partner, a young man who had not yet come of age, a male slave, or a foreigner. The sexual roles could not be reversed, and no reciprocal desire from the passive partner was expected or necessary—these arrangements were structurally identical to the sexual relations the same Athenian citizen would maintain with women. David M. Halperin concludes that "sex in classical Athens" is both "polarizing" and "hierarchical"—polarizing in its division "of participants into . . . radically opposed categories" based on "the penetration of the body of one person by the . . . phallus of another," and hierarchical in its construal of the "insertive partner . . . as a sexual agent" and the "receptive partner . . . as a sexual patient," the two positions identified as domination and submission, reflective of the superior social status of the citizen "sexual agent" to the "proper targets": "women, boys, foreigners, and slaves" (Halperin 30).

The sexual ethos of the Athenian citizen bears a strong resemblance to Frye's depiction of contemporary conceptions of "male heterosexuals," in particular when she denies that the sex of the "passive" partner will affect the social identity of the "active": "When a man who considers himself firmly heterosexual fucks a boy or another man, generally he considers the other to be a woman or to be made a woman by this act" (Frye 134). While this is true in many cultures—including Mediterreanean, some Latin American, and certain Chicano/Latino communities—Euro-American homophobia among men is still more pervasive a controlling principle than that.[15] While I concur with Frye's description of male heterosexuality and the degradation of the person "fucked" being associated with becoming a "woman," I question the easy parallel between heterosexual intercourse and gay male intercourse, the emotional and political equivalence in terms of the presumed nonreversibility of the positions, and the superior status attributed to the penetrator. Just as we should point out that Halperin's essay demonstrates that the Greeks were not "homosexuals," we also need to challenge the implication in Frye's essay that homosexuals are "Greeks."

Halperin's and Frye's portrayals share two other salient features: each describes a sexual system in which phallic dominance delimits the social identity of its subjects, a power disequilibrium crucially enacted in the practice of unilateral penetration; neither describes a system that includes or could accommodate a reciprocal or mobile sexuality, and as such neither description forms a basis for theorizing a non-phallocentrically determined male homosexual desire.[16] The crucial difference between Halperin's and Frye's essays is that Halperin's study is clearly not describing contemporary gay male sexuality, nor does Halperin link his exposition of the ancient Greek case with contemporary situations. This comparison of Frye's and Halperin's essays makes it clear that the real structural parallels in male sexual politics are *not* between classical Greece and modern *male homosexuality*, but between classical Greece and modern *male-dominant heterosexuality*. The "indifference" to the sex of the passive partner in Frye's essay could come about either through an imposition of the Greek sexual system onto contemporary male-male sexual practices, or through an imposition of the current patriarchal heterosexual sexual system onto contemporary male-male sexual practices. The latter simply requires one further step: the rigid associations of biological sex and sociosexual (non)options for women in compulsory heterosexuality must first be metonymized into a law of sexual dynamics, and then imposed on gay male sexuality. In other words, it is the heterosexual model that legislates the "indifference" to the sex of the other—because the other is always (functionally) female, and, quite contrarily, the heterosexual mythos recognizes only "one [male] sex" and "one practice and representation of the sexual" (Irigaray, *This Sex* 86). Elsewhere Irigaray terms this "hommo-sexuality" (*Speculum* 28). Teresa de Lauretis distinguishes "homosexuality," which designates "lesbian (or gay) sexuality," and "hommosexuality, which is the term of sexual indifference, the term (in fact) of heterosexuality" (de Lauretis, "Sexual Indifference" 18).

However accurate Frye's analysis of male heterosexuality and even the gay male politics of the time she wrote the essay (both seem quite accurate, in fact), her presentation allows the historical contingency of these unconscious hetero/homo alliances to be hypostatized into an atemporal, structural inevitability. Where this is particularly evident is in her equation of the male recipient partner in anal intercourse with the woman in heterosexuality, and the exclusion of the former in her analysis of the gay rights struggle. Frye's equation of heterosexual and homosexual "fucking," however, is not singular. While not explicitly drawing these conclusions, Catherine MacKinnon certainly frames male sexuality within one invariant power dynamic when she writes: "If heterosexuality is the dominant gendered form of sexuality in a society where gender oppresses women through sex, sexuality and heterosexuality are essentially the same thing. This does not erase homosexuality, it merely means that sexuality in that form may be no less gendered" (60). MacKinnon's *inclusion* of gender as the invariant meaning of sexual relations here effectively results in the same picture of gay male intercourse as Frye's *exclusion* of the biological sex of the recipient partner as a meaningful variable in the structure: a "feminine" position constituted by a static passivity and an inevitable victimization, transferred from a heterosexual paradigm that is contested politically but whose epistemological pertinence is never questioned. I am not suggesting that there are not many gay men who have enjoyed, continue to enjoy, and even actively participate in this collusion between homosexuality and patriarchal values. What I do contest is the belief that such connections are structurally innate, inevitable, or "natural"; such beliefs can only support sexist and heterosexist norms.[17]

Sexual Difference as Discursive Production

The Heterosexual Sex/Gender System

Frye's and MacKinnon's depictions of the politics of gay male sexuality assume a sexual (in)difference derived from an implicit heterosexual framework inappropriate for a radical consideration of alternative sexualities. The ideological paradigm to which both writers needlessly confine their inquiry thereby distributes the elements of individual identities asymmetrically across the categories of "sex" and "gender"; it also reifies a disequilibrium in the agendas motivating sexual relations. Monique Wittig has observed that there is only one recognized "gender," which is "the feminine, the 'masculine' not being a gender. For the masculine is not the masculine but the general" ("Point of View" 60). This reinforces the relegation of women to the physical and particular, and arrogates to men the exclusive use of "the abstract form" through which "men have appropriated the universal for themselves" (Wittig, "Mark" 66). Conversely, as evidenced in Freud's universal castration complex and Lacan's transcendental phallic signifier, there is only one sex. This asymmetry is sedimented and perpetuated in relations best described in Wittig's term the "heterosexual contract."

Drawing from her interviews with heterosexually identified men and women, and from her own heterosexual history, Wendy Holloway argues that within the heterosexual system, individuals attain socially coherent identity and gendered subjectivity by occupying gender-differentiated discursive positions in relation to sexuality (Holloway 236–37). The relative stability of these identities thus achieved depends upon the degree to which the effective complementarity of those positions can repress or otherwise contain their connections. For example, two of the discourse types Holloway extrapolates from her interviews are the "male sex drive discourse" and the "have/hold discourse." The "male sex drive discourse" is the "commonsense" belief that male sexual desire is a unidirectional biological aggression—or as one of her colleagues described it, an indiscriminate "need to fuck" (231). The "have/hold discourse" displaces the question of female sexuality onto the woman's primary investment in a "relationship with husband and children," at times construing "the sex act for women" as merely a means to obtain her true goals of motherhood and " 'family life' " (232–33).[18]

In preparing for the "have/hold" position, adolescent girls define their femininity in terms of being "attractive to boys," which precludes any sense of an autonomous sexuality, since part of this "attractiveness" often entails having sex with men in order to confirm and maintain a sense of that attractiveness (240–42). The heterosexual institutions that produce these subject positions enforce sexual practices that reproduce the imbalance in the assignations of "sex" and "gender" itself. That is to say, a man as a man is unmarked in terms of gender, but that unacknowledged gendered position is the basis of his "natural" position as a sexual subject (his sexual drives are without inflection and in any event beyond interrogation). Through sex he is simultaneously expressing his autonomous sexuality and denying his gender. Women, however, fulfill their gendered identity as feminine by responding to the man's sexual desire. Heterosexuality for women, therefore, suppresses their sexuality and totalizes their identity as gender.

Holloway's findings resonate with MacKinnon's reduction of "femininity" to a woman's status as object of male desire: "Socially . . . femininity . . . means sexual attractiveness [to men], which means sexual availability on male terms. . . . Gender socialization is the process through which women come to identify themselves as sexual beings, as beings that exist for men" (MacKinnon 530–31). Each of these texts, it seems to me, needs one more step to realize the radical implications of its observations. Holloway is consistently conscious of the heterosexual parameters of her models of gender production, yet she does not venture outside them, even after proving their insurmountable limitations.[19] MacKinnon's depiction of "femininity" is perfectly accurate within a universe of discourse that defines all sexuality as heterosexuality, but it is precisely that heterosexual presumption which installs and perpetuates this definition of female identity in the first place. Both texts, therefore, inadvertently hypostatize heterosexuality as the ultimate determinate limit: Holloway by indicting heterosexuality but situating counterstrategies within its constraints, MacKinnon by analyzing heterosexuality but universalizing its sociopathology as endemic to sexuality itself.

Gay Male Sexuality in Other Discursive Fields

It is obvious that definitions of gender, sexual practices, and sexual difference derived from heterosexual traditions are conceptually inadequate for deviant critical interventions in sexual politics. I begin my particular interventions by reinstating gender, sex, and sexuality as fundamental elements in the social constructions of *both* male and female subjects, however they may be differentially mystified in dominant heterosexual ideologies. By "sex" I simply mean the biological division of male and female; by "gender" I mean the representations of one's sex. These representations include appearance and behavior, but also status, privileges, and restrictions accorded to or imposed upon sexed individuals as part of their gendered identity. One's gendered visibility is further inflected by the relative adherence to or transgressions from the representational norms of the dominant social order.

"Sexuality" includes acts, fantasies, object-choice, and orientation. "Object-choice" denotes the sex of the person desired, and reflects both contingent and variable choices as well as fully defined sexual orientations. I distinguish between "object-choice" and "orientation" because "object-choice" does not always imply an "orientation," and because either a variable or consistent "object-choice" affects an individual's gender identity differently according to the system. I have already considered certain sexual discourses such as those in Classical Greece, in which the sex of his partner does not affect the "gender" of the exclusively penetrative male. The receptive partner, however, is either "feminized" or otherwise reduced to a "noncitizen" in the phallocracy, a "nonperson."[20] In these systems, therefore, the sex of the object-choice is unmarked but the role taken in the sexual act is marked. Within the deadly mythical mass known as the "general population" of the United States, however, any admission—or suspicion—at all of desire between men is often feared as something that will disqualify the individual from full social recognition as men in certain social situations.

My respecifications of sexual difference led me to amend part of Michel Foucault's depiction of the emergence of the "homosexual as a species." Foucault concludes that in the nineteenth century, "homosexuality appeared as one of the forms of sexuality when it was transposed from the practice of sodomy onto a kind of interior androgyny, a hermaphrodism of the soul" (*History* I, 43). Defining male homosexuality as "androgyny" or "hermaphrodism" collapses the distinctions between gender identification and object-choice, which actually reiterates sexual roles as inherently gendered according to heterosexual norms, foreclosing any radical analyses of the dominant sex/gender systems, and recontaining male homosexuality within phallic paradigms of dominance and submission. Unlike Foucault's "homosexual," gay men do not necessarily discard the conception of sodomy as an act when they accept it as a signature practice of their "species." This is not merely a restatement of the obvious fact that not all gay men "fuck," or a recognition of the "tops," "bottoms," and "versatiles" who populate the classifieds (although these options are also important to gay sexual subjectivities). By reinstating the distinction between act and orientation, I refer, rather, to the fluid, contingent, and context-dependent relations of gender identity and sexual practices, and assert that sexual practices (which include fantasies, abstinence, and political and social self-conceptions of one's sexuality) contribute *to* one's gendered subjectivity, rather than simply emerge naturally as transparent signs of an already extant and unitary gender identity.[21]

The relations among these elements contribute to the discrete and contingent signifying totalities that I call "discursive formations," partially derived from Foucault, but closer to the definition of "discourse" developed by Ernesto Laclau and Chantal Mouffe:[22]

> If I kick a spherical object in the street or if I kick a ball in a football match, the physical fact is the same, but its meaning is different. The object is a football only to the extent that it establishes a system of relations with other objects, and these relations are not given by the mere referential materiality of the objects, but are, rather, socially constructed. This systematic set of relations is what we call discourse. . . . It is the discourse which constitutes the subject position of the social agent. . . . The same system of rules that makes that spherical object into a football, makes me a player. ("Post-Marxism" 87)

This theory of discursive formations will prove invaluable to a more rigorous and nuanced analytic of sexuality than conceivable within the constraints of the normative heterosexual model. For example, let us consider the action "deliberately revealing one's penis to another's view" in each of the following discursive formations: (1) a flasher in a park at night, exposing himself at random to lone women; (2) a man posing for a *Playgirl* centerfold; (3) two gay men cruising each other at the baths, each removing his towel to entice the other. The first one is obviously an act of sexual violence. The second is more ambivalent: ostensibly it is a gesture toward "sexual equality" for middle-class white heterosexual women, based on an unexamined equation between male and female arousal or pleasure in looking. It also, however, implicitly questions the "masculinity" of the model, since submission to a desiring gaze is marked "feminine."[23] In the third, both men are simultaneously subject and object, at once asserting masculine privilege and violating its terms.

If we view sexual acts, their meanings, and their representations as three registers of a discursive field, we can also see how alternative discursive formations (such as gay male situations) transform the significations of bodies, body parts, and sexual practices. Guy Hocquenghem echoes Frye's assertion that the penis is the necessary condition of "citizenship," but he also lists the obligations that citizenship imposes: "If you are a boy, you will have relationships with girls. As for your anus, keep it strictly to yourself. Sexual identity is either the certainty of belonging to the master race or the fear of being excluded from it" (Hocquenghem 88). Irigaray discerns in anal eroticism a disavowal of sexual difference; she in fact blames the nonexistence of women in the phallocentric imaginary on an "anal economy" in which sexual difference has not yet emerged (Irigaray, *Ethics* 100–101; *Speculum* 73–75; Whitford, 164–67). Thus "anal erotism" reinforces Irigaray's conflation of phallocentric hom(m)osexuality with the practices and definitions of male homosexuality current in most American urban centers today (*This Sex* 171–71; 192–93). Hocquenghem also acknowledges that the anus is not sex-specific (Hocquenghem 89), but he does not thereby designate it as a site of blindness to sexual difference, but as an erogenous zone that could potentially demystify the penis: "The anus does not

enjoy the same ambivalence as the phallus, i.e. its duality as penis and Phallus.
. . . The desiring use of the anus is inversely proportional to social anality" (83).
The possibility (as threat) of male intercourse underscores how precarious phal-
lic identity actually is:

> Your phallus is constantly threatened: you are in constant danger of losing a
> phallus which was difficult to win in the first place. No one ever threatens to
> take away your anus. There is more of a threat in someone disclosing that
> you too have an anus, that it can be used. . . . [Such a] disclosure . . . chal-
> lenges [a man's] phallic existence. (89–90)

Furthermore, the very image of male-male anal intercourse can be subversive to the sexual identities as established through the heterosexual contract;
this also explains some of the obsessive anxiety about gay male sexuality that
runs through heterosexual male discourse. Lee Edelman argues eloquently that
the real trauma of the "sodomical scene"—the sight of male-male anal intercourse—lies in its potential for ruining the fixed positionality of sexual difference inaugurated and sustained by the castration complex. Edelman illustrates
his thesis with a scene from *Fanny Hill* in which the heroine, finding a peephole
in the wall in her room in an inn, watches two men in the next room fuck:
"His red-topt ivory toy, that stood perfectly stiff . . . shewed that if he was like
his mother behind, he was like his father before" (qtd. Edelman 105). The sentence could mean that the sodomite is like his father in front (penis) and has a
posterior like his mother, but it could also mean that his "behind" is like his
mother "in the front" (the vagina), which refutes the necessity of castration
associated with the "feminized position" in sexual intercourse, prominent in
Freud's interpretation of the Wolf Man's dream (Edelman 106). The *Fanny
Hill* episode suggests that the visibility of the sodomical scene can dispel the
binary logic implicit in castration anxiety.[24]

> Playing out the possibility of multiple, non-exclusive erotic identifications and
> positionings, the spectacle of sodomy would seem to confirm precisely those
> infantile sexual speculations that the male, coerced by the bogey of castration,
> is expected to have put behind him. It threatens . . . [to reveal] that the nar-
> cissistic compromise productive of male heterosexuality, the sacrifice of "ho-
> mosexual enthusiasm" to defend against the prospect of castration, might not
> have been necessary after all. . . . The sodomical spectacle . . . cannot fail to
> implicate the heterosexual male situated to observe it since it constitutes an
> affront to the primary narrative that orients his theory of sexuality. (Ibid. 107)

Hocquenghem and Edelman both write within discursive frameworks in
which male-male anal erotism does not reduplicate the phallic mastery of heterosexuality, nor does the investment in the anus elide sexual difference: rather,
the sexual act and the erotogenic zone liberate social subjects from the hege-

monically enforced consequences of phallocentrically defined sexual difference. The force of Hocquenghem's and Edelman's reevaluations of male sexuality comes from a lived awareness of how the ideological containment of sexual difference under patriarchy impinges upon gay male self-understanding and political agency.[25] Edelman's implied sodomitical therapy for the castration complex succeeds where certain psychoanalytic readings fail—in that he recognizes the reality within phallocratic society of the coercive function of castration anxiety to install rigid gender identities and behavioral taboos, but he rejects its inevitability as well as the gynophobia that is both one of its sources and its residue.[26] Edelman's explication of the internal connections within phallocentric male heterosexuality is informed with a rigorously maintained alienation from the overestimation of the penis and the male obsessions he scrutinizes. Hocquenghem's and Edelman's texts are highly sophisticated critical articulations of the split vision of gay men, one of the components of the model of a specifically gay male subjectivity I outline below.

The Gay Male as Sexually Differenced Subject

Any expression of gay male desire traverses antagonistic and mutually overdetermining configurations of the psychosocial constituents of a sexed identity that condition both the subject's self-representations and his relation to normative masculinity. To repeat Peter Schwenger's supposition with a difference: the male homosexual "may tend to see men in isolation from women and to define men's sexuality exclusively in its own terms. But in that he is no different from heterosexual writers." Here I want it both ways (the gay male is not and yet is very different from the heterosexual male in his definition of his sexuality). Gay men as men live dually within the systems of meaning of the dominant order and within their own constitutive transgressions and betrayals of that order. The gay male subject is an example of a "double articulation," which arises because

> the structure—the given conditions of existence, the structure of determinations in any situation, can . . . be understood . . . as simply the result of previous practices. Structure is what previously structured practices have produced as a result. These then constitute the "given conditions" the necessary starting point, for new generations of practice. In neither case should "practice" be treated as transparently intentional: we make history, but on the basis of anterior conditions which are not of our making. (Hall 95–96)

This double articulation in large degree accounts for the recuperation of male homoerotics by phallocentric social values. But it is also the basis for many of the counterdiscursive strategies I will examine in the following chapters. I will give particular attention to three aspects of gay male subjectivity I discern within the dynamic articulations of the gay male sexual and social subject from this "double articulation" as man and as sexual deviant: (1) an epistemology that transfigures the split belief of the fetishist into the split vision of the internal outlaw; (2) a sexual ontology that is a negating affirmation; (3) a pattern of ego-formative and -transformative desiring identifications constituting an intersubjective narcissism.

These three aspects of gay male subjectivity are empirically derived from my research, and are not meant as universally applicable abstractions, nor do they constitute an exhaustive description of a "gay male subject." I use them chiefly as a means of monitoring and focusing ways in which the contradictions of gay male social and sexual identities are rearticulated as paradigms for critical-creative practices.

Split Vision

Pausing in his survey of cultures in which gender-dysphoric and/or "homosexually" inclined males serve as shamans, priests, or wizards, E. A. Carpenter speculates on the underlying connections:

> Finding himself different from the great majority, sought after by some and despised by others, now an object of contumely and now an object of love and admiration, he would be forced to think. His mind turned inwards on himself would be forced to tackle the problem of his own nature, and afterwards the problem of the world and of outer nature. He would become one of the first thinkers, dreamers, discoverers. (Carpenter 274)

This passage reveals Carpenter's ethnographic fantasy to be a vehicle for the self-portrait of an inner exile from European culture. Carpenter's unannotated sexual identity was a fissure in his society's seamless normative intelligibility. From this fissure Carpenter interrogated the system that had naturalized his exclusion; his unauthorized understanding of the social order led him to develop other criteria for determining the meaningful and the moral.[27] Such a creative skepticism does not arise automatically (there is nothing inherently subversive in men's interest in men, in a male-dominant culture); it is the result of concerted introspection and critical observation, an epistemological askesis of a subject at once inside and outside the center of power.

A gay subjectivity at times manifests itself micropolitically as an insight into ordinary life from a split social identity. On a qualifying examination for a UCLA-Edinburgh student exchange program, Robert Glück was asked to "describe a male friend and describe a female friend." Reading between the lines, he described his friend Larry completely in terms of intellect and accomplishments, and his friend Jennifer chiefly in terms of appearance. He comments: "I deprived Larry of a body—he was just a brain almost in the science fiction sense . . . I had the skill to describe Larry's tapering fingers, cornflower eyes, convulsed laughter [but did not]. The writerly ability to skew these descriptions was bound up with the homosexual's sickening unwanted knowledge of the fiction of gender roles which lead to the knowledge of the difference between an honest fiction and a dishonest one" ("Marker" 20).

Negating Affirmation

The sexual politics of gay male desire exhibit two structural paradoxes. First of all, gay men differ from any other marginal group in that the internalization of the oppressor (the masculinist ideal) "is in part constitutive of male homosexual desire." Gay male desire inevitably "includes the potential for a loving identification with one's enemies" because "a sexual desire for men can't be merely a kind of culturally neutral attraction to a Platonic Idea of the male body; the object of that desire necessarily includes a socially determined and socially pervasive definition of what it means to be a man" (Bersani, "Rectum" 208–209). Secondly, the gay male derives his right to desire from the heterosexist sex/gender system described in Wittig's writings and Holloway's study. At least initially, therefore, the gay male's expression of his desire is not so much an abandonment of his gender identity, but an unanticipated exercise of the privilege that that identity affords him.

By articulating his desire as an elicitation of the desire of another authorized (i.e., male) desiring subject, the gay man becomes an object of desire, and thereby at once creates a dissonance between himself and the sex/gender system that had internalized him, and desecrates the male ideal he had internalized. Gay male desire, therefore, literalizes the sexuality of "sexual politics" when its "subversive potential" is realized "in the fact that in gay men's sexual identification with dominant masculinity, *they never cease to feel the appeal of its being violated*" (Bersani, "Rectum" 209, emphasis Bersani's). Between phallic citizenship and sodomitical forfeiture, there can occur a ruptural shift between the homosexual's "imitation" of men and the gay male's iconoclastic accession to sexual subjectivity by at once claiming his masculine prerogative and contravening its conditions of possibility.

Such alienated resignifications of male experience can be seen in a variety of forms, from the academic essay to the marketing format of a porn video. The vital contradictions of gay male sex are beautifully condensed in the title of a porn film featuring traditionally masculine men engaged in anal intercourse, *Take It Like a Man* (discussed in Pronger 139–41). The title is a macho cliché, whose "naturalness" the sexual activity of the film ruins by overdetermining the semantics of the verb. "Take it" refers to masculine physical endurance and to the receptive role in anal penetrative sex. The insertion of anal sex into the meaning of this cliché violates the standards of male self-affirmation.

A man must meet a challenge and must endure pain: he must "take it." The sexual penetration of the body, however, is physically but not psychopolitically endurable to any masculine subject produced or ensured by this ethos: he must *not* "take it." Dominant male agonistics are suspended in a paradox: any man who refuses a challenge is not a man; but any man who meets *this* challenge is no longer a man. The paradox connotes the coexistence of two incompatible systems of male psychosexual subject formation. The one that survives the paradox as contradiction is the gay male subject, emerging through the negating affirmation inscribed within the film title.

Intersubjective Narcissism

Traditionally desire is figured as coextensive with a gaze polarized according to the same gendered division of masculine subject and feminine object. The visual pleasure of dominant cinema, for example, is predicated upon an irreversible complementarity between a male viewer and a female spectacle, a "sexual imbalance" overdetermined by an "active/passive heterosexual division of labor," which makes it impossible for "the male figure . . . to bear the burden of sexual objectification" (Mulvey, "Visual Pleasure" 18–20). Jacques Lacan describes the objectification of the male subject in the gaze of the Other as an "annihilation" and a castration experience, although he denies a masculinist bias to his formulation (*Four Fundamental* 95–96; 106; 82–85). I discuss Lacan's theory and its symptomatic lapses in chapter 4.

Against this restricted specular economy of desire, the two men at the baths (in my above examples of discursive formations) removing their towels in front of each other engage, therefore, in a dual negating affirmation. Each man asserts his masculine privilege to act as subject of desire in order to elicit the desire of the other; each claims his gendered right to look in order to give his embodied self up to the "annihilation" of the other's gaze. But the significance of the specular economy in gay male sexuality does not exhaust itself in its symmetrical relation to the negating affirmation of the subject-object polarity of desire. While the solicitation of the gaze *negates* the internalized normative male image, it also *affirms* a deviant self-image as desired subject, as recognized ("seen") subject. The encounter is not merely a double negation but also a heterodox reciprocity, unacceptable to the cognitive hygiene of the heterosexual male subject. The syncopations of the joint seduction are operations of an intersubjective narcissism unimaginable within the conceptual systems supportive of normative heterosexuality.

The inadequacy of dominant paradigms is evident in the communication noise that immediately arises. In our received tradition, the phrase "intersubjective narcissism" seems to be a contradiction in terms; in fact, technically speaking, it is virtually redundant. Considering the processes of identification, introjection, and internalization that constitute and reconfigure the ego in various moments of its history, narcissism is inherently "intersubjective."[28] The fact that this is counterintuitive, I think, is partially a function of the trivialization of narcissism in psychoanalytic accounts of the pathogenesis of homosexuality. At times Freud attributed homosexuality to a fixation on a narcissistic stage of development in which the child presumes the object of desire possesses similar genitalia (Freud, "Psycho-Analytic Notes" 60–61). Freud's followers were generally more adamant and simplistic in their etiologies of homosexuality.[29]

Psychoanalytic descriptions of the narcissistic operations constituting and reconfiguring the ego certainly number among the discipline's most sophisticated and suggestive contributions to modern theories of subjectivity. Consider, for example, Freud's "On Narcissism: An Introduction (1914)"; "Mourning and Melancholia (1917)"; *Group Psychology and the Analysis of the Ego* (1921); and *The Ego and the Id* (1923), and Jacques Lacan's theory of the mirror stage. It is quizzical, therefore, that these writers would formulate such elaborate models for narcissism as an intrapsychic dynamic, but then evacuate virtually all such significance from the term when applying it to questions of object-choice. I interpret this contradiction as symptomatic of an unacknowledged commitment to Oedipal male heterosexuality and its radical separation of desire and identification.

This metacritical conjecture also sheds light on another paradox whose standard explanations prove unsatisfactory. Why is the gay male's self-presentation as object of desire so abhorrent in male dominant discourse, given that the male body is the only valorized body in that image reservoir? The negating affirmation of the gay male subject corresponds to the threat that sexual penetration poses to the ego boundaries of the dominant heterosexual male. If, therefore, negating affirmation is a "manifest" violation of the male heterosexual's ego, intersubjective narcissism is a violation, on a deeper level, of the operations that originally constituted and thereafter maintain that ego.

The dominant male heterosexual ego is first consolidated at the concluding phase of the so-called "positive" Oedipus. In this scenario, the castration anxiety the male child experiences in the "phallic stage" of his libidinal organization stimulates a resolution of his Oedipal conflicts conducive to dominant heterosexual object-choice. Until this critical moment in his development, the child could invest his desire in either or both parents. After interpreting female genitalia as a wound marking the absence of a penis, castration becomes a possible punishment his father would exact if the child retained an erotic attachment to the mother. The already accomplished castration of the woman represents the "precondition" for obtaining sexual satisfaction from the father. Thus the boy renounces erotic feelings for the mother in self-defense. He cannot transform his libidinal cathexis for his mother into an identification with her, due to her castration, nor transfer his cathexis to the father, since his mother represents the castration attendant upon desiring a man.[30] He therefore identifies with the father, and transfers his erotic attachments to other "castrated" beings outside the family, with whom he also does not identify.

The sudden resignification of the female body as castrated may "permanently determine the boy's relations to women: horror of the mutilated creature or triumphant contempt for her" ("Some Psychical" 252). Neither the "horror" nor the "contempt" for women, however, necessitates a homosexual object choice—in fact, in the "positive Oedipus" the castration anxiety that incites gynophobia and misogyny also guarantees heterosexuality. This is because such a system demands from the male child a radical separation of identification and desire, while collaterally (but no less significantly) proscribing identification with women in general (whether love-objects or not).

Conversely, identification with the mother is considered a leading cause of male homosexuality, a theory Freud formally introduced in his psychobiography of Leonardo da Vinci (1911), his most illustrious example of this phenomenon: "The boy represses his love for his mother: he puts himself in her place, identifies himself with her, and takes his own person as a model in whose likeness he chooses the new objects of his love. . . . The boys whom he now loves as he grows up are . . . only substitutive figures and revivals of himself in childhood—boys whom he loves in the way in which his mother loved him when he was a child. He finds the objects of his love along the path of narcissism" (*Leonardo and a Memory* 99–100). This passage combines an erasure of homosexuality (the child represses his "true" heterosexual desire for his mother through an identification with her), a prohibition against male identification with women, and the debased narcissism typical of less sophisticated homosexual diagnoses.

To elaborate the psychosexual dynamics of the gay male subject, I want to reclaim both the ego-constitutive identificatory processes and certain aspects of narcissistic nosologies of male homosexuality in psychoanalytic literature. By strategically reinhabiting Freud's "On Narcissism: An Introduction" (1914), I will advance definitions of the heterosexual male subject as an "anaclitic subject" and the gay male as a "narcissistic subject," based on the categories of "object-choice" Freud introduced in that essay. "Anaclisis" is the conventional English translation for *Anlehnung* ("attachment"), a term Freud used to describe the relation between sexual drives and self-preservative instincts that he introduced in his theoretical overviews of human sexual development. I preface my reading of "On Narcissism" with a composite synopsis of Freud's major narratives of sexual maturation, which will explain the meanings of "anaclisis" and "narcissism" as well as the roles each plays in the formation of adult male sexual subjects. Although I include certain significant concepts from later periods, I situate my composite genealogy of sexually differenced male subjects primarily within Freud's writings of 1910–1915, because many of the elements in my argument depend on principal binary oppositions in his thought at that time, particularly the oppositions between sexual instincts and self-preservative or ego-instincts, and between the pleasure principle and the reality principle. (I will return to the latter at the conclusion of this chapter.) I define the anaclitic subject first, for it is in opposition to that subject that the gay male becomes a politically and culturally vital countersubjective possibility.

On Narcissism: A [Re-] Introduction

Genealogies of the Sexual Subject

The Oedipal crisis and its resolution is the culminating narrative in a multiple teleological production of adult sexuality that includes the oral, anal, and genital (or "phallic") stages of libidinal organization; the autoerotic, narcissistic, and extraneous object stages of erotic object type; the gradual separation of self-preservative instincts from sexual drives; and the progressive dominance of the reality principle over the pleasure principle. These progressions and their interrelations are determined by the pecularities of infantile sexuality, which originally "attaches itself to one of the vital somatic functions; it has as yet no sexual object, and is thus auto-erotic; and its sexual aim is dominated by an erotogenic zone" (Freud, *Three Essays* 182–83). The first of these characteristics is epitomized in the oral phase, "in which sexual activity has not yet been separated from the ingestion of food" (ibid. 198). The oral stage represents a complete identification between a "satisfaction of the erotogenic zone" and "the satisfaction of the need for nourishment." A nursing infant does not differentiate the satisfaction of its hunger from the sensual stimulation of the breast and the flow of warm milk over the erotogenic zones of its lips and mouth. The child's autoerotism expresses itself in habits that recapture these nondistinguished satisfactions. Thumbsucking is evidence that "sexual activity attaches itself to functions serving the purpose of self-preservation and does not become independent of them until later" (ibid. 181–82). Although Freud describes this mimetic dependency of the sexual drives on the self-preservative instincts in the original 1905 edition of *Three Essays*, it was first in the 1915 edition that he named this relation *Anlehnung* (attachment), which in English has been conventionally translated as "anaclisis."

As the designations of the phases of sexual organization indicate, infantile autoerotism is an anarchic array of pleasures localized in specific erotogenic zones (*Three Essays* 182–83). It is not the child's "self" but the mouth, the anus, etc. that experiences pleasure. Eventually the constant care (and erotic stimulation) the infant receives encourages it to believe itself to be the center of the universe, a grandiose self-conception Freud calls the ideal ego. The formation of the ideal ego allows the transition from objectless autoerotism to a narcissism taking one's "self" as erotic object. The infant, therefore, does not simply transfer libidinal cathexis from an isolated erotogenic zone to an already constituted ego; rather, the libidinal energies constitute the ego in which they are invested. Freud notes that "a unity comparable to the ego cannot exist in the individual from the start; the ego has to be developed," and infers from this that "there must be something added to auto-erotism—a new psychical action—in order to bring about narcissism" ("On Narcissism" 76–77). I would invert this logic: narcissism is the "new psychical action" that serves to "bring about" the ego.

This narcissistic stage also affects the child's relations to those responsible for its care. In other words, the overestimation of its own importance conditions the child's perception of those who preserve its life. This "affectionate current" of the libido is based on "the interests of the self-preservative instinct and is directed to the members of the family who look after the child." It is in this relation that Freud locates the tendency of the sexual instincts to "find their first objects by attaching [anaclisis] themselves to the valuations made by the ego-instincts, precisely in the way in which the first sexual satisfactions are experienced in attachment to the bodily functions necessary for life" (Freud, "On the Universal Tendency" 180–181).

The increasing expectations that socialization places upon the maturing infant make it impossible for it to retain its ideal ego as an immediate self-conception. It therefore attempts to refashion a new ideal ego through adjustments according to the standards and judgments it encounters, and by taking on a model, an "ego ideal" from among the others with whom the child interacts (Freud, "On Narcissism" 92–94). This ego ideal can be a composite of several people, or merely aspects of them, or simply internalized voices. One of the most important admonitions figured within ego ideals is the the prohibition against incest. Because the primary caregiver in patriarchal societies is typically the mother (or other female surrogates), the identifications in the process of establishing ego ideals, and the gendered difference in response to the incest taboo, indicate the importance of sexual difference which arises at these junctures in sexual development; and sexual difference in these contexts necessarily implies the Oedipus.

Although Freud uses both the terms "ideal ego" and "ego ideal" in "On Narcissism," in my discussion I maintain distinctions between the two that had not been fully developed in Freud's 1914 text. My understanding of the ego ideal, as the internalization of parental and other authority figures' prohibitions, and external people as models, comes in part from Freud's 1921 *Group Psychology and the Analysis of the Ego* and to some extent *The Ego and the Id*.[31] My conception of the ideal ego is indebted to Jacques Lacan, an understanding of which requires a brief synopsis of the Lacanian system from which it emerges.

Lacan explains the emergence of the adult subject in terms of his three registers of experience: the Real, the Imaginary, and the Symbolic. About the "Real" nothing can be said, as it is always mediated by the other two registers and unavailable to direct experience. The Imaginary, which predates but coexists within the Symbolic, is a system of binary structures of identifications with images and counterparts. The Symbolic refers both to the structures that organize and motivate heterogeneous elements as signifiers, and to the law that establishes such structures, a law Lacan calls "the Name-of-the-Father" (Laplanche and Pontalis, *Language* 440).

The pre-Oedipal infant's psychic life is dominated by the Imaginary. The shift from autoerotism to narcissism that marks the crystalization of the ideal ego occurs during this time at a mythically structuring event Lacan calls the mirror stage. The "mirror stage" designates the infant's initial self-recognition in a mirror, an identification with the image as an anticipated totality that is not as yet fully experienced due to the infant's lack of bodily coordination, muscular control, and its continued dependence on the care of others (Lacan, *Écrits* 18–19). The identification of infant and mirror image is an extension of the dyadic unity between mother and child, which is interrupted by the intrusion of the Law of the Father prohibiting incest and establishing the Oedipal boundaries of desire and identification that also resituates the child in a "Symbolic Order" of language, kinship structures, and community obligations. Leaving the Imaginary dualism of self and mirror for the entry into the Symbolic of language acquisition and social relations, the child cannot retain the immediacy of his earlier sense of self as ideal ego. The child's ego at the mirror stage is a hallucination achieved through optical technology, whose affective stability can be regained only in the Symbolic through adaptations to social norms and specific internalizations of imposed standards and capitulations to patriarchal law.

The interlocking progressions of Freud's model of sexual maturation evince a mutually supportive oscillation between "anaclitic" and "narcissistic" adjustments to the changes in conditions brought about by maturation. The emergence of the child's primary narcissism stimulated the child's overvaluation of its caretakers, thus facilitating the first external "object-choice" that is marked with the same anaclitic (attachment) relation to self-preservative instincts that had characterized the original erotogenic pleasures. Similarly, the child responds to the loss of the ideal ego with a narcissistic adjustment—the internalization of ego ideals. The acceptance of the incest taboo stimulates an anaclitic adjustment: the erotic cathexes in caregivers is transferred to more appropriate objects outside the family, but these attractions are modeled on memories of the earlier familial relations.

In its earliest and most basic meanings in Freud's work, the "anaclitic" nature of human sexuality referred to the modes of its manifestation. A function of the peculiarities of human physiology and the long period of helplessness, the mimetic dependency of sexuality on activities and experiences of the self-preservative instincts was considered a common tendency, regardless of biological sex or later sexual orientation. Three years before the term "anaclisis" was added to the third edition of *Three Essays*, however, Freud had already begun a shift to a gender-based inflection of the concept's sphere of pertinence. In a 1912 discussion of the anaclitic process of modeling adult object-choice on the primary caregivers of infancy, Freud observes that the fusion of sensual attraction and affection present in the infantile relations with caregivers is carried over into adult love relations, and claims that the preservation of these two "currents" of libidinal interest is a chief cause of "the normal overvaluation of the sexual object on the part of a man" ("On the Universal Tendency" 181), although he fails to explain why this "overvaluation" is a particularly male characteristic, given that it is an effect of the primary narcissism of children of both sexes.[32] "On Narcissism: An Introduction" provides an answer which I will question.

Anaclitic/Narcissistic: From Object to Subject Types

"On Narcissism" presents two definitions of "narcissism": first, a range of identificatory operations that form and refigure the ego; and second, a classification of object-choice. The former offers a potentially compelling descriptive model of the dynamic interchanges constituting psychosocial subject formations (and the economic fluctuations of external or internal libidinal investments); the latter is merely part of a two-term typology of sexual relations, and one which is thoroughly implicated in a gender-hierarchized value system. After considering the implications of the role of narcissistic identifications and introjections in constituting the ego, it is difficult to accept Freud's reduction of "narcissism" to a pattern of object-choice. It is, however, virtually in the center of this essay that Freud claims:

> The sexual instincts are at the outset attached to the satisfaction of the ego-instincts; only later do they become independent of these, and even then we have an indication of that original attachment in the fact that the persons who are concerned with a child's feeding, care, and protection become his earliest sexual objects. . . . Side by side, however, with this type and source of object-choice, which may be called the "anaclitic" or "attachment" type, psycho-analytic research has revealed a second type . . . especially [pronounced] in people whose libidinal development has suffered some disturbance, such as perverts and homosexuals . . . a type of object-choice which must be termed "narcissistic." In their later choice of love-object they have taken as a model not their mother but their own selves. (87–88)

Because of the "primary narcissism" Freud postulates as a common human characteristic, he admits that either type of object-choice is available to any individual. Generally speaking, however, Freud finds that "object-love of the attachment type is . . . characteristic of the [heterosexual] male," and its narcissistic counterpart more common in women (88). He also enumerates the criteria operative in each object-choice type.

> A person may love: (1) According to the narcissistic type:
> (a) what he himself is (i.e. himself),
> (b) what he himself was,
> (c) what he himself would like to be,
> (d) someone who was once part of himself
> (2) According to the anaclitic (attachment) type:
> (a) the woman who feeds him,
> (b) the man who protects him,
> and the succession of substitutes who take their place. (90)

We have already observed that the primary narcissism of the child is initially personified by the ideal ego whose subsequent demise the child compensates through internalizations of ego ideals. However generally supportive these internalizations are to patriarchal authority, they are nevertheless narcissistic operations. The two nodal points of the subject's history, the ideal ego and the ego ideal, moreover, correspond to the second and third (respectively) of Freud's four options for "narcissistic object-choice": "(b) what he himself once was; (c) what he himself would like to be."[33] In contrasting these narcissistic options of object-choices with the intrapsychically trivial anaclitic options, it is difficult to understand why Freud characterizes male heterosexuality as an anaclitic object-choice pattern.

How Freud distinguishes the anaclitic type from the feminine "narcissistic" type does not clarify his emphasis either. The anaclitic object-choice "displays the marked sexual over-estimation which is doubtless derived from the original narcissism of the child, and thus corresponds to a transference of that narcissism to a sexual object"; the narcissistic object-choice is not "a true object-choice" as such, but a behavioral pattern resulting from "an intensification of the original narcissism," which Freud finds "unfavourable to the development of a true object-choice with its accompanying sexual overvaluation" (88). The logic of the contrast, however, ultimately does not bear scrutiny. In both cases the object-choice developed out of the "original narcissism," which not only makes Freud's evaluative judgment rather arcane (the "real" object-choice and "unreal" having the same origin), but it also suggests a primacy to narcissism that the emphasis on the man's "anaclitic" pattern does not address.

The importance of a sexually differentiated anaclisis becomes clearer, however, when we consider its value to the continuation of dominant heterosexual institutions: "Women, especially if they grow up with good looks, develop a certain self-containment which compensates them for the social restrictions that are imposed upon them in their choice of object. . . . It is only themselves that such women love with an intensity comparable to that of the man's love for them. Nor does their need lie in the direction of loving, but of being loved: and that man finds favour with them who fulfills this condition" (88–89). The complementarity of the man's anaclitic "overvaluation" of love-object and the woman's narcissistic self-involvement foreshadow Lacan's schematization of heterosexual relations as a phallically mediated masquerade-comedy.

Desire is motivated by lack, and in the post-Oedipal logic that informs heterosexuality, each subject will experience that lack according to how the castration complex fixes his or her sexed identity. The male experiences the sense of lack as a threat of possible castration; the woman experiences it as a recognition of her having already been castrated. Each subject seeks compensation for this lack in the phallus, the transcendental signifier of desire; each must signify the phallus for the other. The woman, therefore, becomes the phallus for the man; the man in turn, "has" the phallus for the woman (Lacan, "Meaning" 83–84). The woman's "feminine" narcissism allows her the self-immersion to transform her body into the signifier of the male's desire, while the man's anaclitic object-choice as an "overestimation" of the love object allows him to believe in her masquerade, and his socially enjoined "overestimation" of the penis as phallus allows him (indeed requires him) to believe in her misrecognition of his penis as phallus. Both roles in this comedy are played out in terms of male sexuality and for the purpose of stabilizing the male's psychosexual identity. Although in a radically different idiom and describing a completely different sphere of subjectivity and intersubjectivity, the dynamics of Lacan's psychic scenario resonate with those of the asymmetrical discursive achievements of gendered subject positions within the heterosexual relations extrapolated in Wendy Holloway's study summarized above. Freud's object-choice model also elides female sexuality, since the woman's "narcissism" is not "a true object-choice" and her participation in the relation neither expresses nor serves her desire as much as it accommodates the male's desire; Lacan's model emphasizes the woman's role in meeting the male's sexually articulated need to deny lack and allay anxiety.

The weird practicality of the heterosexual dynamic in Lacan's description reveals the sexual politics served by the conflation, in Freud's "On Narcissism," of the heterosexual male's transformation of his primary narcissism into an overvaluation of the love object, with the self-preservative intentionality of anaclitic object-choice. The socialization of young boys into normative heterosexuality depends largely on a terrorized discovery of sexual difference. Freud readily admits that the young boy's first sight of female genitalia does not immediately stimulate the castration fear; this comes about subsequently, "when some threat of castration has obtained hold upon him" ("Some Psychical" 252)—in other words, once he has been sufficiently indoctrinated to fear the absence of the penis, and to internalize the ideologically naturalized relation between women's anatomical difference from men and the former's disenfranchisement. In emerging as a self-consciously gendered entity, the boy is faced with two alternatives in his attitude to women: terror of her ("horror of the mutilated creature") or terroristic impulses toward her ("triumphant contempt for her"). The successfully Oedipalized heterosexual male, therefore, reaches an impasse: in order to enter the symbolic position whose alternative is the castration the woman's body has proven a possibility, he must desire that body which represents that very threat. This is why his anaclisis requires an overvaluation of the love object he also holds in contempt. He must desire it as the phallus, so that his possession of it will suffice to neutralize both his knowledge of sexual difference and the possibility of his own constitutional "lack" (which desire is, in fact, predicated upon). In other words, male heterosexuality is "self-preservative" because the female body is experienced as life-threatening. This threat is alternatively overcome by villification of the woman as castrated, or by fetishizing her as the Phallus whose irreducible absence is first incarnated in and then disavowed through her body.

When Freud uses the Medusa myth as an allegory for the male subject's paradigmatic encounter with female genitalia, he inadvertently exposes the conflicting agendas within Oedipalized male heterosexuality:

> The terror of Medusa is . . . a terror of castration. . . . It occurs when a boy . . . catches sight of the female genitals, probably those of an adult, surrounded by hair. . . . The hair upon Medusa's head is frequently represented . . . [as] snakes, and these once again are derived from the castration complex. . . . They serve actually as a mitigation of the horror, for they replace the penis, the absence of which is the cause of the horror. ("Medusa's Head" 273)

Freud also interprets the paralytic effect of looking at the Medusa as another phallic comfort, the "stiffening" of the body suggesting erection, thus reminding the male of the continued existence of his own penis. The erection is not only an internal comfort, but its display to the woman "has an apotropaic effect. To display the penis (or any of its surrogates) is to say: 'I am not afraid of you. I defy you. I have a penis.' Here, then, is another way of intimidating the Evil Spirit" (ibid. 274).[34] His sexual arousal is a means by which he exorcises the threat of sexual difference the woman represents. The erect penis is a weapon of both defense and offense, a talisman wielded in a sexual act that functions as preemptive aggression. His erection is "caused" by the woman, but as a response it expresses sexual desire and murderous defensive hostility (or sexual desire *as* murderous defensive hostility). Male heterosexual relations with women are determined to a great degree by the "successful" resolution of the Oedipus through the castration anxiety of the phallic stage at which point "maleness exists but not femaleness" (Freud, "Infantile Genital" 145)—meaning that the principal binary is not male-female but male-castrated. Therefore, a male encounter with a female is an encounter with non-existence: both hers and the possibility of his. In the anaclitic subject, therefore, self-preservative instincts are not merely the models for adult object-choice, but they are thematized as self-preservative within that object-choice and that sexuality. Male heterosexuality is anaclitic because it is "attached" to self-preservative instincts, but also because it is realized as a complex of self-preservative maneuvers against the life-threatening encounter with sexual difference.

Resituating the heterosexual anaclitic object-choice in its earlier developmental history in Freud's thought brings to light the implicit associations with male heterosexuality and the self-preservative instincts, since this object-choice fits so well into the other anaclitic instincts based on survival needs. The anaclisis of the heterosexual male is based on the anaclitic/narcissistic dovetail of the heterosexual contract (the man has the phallus, the woman is the phallus, the man is relieved of his castration anxiety through the woman's willingness to transform herself into the phallus). Such associations, furthermore, imply an instrumental view of the (female) object: the (female) object is chosen and used primarily for the benefit and maintenance of the (male) subject.

Synthesizing the disparate meanings of "narcissism" as object-choice category and ego-forming functions of identification and introjection, on the other hand, enables us to reenvision gay male desire as integral to the processes of subject constitution and intricately related to operations of representation and self-representation. If the narcissism that inaugurates the infant's self-conception as ideal ego is to be understood in terms of the structuring fantasy of the mirror stage, we must remember that the child is held up to its reflection by its primary caregiver (probably its mother), and that the caregiver's role is crucial to understanding that the infant's recognition of itself as ideal ego is the paradigmatic instance of narcissistic intersubjectivity—a web of scopic and libidinal investments constituting the ecstasis of the sexual subject. The infant seeing itself, sees itself sexually stimulated by the physical contact with the caregiver and sexually aroused by its apperception of its own totality. These perceptions are also mediated by the caregiver's sexuality (the erotic energies the caregiver invests in the infant)[35] and the caregiver's look (visible in the mirror as he or she holds the infant before it).[36] In the intersubjective narcissistic sexual encounter among gay men, these erotic and scopic vectors of sexual subject formation are consciously experienced and manipulated.

In the body of the other, the gay male recognizes his (somatic) like and object of desire; in the look of the other, he sees himself as object of desire. The other's desire and the other's look are means by which he can reconstitute himself as a transitory ideal ego, confirmed in the "annihilation" of the other's desiring look. From the perspective of the anaclitic subject, gay male sexual behavior would endanger and disperse one's "identity" as subject rather than actualize it. This contrast provides, among other things, two different erotic bodies in opposing sexual-political imaginaries; it also returns us to a variable confluence of the negating affirmation and intersubjective narcissism of gay male subject processes I first noted in introducing the latter term.

Sexually Differenced Male Subjects of Representation

The identification of the ego or the subject with a body is first achieved in the Imaginary, in the narcissistic identification of the mirror stage;[37] for the adult, the representation of the subject as body remains an operation of the Imaginary, but is intelligible only through its relation to the Symbolic. Although the subject is en-visioned as a body within the Imaginary, the overdeterminations of both the subject-as-body and the physical correlative of that body are played out within the Symbolic through the narrativization of the body's psychic history and the political ramifications of the body's performative expressions and phantasmatic valences. In other words, the subject imagined as its corporeal extension is further adumbrated by the serial manifestations of its possibilities within its interaction with the "external world." The body is not merely a biological fact but a network of often contradictory psychological, cultural, and social meanings. It is always simultaneously its material substance, the images generated around it, its actions, and its possibilities. The body is an imaginary accomplishment in which are intermeshed the libidinal configurations of the drives and the potentials for action that will partially determine the subject in its specific relationship with its environment.[38]

If the subject finds its specular coherence in an ego-imago that is identified with a body (at least contiguous to, but necessarily not identical to, the facticity of its being-in-the-world), in what way does the gay male body differ from the heterosexual male body in the dominant political Imaginary? The very fact that its being-in-the-world makes the body available to the phantasmatic appropriation of others renders the gay male body an intersection of conflicting semiotic practices upon the circuitry of meanings and values attributed to the body. In order to map the generation and polyvocalizations of this body, it is necessary first to outline the social nexuses in which the political Imaginary eventuates and subtends identities.[39] As Bersani has claimed, the aspect of gay male sexuality that is seen as most threatening to the heterosexual male subject is the prospect of a male willfully and pleasurably submitting to anal penetration by another male ("Rectum" 210). Central to the revulsion this practice evokes are the definition of the male and the sexual hierarchies based on a rigid binarism of active-passive roles defined by penetration. To be penetrable is part of the phallocratic definition of woman, and conversely, the male is defined as impenetrable—any act of sodomy is a "crime against nature, male nature" (Dworkin, *Intercourse* 152). In the heterosexual male imaginary, the horror of penetration has a more subtle corollary in the aversion to ecstasy, or any excess (sexual or otherwise) which would threaten to disintegrate the psycho-physical boundaries of the self. Women are viewed ambivalently as the source of erotic excitation, the object of sexual attraction, yet also as the threat of dissipation into otherness, into a bliss (*jouissance*) that would permanently dissolve the male subject's solidity. The chaotic dispersion that woman represents to this type of heterosexual male imaginary is configured in the iconography of syphilis since the Enlightenment, when depictions of the syphilitic shift "from male to female, and with this shift comes another: from victim to source of infection," which is also a "change . . . from the innate corruption of the female to her potential for corrupting the male" (Gilman 95–96).

In his socio-psychoanalysis of the fascist male (which I view as the logical extreme of the male heterosexual subject produced under the regime of misogynist compulsory heterosexuality), Klaus Theweleit describes the role played in the male imaginary by threatening images of the woman-as-other as paradigmatic for the political and social "deviancies" against which the "soldier male" develops his lethal defense mechanisms.[40] The thing that threatens the coherence of the male body/mind is the dissolution in orgasmic pleasure; its possibility is engendered as female, and the drives toward such pleasure are considered a disease. The Wilhelmine German fascist male obsessively identified the feminine disease of pleasure with Jewishness. "The focus of repression in the soldier male is the 'desire to desire'; concomitantly, the core of all fascist propaganda is a battle against everything that constitutes enjoyment and pleasure. Pleasure, with its hybridizing qualities, has the dissolving effect of a chemical enzyme on the armored body. . . . The Nazi program for the masses [is]: a combating any hope for a real 'heaven-on-earth,' a real life in pleasure; a naming of the desire for a better life as an illness, of human pleasures as a contagious disease whose prime carrier is the 'Jewish element' " (Theweleit 2: 7–8). One need hardly note how readily the "Jewish element" slot in this pathological system can be replaced (or doubled) with "male homosexual."

In his attempt to sketch an "articulation of the male body and male imaginary in the construction of a preoedipal register for masculinity," Paul Smith relies heavily on Michèle Montrelay's article "L'appareillage" in order to displace the primacy of the phallus in his discussion, something which, he notes at several points in his essay, does not always work. Of the four meanings Montrelay lists for *appareillage*, the most important for both her and Smith is " 'the taking off itself, the orgasmic experience of having taken off" (Smith, "Vas" 97). Smith defends Montrelay against suspicions of biological essentialism by explaining "the importance and crucial place of ejaculation in the male imaginary" as "something more akin to an ontological than a biological event" (ibid. 98). Montrelay's theory of the male imaginary stems in part from the frequency with which her analysands speak of a fear of a "loss of self" in the orgasm, a fear which these men find substantiated by the loss of "the male seed" in the ejaculation (98–99). It is at this point, Smith admits, that "her theory . . . eventually defers to the metaphor of the phallus" (99).

Smith also draws from Montrelay's *L'Ombre et le nom*, where she characterizes femininity in terms of its "specific access to the 'abyss of non-meaning which is opened in every discourse and which is the real of every discourse' " (ibid. 96). Some of the dangers of using Montrelay's already tenuous description of the feminine imaginary in a discussion of masculine anxieties become apparent here. In his discussion of Montrelay's observations on the fears of her male analysands, Smith conjoins the above metaphor of the "abyss" with the male reluctance to ejaculate: "[Montrelay] understands the male imaginary as having in part 'the function of deploying and marking out a possible space to prevent ejaculation from leading to a destruction of the subject' . . . through flight or evanescence, thus preventing the subject's having to confront the abyss of the Other or of non-meaning" (98–99). Smith very admirably factors into his account that he is writing from a heterosexual perspective (103), which may be one reason that the "metaphor of the phallus" seems so insurmountable.[41] We must be able to distinguish gay male sexuality from this "male fear of nonmeaning" without in any way affirming the implicit equation of woman as "non-meaning," or the not-so-hidden image of the female body in the heterosexual dynamic as a nonsignifying repository for male plenitude.

To situate Smith's thesis within a discussion of comparative models of male sexual subjectivity, one must re-envision the heterosexual male's equation of ejaculation with a "loss of self" according to a dialectic that arises between two sexually involved men, a dialectic based on an intersubjective narcissism (an at least physiological empathy) in which self and other intermesh, and such that the ejaculation "lost" is "regained" in the partner, and vice versa.[42] Gay male lovemaking is a pulsation of inter-ruptions of subjectivity, of inter-irruptions into the subject's somatic extension of his imaginary selfhood by the subject whose object he has ec-statically become. Subjectivity within male coupling is episodic, cognized and re-cognized as stroboscopic fluctuations of intense (yet dislocated, asymmetrical, decentered) awareness of self-as-other, self-for-other, via interlunations of psychic and sexual exuberance. If the heterosexual male imaginary includes a defense against ejaculation as loss of self, risk of nonmeaning, or abyss of meaning, gay male sexuality (with the anal drives restored) is a circulatory system of expenditure and absorption, taking/giving and giving/taking.

We can summarize these comparisons by typifying the heterosexual male body as monocentric (phallic) and apotropaic, sexually actualized as a weapon in defense of its own paranoic integrity: it cannot—must not—be penetrated.[43] The erect penis wards off bliss and metonymizes the rigidity of the heterosexual male psyche.[44] The gay male body, on the other hand, is polycentric and ludic, sexually actualized as a playground. Understanding the extensions of these subjects into cultural representations that at once reflect and constitute them requires a multidimensional appreciation of the dynamisms of sexually differenced subjects and the roles sexualities play in the modes of those subjects' visibility. It also indicates the crucial interrelations between these imaginaries and radical expressions thereof. I now turn to cultural representational strategies reflective of the patterns of negating affirmation and intersubjective narcissism in gay male subject processes.

Deviant Agencies of Representation

Negating Affirmation: The Politics of Jouissance

In sketching the theoretical framework of this book at the opening of this chapter, I noted that I consider the subject an effect of signification rather than its source. The political importance of this distinction is evident if we consider the ways in which conceptions of a "self" as a preunderstood ground of experience or psychologically coherent entity antecedent to its material history naturalize or otherwise support structures of domination, in the construction both of the master subject and of those sub-jected to that mastery. Descartes's self-certain *cogito* abetted the mystification of the hegemonic (white male) western European subject as a universal principle, whose imperialist expansionism was the essential radiance of Reason. Michel Foucault argues that the various formations of the subject in history represent innovations in power and subjugation rather than the emergence of an autonomous individual consciousness.[45] The present overview of the dominant sex/gender system bears Foucault's theses out. Wendy Holloway's study, for example, indicates that modern middle-class "normal" and "well-adjusted" heterosexuals are not self-realized individuals but subject positions taken up within a discursive system that delimits them within the very gendered identities it imposes upon them.

The ideological fixing of the subject is a central concern in post-1968 Marxism, feminist theory, and poststructuralist semiology. While the history of this critical attention to this political function of representation can be traced to Louis Althusser and his 1970 essay "Ideology and Ideological State Apparatuses," his theory has been challenged, expanded, and improved upon by several writers whose work informs my argumentation throughout this book.[46] For our purposes Althusser's most important formulation is the relation of the subject to ideology: "The category of the subject is constitutive of all ideology, but at the same time . . . the category of the subject is only constitutive of all ideology insofar as all ideology has the function . . . of 'constituting' concrete individuals as subjects. . . . All ideology hails or interpellates concrete individuals as concrete subjects, by the functioning of the category of the subject"

(Althusser, "Ideology" 173). The "Copernican revolution" proposed by semiotics and other disciplines serves to demystify the hegemonic (white male) subject's transcendence and "universality" and to destabilize those subjects whose fixity is a measure of their subordination to the dominant order.

The ecstatic deontologizing articulation of the gay sexual subject, most intensively realized in his negating affirmation, provides a model for representational practices that deconstruct the "whole subjects"—either the hegemonic "transcendental subject" or the interpellated subject of ideology. In this light, it seems neither accidental nor incidental that two very influential poststructuralist essays of the 1970s, "What Is an Author?" and "The Death of the Author," were written by gay men, Michel Foucault and Roland Barthes, respectively. In each case, the writer's disarticulation of the Cartesian *cogito* entails a self-subverting manipulation of the paradoxical social construction of a gay male subject. In other words, each writer used his rhetorical gift and public status to dissipate the metaphysical underpinning of his own enunciative position.[47] This is consonant with the pattern I have outlined above of negating affirmations, in which the gay subject expresses itself by accessing male privileges to annihilate the very identity that those privileges initially made possible.

These deconstructive gestures, however, have their own political ambivalence that cannot be ignored. Both Barthes and Foucault are often taken to task for their inattention to questions of gender, race, and ethnicity. Many scholars and intellectuals involved in women's studies, ethnic studies, and other "minority discourse" disciplines have responded negatively to the dissolution of the "self" or the "subject" as promoted by the French structuralists and poststructuralists.[48] Reflecting on his experience in graduate school at Yale, José David Saldívar finds a suspicious irony in the fact that, at the time when "Chicanos, peoples of color, and feminists, [first were beginning] to see themselves as subjects, as capable of action instead of just being acted upon . . . mainstream critics [began] talking about the end of the subject" (qtd. Chabram 132–33).

The black, gay, profeminist writer Samuel R. Delany, on the other hand, has diagnosed the promulgation of an ideal, "whole" self as a form of ideological violence. Deployed in support of "the white, western, patriarchal nuclear family," this "self" is an "ideological mirage . . . that necessarily grew up to mask the psychological, economic, and material oppression of an 'other' " (Delany, *Stars* "Afterword" 384). I have no intention of exonerating Foucault or Barthes or defending the indefensible lacunae in their critical formulations. I do, however, want to reconsider particularly Barthes's dissolution of the subject in the context of the present discussion, and to foreground its radical potential by reading it through Delany's work.

In *The Pleasure of the Text* Barthes introduces a bipartite typology of texts distinguished by their effects on the reading subject: the text of pleasure and the text of bliss (*jouissance*). Barthes's adaptation of *jouissance* includes its usual associations with orgasm, but also refers to a less physiologically localized extreme of pleasure, one whose intensity shatters the subject's boundaries and exceeds stabilizing representation. For Barthes, the text of pleasure "contents, fills, grants euphoria; comes from culture and does not break with it, is linked to a *comfortable* practice of reading," but the text of *jouissance* is "the text that imposes a state of loss, the text that discomforts," that "unsettles the reader's historical, cultural, psychological assumptions, . . . [and] brings to a crisis his [*sic*] relation with language" (*Pleasure* 14). The texts of pleasure and bliss generally correspond to one of Barthes's subsequent categorical binaries, the "readerly" and "writerly" texts. The readerly text, like the text of pleasure, includes any form of bourgeois text, from the classical realist novel to the romance or adventure, anything that confirms the reader in his/her culturally allocated subject position; the text of bliss and the "writerly" text are, generally speaking, the avant-garde texts that violate the norms of intelligibility securing the reader's wholeness, destabilizing both the social order and the ego fixed securely within it.[49]

The code that founds the operations of the text of pleasure or readerly text "is a perspective of quotations . . . (The Kidnapping refers to every kidnapping ever written); they are so many fragments of something that has always been already read. . . . The code is the wake of that already. Referring to what has been written, i.e. to the Book (of culture, of life, of life as culture), it makes the text into a prospectus of this Book" (Barthes, *S/Z* 20–21). That recognition of the code is the response to the text of pleasure. The "already read" is what allows the individual to recognize the codes of the social order as natural, the process whereby the realist novel (Barthes's "text of pleasure") confirms the reader as a "proper" subject through its seductive reassurance of comfortable intelligibility—in fact, the "subject is fixed at the point of that intelligibility" (Heath, "Film and System" 98).

Contrarily, the text of *jouissance* or the writerly text dissolves that certainty, exposing the "I" as a network of textual relays. "This 'I' which approaches the text is already itself a plurality of other texts, of codes which are infinite or, more precisely, lost (whose origin is lost). . . . I am not hidden within the text, I am simply irrecoverable from it: my task is to move; to shift systems whose perspective ends neither at the text nor at the 'I' " (Barthes, *S/Z* 10). The *jouissance* in this text-reader dynamic activates the volatility of the subject's significatory constitution; the "already read" now facilitates dispersal of the self rather than its consolidation.

An incident in his personal history that Delany recounts in his autobiography, *The Motion of Light in Water*, illustrates the political implications of Barthes's intertextualized subjectivity. After a nervous breakdown in 1964, Delany attended group therapy as an outpatient. Although at first he discussed his homosexuality only with his doctor, he eventually told the group, but "it was the most abject of confessions. . . . I had the problem—I was homosexual, but I was really 'working on it.' I was sure that, with help, I could 'get better' " (*Motion* 245). His speech omitted everything about his sex life that was meaningful to him: "the physical pleasure of homosexuality, the fear and power at the beginnings of a political awareness, or the moment of community and communion with people from over an astonishing social range, or even the disappointment that came when fear or simple inequality of interest kept encounters for one or another of us too brief" (ibid. 246). It occurred to him later that everything he had said had come from texts he had *already read*: one "by the infamous Dr. Edmund Bergler that had explained how homosexuals were psychically retarded," another from "an appendix to a book by Erich Fromm . . . that told how homosexuals were all alcoholics who committed suicide"; Delany's tone echoed "the pathos of Theodore Sturgeon's science fiction story 'The World Well Lost' and his western story 'Scars' " (246–47). Delany realized then that when "you talk about something openly for the first time— and that, certainly, was the first time I'd talked to a public group about being gay—for better or worse, you use the public language you've been given." In this case "that language had done nothing but betray me" (247). That language could only articulate Delany's disclosure as a confession; the only subject position it provided him was that of a "homosexual" observant of the "heterosexual exhortation to silence" (248).

In *Camera Lucida* Barthes compares his wayward private "I" with the stolid image of his "I" that photographs preserve. "What I want . . . is that my (mobile) image, buffeted among a thousand shifting photographs . . . should always coincide with my (profound) 'self'; but . . . 'myself' never coincides with my image; for it is the image which is heavy, motionless . . . (which is why society sustains it), and 'myself' which is light, divided, dispersed" (12). Paul Smith reads this passage as Barthes's metaphor for the tension between the "coherent ideological 'subject' " and the subject's personal experience of itself as "I." Barthes's recognition of the division between the two, and the flux of their relations, is a space in which the subject might subvert the ideologically imposed stasis of the proper identity. Smith also identifies the transgression of the fixed subject as Barthes's *jouissance*, in contradistinction to the "pleasure" of the "texts of pleasure" that relies on "the fixity of the subject within the codes and conventions it inhabits" (Smith, *Discerning* 106–107). Delany's "confessional homosexual" is a "whole readerly self" that the gay male subject's *jouissance* (his negating affirmation) can shatter. The position of either enunciator or addressee of a readerly text would contain both gay male subjects (reader and writer) within an ideological paralysis. The *jouissance* Barthes introduces into critical discourse and Delany politicizes informs an engaged disarticulation of the fixed subject. The double meaning of *jouissance* as orgasm and as radical dispersal of the subject nicely literalizes the correlation of this textual practice to the negating affirmation of the gay male subject.

Intersubjective Narcissism: Ludic Resistance

Many of the cultural practices of the anaclitic subject manifest the same defensive ambivalence that characterizes his sexual life. The female image dominant cinema renders a sexual spectacle for the male viewer also embodies a crisis in that it "always threatens to evoke the [castration] anxiety it originally signified." The anaclitic viewing subject has two means of defense against this anxiety, a "sadistic voyeurism," arising from a "preoccupation with the original trauma (investigating the woman, demystifyng her mystery)," or a "fetishistic scopophilia" that affords the subject a "complete disavowal of castration by substitution of a fetish object or turning the represented figure itself into a fetish so that it becomes reassuring rather than dangerous (hence overvaluation, the cult of the female star)" (Mulvey, "Visual Pleasure" 21–22). In both sexual relations and film spectatorship, anaclisis comprehends both heterosexual object-choice *and* self-preservative instincts. In both cases the man's motivation is self-defense *from* the woman *by means of* the woman.

By the same token, the narcissistic subject engages in forms of specular play that foster an efflorescence of the identificatory subject processes and the libidinal investments beyond anything Freud could have anticipated in conflating these meanings of "narcissism" in his diagnosis of homosexual men.[50] I will discuss the relations of these psychosexual processes to the cinematic apparatus in chapter 4. There are also less obvious implications of my reinhabitation of "narcissism" for other deviant representational strategies. In my reading of Delany's rearticulation of Barthes's *jouissance*, I specified ways in which negating affirmation can model a pleasure-inflected ethics in gay male cultural interventions. Here I want to explain how intersubjective narcissism can also serve this function. To do this, I return briefly to the multiple teleologies of the sexual subject circumscribing Freud's "On Narcissism" essay, in particular the one I have not yet discussed: the gradual mastery of the reality principle over the pleasure principle.

The pleasure principle is the "primitive" psychical mechanism that seeks the most direct and immediate elimination of an experience of "unpleasure" or satisfaction of a wish.[51] An infant reacting to an internal stimulus of "unpleasure" remedies it by recalling an experience of satisfaction, "an essential component" of which "is a particular perception (that of nourishment), the mnemic image of which remains associated thenceforward with the memory trace of the excitation produced by the need." When the "need arises a psychical impulse will at once emerge which will seek to re-cathect the mnemic image of the perception and to re-evoke the perception itself, that is to say, to re-establish the situation of the original satisfaction" (*Interpretation of Dreams* 5. 565–66). Sexual behaviors in effect pantomime the infant's confusion of the satisfaction of an instinct (such as hunger) with the stimulation of an erogenous zone (such as the mouth and the lips). While modeled on a self-preservative instinct, the sexual pleasure the infant derives from the experience is characterized by important differences. Self-preservative instincts represent needs that require a specific (real) object for their satisfaction; sexual wishes can accept an infinite variety of substitutes, and the sexual drive, operating under the pleasure principle, is indifferent to the reality of the object: hallucination, memory, daydream, fantasy, are perfectly viable, which is why thumbsucking, for an infant, is an effective means of self-pacification.

Of course, however convenient this means of satisfaction may be temporarily, if real food and memories or fantasies of the experience of eating remain undifferentiated, the infant would never adapt abilities necessary for survival. That adaptation becomes possible with the emergence of the "reality principle" beginning when the hallucinated experience fails to produce satisfaction. At this point "the psychical apparatus [has] to decide to form a conception of the real circumstances in the external world and to endeavour to make a real alteration in them. A new principle of mental functioning [is] thus introduced; what was presented in the mind was no longer what was agreeable but what was real, even if it happened to be disagreeable. This setting-up of the reality principle [proves] to be a momentous step" (Freud, "Formulations" 219–20).[52]

The ascendancy of the reality principle over the pleasure principle takes on an ominous cast as the teleologies convene. Freud's initial celebration, in the *Three Essays*, of polymorphous perversities, component drives, and sexual fluidity is inexplicably overshadowed by a biological master narrative that spoils the party. In "infantile sexual life . . . individual component instincts are . . . disconnected and independent of one another in their search for pleasure. The final outcome of sexual development lies in what is known as normal sexual life of the adult, in which the pursuit of pleasure comes under the sway of the reproductive function and in which the component instincts, under the primacy of a single erotogenic zone, form a firm organization directed towards a sexual aim attached to some extraneous sexual object" (*Three Essays* 197). The lifesaving capacity of the reality principle is connected here at least subtextually with the life-producing act of reproduction. Pleasure (like the life-threatening fancifulness of the pleasure priniciple) is brought under firm control.

In the concluding section of the *Three Essays* Freud adopts a peculiar attitude toward sexual pleasure that parallels his recontainment of perversions in the same text. Freud distinguishes two types of sexual pleasure the adult experiences: "forepleasure," which he associates with the autoerotic, polymorphous perversity of the pre-Oedipal child, and the orgasm or "end pleasure," which he associates with the postpubertal genital stage at which it first appears. Just as the component instincts of infantile sexuality become subordinated to the serious reproductive faculty of the genital organization, the pleasures of a sexual experience (the "forepleasure") are begrudgingly tolerated (but hastened and regimented) toward the all-important discharge of semen (the "end-pleasure") that might fertilize an egg (210–11). This qualification exposes the exclusively male bias in this theory of sexuality, since it is only the male's orgasm (end pleasure) that can be identified as a necessary moment in the reproductive process.

While "pleasure" is physiologically necessary for the male's sexual performance (as it is not for the female), Freud delimits the validity of the forepleasures to their inconspicuous and efficacious contribution to the attainment of the end pleasure, to "the production of the greater pleasure of satisfaction" (211). This phrase is similar to ones Freud uses to distinguish the superior reality principle from the pleasure principle: "A momentary pleasure, uncertain in its results, is given up, but only in order to gain along the new path an assured pleasure at a later time" ("Formulations" 223). The association of end pleasure with the reality principle supports an association between male heterosexual ejaculation and life-preserving instincts (since the reality principle is the life-preserving adaptation to reality), an association central to the pattern of the "anaclitic" subject I have delineated here.[53] Conversely, like the other aspects of the anaclitic subject's sexualized self-defenses, this association also is implicated in a specific delegitimization of gay male sexuality and a heinous programmatic exploitation of women.

Freud numbers among men who make narcissistic object-choices "perverts" and "homosexuals" due to a "disturbance" in their "libidinal development" ("On Narcissism" 88). One may assume that the "development" so disturbed is the progression of "the sexual instincts . . . from their original auto-erotism . . . to object-love in the service of procreation" ("Formulations" 224). Rather than contest this, I wish to accept it with radical and deviant literalness. The implicit logic herein is responsible for the association of male homosexuality with "arrested development" as well as "inauthenticity," "frivolity," "artifice," "inutility," in fact, art. This is because a cessation in the development toward the intrapsychic hegemony of the reality principle keeps the homosexual male more within the realm of the "pleasure principle" than is considered acceptable in mature adult males. The contrast between heterosexual reproductive responsibility and the purely recreational sexuality of homosexuality is the basis of a moralizing phenomenology of dominant heterosexuality that delegitimates homosexuality as ontologically bereft, epistemologically deranged, and procreatively recalcitrant.

One of Freud's definitions of a "perversion" is the "linger[ing] over the intermediate relations to sexual object which should normally be traversed rapidly on the path towards the final sexual aim" (*Three Essays* 150). Sadism and masochism, however, when installed within the agenda of dominant heterosexual reproduction, are not necessarily perversions, but complementary forms of masculine aggression and feminine submission functioning to ensure the continuance of the lineage (on these terms): "The sexuality of most male human beings contains an element of *aggressiveness*—a desire to subjugate; the biological significance of it seems to lie in the need for overcoming the resistance of the sexual object by means other than the process of wooing" (157–58).[54]

The gay science fiction writer Thomas A. Disch expresses a very situated alienation from this kind of heterosexual pragmatism in his story "Planet of the Rapes," set in a distant future society in which all women live on earth and all men live as perpetual space cadets among the colonized moons and planets. Men and women meet only in governmentally controlled mating situations. Beginning at age seventeen, women are regularly sent to "Pleasure Island" for one month, during which time they are raped repeatedly by selected males who have been stationed there for the same period. "Planet" chronicles the first sexual experience of seventeen-year-old Colly and the equally virginal Space Marine Ensign 17-J. The story opens with Colly's distress over her scheduled visit to Pleasure Island. "Colly felt . . . that she was too young to be raped" (162). Ensign 17-J, however, anticipated his visit to the island with more pleasure, "wondering whether the reality of his first rape would measure up to the long-cherished dream" (165). He had also been given much more specific preparation. From ages eleven to fifteen, boys are required to have sexual intercourse with specifically designed artificial women, in special gymnasium settings where pornographic video tapes are played repetitively to stimulate and maintain arousal. If a cadet fails to ejaculate within two minutes, he will be given "a punishing jolt of electroshock direct to the cerebral cortex instead of the lollypop of orgasm" (166).

Ensign 17-J was trained exclusively on the "Polly Doll . . . British Leyland's answer to Ford's prize-winning Susie Tawdry model. They had red hair, red hoopskirts, and blue tits with little tassles." His standard workout prior to arrival on earth shows him to be in top form: "He toned up . . . with ten minutes of incline sit-ups, seventy-five push-ups, and a nice spring eight times around the . . . track . . . four rounds with a Norelco Electropuncher . . . following which . . . he went straight to the Men's Room and threw a quick fuck into the Polly Doll. Whap-Blap. Exactly 12 strokes, whereupon he shot his load with a satisfying sense of dispatch" (166). On Pleasure Island the cadet finds Colly standing blindfolded and immobilized on a display carousel, dressed and made up to be an exact replica of the Polly Doll. Enraptured, he carries her off to the De Sade Hilton, where he chains her to the wall and rapes her repeatedly for three days, following instructions in his *Marital Love* guidebook.

This arch parody indicts dominant heterosexuality for several of its fundamental characteristics, some of which my earlier analyses have touched upon: (1) a prohibition of identification across genders; (2) a reduction of sexuality to the reality principle of reproduction—which (a) erases female sexuality altogether; (b) allows for sexual pleasure for the man—but a restriction of the degree of permissible pleasure to that necessary to bring about a quick and effective ejaculation; (c) identifies impregnation and masculine identity as athletic performance (and duty) that serves as a compensation both for the minimalization of pleasure and for the anxieties regarding the loss of self in the orgasm.

Disch's story also illustrates the grotesque implications of Freud's reservations about classifying "sadism" as a perversion, since it served the function of reproduction when it enabled a male to fulfill his duty independent of the woman's consent. The sadism in "Planet of the Rapes" dramatizes the two ways in which sadism is implicitly desexualized in that passage of Freud's *Three Essays*: the pragmatics of enforced reproduction, and the repression of empathy. As Freud explains in "Instincts and Their Vicissitudes," the "sexual" sadist identifies with his or her "victim," recognizing the masochistic pleasure the sadist's enacted violence incites (128–29).[55] A "sadism" that precludes identification with the object of the aggression is therefore not sexual. As such, this heteroaggressive, goal-oriented sadism is strangely grafted onto two stages in the sexual history of the male child: the anal-sadistic stage of male sexual maturation in which the "active/passive" opposition has not yet given way to a conception of "male/female" (*Three Essays* 198, 219–20), and the phallic stage at which "maleness exists but not femaleness" (Freud, "Infantile Genital" 145). The threat from the "abyss of non-meaning" is warded off anaclitically by proving one's manhood through the end-driven heteroaggressive intercourse economically dispatched. It is no wonder that the "Polly Dolls" are known as "fetishes" ("Planet" 166). All things considered, Leonardo's identification with his mother (along "the path of narcissism") does not seem like such a terrible idea after all.

In later chapters I go into more specific detail on the two features of intersubjective narcissism I sketch here, namely the suspension of the primacy of "reality" over "artifice," and the transgressive mobility of identifications. I will also demonstrate specifically how intersubjective narcissism thus constituted facilitates deviant reinhabitations of the most typically oppressive representational traditions: the historical narrative (in chapter 2) and visual pornography (in chapter 4).

The Stakes of Representation

Representational Politics

"Representation" names both the practices in which the subject's accession to agency is enacted, and the cultural productions within which subjectivity and agency are materially inscribed. The peculiar interiority to the dominant order from which gay male subjectivity emerges often imbues gay cultural expressions with a metatextual ambivalence. The strategic efficacy of gay male appropriation of conventional forms of representation should be evaluated on a case-by-case basis. Whatever pertinence Fredric Jameson's perspective on the "third world novel" may hold for gay male cultural politics must be assessed within critical considerations of the relations of white Euro-American gay men to power, in ways Jameson's theory does not accommodate. He writes:

> In its emergent strong form a genre is essentially a socio-symbolic message.
> . . . That form is immanently and intrinsically an ideology in its own right.
> When such forms are reappropriated and refashioned in quite different social
> and cultural contexts, this message persists and must be functionally reckoned
> into the new form. . . . The ideology of the form itself, thus sedimented, per-
> sists into the latter, more complex structure, as a generic message which co-
> exists—either as a contradiction or, on the other hand, as a mediatory or
> harmonizing mechanism—with elements from later stages. (*The Political Un-
> conscious* 141)

Because of the social privileges of (particularly white) men, the accidental congruence of male-male homoerotic bonds with masculine orthodoxy, and the ease with which male homoerotic desire can be sublimated within phallocentrism, the "mediatory or harmonizing" mechanisms within any standard genre could easily nullify the radical potential of any gay male cultural production.[56]

This complication seems particularly true of the novel, since it achieved its normative realist form in the nineteenth century, "the age of discipline" characterized by "hierarchical surveillance, normalization, and the development of a subjectivity supportive of both" (D. A. Miller 18). In fact, the nineteenth-century novel functioned to domesticate the mind—interiorizing and privatizing the individual in the act of reading, a cultural extension of the social function of the nuclear family (ibid. 80–81). When one of the characters in Kevin Killian's novel *Shy* reads *Bleak House*, the narrator observes that the novel is "one of Dickens' 'social' novels . . . calculated to make its readers feel guilty, as indeed all novels are so calculated" (115). Moreover, Barthes's opposing typologies of the readerly and writerly texts (or texts of pleasure and *jouissance*) and the ideological critique of mainstream cinema strongly suggest the gay male subject requires experimental or avant-garde representational forms if that subject is not to be coopted by the very form of its self-representation.[57]

Several reasons have already presented themselves, however, why a critical engagement with gay cultural practices cannot be based upon a presumed adequation between a "radical" subject and a correspondingly "radical" mode of expression. First of all, many of the textual forms I examine here are rather conventional—some of them are even frequently associated with conservative or oppressive cultural agendas: the biography, the memoir, science fiction, sword-and-sorcery, and pornographic film, for example. Secondly, in a phallocratic social order, there is nothing inherently "radical" about male homosexuality. Thirdly, the reduction of the representational practice to an ideal dovetail between subject and expressive form preserves a Cartesian metaphysics of self that is both theoretically impoverished and, as demonstrated in my joint reading of Delany and Barthes, politically disempowering.

A text's subversive potential is not dependent upon its generic innovation, but on how it maps and motivates the antagonisms constituting the subject(s) of representation, and on how it transfigures and recathects the available forms of cultural expression. The paraliterary genres of Samuel R. Delany, the deliberate fragments of Barthes, Kevin Killian's idiosyncratic autobiographical narratives, Almodóvar's adaptations of melodrama and pornography, etc., are all examples of "disconcerting text[s]" that seem "to rewrite the genre or to take part in a continual founding and altering of expectations" (La Capra 140–41). This rewriting is coextensive to the articulation of gay male identities-in-process as these deviant subjects confront culture and enter into representational agency within it. The most radical representational practices of deviant subjects not only challenge the official versions of their lives, but also transvalue the notion of deviance, and interrogate the mechanisms and meanings of representational practices—including their own.

The Narrative and the Specular

I include both prose and film in this study not only for their own considerable inherent interest, but because each offers the most literal realization of the two representational modes on which I will focus: the narrative and the specular.[58] I define "narrative" as a "meaningful" organization of events that at least provisionally posits a "narrator" (of varying degrees of textually explicit "presence") as a generative source of the text's coherence and a privileged relation to its significance. The "specular" refers to the demarcation of subject positions in relation to an image or images and to the schematics of intersubjective differences (subject-object, passive-active, knower-known, self-other) established in the direction and "command" of the look.[59]

Considering these two representational categories brings into focus the relevance of Jameson's claim that the "form" of "a genre is . . . immanently and intrinsically an ideology in its own right," and that the sedimented "ideology of the form itself" must be taken into account when that form is reappropriated in "quite different social and cultural contexts." Both the narrative and the specular are deeply entrenched in the hierarchized binarisms of sexual difference and the epistemological imperialism of the white male subject in Western Euro-American history. The masculine privilege of knowing and interpreting the world is coeval with the practices of narrative as the production of truth, most notably in the disciplines of history and science.[60] The dominant traditions of image production and consumption are founded on the absolute bifurcation into male spectator and female spectacle. In its traditional forms from myth, folktale, to psychoanalytic case history (and certainly the Oedipus), to mainstream film, the practice of narrative itself has played crucial roles in the social embedding of men and women in unequal sociosexual relations as mediated by their respective relations to desire (de Lauretis, *Alice* 103–57).

Even narratology extends and reinforces the teleology of (heterosexual) male sexuality as the standard structure and movement of intelligibility. Susan Winnett takes up some of de Lauretis's insights in her own deconstruction of (heterosexual) male-centered narratology. Winnett's critical project is, first, an elucidation of sexual stereotyping and the elision of feminine sexuality implicit in "the analogy between the representability of the [male] sex act and a possible erotics of reading"; secondly, it outlines the possibility of a narratology based on (heterosexual) female experience, particularly on the different relation of female sexuality to representation (507–508). Winnett takes Peter Brooks's ex-position of Freud's *Beyond the Pleasure Principle* as paradigmatic of the male-centered narratology she interrogates. Male sexual pleasure constitutes a visibly articulated sequence of tumescence and detumescence which begins with a per-ceptible " 'awakening, an arousal, the birth of an appetency, ambition, desire or intention.' " The male organ registers the intensity of this stimulation, rising to the occasion of its provocation, becoming at once the means of pleasure and culture's sign of power. This energy, aroused into expectancy, "takes its course toward 'significant discharge' and shrinks into a state of quiescence . . . that minutes before would have been a sign of impotence" (Winnett 505–506 [phrases in quotation marks are from Brooks]).

Within the linear progression toward "significant discharge," Winnett dis-cerns a negativity that informs and conditions the telos of male-centered sexu-ality itself:

> According to Brooks, Freud's discussion of the pleasure principle charts the route an organism takes when, stimulated out of quiescence, it strives to re-gain equilibrium by finding the appropriate means of discharging the energy invested in it. According to this scheme, desire would be, even at its inception, a desire for the end; birth . . . would be evaluated proleptically through the significance it acquires in the light of the death that consummates and total-izes the life history. (507–508)

Winnett offers as counterexamples two texts (*Frankenstein* and *Romola*) that support her argument for alternative criteria for narrative pleasure outside the phallocentric constraints upon intelligibility legislated by and incessantly rehearsed through the institutions of compulsory heterosexuality. What is more relevant to the present project than Winnett's specific examples, however, is the methodological aperture she provides within the psychosexual modeling of narrative paradigms. Winnett's critical rigor is evident in her refusal to reify her own examples as *the* oppositional narrative form; she explicitly qualifies her reading of her chosen texts as "ultimately more valuable for its relativizing function than as a scheme competing for authority with the Masterplot" (508).

My major criticism of Winnett's strategies, however, concerns her binary opposition between a uniform "male sexuality" and the repressed and potentially subversive plurivocity of female experience. Of course, the presumption that a particular kind of male sexuality is both unmarked and universal is a grounding feature of the kind of male-dominant discourse she is arguing against. Winnett does not foreclose the possibility of male-based countercultural production when she indicts the universalization of conventional male heterosexuality: "male narratology conceptualizes narrative dynamics in terms of an experience it so swiftly and seamlessly generalizes that we tend to forget that it has its source in experience—in fact, in experience of the body" (508). Although she never explicitly states it in these terms, Winnett provides the possibility of alternative male sexualities generating alternative narrative structures: "The existence of two models implies . . . the possibility of many more; neither the schema I am criticizing nor the one I develop here exhausts the possibilities offered by the psychoanalytic model" (ibid.).

Therefore, even though Winnett's depiction of male sexuality is confined to its most oppressive and static form, her strategic proposal of (heterosexual) female-based narrative structures subtends a discursive space in which nondominant male sexualities could also be productive of texts and meaning systems that phallocentric narratology cannot accommodate. If we allow other male experiences—in particular male homosexuality—to ground and contour narrative expression, the specificity of these bodily experiences would be foregrounded in their oppositional relationship to the hegemonic definitions of masculinity and the hierarchized binarisms of sexual difference. The gay male-based narrative would yield other forms of subjectivity, as well as an alternatively eroticized body within the psychosexual politics of postmodern culture.

With differing emphases, both Teresa de Lauretis and Laura Mulvey identify narrative with the male subject and associate the cultural construction of "woman" with an image-bound hindrance to narrative progression. De Lauretis notes the tendency in narratives—from myth to folktale to popular film—to designate the male figure as the mobile hero of the action, and the female as a stationary obstacle (often monstrous) or as the terrain through which the male passes (de Lauretis, *Alice* 109–24).

In her spectatorship model for dominant cinema, Mulvey has convincingly argued that the different representational planes of the Hollywood film are asymmetrically en-gendered: the woman as passive exhibitionist display represents the nondiegetic spectacle, and the male protagonist personifies the motivation of narrative progression ("Visual Pleasure" 18–19). These oppositions also structure the heterosexual male spectator's relation to the screen, in that he finds erotic pleasure in looking at the female figure as specularized object, and identifies with the male protagonist as the person whose actions control and shape the events of the filmic world.

The Oedipus, which is also the principal ideological narrative in de Lauretis's analysis, is evident in the way that the psychical operations of the male spectator reenact the injunctions of the so-called "positive" Oedipus, the mutual exclusivity of desire and identification. The pleasure in looking in dominant cinema for the male heterosexual viewer is predicated upon the "sexual imbalance" organizing socially defined subjects, reflected here as a tension between an active male viewer (the "bearer of the look" ["Visual Pleasure" 18]) and a passive female object of that male gaze, and overdetermined by an "active/passive heterosexual division of labor," which makes it impossible for "the male figure . . . to bear the burden of sexual objectification" (ibid. 20). The heterosexual constraints on the male gaze are supported by the construction of the "hero" as the embodiment of the narrative drive. The on-screen hero's narrativity, functioning to reinforce the absolute division between identification and desire in the scopophilic economy of the male viewer the film addresses, furthermore, reveals the structural relations among the cinematic apparatus, narrative deployed as a specifically gendering technology of the subject, and the Oedipal complex.

The Oedipal narrative that seems to collapse homosexuality and phallocentrism also invalidates "real" homosexuality as an antinarrative anomaly. The association of male heterosexuality with the reality principle, the self-preservative drives, and the "appropriate" resolution of the Oedipal prohibitions crystallizes a conception of the male heterosexual (anaclitic) subject as both the result of and protagonist in a series of linear, goal-directed, pleasure-sublimated narratives. The male has gone through the three stages of oral, anal, and phallic sexual development in the correct order without lingering or diversion, and has confronted the Medusa of sexual difference and submitted to paternal Law. This male then becomes the hero in the battle narratives of heterosexual phallic masquerade-courtship, apotropaic conquest, and patrilineal destiny.

The adult male homosexual, in contrast, is a pastiche of interrupted narratives: a maturation "arrested" at the narcissistic stage; a "disturbance" in his libidinal development, suspending him within the sway of the pleasure principle; a failure to understand the riddle of the castration complex, thus sabotaging Oedipal resolution and fomenting a capacity for transgressive identifications. Even the polycentric erotic body of the male homosexual figures a coexistence of the oral, anal, and phallic phases of libidinal organization that should be discrete and unrecoverable moments in the subject's pre-Oedipal history. Of course, to suggest that the erotic choices of the "homosexual male" evolve from an identifiable preservation of these phases is to conflate the somatic and specific practices of adult individuals with the metaphoric and emblematic uses of body parts to designate an abstract outline of psychosexual development. It may be just such a series of conflations, however—between the metaphoric and the referential, between the figurative and the experiential—that are operative within the political imaginary of the dominant culture which makes the male homosexual an embodied crime against "nature" and his sexuality an aberration within the narrative logic of phallic truth. The gay male body (or gay male subject) therefore lends itself to representation as picture (perhaps a cubist picture)—with a simultaneity of erogenous zones—rather than as a history (a narrative).[61] In discussing gay male representational practices, therefore, I use "narrative" and "specular" in three distinct but often interrelated senses: as broad categories of representational genres, as metonyms for registers of subjectivity (the specular and the narrative corresponding to Lacan's "Symbolic" and "Imaginary," respectively), and as metaphors for specific conceptualizations of sexual identities, such as the specularity of homosexuality and the narrativity of male heterosexuality.

Mapping Deviant Strategies of Representation

If gay male sexuality lends itself to representation as a saturated specularity, the narrativized, stoic sexuality of the anaclitic subject, in fact, finds its own optimal representational correlatives in the scientific study and the historical treatise. The proscription of "superfluous" pleasure and the fervent priority of accomplishment over process suggest a signifying practice delimited by a determinate exteriority: the Truth as the transcendent end of a disciplined progression. The reality principle governs the anaclitic male's sexual agenda (apotropaic erection, efficient attainment of end pleasure in the service of procreation) and the scientist's narrative priorities (the domination of nature, the establishment of Truth). Chapter 2 opens with a reading of Freud's psychobiography of Leonardo da Vinci, one of the most overdetermined examples in Freud's canon of such sexualized epistemological contests. Freud's characterizations of the dual aspects of Leonardo's "genius" as artist and as scientist display structural associations between representational form and sexual orientation I have just suggested, by marking Leonardo's "artistic" or "pictorially inclined" activities as more "homosexual" than his scientific curiosity (Freud, *Leonardo and a Memory*, 76–77; 130–34; Laplanche, "To Situate" 10–11).

Deviant readings of texts such as "On Narcissism" and the *Leonardo* monograph clarify the dialectical logic of a significant pattern of gay male cultural resistance to the heteropatriarchal fixing of male homosexual difference from heterosexuality in structurally paralleled binary oppositions, among them the pleasure principle and the reality principle; play and work; sexual desire and sublimation; inauthenticity and authenticity; and appearance and reality. I will trace such antagonisms in chapter 2 by contrasting Freud's "sublimated" scientist's narrative commitment to Truth with the desublimated fantasy investigations of Oscar Wilde and Derek Jarman. The uses of "artifice," "camp," and the self-conscious fictivity of the subject in the works examined in the other chapters attest that the pleasure principle of the artist and the sexual deviant is not so much a failure to mature into an obedience to the reality principle and the often grim tasks of heterosexual genitality, as it is a resistance to the stultifying purposiveness of (literally) reproducing the current social order. There is a playfulness in gay sexuality that serves neither the goal-directed realism of reproductive altruism nor the defensive maintenance of anaclitic male heterosexuality.

The ludic insubordination to the reality principle is a motivating force in gay male cultural politics. In chapter 3 we will see other forms of resistance to the "reality principle" and "truth" in Samuel R. Delany's science fiction, sword-and-sorcery, and theoretical writings. Science fiction is a type of writing that consistently counterposes the presumed "real," the possible, and the conceivable, in mobile and innovative conceptual systems. Deviant science fiction writers might exploit the transpersonal semantic capacity of language to advance specific forms of the subject as a cognitive entity beyond the referential myopia of realism or the "already read" histories of Truth. Delany has adapted the genre for speculation on unanticipated epistemes and for the projections of currently unauthorized identities. One of the stories featured in this chapter deconstructs the ineluctability of dominant male sexual narratology, and vividly distinguishes the politically oppressive, involuntary sadism (of compulsory heterosexuality) from intersubjectively engaged sexual S/M.

In the first section of chapter 4 I develop contrasting cinematic spectatorship models for the anaclitic and narcisstic subjects, paying particular attention to how the specular modalities of gay male subject processes emerge from transgressive internalizations of the dominant polarities of vision (in terms of the failed Oedipus, negating affirmations, and intersubjective narcissism). My examples are drawn primarily from gay male pornographic film and the peculiarities of their exhibition. In the second section I discuss the adaptation of pornographic representational practices among filmmakers closer to the mainstream, in particular Pedro Almodóvar and Derek Jarman. The pornographic apparatus supports Almodóvar's reappropriation of the dominant constructions of male homosexuality as specular and heterosexuality as narrative. In *Law of Desire*, the gay porn film symbolizes the gay male subject's "specular" interruption of the heterosexual Oedipal narrative. The specular excess of pornography as an emblem for gay male sexuality in *Law of Desire* is in turn juxtaposed to the murder mystery as an emblem of heterosexuality in *Matador*. This juxtaposition demonstrates that the representational modes (and what the modes represent) can be manipulated not only to provide allegorical illustrations for the psychic and social constructions of the subject, but even to intervene in that process.

In Victorian England, overt expression of same-sex desire among men was repressed by the possibility of scandal, and reinforced by those "scandals" that were publicized as examples of the impunity with which homoerotic visibility would be punished.[62] At least since Genet, but certainly after Stonewall, "scandal" is no longer a pressure from without to prevent disclosures of a perverse identity, but rather the fissure in public discourses that enables contestatory articulations of deviant sociosexual subjectivities. Chapter 5 showcases three of the "New Narrative" writers who have explored and actualized the dynamics of "scandal" in their works: Dennis Cooper, Robert Glück, and Kevin Killian.

The "revolutionary" element of New Narrative writing is not so much in the form, but in the politics of expression. These writers abandoned the narrative traditions of the quest for an objective or transcendent "Truth" in favor of storytelling that produces meanings as an intensely localized event. In specifically gay "New Narrative," language takes on dual purposes: communal identification ("I'm interested in the way we exist for each other in language" [Glück, "Truth's Mirror," 40]); and countercultural defiance, since such texts are written against the dominant social "tenet that homosexuality does not exist verbally" (Glück, *Elements* 15). For these reasons, New Narrative represents an "avant-garde" that is neither "difficult" nor exclusionary. The most radical elements of New Narrative actually increase the accessibility (or relevance to the reader) of the represented world, and encourage participation in the production of the text's meaning. But the use of "real people" in the narrative that accomplishes this has other, contradictory purposes. Glück "names names" not only to "make the work co-extend with the world and history" but also "to examine the fiction of personality" (Glück, "Fame" 2). Just as the narrative progression is not subordinated to the reality principle toward an unmediated Truth, the narrator's textualized subjectivity is a scandalously publicized *jouissance* not effaced in the pure abstraction of the Cartesian *cogito*, nor bound as the psychosocially fixed "self" of bourgeois realism.

In his discussion of the shifting historico-cultural valences of Barthes's textual categories, Delany maps an ethics of representational response, accentuating the political import of the concepts often eclipsed in Barthes's texts by the apparent hedonism of his preferred critical metaphors. Delany characterizes "writerly texts" as those which directly confront "all the problems of writing," and "readerly texts" as those which avoid problems and possibilities of writing "by accepting some standard of 'the real' that is nowhere a correspondence between the word and the world but is rather a set of language conventions that mystify whatever correspondences there might be for the sake of bourgeois exploitation." Prior to the twentieth century, "it was possible to write the readerly text in good faith," but when it became "necessary to write the writerly text, it became impossible to write the readerly text in good faith any longer" (Delany, *American Shore* 169 n. 2).

Delany's distinctions here speak to the cultural lineage of the doubly articulated male homoerotism I traced from the Renaissance to the turn of the nineteenth century. Like the Renaissance sodomite, the nineteenth-century "Uranian" relied on phallocentric mythographs of masculine self-overestimation to disguise his fantasies—he sought a visibility through which he could remain unseen. This defense allowed the writers or artists to elude surveillance while conveying their hidden meanings to those whose desires also enabled them to read the codes. Such appropriations of masculinist discourse were repetitions with perverse internal differences whose exposure might have denaturalized the male ideals these gestures putatively exemplified. Any signifying practice always exceeds its normative limitations; although "symbolic schemes" are "experienced as received knowledge," they, like language itself, "contain the conditions for their own reformulation" (Boon 83). There is, however, as much ambivalence as dissonance in this subterfuge: the mere existence of male homosexuality within these representations is not inherently subversive, nor are such practices automatically transformative; in fact, practice is the means by which "a structure is actively reproduced" (Hall 96). Although the perverse resignifications of dominant masculine iconography provided a cryptography for an "outlaw" community, its mimesis of patriarchal autoaffection was too well executed to disturb the dominant meanings of those expressions.[63]

The tradition of culturally encoding homosexual desire with the neo-Platonic euphemistic rationalizations of Greek homoerotic expression resembles Freud's characterization of hysterical symptoms and the manifest content of dreams as forms of "compromise" in the struggle between the unacceptable wish and the repressive force of the ego—or the "sexual instincts" and the "ego instincts" (Freud, *Introductory Lectures* 347–51). The symptom arises when these antagonistic forces reach a reconciliation; the symptom in fact is the form that that reconciliation takes. "It is for that reason too that the symptom is so resistant: it is supported from both sides" (ibid. 358–59). The dream is a compromise between the unconscious and preconscious. The form the unconscious wish takes in order to elude the censorship of the preconscious expresses both the power of repression and the opposition to that repression in the unconscious (359). We need to remember, however, that the symptom's constancy and the dream's occurrence at all are due to the fact that each serves the interests of repression (the repressive order) *more than* the interests of the repressed desire.

While Symonds, Wilde, Pater, and their contemporaries had no choice but to disguise their desires within expressions derived from traditions of masculinist self-worship, similar strategies now would prove worse than nostalgic. Just as Delany argues that historical and social changes made the "readerly text" no longer an ethically feasible option, the social and cultural transformations wrought by the civil rights movement and by second-wave and "third world" feminisms render insupportable the formally self-preservative "anaclisis" (attachment) of homoerotic desire to male-dominant cultural forms.[64]

As I stated above, the narrative and the specular have been instrumental in the establishment and maintenance of white male authority. As men within this history, gay men express their subjectivities through the same traditions and privileges; the deviant strategists do so with destabilizing differences. The disruptive, intersubjective narcissism of the gay male *desidero* (replacing the Cartesian *cogito*) elaborates itself in print and visual texts whose recursive reflexivity mirrors the constitutive narcissism of their own representational processes and illuminates the contingencies of subject production that are assiduously obscured in patriarchal culture. Such recursive reflexivity also contours the project at hand: this book is about gay male texts, and is itself a gay male text; it examines expressions of gay male subjectivity, and is itself an expression of a (my) gay male subjectivity. The titles of the last two chapters, "Graphic Specularity" and "Scandalous Narratives," also suggest the gay-inflected metasignifications of the mutually implicative relations between the representational mode and the text that instantiates it. The reciprocity or mutual inscriptions of voyeurism and exhibitionism and scopophilia and identification in gay male visual media are not only instances of "specularity," but *the specularity itself is also graphic*, explicit: the processes of the looks, the exchanges, and their phantasmatic confirmations of the subject are rendered visible. The prose texts narrate the realities of sexual identities that are scandals, but *the act of narrating them itself is also a scandal*. These texts affirm their deviance in negating the masculinist metaphysics of their tradition. Its intertextual, intrageneric, and metadiscursive narcissism allows a given text to represent both a representational practice and a subject of that representation whose articulation in that text also represents a rupture from the traditions that this act of representation and its subject reinhabit. This radical rupture comes not from hiding within dominant male identity, but from articulating a countersubjectivity through that identity's constitutive impossibilities. Deviant strategies enable ruptural reinhabitations of cultural practice. Deviant cultural production inscribes within its texts the historically necessitated break between the encrypted subject and the scandalous subject, an inscription whose double-cross-hatching maps where and how gay male subjectivity and representational agency intermesh.

2

History and Its Desublimations

"I think," he said, "in this world it is very important not to have a father if you
want . . . to know anything."

—Samuel R. Delany, *Stars in My Pocket Like Grains of Sand*

NAMING "GREAT PEOPLE" throughout history who in all likelihood har-
bored and even acted upon same-sex desires is a time-honored antihomo-
phobic strategy. Uncovering these aspects of those famous lives and the mechanisms of their exclusion from "official" histories has been an important part of
lesbian and gay studies. In considering such historiographic revisions, however,
we must clearly distinguish between apologetics and critical intervention, between "homoerotism" and "homosexuality," and between premodern and
modern historical periods. To elaborate the importance of Walt Whitman's or
Hart Crane's homosexuality to their poetry is easily justified; to declare Plato
or Shakespeare "homosexual" or "gay" is quite another story. Projecting an
unproblematized "homosexual identity" onto figures from historical periods
prior to the invention of the homosexual in the nineteenth century simplifies
questions of sexual identity that lesbian and gay studies should complicate; it
also reinforces the popular associations between male-dominant culture and
male homosexuality that need to be severed (Jackson, "Responsibility" 136–37).[1]

The first major text to insist on the homosexuality of a "great man" of
European civilization and the importance of his sexuality to understanding his
work, moreover, was not written by a "queer theorist," nor was it intended as
a validation of "gay" desire. I refer to Freud's *Leonardo da Vinci and a Memory
of His Childhood* (1910), a text basic to one tradition of the institutional pathologization of male homosexuality. On the other hand, our preliminary overview
of deviant strategies in the previous chapter strongly suggests that even the
most oppressive signifying practices can be in some way reappropriated, by virtue of, for example, the double articulation of the gay male sociosexual subject,
the "split visionary" epistemology a gay male subject may develop from that
double articulation, and the logic of Foucault's reverse discourse that often
structures gay representational agency. I will illustrate the counterdiscursive potential of the political indeterminacy of Freud's homosexual historiography by

juxtaposing my reading of *Leonardo* with readings of Oscar Wilde's "The Portrait of W. H." and Derek Jarman's writings on Michele Caravaggio.[2]

The History of an "Ideal" Homosexual: Freud's *Leonardo*

"History" in Freud's Leonardo

In 1902 Freud began hosting weekly meetings among professionals interested in psychoanalysis and its broader critical implications. These "Wednesday evenings" evolved into the Vienna Psychoanalytic Society, founded in 1908. Several biographical studies of historical and literary figures emerged from these meetings, including *Leonardo da Vinci and a Memory of his Childhood* (1910) (Gay, 136; 268–74). This monograph was one of Freud's first attempts to demonstrate the relevance of psychoanalytic method for other areas of cultural investigation, an interest he pursued throughout his career.

Freud relies on traditional historical methods of documentary research to present a coherent synopsis of the pertinent "facts" of Leonardo's life; he appeals to psychoanalysis to discover the meaning of those facts and the internal dynamics constituting that life. With this dual methodology Freud intended to bring to light elements of da Vinci's "genius" that would otherwise remain enigmatic. The enigmas on which Freud focused include Leonardo's tendency to leave paintings unfinished or to declare apparently completed works unfinished; his insatiable scientific curiosity; the relation between his artistic practice and his scientific research (*Leonardo and a Memory* 64–67); and his apparent disinterest in sexuality—either as a topic of investigation or as an aspect of his personal life (ibid. 69–70). Freud's solutions to these Renaissance mysteries were also presentations of theories Freud had formulated from his contemporary clinical practice, in particular a specific etiology of male homosexuality, and a theory of sublimation.

The Etiology of Male Homosexuality

The second edition of the *Three Essays*, published a few months before *Leonardo*, contained a new footnote in which Freud introduces a theory on one of the causes of male homosexuality that figures importantly in the Leonardo monograph. In this footnote Freud asserts that "in all cases we have examined, we have established the fact that future inverts, in the earliest years of their childhood, pass through a phase of very intense but short-lived fixation to a woman (usually their mother), and that, after leaving this behind, they identify themselves with a woman and take themselves to be their sexual object" (144–45 n. 1). In the *Leonardo* text, Freud closely paraphrases the *Three Essays* note, but adds that the "intense erotic attachment" of the fledgling invert "was evoked or encouraged by too much tenderness on the part of the mother herself, and further reinforced by the small part played by the father during their childhood" (*Leonardo and a Memory* 99). Among his homosexual analysands, Freud was "impressed by [the number of] cases in which the father was absent from the beginning or left the scene at an early date, so that the boy found himself left entirely under feminine influence" (ibid.).

Prior to arguing for Leonardo's homosexuality, therefore, Freud had to establish a familial situation that resembled those of his homosexual patients. Freud's "historical" evidence is quite plausible. Leonardo was born in 1452, the illegitimate child of a peasant woman and Ser Piero da Vinci, a nobleman. Leonardo's father married another woman the year of Leonardo's birth, but the couple remained childless. A 1457 land register lists Leonardo living in the da Vinci household "as the five-year-old illegitimate son of Ser Piero." No records of da Vinci's biological mother exist (*Leonardo and a Memory* 81). The land register proves that Leonardo was raised with his biological father and his father's wife from the age of five. Freud speculates, however, that the child was probably raised alone by his biological mother for at least the first three years of his life. He reasons that the newly married couple would not be likely to take the child immediately, since "the young bride . . . still expects to be blessed with children of her own." It would only be after "years of disappointment" that the couple would adopt the illegitimate child "as a compensation for the absence of the legitimate children" that were not forthcoming (91).

For clinical evidence of Leonardo's homosexuality and its origin in an intense, isolated relationship with his mother in early childhood, Freud turns to one of Leonardo's scientific notebooks. In an essay on flight, Leonardo remarks that one of his earliest childhood memories is of lying in his cradle when " 'a vulture came down to me, and opened my mouth with its tail, and struck me many times with its tail against my lips' " (qtd. *Leonardo and a Memory* 82). Freud surmises that this apparent "memory" is actually a fantasy from later life projected backward onto the artist's infancy. Within this fantasy, the vulture's tail represents both the mother's breast and a penis; the child is at once nursing and engaged in fellatio (82–84). Freud then traces possible cultural associations surrounding vultures that would support this image complex in da Vinci's psychic life. He notes that the Egyptian mother goddess Mut was often depicted with the head of a vulture, and endowed with breasts and a penis (88; 93). Furthermore, the Egyptians believed that all vultures were female, and were impregnated by the wind (88–89). The latter legend was taken up and widely disseminated by the Roman Church as an illustration of "virgin birth," and was thus a legend with which Leonardo would have been familiar. Freud concludes that in Leonardo's fantasy "the replacement of the mother by the vulture indicates that the child was aware of his father's absence and found himself alone with his mother," for at least the first several years prior to adoption into the da Vinci household (90–91).

The vulture fantasy functions in Freud's narrative as a palimpsest of the psychic consequences for Leonardo of the situation of his birth. Within the fantasy Freud finds inscribed the sexual frustrations of Leonardo's mother channeled into erotic attentions to her child, the child's initial response to this attention, and the germinal moments of his subsequent repression of his erotic feelings for his mother in homosexuality. Freud "translates" da Vinci's phrase "[the vulture] struck me many times with its tail against my lips" to read: " 'My mother pressed innumerable passionate kisses upon my mouth' " (107). The erotic overstimulation Leonardo received from his mother is offered as evidence of the exclusivity of their relationship and as a cause of his homosexuality. The "forsaken mother . . . compensat[ed] herself for having no husband, and also compensated her child for having no father to fondle him. So, like all unsatisfied mothers, she took her little son in place of her husband, and by the too early maturing of his erotism robbed him of a part of his masculinity" (116–17).[3]

The homosexuality that results from this scenario arises when the child, unable consciously to acknowledge his inordinate love of his mother, transforms it into an identification with her, and then selects as objects of his desire young men that resemble himself when his mother and he were the primary bond. The number of "homosexual patients" Freud and his colleagues have encountered of this type supports the conclusion Freud draws from his analysis of the vulture fantasy of "a causal connection between Leonardo's relation with his mother in childhood and his later manifest if ideal [sublimated] homosexuality" (98).

Sublimation

His mother's mutual erotic solace stimulated Leonardo into a "precocious sexual maturity," manifested in "the intensity of his infantile sexual researches. . . . The instinct to look and the instinct to know were those most strongly excited by the impressions of early childhood" (131–32). The "intensity" of Leonardo's "infantile sexual research" was partially caused by the mysteries of his parentage: Leonardo "pondered this riddle with special intensity, and so at a tender age became a researcher, tormented as he was by the great question of where babies come from and what the father has to do with their origin" (92). His urgent curiosity was abetted by an inquiry unrestrained by paternal authority. The father's presence might have prevented his homosexuality (99), but it also would have inhibited his later development as a natural scientist (122).

Freud attributes the origin of all investigative impulses to the child's first sexual curiosity, which persists until a period of prepubertal repression sets in. The manner in which these early investigations end determines how this "instinct for research" will emerge from that repression. There are three possibilities. If the sexual repression is severe, the "curiosity remains inhibited and the free activity of intelligence may be limited" for life; if some of the repression is partially overcome, curiosity reemerges as "compulsive reasoning" which at times is "sufficiently powerful to sexualize thinking itself and to colour intellectual operations with the pleasure and anxiety" typical of sexuality, but which remains bound to repetition and frustration (79–80). The instinct may elude repression altogether, however, by sublimating the libido "into curiosity" that can be freely put "in the service of intellectual interest" (80). Sexual repression is still a factor in this operation in that the instinct "avoids any concern with sexual themes." Leonardo is "a model instance of the third type" of postpubertal curiosity because of "the concurrence . . . of his overpowerful instinct for research and the atrophy of his sexual life (which was restricted to what is called ideal [sublimated] homosexuality)" (80).

Like all children, Leonardo's early "sexual researches" were "brought to an end" by "a powerful wave of repression" whose transformations would "become manifest in the years of puberty." Because of his early, intense sexual curiosity, "the greater portion of the needs of his sexual instincts could be sublimated into a general urge to know, and thus evaded repression." His artistic practice was conceivably a sublimation of the "scopophilic instinct" prematurely awakened by his mother's libidinally charged caresses (132), his scientific career a sublimation of his early sexual investigations unchecked by a father's prohibitions. Because Leonardo's sexual feelings for his mother also succumbed to repression, "this portion [of his libido] was driven to take up a homosexual attitude and manifested itself in ideal love for boys" (132). As a master painter, Leonardo was able to maintain the fixation on his mother according to this pattern: he "took only strikingly handsome boys and youths as pupils. He treated them with kindness and consideration, looked after them, and when they were ill nursed them himself, just as a mother might have tended him" (102). Leonardo's painting sublimated his scopophilia, and his reputation as an artist allowed him to sublimate his homosexuality (in itself a repression of his heterosexual desire for his mother) into nuturing the young male surrogates for himself.

(Mis)Constructions in Analysis

It seems that the plural itinerary of the Leonardo text would dissipate any unity of "knowledge" it might produce. In fact, however, the historical detective work and the presentation of psychoanalytic theory constitute mutually supportive operations: each functions to supplement the deficit in the narrative logic of the other. The circularity of the investigation is most conspicuous in the passage in which Freud interprets the vulture fantasy as evidence of Leonardo's homosexuality and its origins in his mother's excessive love. Freud pauses in his close reading of the fantasy images to ask: "When we remember the historical probability of Leonardo having behaved in his life as one who was emotionally homosexual, the question is forced upon us whether this phantasy does not indicate the existence of a causal connection between Lzonardo's relation to his mother in childhood and his later manifest, if ideal [sublimated], homosexuality" (98). He immediately qualifies this speculation by referring to scientific data from modern case studies of homosexuals without which he would not have "venture[d] to infer a connection of this sort from Leonardo's distorted reminiscence." Freud's apparently wild association is actually, therefore, an educated guess, because "the psycho-analytic study of homosexual patients" has proven "that such a connection does exist and is in fact an intimate and necesssary one" (ibid.). After a lengthy (and heavily annotated) discussion of the details of this etiology of male homosexuality, Freud justifies this digression by declaring the vulture fantasy proof of the validity and relevance of this theory of homosexuality, even though the modern case studies were introduced into this discussion as vindication of Freud's interpretation of the vulture fantasy. He writes: "We should not have had any cause at all for entering into the psychical genesis of the form of homosexuality we have studied if there were not a strong presumption that Leonardo, whose phantasy of the vulture was our starting point, was himself a homosexual of this very type" (101). Freud assumes a circumstance that he sets out to prove.

The deduction of Leonardo's homosexuality from the bird fantasy contains another faulty syllogism, but the very lapses in the logic of the explanation accord with the mythic structuration of phallocentric patriarchy. Freud, in fact, begins his analysis of the bird fantasy by drawing an analogy between early male sexual development and mythological thought. He focuses on an irrecoverably mythic period in male psychic history, that stage "when [the boy] still held the woman at her full value." This attitude arises from the child's narcissistic fascination with his own penis and his presumption that everyone was possessed of one. When the sight of female genitalia shatters his assumptions, the boy's desire for his mother becomes "disgust, which . . . can become the cause of psychic impotence, misogyny, and permanent homosexuality" (96). The former belief in the woman's penis leaves psychic imprints on the child, collective traces of which are found in the mythical mother goddess figures such as Mut, depicted with prominent breasts and penis (97–98).

There is nothing at this point in the explanation that differentiates a homosexual and a heterosexual male. Freud locates Leonardo's homosexual difference in the syntax of the vulture fantasy itself, the fantasy's transformation of "sucking at the mother's breast into being suckled, that is, into passivity, and thus into a situation whose nature is undoubtedly homosexual" (98). What is the difference between sucking at the breast and being suckled? "The child sucks at the mother's breast" and "the mother suckles the child" essentially describe the same activity of nursing, from opposite perspectives. In the former, the child can suck on the breast only if the mother has given it to the child (which is what "to suckle" means); in the latter, nursing is described in terms of the activity of the mother, but it is a pointless action unless the child then sucks on the breast once it is inserted in the mouth. What "passivity" does Freud mean? Why is "passivity" the mark of homosexuality and not the sexes of the persons involved?

The "passivity" in this sentence is the conjunction of two separate transfigurations of the concept of the "passive": one grammatical and one a sexual positionality. Freud's oversimplification of the operations involved to derive "being suckled" from "sucking" is not merely linguistically unsophisticated. The passive form of "to suck" (*saugen*) is "to be sucked" (*gesaugt werden*), not "to be suckled" (*gesäugt werden*), which is the passive form of "to suckle" (*säugen*). "*To suckle*" (*säugen*) is a causative form of "to suck," meaning "to make or allow to suck." Freud used "to suckle" only a few pages prior to the analysis of the fantasy, but significantly "corrects" himself: "The mother who suckles her child—or to put it better, at whose breast the child sucks" (93). Here the mother's agency, her position as subject of an active verb, is displaced by substituting a verb in which the child becomes the subject. In the passage at hand, the transformation of "sucking at the mother's breast into being suckled," the previous verb is restored, not in its active form (for which the mother would be the subject) but in its passive form (in which the subject is suppressed).[4] In the earlier passage the replacement of the verb "to suckle" with "to suck" denied the mother the subject position in favor of the (male) child. The "transformation" from "to suck" to "to be suckled" revokes the male child's prerogative as subject because of his homosexuality, but tautologously this revocation (the "passivity") is offered as *proof* of his homosexuality. The grammatical transformation into "being suckled" denies a subject position to both the mother and the child, the woman and the "homosexual." The marginalizations played out within this grammatical fantasy are obscured by the assumption that the "transformation" in the verb reflects a concrete physical or intrapsychic event independent of this linguistic construction imposed upon it. The politics of representation here are mystified by the common-sense belief in a language transparent to a preexisting referential reality. This is the language philosophy of the historical narrative, not the psychoanalytic narrative, a distinction to which I will return below.

The "passivity" that is transferred from a grammatical designation to a sexual subject position is another end product of a suppressed chain of substitutions. The "passivity" at the heart of male homosexual difference is the so-called "passivity" of the receptive partner in male-male anal intercourse. Even this, however, is not an objective description of the roles, but an evaluative binary based on dominant sexual politics, mystified through a metaphor based on the grammar of the Indo-European verbal system (active/passive voice) just as gender inequities are systematically naturalized through metaphors based on the grammar of nouns (masculine/feminine). In the case of male-male fellatio, the "passivity" of the oral insertee is a conventional attribution derived from an imperfect analogy with the recipient partner in anal intercourse: each person receives the penis into a bodily cavity. The analogy does not hold, however, when comparing the distribution of exertion required to produce orgasm in each act. In anal intercourse, the insertee could conceivably remain motionless; the effort is required of the insertive partner. In fellatio, however, the stimulation of the genitals depends on the efforts of the insertee; the insertive partner may remain entirely motionless. The oral insertee is, technically speaking, exerting more effort, more decisive activity, than the oral insertive partner. This is just as true for the nursing child, whether the act be described as the child sucking the breast, the mother suckling the child, or the child being suckled. Freud's equation of "being suckled" with passivity, and that "passivity" with the infant's homosexuality, requires two serial misprisions: one based on the elision of one of the transformations in the grammar of a verb, and one based on the conflation of effort-based active-passive binarism of anal intercourse with the incertive-receptive roles, that conflation transferred to fellatio.[5]

The argument for the "passivity" in the vulture fantasy as the mark of Leonardo's homosexual difference, therefore. is a grammatical sleight of hand that cancels itself out. Without this difference, the steps of Freud's proof of Leonardo's homosexuality deduced from his analysis of the vulture fantasy are as follows: (1) at a certain stage in sexual development, all boys think that everyone has a penis; (2) at this stage a boy's sexual interest in his mother revolves around her imagined penis; (3) when a boy discovers that women do not have penises, he is traumatized; (4) the early belief in the mother's penis is so transculturally pervasive that many mother goddesses have penises; (5) Leonardo had a fantasy of being nursed by his mother that figured a belief in her breasts and penis; (6) Leonardo is a homosexual.[6]

Such a proof once again neutralizes the difference between a homosexual and the phallocentrically defined heterosexual male. (Leonardo is "homosexual" because he is not different from the other men.) These are the kinds of internal contradictions of dominant masculinity that give rise to feminist interventions such as those of Luce Irigaray, who, as I noted in chapter 1, characterizes patriarchies as "homm(m)osexual" social orders. Freud supports such identifications when he characterizes Leonardo as exemplary of the kind of male homosexual who does not indulge in sexual contact with men. Freud does not view this as a repression but as a metaphysics which he terms "ideal [sublimated] homosexuality" (*Leonardo and a Memory* 98).

Even if the logic of Freud's deductions were to hold up, however, the assertions listed above are an extraordinary amount of speculative weight to balance on the capricious tail feathers of a fantasized bird. In fact, the maternal origin of Leonardo's homosexuality proves to be insupportable: *nibio*, the bird in Leonardo's text, is not a "vulture" but a "kite" ("Editor's Note," ibid. 61). While this does not invalidate the associations of suckling and fellatio, it obliterates Freud's evidence that Leonardo spent any time at all with his biological mother in his infancy, since this supposition depended upon the legend of the vulture's virgin births. The image of a large bird placing its tail in an infant's mouth may indeed not be a childhood memory but an adult's fantasy; but the psychobiography this image inspired is not Leonardo's history but Freud's fiction.

In more purely psychoanalytic contexts, the term "fiction" does not necessarily carry the pejorative connotation it acquires here from the historiographical burden placed on the *Leonardo* text. After all, "fictions" are a large part of both the object and the method of psychoanalysis: dreams, fantasies, symptoms are fictional objects of psychoanalysis; "constructions in analysis" and the role of the psychoanalyst are fictional instruments of psychoanalytic practice. Freud's respect for fiction as an interpretative model is evident in his admiration for D. S. Merezhkovsky's novel *Leonardo da Vinci* (1902), which he considered one of the few serious psychological portraits of the artist and scientist (*Leonardo and a Memory* 73).[7]

History and psychoanalysis are both narrative practices which intend an intelligible model of the past.[8] But traditional historiography postulates a referential truth antecedent and external to the narrative that is meant to attain it. Psychoanalysis views the past as multiply realized and continually transformed in the processes of interpretation; the psychoanalytic narrative, like any signifying operation, produces meanings that exceed any stable referent—in fact, referentiality is not generally of primary relevance in determining the meaning or significance of what is observed or produced. Freud's mistranslation of *nibio* is the accidental reason why the psychoanalytic reading of this anecdote renders groundless the historical situation it was meant to prove. This accident, however, ironically suggests irreconcilable epistemological differences between psychoanalytic and historical explanation. For the historian, the incident of the bird is potentially significant only *if it occurred*; for the psychoanalyst the bird incident is significant only *if it did not*. The psychobiography fails when Freud presents material within the historiographical presumptions of referential language in the service of "Truth," while the meanings he activates are from psychical operations that displace the possibility of truth.

The historical "Leonardo" Freud intends to "discover" through his investigation is actually produced by Freud's narrative and like a fantasy or a dream, is constituted by a specific and idiosyncratic constellation of its elements. But the "historical" presentation of these elements shifts the burden of the argument from the construction of a conceptual schema of a signifying formation to the restoration of the true story from verifiable evidence. This means that Freud must advance and maintain the following axioms as "true" and noncontradictory: (1) Leonardo was a "homosexual"; (2) his homosexuality was determined by his close relationship with his mother and the absence of his father in his formative years; (3) his artistic experimentation and scientific investigation resulted from a successful sublimation of his sexual drives; (4) he seldom—perhaps never—engaged in sexual activity with men or women. As a "construction in analysis," the contradictory elements can be subsumed in the structural particularity of "Leonardo" as a specific psychosexual dynamic system. As a historical text, however, Freud's insistence on the fourth axiom undermines the logic of his arguments and the credibility of the life they portray. Without accepting the sublimation as an integral element in the entire gestalt of "Leonardo da Vinci," it is difficult to understand Freud's dismissal of the implications of the "facts" he himself presents.

Freud's commitment to Leonardo's homosexual celibacy obligates Freud to accept evidence of *homosexual desire* while refusing to admit evidence of *homosexual behavior.* Because, as Freud notes, Leonardo chose them "for their beauty and not for their talent," none of the "handsome boys and youths" in Leonardo's retinue achieved notable careers as artists, not even his last pupil, Francesco Melzi, who fled with Leonardo to France, where he stayed with him until Leonardo's death and was Leonardo's designated heir. Nevertheless, Freud saw no reason to suspect overt sexual relations between Leonardo and any of his wards (72–73; 102). Although the opposite assumption may reflect a twentieth-century perspective on a fifteenth-century circumstance, I would still venture that these "facts" might be more conducive to a suspicion of the *occurrence* of sexual relations than to their *nonoccurrence*—a suspicion that should be supported rather than thwarted by the "historian" who presents these "facts" as proof of Leonardo's homosexuality.

The presence or absence of textual testimony is subject to extremely variable criteria of interpretation. Freud builds his case for da Vinci's celibacy by pointing out that da Vinci never writes anywhere of actual carnal lust for or experience with any of his pupils or any men at all. Given that sodomites were regularly burned at the stake at that time, Leonardo's omission seems hardly surprising. Contrarily, Freud's certainty of da Vinci's atheism is not lessened by the absence of any such declaration by da Vinci; the discretion that eluded Freud's consideration in the sexual issue supports his conviction in this one: "In view of the extraordinary sensitiveness of his age where religious matters were in question, we can understand perfectly why even in his notebooks Leonardo should have refrained from directly stating his attitude to Christianity" (124).[9]

Even during his lifetime, Leonardo's reputation was occasionally shadowed by suspicions of sexual improprieties with boys, and Freud refers to such reports frequently, but relies on them ambivalently. Freud admits that "few details are known about [Leonardo's] sexual behavior," and assumes that "the assertions of his contemporaries were not grossly erroneous" (101).[10] Yet when Freud appeals to those "assertions" he affirms the reliability of the sources but *disavows their message.* Freud alludes to Renaissance documents implicating Leonardo in cases of "sodomy" as corroboration of Leonardo's homosexuality, but forecloses from consideration any inference of Leonardo's overt expression thereof. Freud's assurances that "tradition does in fact represent Leonardo as a person of homosexual feelings" (87) and his reiteration of "the historical probability of Leonardo having behaved in his life as one who was emotionally homosexual" (98) are conceptual anachronisms. When Freud accepts the testimonies of Leonardo's contemporaries that the painter was "a homosexual" or had "homosexual feelings," he is assenting to statements no one could have made in the fifteenth or sixteenth centuries: "homosexuality" was not conceived of as an innate characteristic or a personal proclivity until the nineteenth century.[11] Sodomy, on the other hand, is a variously defined category of transgressive sexual behaviors predominantly associated with male-male sexual contact. Any early modern sources would have to be referring to *behavior*, and not an abstract (and particularly not an unrealized) sexual *orientation*. (It stands to reason that anyone who had not indulged in sodomy was a potential sodomite, which makes the question of "latency" redundant.)[12] My point is not to "prove" that da Vinci actually did engage in sex with men, but rather to call attention to the degree to which the "Leonardo" Freud "discovered" was predetermined by the suppositions he had set out to verify.

Freud's Leonardo *in "History"*

The readiness of the psychoanalytic and psychological establishments to accept the self-vindicating speculations of the *Leonardo* biography as firm evidence of the etiology of male homosexuality is astonishing. At the International Psychoanalytic Congress in 1911, Sandór Ferenczi presented a paper on male homosexuality heavily influenced by the theory Freud showcased in *Leonardo* (Ferenczi, "Nosology" 296–300). Some of the most conservative views on male homosexuality were attributed directly to the da Vinci text for years to come (Boehm; Lewes 56–58).[13]

There is a passage in *Leonardo* in which Freud sketches the implicit politics of history writing that can serve as an allegorical explanation for the scientific credence granted the text. Freud writes that only powerful nations find a need to write their own history, which inevitably becomes "an expression of present beliefs and wishes rather than a true picture of the past," motivated not by "objective curiosity but a desire to influence their contemporaries, encourage and inspire them, or to hold a mirror up before them" (83–84). Given that the "powerful nation" behind the more repressive forms of clinical psychotherapy is phallic heteropatriarchy, the usefulness of the *Leonardo* study becomes clearer. One of the unnamed narrative structures in the account of Leonardo's childhood is the Oedipus complex.[14] The text can be read, therefore, as a negative reinforcement of the repetitive history of the normative heterosexual male, Leonardo an example of a failure to conform to Oedipal orthodoxy. The acceptance of Freud's psychosexual sleuthing provides the conservative medical establishment a new theoretical justification of a belief in a sexual history phallically determined for both men and women, and for rigid adherence to the dominant sex/gender system, since the influences of a "strong mother" and an "ineffective father" may produce homosexual sons. (To warn parents, however, that their children may turn out to be like Leonardo da Vinci hardly seems an effective deterrent.)

The adoption of Freud's *Leonardo* as a canonical support of ego-adaptive therapeutic enforcement of the dominant form of Oedipalized heterosexuality requires a reduction of the text to its theses, a radical separation of content from form that models itself on Freud's bifurcation of Leonardo's genius into the evaluatively imbalanced binaries of "science" and "art." While Freud keeps both aspects in play, the scientists who read his monograph distill the "science" from the art of its presentation. *Leonardo*'s distracting forepleasures and polymorphous perversities were foreclosed from the reality principle guiding the disciplined appreciation of the readers whose pragmatics ensured a linear progression to a univocal and productive climax. Through a selectively literalizing reading, these interested parties focus on a conclusion whose "scientificity" at once validates and eclipses the signifying excesses that produced and mediate it.

Freud generally depicts Leonardo's science as of greater value than his art, on several levels. In terms of Leonardo's psychosexual history, his scientific investigation is seen as a more mature sublimation, a more profitable negotiation with the reality principle, than the earlier sublimation of scopophilia into his art (131–33). Jean Laplanche observes that Freud marks Leonardo's "artistic" or "pictorially inclined" activities as more "homosexual" than his scientific curiosity (Laplanche, "To Situate" 10–11; 23–25). Leonardo's scientific thinking was also a contribution to Western civilization whose sophistication exceeded his own time. While his contemporaries immediately understood da Vinci's value as an artist, his brilliance as a scientist required twentieth-century minds to appreciate (Freud, *Leonardo and a Memory* 63–66).

But even when specifically extolling Leonardo's empirical audacity, Freud estimates Leonardo's scientific research as "*perhaps* an equally sublime accomplishment" to that of his art (122; emphasis mine). Furthermore, Freud's ambivalence can be discerned in the presentations of the emergence of scientific inquiry in da Vinci's career as an intellectual triumph with debilitating repercussions for his artistic practice: "The investigator in [Leonardo] never in the course of his development left the artist entirely free, but often made severe encroachments on him and perhaps in the end suppressed him" (64–65); "Leonardo's scientific research began in service of his art. Finally the instinct swept him away until the connection with the demands of his art was severed" (76).[15]

The locus of Freud's identification with Leonardo is not always to be found in the pioneering scientist but rather in the defeated artist, reflecting Freud's personal frustration that his success as a "scientist" foreclosed exploration of his creativity, his desire to be "a novelist" (Jones 2: 432). It is no wonder that Freud's chief text of comparison is Merezhkovsky's novel, and that in Freud's disclaimer concerning the accuracy of his own portrait of Leonardo, he does not seem eager to refute the anticipated denouncements of the monograph as a "psycho-analytic novel" (*Leonardo and a Memory* 134).

Freud did not make his psychobiographical experiment any easier to assimilate to a scientific psychological canon in either his admissions of profound identification with Leonardo, or the symptomatic slippages in logic through which those identifications are inscribed within the text's legible unconscious. Freud acknowledges the role his identification with Leonardo plays in his research. Toward the conclusion of the monograph, he confesses, "Like others I have succumbed to the attraction of this great and mysterious man" (ibid.). Of course, conscious awareness of them does not prevent identifications from affecting the interpretative practice. Freud's eloquent insistence on Leonardo's atheism (122–25) is clearly an expression of this identification, and one which does not allow him to see the difficulty in asserting something with no evidence other than what seems personally logical (that may not be "self-evident" within the intellectual and social contexts of fifteenth-century Florence).

This identification also at times leads Freud into inconsistencies. For example, against readers who might consider the sexual investigation of Leonardo an affront to such a "great man," Freud invokes Leonardo in his defense: "Leonardo himself, with his love of truth and his thirst for knowledge, would not have discouraged an attempt to take the trivial peculiarities and riddles in his nature as a starting-point, for discovering what determined his mental and intellectual development" (130–31). This is in direct contradiction to one of the "enigmas" that Freud enumerates at the beginning of the monograph which he sets out to solve: Leonardo's absolute disregard for sex. Freud notes that in all of da Vinci's works, neither the scientific nor the frivolous deals with the erotic at all; in fact, the conspicuous absence of sexual topics suggests a presumption that "Eros alone . . . was not worthy material for the investigator in pursuit of knowledge" (69–70). Leonardo, therefore, would be the *least* likely reader to approve of Freud's avenue of inquiry.

The scientific reader cannot afford to recognize these identifications, par-

ticularly in view of the association of the "artist" with the "homosexual" da
Vinci. The necessary disavowal of Freud's heterogeneous narratorial persona
and multiple relations to the text recalls a pattern of disavowal Freud deployed
in compiling evidence for Leonardo's sublimated homosexuality, accepting the
truth of the contemporary sources that Leonardo had "homosexual desires"
but rejecting the content of those sources that Leonardo had "homosexual
experiences." It is as if underneath his statements Freud were saying, "The
sources are reliable but I do not believe them"; "I know very well that Leonardo
was a homosexual, but all the same. . . . " This pattern of simultaneously affirming and negating a circumstance, of claiming knowledge and refusing it at
once, is precisely the pattern of the split belief that operates within the psychic
defenses against castration anxiety in the fetishist. Freud maintains that a fetish
is invariably a penis substitute, and in particular the substitute for the "mother's
phallus which the little boy once believed in and does not wish to forgo" ("Fetishism" 149–50), the very phallus memorialized in the statues of the vulture-
headed mother goddess Mut.[16]

Since the scientific reader of Leonardo undertakes certain disavowals in the
service of the Oedipus, the fetishistic pattern of Freud's presentation of evidence may be more important for the scientist as a phantasmatic reinforcement
of the interpretative agenda than the same pattern (as fetish) was for the elaboration of Freud's presentation. In the next section I will examine the fantasy
operations that are intimately related to the narrative processes of the *Leonardo*
text, but the fetish is not one of them. The split belief Freud uses here is a
contingent necessity for establishing Leonardo's sublimation of his homosexuality, but the method seems extrinsic to the narrative's endogenous phantasmatic operations. Even the limited deployment of the split belief, however, may
engage the fantasy operations of the patriarchal scientist. The scientist can disavow the phantasmatic elements of Freud's text in order to make it a textbook,
but that scientist therefore also disavows his or her own phantasmatic process
of disavowal in the reading. While Freud clearly identified with Leonardo both
as an artist and as a scientist, the reading of the fetishistic scientist admits only
Freud's identification with the scientist-Leonardo: like any fetishist, the scientist seeks to render difference as sameness, heterogeneity as uniformity, otherness as a reflection of an already stabilized self.

The split belief that patterned the way Freud evaluated or qualified evidence in the Leonardo text was made necessary by attempting to prove not
Leonardo's homosexuality but his *sublimated* homosexuality. Therefore, to continue this metacritical associative logic, if a fetishistic discourse implies a specific fetish as its object or source, modeled upon the continued belief in the
mother's phallus that the fetish originally accomplished, for this narrative line
of Freud's text, the fetish would be the "sublimated" or "ideal" homosexual.
The so-called "positive Oedipus" of the heterosexual male desexualizes earlier
libidinal investments in other males and redirects them into "social instincts

... comradeship ... and to the love of mankind in general" ("Psycho-Analytic Notes" 61). In fact, "psychoanalysis" considers "social feeling ... a sublimation of homosexual attitudes towards objects" ("Some Neurotic Mechanisms" 232). A proper "sublimation of erotic instincts" can transform "manifest homosexuals" into "ideal homosexuals," who, like Leonardo, "struggle against an indulgence in sexual acts, distinguish themselves by taking a particularly active share in the general interests of humanity" ("Psycho-Analytic Notes" 61).[17] If, however, this sublimation either does not occur or is disturbed, the heretofore pastoral citizen becomes the agent of potential social disorder.[18] Sublimated, homosexuality becomes an indifferent enclave of the "overestimation of the phallus" basic to the dominant ideology. The sublimated homosexual does not have sex with men, and therefore can be assimilated into a devotion to masculinist principles without the subversive dissonance of a manifest sexually deviant practice that would violate the body politic of a hom(m)osexual male supremacism which the ideal homosexual should serve as "ardent priest."[19] The "ideal" or "sublimated" homosexual becomes a fetish object that protects the phallic integrity of the male subject far more homogeneously than a phallic mother goddess, because of the ideal homosexual's absolute indifference.

Although Freud originated the fetishistic interpretative method that generates this dystopian hom(m)osexual fantasy, he was not overly interested in it. Like Leonardo, Freud occasionally invented mechanisms he left for others to utilize. Unfortunately, as in this case, others often did—and they often did this without Freud's theoretical acumen or ethical restraint. It is significant, I feel, that of all the categories of psychical structures operationalized in *Leonardo*, the one Freud seems to discard, to relinquish to the historians and the scientists, is the fetish. The fetish object is the memorial to an act of self-deluding signification—a signification that seeks to elide the primacy of signifying processes over the meanings and referents those processes constitute. The fetish mimics an object that never existed, but denies even the mimicry; it masks the absence that motivated it, an absence the fetish incessantly signifies as it defers that signification. The "objective fact" is the fetish object that stands in for "truth" in both historical and scientific narratives whose operations of meaning constantly connote yet disavow the impossibility of the object (Truth) that is their telos and irreal foundation. If Freud left the realists the fetish, among the fantasy processes he retained, some will prove useful even in constructing countervailing discourses in response to the "Truth" of the fetishists and the good citizenship of the ideal homosexuals.

Leonardo in Freud's History

I do not mean to demonize Freud himself in either the preceding or the following analyses of this very problematic text. Nor do I impute to Freud the same degree of commitment to the text's most egregious conclusions that is evident among his more conservative and less nuanced readers. Although Freud certainly did not do homosexuals any favor by writing *Leonardo*, neither did he intend it as an attack. It is important to remember that this is also the writer who, in 1915, declared that "the exclusive sexual interest felt by men for women is also a problem that needs elucidating and is not a self-evident fact based upon an attraction that is ultimately of a chemical nature" (*Three Essays* 146 n. 1).

Freud's exegesis of the "vulture" fantasy, of course, is difficult to defend. Presented as a step-by-step deduction of Leonardo's type of homosexuality from the "evidence" and established scientific principles, the text in fact betrays a bizarre logic that seems to have been necessitated in advance by the sexist and heterosexist conclusions it reaches. Even here, however, I do not see a deliberate, ideologically motivated sophistry on Freud's part, but rather lapses in his control over the signifying processes he engages. A major structuring cause of such lapses lies in Freud's attempt to synthesize the historical narrative and the psychoanalytic narrative without factoring in the differences in their respective epistemological and semiological presuppositions.

It will be easier to tease these narratives apart by distinguishing between Freud's "public" agendas in writing the monograph and what I perceive to be more personal agendas. The public agenda of the validation of psychoanalysis as a science calls for a recognized disciplinary method, provided by the historical narrative. The personal agendas are inscribed within the psychoanalytic narrative because its critical apparatus also engages the processes it describes: identification, disavowal, projection, introjection, internalization, and transference. The latter narrative is immediately insinuated within the former, because every public agenda is implicated in the personal. For example, Freud's decision to write a biography is part of the "public" agenda; his choice of "subject" is part of the personal agenda, based on his long fascination and identification with the artist-scientist.[20]

There are other ways in which public agendas are informed by personal histories and private meanings. The attempt to demonstrate the critical capacity of psychoanalysis the psychobiography represents may also have been a reworking of a previous failure. At the turn of the century, Freud had placed his hopes for a general recognition of the scientific legitimacy of psychoanalysis in the anticipated success of his analysis and treatment of the hysterical young woman who became known as "Dora." When Dora suddenly withdrew from treatment, Freud was reportedly seriously disheartened.

In his postscript to the case history of Dora, "Fragment of an Analysis of a Case of Hysteria" (1905 [1901]), Freud attributes Dora's decision to leave analysis to transference (i.e., relating to Freud as she would to her father), and blames his failure to adjust his responses accordingly to his underestimation of the severity of the transference ("Fragment" 115–16). He defined "transferences" as "new editions or facsimiles of the impulses and phantasies which are aroused and made conscious during the progress of the analysis . . . [which] replace some earlier person by the person of the physician" (116). During Dora's analysis, Freud considered transference occasional and epiphenomenal to the analytic situation. He resituated it as central to analysis after the implications of the Oedipus complex became so crucial to his thought (Laplanche and Pontalis, *Language* 457–58). It would be several years before Freud developed a theory of "countertransference," the response the analyst has to the analysand based on the ways in which the analysand affects the analyst's unconscious. Freud's own countertransference, however, is everywhere in evidence in "Fragment of an Analysis," and has been a major focus of subsequent interpretations of this case history. Steven Marcus, in fact, considers the unacknowledged countertransference to be the organizational principle and narrative drive within the case history itself (Marcus 309–10).

There are textual resonances between the Dora case history and the Leonardo biography that suggest a significant relation between the two. The preoccupation with virgin birth and the fantasy of fellatio Freud discovered in Leonardo, he had already discovered in Dora ("Fragment" 96; 50–51).[21] One of the causes of Dora's "hysterical" cough Freud postulates is a "displacement of sensation" from lower body regions (the clitoris) to upper regions (the throat) (ibid. 29–30). This is precisely the hysterical operation by which Freud transfers the homosexual "passivity" conventionally associated with receptive anal sex to fellatio in the explanation of the vulture fantasy.

Donald Moss speculates that Freud chose to study Leonardo as a means to recover the stable object of scientific inquiry his interrupted sessions with "Dora" did not ultimately provide (Moss 66). Even during his analysis of Dora, Freud perceived her transference as seriously jeopardizing the accuracy of his interpretations: "Everything fits together very satisfactorily, but owing to the characteristics of transference its validity is not susceptible of definite proof" ("Fragment" 74; qtd. Moss 67). Da Vinci may have also been an attractive case, Moss suggests, because a dead individual would be "transferentially inert" and thus more susceptible to an analysis that might yield "a theory capable of generating narratives whose endpoint is 'certainty,' " in contradistinction to the Dora sessions, replete with the "epistemologically destabilizing network of transference forces" (Moss 73).

There are several ways in which the *Leonardo* text is implicated in the conceptual history of "transference" that support Moss's extremely interesting thesis, not least of which would be the subtextual presence of the Oedipus underlying the psychogenesis of the "type" of homosexual Freud claims Leonardo to have been. Freud began research on *Leonardo* in November of 1909, and completed the manuscript at the beginning of April 1910. At the end of March 1910, Freud addressed the Second Psychoanalytic Congress, where he mentioned for the first time "countertransference," which he does not define but claims that it "arises in [the analyst] as a result of the patient's influence on his unconscious feelings." Freud insists that the analyst must "recognize [it] in himself [*sic*] and overcome it" through "self-analysis" ("Future Prospects" 144–45). Ironically, self-analysis was subsequently condemned as a narcissistic resistance to analysis which "bypasses transference" (Laplanche and Pontalis, *Language* 413). "Bypassing transference" may have been precisely what Freud wanted to do in his da Vinci project, if we accept Moss's proposal. I do, in fact, accept Moss's thesis, but I want to modify it by demonstrating that this desire to "bypass transference" would be only one agenda inscribed within the textual project of *Leonardo*, which would dynamically and/or topographically coexist with other agendas conditioned by Freud's increasingly more complex conceptualizations of "transference" subsequent to the aftermath of Dora's aborted analysis. If on one level *Leonardo* represents a desire to "bypass" the negative transference embodied in Dora, on other levels the text reflects a self-conscious appeal to the analytic potential of countertransference that was manifested only unconsciously and symptomatically in "Fragment of an Analysis." Finally, in writing *Leonardo* Freud adapts specific modes of transference as models for a speculative critical methodology.

The psychoanalytic dismissal of "self-analysis" is ironic considering that a great deal of psychoanalysis as a theoretical field (including the Oedipus complex) was initially formulated within the self-analysis Freud began in 1897. His self-analysis is thoroughly documented in his letters to his friend, the Berlin physician Wilhelm Fliess.[22] This correspondence also includes extended excerpts from Freud's dream journals that would become the basis of *The Interpretation of Dreams*. Freud's intense and prolonged self-disclosure in these letters created a transference relation to Fliess comparable to that which Freud later discovered to be a structural inevitability of the psychoanalytic session. It has been argued that one of the reasons the Dora case was so important to Freud was his hope that its success would serve to dissolve his transference to Fliess (Marcus 302–303). Years after the disastrous end of this friendship, Freud admitted to Ferenczi that his transference had had a significant "homosexual cathexis" (qtd. Jones 2:92). The single mention Freud makes of Leonardo in the extant correspondence to Fliess occurs in an overdetermined context: "Leonardo—no love affair of his is known—is perhaps the most famous left-handed person. Can you use him?" (Letter of October 9, 1898, Freud, *Complete Letters* 331). Freud refers here to Fliess's theory that left-handedness was related to bisexuality—a theory which later became one of the points of disagreement between the two men that led to their irreconcilable break in relation.[23] The overdetermination of Leonardo certainly carried over into the psychobiography and its multileveled agendas.

Even in the rudimentary formulation of transference in the postscript to the Dora case history, Freud notes the ambivalent potential within the dynamics of transference: "In psycho-analysis . . . all the patient's tendencies, including hostile ones, are aroused; they are then turned to account for the purposes of the analysis by being made conscious. . . . Transference, which seems ordained to be the greatest obstacle to psycho-analysis, becomes its most powerful ally" ("Fragment" 117). He also distinguishes among gradations of mimesis in the transferences of the patient: "Some of these transferences have a content which differs from that of their model in no respect whatever except for the substitution. . . . Others are more ingeniously constructed; their content has been subjected to a moderating influence—to *sublimation*, as I call it" (116; emphasis mine). Considering the cognitive dissonance that characterizes so much of the narratorial rhetoric and interpretative maneuvers in this case history,[24] it seems reasonable to transpose the patient's "sublimation" of transference to Freud's sublimation of countertransference in a narrative strategy for constructing and asserting interpretative authority.

As Freud's conception of transference became more complex, he introduced the distinction between a "positive" and a "negative" transference. The "positive" transference manifested itself as an affectionate attitude toward the analyst ("Dynamics of the Transference" 104–105). This attitude supported a belief in the analyst's omniscience, granting the analyst a "transference authority" (Glover 406). The positive transference, therefore, could be manipulated in persuading the patient to accept interpretations that could not be corroborated by the patient's memory because of repression or other resistances. Returning to Moss's theory on the reasons behind Freud's study of Leonardo, it seems feasible that, just as Freud sublimated his countertransference into the narrative of Dora's case history, he could sublimate a positive transference to write the Leonardo biography.

The analogy of the scholar-text relation to the analyst-analysand relation recasts the confrontation of "active" reader with the "dead" text as the nonreciprocal relation of doctor and patient that contractually produces the doctor's hermeneutic infallibility as the text's "positive transference" to the critic. This scenario allows Freud to project the "positive" transference an "ideal" patient would have for him onto the text of Leonardo's life, and internalize this "ideal" [homosexual] patient in a fantasy analytic session that provides the phantasmatic guidelines of Freud's historical investigation. Clinical acumen becomes critical solipsism, as the text's silence ensures assent to any of Freud's interpretations. Having assumed the unquestioned authority of the analyst's position, and introjected the compliant analysand, Freud can posit questions and bequeath to himself answers which, in the tautologous rules of this truth game, find their validation in Freud's articulating them.[25]

Those passages in the psychobiography in which Freud writes in the first person as Leonardo synthesize his identification with da Vinci and the fantasy of a positively transferential analysand, while they dramatize the traditional historian's attitude of making the documents "speak" the "truth" of the past.[26] Freud's attitude toward "official" history may ameliorate the completely repressive nature of this technique as I have described it so far. Freud assumes that histories are not disinterested texts, and that their agendas largely determine their production of the truth of the past. Freud's metahistoriographical description of "history writing" I cited above is not a response to an actual "history" or "historical" text, but an analogy to the process of adult fantasies that retroactively create childhood experiences: in fact, he offered this analogy to explain Leonardo's belief in the bird fantasy as an actual memory. Memories can be fantasies, and psychoanalysis can make even the person who holds the "memory" aware of this. Freud's analyses of some of his dreams are records of the self-discovery of the irreality of some elements of one's personal "history." History as a discipline, however, is a politically motivated fixing of memory, a canonization of fantasies that disavow their phantasmatic production.

Two of the chief tasks of traditional history writing are the establishment of facts and the determination of their significance.[27] The historical narrative is a means of regulating "truth" because "evidence . . . only counts as evidence and is only recognized as such in relation to a potential narrative, so that the narrative can be said to determine the evidence as much as the evidence determines the narrative" (Gossman, qtd. Scott, "Evidence" 776).[28] The interpretative license Freud grants himself in writing *Leonardo* through his deliberate internalization of the positive transference is a way to adapt the unfair advantages of the historian for the psychoanalytic narrator. But the circular guarantees of knowledge Freud maintains in the psychoanalytic narrative he doubly denies himself in his own historical narrative of Leonardo. By insisting on proving da Vinci's sublimated homosexuality, Freud asserted "facts" from "historical documents" but divested them of historical "truth."[29] Even in his historical narrative, therefore, Freud undermines the historical project by denying referentiality any *a priori* significance.

Of course, the logic internal to historiographical practice contaminates the psychoanalytic narrative of *Leonardo*, as much as the psychoanalytic subverts the historical. Freud does not fulfill the radical potential of his textual strategies because the truth games of history and science he infiltrates ultimately recuperate the destabilizations he introduced. This is what allows his "scientific" readers to transform the Leonardo fantasy into *the* textbook case of mother-dominated male homosexuals. The sublimated transference narrative of "sublimated" homosexual desire in turn becomes a fetishistic point of identification for interested professional readers from medical, clinical, and legal institutions supporting heteropatriarchal orthodoxy. Through their various disavowed fantasy operations of disavowal, projection, and transference, for example, the possibility of "sublimated homosexual desire" Freud postulated in his fantasy of

Leonardo's fantasy becomes a justification for demanding such sublimation as essential to healthy social engineering.

Like Leonardo's art, Freud's subversive narrative succumbed to the reality principle of the historian and the scientist. What if unsublimated (nonideal) homosexuals were to become unsublimated (or desublimating) investigators? The gay "researcher" whose investigation aims at finding reflections of his own sexuality within culture has not only not sublimated his sexuality into his research, but expresses and to some extent creates it through his intellectual endeavor. Like psychoanalytic discourse at its most radical, the desublimated histories will present "evidence" that acknowledges its own constitutive fictionality. The narcissistic narrator of such desublimated investigations does not aggrandize a solitary ego at the expense of the libido, but proliferates the ego's multiplicities and volatilities as generative mobile loci of identificatory desire. The politics of the pleasure principle informing these narratives expropriate truth games for countertruth games.

The Fantasies of Nonideal Homosexuals

At Play with the Tools of the Master: Oscar Wilde's "W. H."

Some of the principal operations of Freud's narrative in *Leonardo* are anticipated in Oscar Wilde's "The Portrait of W. H.," a story concerning the identity of the "young man" of Shakespeare's sonnets, a preoccupation of Shakespearean criticism practically since their publication, and a point of debate long after Wilde's death. The mystery originates from the dedication on the title page of the first printing, to "Mr. W. H.," which are not the initials of Lord Southampton, Shakespeare's patron at the time, and the presumed addressee of the poems.[30] Wilde proposes that "W. H." is "Willie Hughes," a boy actor in Shakespeare's troupe. Wilde published a version of this story in 1889; a much longer version, completed in 1893, was not published during his lifetime.[31] Wilde took the "Willie Hughes" theory from Thomas Tyrwhitt, who originally published it in 1766; Tyrwhitt's speculation was also included in the 1780 edition of the sonnets, establishing this supposition as an apocryphal tradition. Wilde also pastiched information he had gleaned from an article on Shakespearean boy actors by Amy Strachey which he had edited for *Women's World* in 1888 (Gagnier 41).[32] Both versions of Wilde's story combine actual scholarship with elements that parody both contemporary Shakespearean criticism and Wilde's project itself.[33]

The story is told from the perspective of an unnamed first-person narrator. It opens with a discussion between the narrator and his friend Erskine on "literary counterfeits." Erskine tells the story of his friend Cyril Graham's tragic use of a "counterfeit" painting to prove his theory of the identity of the "W. H." of the sonnets. Graham had acted in Shakespeare in college (excelling in women's roles) and convinced himself that "W. H." was "Willie Hughes," a boy actor in Shakespeare's troupe, who at one point abandoned Shakespeare to act in a rival company, but then later returned. Despite Graham's ingenious compilation of "internal evidence," Erskine insisted on the need for historical verification, which Graham provided: an Elizabethan painting of a beautiful young man, pointing to the dedication page of an open copy of the sonnets. Graham claimed to have found the painting in a chest initialed "W. H." When Erskine later discovered that Graham had commissioned the forgery, they quarreled, and Graham committed suicide that night, leaving Erskine a note saying that he killed himself to express his devotion to the truth of his theory. The narrator finds the theory intriguing and, despite Erskine's objections, attempts to prove it.

The narrator's research takes up nearly all of the remainder of the published version. The text's structure consists of several semi-autonomous progressions: the main plot (the story of the narrator's involvement with the sonnets); interpretation (the gradual deduction of "truth" from evidence); and sequence construction (the story of Shakespeare's romance with Willie, "read out" of the sonnets through the narrator's theoretical apparatus). The main story progresses in terms of the narrator's accumulation of "knowledge" and interpretative mastery over the sonnets, which authorizes another progression as an increase in *homosexual* truth. At first the narrator had assumed, as had Graham before him, that Willie had left Shakespeare's company to perform for Chapman (Wilde, "Portrait" 148). But closer readings of the poems reveal to him that Willie actually left to join Marlowe's theater, to perform as Gaveston in *Edward II* (160–61). Therefore the progression in the plot eventuates a new sequence from the sonnets (the story of Marlowe) and a proliferation of homosexual subplots.

Like Leonardo, "W. H." is advanced by an investigative method that determines its evidence—both internal and external. That there is no "Willie Hughes" listed in the first folio of Shakespeare's plays is twice cited as "proof" of his existence: "the absence of Willie Hughes's name . . . really corroborated the theory, as it was evident from Sonnet LXXXVI that Willie Hughes had abandoned Shakespeare's company to play at a rival theatre" (Wilde, "Portrait" 148; repeated 166). In the longer version of the story, the reiteration of this reasoning is given further support. Because of the " 'very strong prejudice against the theater,' " Erskine conjectures that Hughes would have likely used an " 'assumed name' " in deference to his family, and therefore it would have been his stage name placed in the folio as he was known in the public, but " 'the Sonnets were of course an entirely different matter' " (Wilde, *Portrait* 84–85).[34]

The narrator's exegesis becomes axiomatic: he assumes that his reading of a sonnet is incomplete or inadequate until it supports Graham's theory. Wilde's narrator openly operates on a methodological circularity similar to that implicit in the Leonardo text: " 'You start by assuming the existence of the very person whose existence is the thing to be proved' " ("Portrait" 153). As in Freud's narrative, the "W. H" theory is also dependent on proving collateral elements of the investigator's initial suppositions. The addressee of the sonnets could not merely be male, but had to be a favorite boy actor of Shakespeare's troupe, just as Leonardo had to be both "homosexual" and celibate: "Who was he whose physical beauty became . . . the very incarnation of Shakespeare's dreams? To look upon him simply as the object of certain love-poems is to miss the whole meaning of the poems: for the art of which Shakespeare talks in the Sonnets is . . . the art of the dramatist . . . and he to whom Shakespeare said 'Thou art all my art, and dost advance / As high as learning my rude ignorance' . . . was surely none other than the boy-actor for whom he created Viola and Imogen, Juliet and Rosalind, Portia and Desdemona, and Cleopatra herself" (146–47).

By continually exposing its own fraudulence, Wilde's story also exposes the mechanisms of interpretative authority and their inherently interested nature. To demonstrate how a "master narrative" (a preestablished criterion for truth and intelligibility) determines the limits of a text's signification, I will briefly compare some of Wilde's narrator's glosses on the sonnets to that of an "official" Shakespeare scholar, A. L. Rowse, "renowned" for having "discovered" the identity of the "Dark Lady" of the sonnets. Rowse's interpretation of the sonnets, therefore, is as committed to Shakespeare's *exclusive heterosexuality* and Southampton as the addressee of the sonnets as Wilde's investigator is contrarily committed.

In his introduction to his third edition of the sonnets, Rowse proclaims that all "the problems of Shakespeare's Sonnets . . . have now been solved," meaning that he personally had solved them. He had solved all but one in his 1964 Shakespeare biography, and subsequently solved the last, the name of the Dark Lady (Rowse ix).[35] Having established his unquestionable authority, Rowse then dismisses all questions of W. H., explaining that he was merely the man to whom the publisher had dedicated the first printing, which Rowse assures us closes the question of possible homosexual themes in the sequences (ix–xii). But this is merely diversionary. Even if this were true, it would mean only that the addressee of the sonnets would be Southampton after all, which keeps the question of the sexuality in the sonnets open. The passionate language in the sonnets Rowse ascribes to an Elizabethan convention of writing to one's patron in courtly language, a practice intensified by Shakespeare's often excessively exaggerated and elliptical expressive tendencies (xii). Rowse concludes that "the Sonnets are not homosexual. . . . Shakespeare makes it perfectly clear in Sonnet

20 that he is not interested in the youth sexually—if only he were a woman! Everything in his life and work shows that Shakespeare was an enthusiastic heterosexual, very susceptible, even inflammable where women were concerned" (xiii).[36]

Ironically, it is the same Sonnet 20 that Graham had considered conclusive proof of Shakespeare's sexual desire for the boy actor, and he even finds Willie's name embedded in word plays within the couplets (another "Elizabethan convention") (Wilde, "Portrait" 147–48).[37] Sonnet 78 contains several clues: "Every alien pen has got my use / And under thee their poesy disperse"—"use" is a play on "Hughes," and the rest of the couplet means " 'by your assistance as an actor bring their plays before the people' " (ibid. 148), and the final couplet also attests to the importance of Willie's talent to Shakespeare's art: "Thou art all my art, and dost advance / As high as learning my rude ignorance" (146). Rowse interprets this sonnet as a dry message to Southampton, expressing Shakespeare's bitterness over not having gone to the university, and his anticipation of rivalry from other poets for Southampton's continued support (Rowse 159).[38]

According to Wilde's narrator, Sonnet 53 refers to Willie's particular skill in female leads, a poem extolling the actor's versatility in performing roles "from Rosalind to Juliet, and from Beatrice to Ophelia": "What is your substance, whereof are you made, / That millions of strange shadows on you tend? Since every one hath, every one, one shade, / And you, but one, can every shadow lend"—the narrator explains that these lines "would be unintelligible if . . . not addressed to an actor, for the word 'shadow' had in Shakespeare's day a technical meaning connected with the stage" ("Portrait" 154). Other lines in the sonnet the narrator does not quote also suggest sexual and gender ambiguity, comparing the addressee to Adonis and to Helen. Rowse, however, ignores the dramaturgical terminology to render this poem a simple song of the poet's gratitude to his new patron. Even the personae evoked pose no problems for Rowse: he explains that "Adonis" refers to "Venus and Adonis," which Shakespeare was writing at this time; the ambisexual comparisons are part of the Elizabethan tradition of praising someone as having the "best of both masculine and feminine attractions . . . as in the court poems of Henry III" (Rowse 109).

It is not only Rowse who has to come up with some extremely creative interpretations to overcome fairly large empirical obstacles. Graham's successor, for example, had to explain the recurrent attempt of the poet to persuade "Willie" to marry and beget heirs. The narrator reconciles this theme with the romance between Shakespeare and Willie through a reading of Sonnet 82: "I'll grant thou wert not married to my Muse"—which marriage would result in children not "flesh and blood, but more immortal children of undying fame," that is, the heirs of a union of the actor's skill and the poet's plays (Wilde,

"Portrait" 156–57). The implicit reference here to the esoterica Diotima granted Socrates in the *Symposium* is elaborated in the longer version of the story. There Wilde included a long excursus on Neo-Platonism, tracing its influence in England to the 1492 translation of the *Symposium* by Marsilio Ficino, and asserting that Shakespeare had read it and was fascinated by its doctrine (Wilde, *Portrait* 42). This assertion allows the narrator to draw an explicit connection between Neo-Platonism and the sonnets: "When he says to Willie Hughes, 'he that calls on thee, let him bring forth / Eternal numbers to outlive long date' [Shakespeare] is thinking of Diotima's theory that Beauty is the goddess who presides over birth . . . and exhorts his friend to beget children time cannot destroy" (ibid. 43).

This interruption in the narrative of the longer version of "W. H." amounts to a capsule history of male homoerotic discourse and its relation to both heterosexual sublimation and suppression, which I sketched in the previous chapter. The narrator reflects on the Renaissance rediscovery of the Greek ideals of masculine companionship. In adopting these "secrets of Hellenism" and refashioning male friendship as "a mode of self-conscious intellectual development" (Wilde, *Portrait* 43), Renaissance thought and art became imbued with "the soul, as well as the language, of Neo-Platonism" (42). A failure to appreciate this often led to misinterpreting "the true meaning of the amatory phrases and words with which friends were wont, at this time, to address each other" (43) as evidence of "excessive and misplaced affection" (46)—not realizing that these expressions of intellectual passion were completely "removed from gross bodily appetite" (43–44).

Wilde's examples of historical figures who subscribed to this philosophy, however, totally belie the purportedly chaste nature of the tradition. Wilde's list comprises the who's who of sodomitical probability: Edward Blount, Marlowe, Bacon, Michelangelo, Montaigne, Philip Sidney, Hubert Languet, Giordano Bruno, Richard Barnfield, and Winckelmann. His comparison of Shakespeare's sonnets to Michelangelo's for Tommaso Cavalieri actually exacerbates rather than allays suspicion of homosexual passion in the former. Mentioning the influence of Montaigne on Shakespeare in this context also gives a homosexual coloration to a usually unmarked "fact" of literary history (45). Wilde even mentions two of his own contemporaries, J. A. Symonds and Walter Pater, in openly sarcastic passages. In explaining the fervor of Michelangelo's sonnets to Cavalieri, Wilde writes: "Rightly interpreted they merely serve to show with what intense and religious fervour Michael Angelo [*sic*] addressed himself to the worship of intellectual beauty, and how, to borrow a fine phrase from Mr. Symonds, he pierced through the veil of flesh and sought the divine idea it imprisoned" (44). "Neo-Platonism" becomes in this text a code word for perverse sexual arousal—apparent in the "proper interpretation" of Michelangelo's sonnets, it is outrageously transparent near the end of the passage:

"When Pico della Mirandola crossed the threshold of the villa of Careggi, and stood before Marsilio Ficino in all the grace and comeliness of his wonderful youth, the aged scholar seemed to see in him the realisation of the Greek ideal, and determined to devote his remaining years to the translation of Plotinus . . . in whom, as Mr. Pater reminds us, 'the mystical element in the Platonic philosophy had been worked out to the utmost limit of vision and ecstasy' " (47).

The inclusion of Symonds and Pater ostensibly reinforces the intellectual integrity of Neo-Platonism, but it also ensures the homosexual implications of the Renaissance anecdote and obliquely attests to the continuity of homoerotic desire and its neoclassical camouflage. Although these sentiments as expressed here are clearly satirical, the viability of this pose is costly, and the comic relief it provides comes from a tragic moral code. Wilde was forced to use the same kinds of arguments "seriously" in his own defense at his trial (Hyde 132–36).[39] Furthermore, the ambivalence of the text derives from the long tradition of eliding or assimilating male homoerotic desire in dominant masculinist rhetoric.[40]

On the other hand, besides exposing the hypocrisy of the Platonic euphemistic dismissal of male homosexuality, Wilde's satiric virtuosity also anticipates a specifically gay purchase on a new role for intellectuals, as Foucault would reconceive it, in questioning the institutions of truth production, defining "truth" as "a system of ordered procedures for the production, regulation, distribution, circulation and operation of statements . . . linked in a circular relation with systems of power which produce and sustain it, and to effects of power which it induces and which extend it" (Foucault, *Power/Knowledge* 132–33).

Although the act of establishing evidence for the existence of "Willie Hughes" was an admitted pseudo-interpretation, the text's indictments of the institutions of knowledge and knowledge production are far from whimsical. In its aggressive transparency to the processes of its duplicity, "W. H." demonstrates how "truth" is fabricated. The self-acknowledged artifice of the exercise is foregrounded and critically recuperated in the opening episode in which Erskine and the narrator are discussing literary forgeries. The narrator defends Chatterton's bogus medieval monk poems as stemming from "an artistic desire for perfect representation," reserving for the artist the right to decide "the conditions under which he chooses to present his work." Since all "Art" was a form of "acting, an attempt to realise one's own personality" outside the "limitations of real life," to condemn an artist for forgery was senseless (Wilde, "Portrait" 139). Wilde's apparent sophistry here can be appreciated as a political and moral rejection of the status quo if "reality" in his text is read to mean the "official reality" of the exclusively heterosexual normativity so vehemently enforced. Homosexuals as literary counterfeiters deal in the politics of encoded expressions of a socially proscribed desire, representational "criminals" whose lives are likewise condemned as false versions of the truly valuable institutions of marriage and patriarchal domesticity.

If counterfeits and forgeries are the necessary instruments of communication under the regime of "reality," the tautologically ensured search for "W. H." is a vital process of self-formation. The narrative is motivated by two logically antithetic cognitive processes that are coextensive within the narrator's self-expression of a textual persona: his analysis of the sonnet text, and his constriction of "Willie Hughes." Taking Shakespeare's text as analysand (or the symptom-dense utterances of the analysand), as Freud did with Leonardo, the narrator-critic becomes an analyst who engages in dream interpretation of the text in order to engage ultimately in the analyst's own conscious dream work. "Dream work" refers to the operations that transform the latent dream thoughts (those that must be repressed) into a manifest dream content (which can escape repression) (Freud, *Interpretation of Dreams* 4: 278–79). Dream interpretation is the act of discovering the latent thoughts disguised by the dream's manifest content. By revealing the latent thoughts of erotic desire for W. H. in the sonnets, Wilde's narrator performs a "dream interpretation" on Shakespeare's sonnets, and in turn imagines a "Shakespeare" as a desiring subject with which to identify, thus creating his own desiring persona as a kind of self-conscious dream work, or more precisely a series of identifications and internalizations of ego ideals the narrator discovers/posits within his investigations. In other words, this is a narcissistic and desublimated version of Freud's project in *Leonardo.*

The sonnet text requires interpretation because, generated from the poet's dream work, it was not "*made with the intention of being understood*" (Freud, *Interpretation of Dreams* 5: 341; emphasis Freud's). The poet's meanings are translated through the poet's dream work according to "considerations of representability . . . for the most part, . . . representability in visual images" (344), that can "escape censorship" (349). In this "dream" the role of intrapsychic censor is played by society at large. As the analyst, Wilde's narrator on one level pursues "historical investigation" in the clinical sense of ascertaining the text's "whence" and "whither," the former referring to the symptom's (the poem's/ the dream's) external causes and the latter to "its purpose," which is "invariably an endopsychic process" (Freud, *Introductory Lectures* 15: 284). In this case, the "whence" is Shakespeare's relationship with Willie Hughes and the "whither" the crystallization of Shakespeare's emotive and aesthetic responses to that relationship.[41]

The meanings Wilde's narrator extracts from his dream interpretation of the sonnets become the components of his own dream work. One passage in particular marks the dovetailing of analysis and fantasy formation: "Every poem seemed to me to corroborate Cyril Graham's theory. I felt as if I had my hand upon Shakespeare's heart, and was counting each separate throb and pulse of passion. I thought of the wonderful boy-actor, and saw his face in every line" ("Portrait" 154). The narrator comes to identify with the subject of desire his reading discerns within the sonnets, and begins to internalize that desire as a capacity within himself by focalizing his research through the image of Willie Hughes as its goal (Willie Hughes as goal of research and object of desire). The narrator identifies with Shakespeare as the desiring poet-subject, but only the Shakespeare whose object of desire is the "Willie Hughes" the narrator presupposes to have existed. Therefore the narrator's identification with Shakespeare depends upon the existence of Willie Hughes.

Although the external structure of the narrator's intellectual activity resembles the "scientific" analysis that Freud defines in *Interpretation of Dreams* and the *New Introductory Lectures,* or the "historico-scientific" method Freud deploys in the *Leonardo* text, the internal operations of the narrator's activity are closer to the identifications and introjections of real and imaginary models for both the ideal ego and the ego ideal of the researcher—thus they have more in common with the processes described in "On Narcissism" and "Mourning and Melancholia."[42]

The process of internalization is more explicitly realized in the longer version of Wilde's story. As the narrator's research nears its conclusion, he writes, "It seemed to me that I was deciphering the story of a life that had once been mine, unrolling the record of a romance that, without my knowing it, had coloured the very texture of my nature. . . . I felt as if I had been initiated into the secret of that passionate friendship, that love of Beauty and beauty of love, of which Marsilio Ficino tells us" (*Portrait* 77–78). It was through the identification with the world of the sonnets that he could claim "Hellenism" as his own homoerotic desire: "Yes I had lived it all. . . . I had never seen my friend, but he had been with me for many years, and it was to his influence that I owed my passion for Greek thought and art, and indeed all my sympathy with the Hellenic spirit. . . . A book of sonnets, published nearly three hundred years ago, written by a dead hand and in honour of a dead youth, had suddenly explained to me the whole story of my soul's romance" (78–79).

Wilde's narrator investigates the "mystery" of the sonnets out of personal, political, and cultural interests. But his research is also sexually motivated; the initial glancing recognition of a certain kind of desire in the sonnets (or, more precisely, in Graham's reading of the sonnets) incites a vital curiosity—a need to identify positively that which one suspects, that suspicion being a proleptic identification with that which the dominant interpretative institutions insist is not there, and which the gay male subject knows is there, because he will create it out of what he finds. In its intensity, this passion for knowledge resembles the epistemophilia Freud attributed to Leonardo, but without the sublimation. As a social commentary, "The Portrait of W. H." exposes "knowledge" as a process whereby beliefs advantageous to the dominant group are transformed into "truth." For gay men, Wilde literally demonstrates how desire can mobilize a libidinous critical imagination and incite deviant semiotic sabotage to fashion a "self" out of the textual networks of a culture whose "official investigator" would never "discover" such selves or such desires.

From an "authorized" investigation that "proves" the homosexual desire of a Renaissance artist based on the absence of its expression, and yet absolutely insists on its accuracy, denies its artistry, and sublimates its emotive dynamics, to a counterfeit investigation that "proves" the existence of a male object of desire in the sonnets, but incessantly announces its fictive contexts and spurious claims while thematizing the sexual drives that motivate its search and predetermine its (self-)discovery, I now turn to an unauthorized psychobiography of another Renaissance painter, in which the "analyst" celebrates his transferences as much as his truths.

Improper Identification: Derek Jarman's Self-Portrait of Caravaggio

In 1606 Michele Caravaggio stabbed to death Ranuccio Thomasoni in a drunken brawl, and fled Rome to spend the last four years of his life in exile. Derek Jarman's film *Caravaggio* (1986) is based on Jarman's premise that Thomasoni had been Caravaggio's lover, and the model for some of his most important paintings, including *The Martyrdom of St. Matthew*. Jarman's basis for this fantasy includes some detective work that rivals Freud's on Leonardo. In his notes to the screenplay, Jarman writes that Caravaggio carried a painting of a nude "St. John" with him for the final four years of his life. When the painting presumed to be the one in question was cleaned in the 1970s, the curators discovered Caravaggio's signature (his only one) "scrawled into the blood which splashed on the floor from the Saint's severed artery. The signature says, 'I, Caravaggio, did this.' The [executioner's] knife . . . in the painting, is very unusual, and it probably refers to the knife that was the murder weapon in the fight with Ranuccio . . . which Caravaggio always carried" (Jarman, *Caravaggio* 48).[43]

In establishing Caravaggio's homosexuality, Jarman departs from Freud's methods, by believing the testimony of the historical sources he cites. Jarman also, however, relies on "evidence" far more subjective than Freud had. Because of the scarcity of explicit documentation, Jarman reads Caravaggio's paintings as self-proclamations of homosexual desire. Jarman is particularly certain of this message in *The Martyrdom of St. Matthew*, in which Caravaggio painted himself in, looking at the near-naked youth in the center of the painting. For the accuracy of his interpretation, Jarman appeals to his own lived experience as a gay man: "Michele [Caravaggio] gazes wistfully at the hero slaying the saint. It is a look no one can understand unless he has stood till 5 a.m. in a gay bar hoping to be fucked by that hero" (Jarman, *Dancing Ledge* 22). This is identification posing as explication, similar to Freud's certainty of Leonardo's atheism.

Jarman's identification with Caravaggio in *The Martyrdom* bears an intriguing structural affinity to the dilemma Basil Hallward finds himself in after painting Dorian Gray's portrait. Wilde essentially pioneers a theory of queer representation in Hallward's confession to Dorian concerning his problem. In his adulation of his model, Hallward sketched Dorian in the guises of mythical figures, from Adonis to Narcissus, but "one day . . . I determined to paint . . . you as you actually are . . . in your own dress and your own time. . . . As I worked at it, every flake and film of colour seemed to reveal my secret. I grew afraid that others would know of my idolatry. I felt, Dorian, that I had told too much, that I had put too much of myself into it" (Wilde, *Picture* 128).

The danger to Hallward comes from removing his images from the euphemisms of Winckelmannian antiquity and situating Dorian in the contemporary world. The painting fascinates its model (its subject?) because it reflects him to himself, but enthralls and horrifies the painter because it depicts both the *object* of desire *and the painter's desire itself.* It is not merely Dorian but Dorian's beauty as realized in the eyes of a would-be lover—the artist's gaze is inscribed in the figure that it captured (and was captured by). It is at once a portrait of Dorian and a self-portrait.[44] Hallward's desire is disseminated in the object; to Jarman's eye, in *The Martyrdom* Caravaggio's desire is doubly represented: in the desired object, and in his self-representation as desiring subject. The desiring gaze—only thematized in Dorian's image in Hallward's picture—in *The Martyrdom* is split into the central figure of the fantasy and the embodied subject of the desiring gaze. Jarman's aesthetics and critical method are an expansion of Hallward's desiring self-inscription in his painting. Hallward's anxiety is the principle Jarman presumes in order to establish Caravaggio's homosexuality.

Jarman defends his use of Caravaggio's paintings as evidence of the painter's homosexuality, by reasoning that, because "all the work was painted from life, it is much easier than might be imagined" (*Dancing Ledge* 21). In other words, because Caravaggio adhered to the same realism Wilde's Hallward stumbled upon, his desire for his male models is also recorded therein. Hallward assumed that his desire was legible to the viewer of the painting; Jarman assumes that he can read Caravaggio's desire in the latter's paintings.

Just as Hallward infused his desire into his portrait of Dorian, Jarman inscribes his own desire into his reading of *The Martyrdom*, and in turn his own sexuality, politics, and aesthetics into his cinematic portrait of Caravaggio. Although he thoroughly researched Caravaggio's life and times, and "followed the pattern of [Caravaggio's] life in the film," Jarman plainly states that Caravaggio's story "allowed me to recreate many details of my [own] life" (*Caravaggio* 132). In fact, Jarman's early difficulties in getting his script understood by potential collaborators were often because he had "written a self-portrait filtered through the Caravaggio story" (*Dancing Ledge* 28).

Jarman himself admits that "it's difficult to know how the seventeenth century understood physical homosexuality" (ibid. 21), which suggests that he recognizes that his associations surrounding sexual identity and desire are not necessarily literally applicable to Caravaggio. My historical constructionist objections to Freud's classification of Leonardo as a "homosexual" may appear inconsistent with my engagement with Wilde's "homosexual Shakespeare" or Derek Jarman's celebration of a "gay Caravaggio" or a "Queer Edward II." Wilde's and Jarman's projects differ from both the essentialist homogenization of all cultures and times into one indistinguishable fruit cocktail, and the assimilationist apologetics that bid for tolerance by name-dropping Plato and Michelangelo. Wilde and Jarman are fully aware of the differences between "veridical" and "consensual" truths. Their texts are cultural engagements with the present via a mythologized past; the tension between the two circumscribes a contested and contestatory space of cultural intelligibility and occlusion.

Jarman's exposition of Caravaggio's "homosexuality" also differs significantly with the projects of gay male academics who seek to reclaim the homosexuality of artists and writers. These gay scholars work either to establish the sexuality of their subjects or to explicate how their sexuality is crucial to a fuller appreciation of their work. Such projects usually have dual foci: the artists under examination, and the homophobia operative in the denial or trivialization of the artists' sexuality, since the gay revisionists are usually challenging critics who either refuse to believe in the artist's homosexuality or see it as an inconsequential detail. In these cases, gay academia's demand for and appeals to "historical accuracy" necessitate definitions of both "history" and "accuracy" that would constrain Jarman's project beyond feasibility. After all, even after bracketing the "objectivism" of traditional historians and scientists, "situated knowledge" is not a license for basing historical observation on personal phantasmatic relations to the past (as in Jarman's identification with Caravaggio's gaze in *The Martyrdom of St. Matthew*).

The ways in which Freud and Jarman each exploit psychical operations and phantasmatic structures to assume a specific position of interpretative authority in their respective "historical portraits" reflect different relations to the representational politics involved. Dominick La Capra observes that "point of view or narrative perspective . . . can become more of an issue when one attempts to come to terms with a transferential relation to the past" (124). Through his self-referential "indulgences" Jarman is the more accountable of the two narrators. Jarman explicitly states and thematizes his position within his reimagining of Caravaggio, something which Freud does not do in his "examination" of Leonardo. Jarman thereby avoids a pitfall that Freud does not, since, in such historical investigations, the "question is not whether transference takes place;

it is how it takes place and what the nature of the ensuing interchange with the 'object' is and should be" (ibid.).

Both Wilde's use of the sonnets and Jarman's of Caravaggio are obviously in part motivated and fully informed by the respective artist's sexuality and the need to express it in culturally recognizable forms—both in their creations of such forms and in the recognition of its historical existence in already accepted works of art. Their maverick readings, however accurate or fanciful, are also serious responses to the silence imposed on the possibility of homosexuality as such. Their revisions of history constitute "a way of reacting to enunciative poverty, and to compensate for it by a multiplication of meaning; a way of speaking on the basis of that poverty, and yet despite it" (Foucault, *Order* 120). Such self-interest is also a critical perspective outside of the received interpretations of these texts and these lives in the dominant culture, which allows Wilde and Jarman to illuminate and activate meanings and values within those works that the dominant culture either unconsciously or willfully elides in support of its own official version of itself. Both Wilde's and Jarman's readings of "Great Works" make it clear that "texts hailed as perfections of a genre or a discursive practice may also test and contest" societal values; their deviant reinterpretations raise (and confirm) suspicions that "texts classified as 'great' or as 'classics' . . . may . . . engage in processes that are repressed or downplayed in canonical interpretations—processes that may . . . have broader social and political consequences" (La Capra 141).

Wilde's and Jarman's rereadings also demonstrate Richard Brodhead's insight that "no past lives without cultural mediation. The past, however worthy, does not survive by its own intrinsic power," which leads Henry Louis Gates, Jr. to observe that one function of dominant " 'literary history' is . . . to disguise that mediation, to conceal all connections between institutionalized interests and the literature we remember" (Gates 105). Wilde's and Jarman's histories prominently display their countermediations on texts already hallowed by the more clandestine arbitration of the Academy. Furthermore, Wilde's and Jarman's reappropriation of historical figures is a strategy which determines the "resistance narrative" of their respective texts, since both "experiment with structures of chronology and temporal continuity . . . [as] part of their historical challenge, their demand for an access to history which necessitates a radical rewriting of the historiographical version of the past" (Harlow 85–86) that founds and sustains the dominant order.

Desublimated Narcissistic Investigations

The Narcissistic Subject and the Pleasure Principle

Although "sublimation" in Freudian thought refers to any "instinct's directing itself towards an aim other than, and remote from, that of sexual satisfaction" ("On Narcissism" 94), Freud and his contemporaries were particularly adamant about the benefits of the sublimation of homosexuality. In considering the implications of Freud's unfortunate use of the terms "sublimated homosexuality" and "ideal homosexuality" as synonyms, and the sexual politics of the more conservative institutions of psychology in the first decades of the twentieth century, I suggested that sublimation facilitated the assimilation of the male homosexual into the privileged "indifference" of phallocratic patriarchal privilege. This, however, strikes me as a rather obvious and insufficient explanation. Toward formulating a more complex understanding of the political and cultural stakes surrounding "sublimation," I wish to consider the opposition of the sublimated-nonsublimated investigator types in terms of the opposition of the anaclitic and narcissistic subject types I began to develop in my deviant reinhabitation of Freud's "On Narcissism" in the first chapter. First I will recall certain key elements of Freud's thought circumscribing the "Narcissism" essay, and consider other implications of this conceptual system for further critical appropriation.

In the texts of 1910–15, Freud conceived of the ego instincts as self-preservative instincts that opposed the anarchy of the sexual instincts, and posited as organically related parallels the antagonisms between the ego instincts and the sexual instincts, the reality principle and the pleasure principle, and their respective agencies, the reality ego and the pleasure ego. The pleasure ego, which can only "*wish*, work for a yield of pleasure," is protected against its own excesses by the reality ego, whose function is to "strive for what is *useful* and guard itself against damage" ("Formulations" 223). In the narrative of sexual maturation these antagonisms enclose, the healthy progression from autoerotism to heterosexual procreative genitality occurs in tandem with the ascension to prominence of the reality principle over the pleasure principle, and "the transformation of a pleasure-ego to a reality-ego" (ibid. 221–24).

If, as Freud contends in "On Narcissism," the "narcissistic object-choice" of male homosexuals arises from a "disturbance" in their "libidinal development" (88), this interruption in the narrative of Oedipal sexual formation would entail an arrest across all the interlocking progressions listed above. The narcissistic subject, therefore, describes a "between-space" in which the psychic components of subjectivity—the pleasure and reality principles and their eponymous egos—do not attain the absolute antipathy that characterizes their oppositional relations within the constitution of the anaclitic heterosexual male subject.

Freud's capitulation to "History" in *Leonardo* subordinated the signifying processes of his narrative to an external "Truth" to be discovered as the telos of the text and justification of his research, characterizing the implied narrator as a "reality ego," and his inquiry as a function of the reality principle. The reality principle in the narrative of *Leonardo* is a self-confirming politics—a vindication of an already accepted social truth in its motivation and narrative teleology. The preordained meaning that that realist narrative yielded—the significance of Leonardo's sexuality and the centrality of the Oedipal father to social order—assumed by the medical establishment, becomes a monolithic truth in the service of a socially enforced sex/gender uniformity.

Both Wilde and Jarman reject official "History" as a set of narrative constraints on signification supporting an oppressive "reality." Instead they engage in desublimated investigations that literally put the pleasure principle into practice. It is under the sway of the pleasure principle that the unconscious processes replace "external reality" with a kind of wishful thinking that constitutes "psychical reality" (Freud, "The Unconscious" 187). "Psychical reality" is a concept that emerges after Freud abandoned his theory of seduction, in favor of a theory of fantasies (often manifest as memories) as the causes of neurosis, even in place of actual events (Laplanche and Pontalis, "Fantasy" 8–10). It is such a theory of fantasy-become-memory that Freud develops in the Leonardo biography to explain both Leonardo's "vulture" fantasy and the politics of "history writing." Freud, in fact, compares the fantasies of the neurotic analysand "with which he [*sic*] has disguised the history of his childhood" to the "legends" every nation constructs to disguise "its forgotten prehistory," in the same text in which he proposes a strategic acceptance of these childhood memories independent of their veracity. Freud argues that even the purely fantasized memories "possess a reality of a sort," and the fact that the analysand has produced them "is scarcely less important for his [*sic*] neurosis than if he had really experienced what the phantasies contain. These phantasies possess *psychical* as opposed to *material* reality . . . and *in the world of the neuroses it is the psychical reality that is the decisive kind*" (*Introductory Lectures* 15: 368; emphasis Freud's).

The associations of male homosexuality with nonproductive aestheticism, informing tandem traditions of dominant delegitimation and countercultural reappropriation of those stereotypes from Oscar Wilde to Kevin Killian, have their psychoanalytic roots in this binary opposition between the pleasure principle and the reality principle, and the diagnosis of "narcissistic" homosexuality as an anachronistic adherence to the former. The delegitimation of gay male sexuality as "counterfeit" or "nonproductive" betrays a politically interested misconstrual of the reality principle and the pleasure principle as mutually exclusive opposites; the valorization of the former as the epistemological and moral superior of the latter depends upon a conflation of "reference" and "significance," a reduction of "reality" to a metaphysically conceived "Truth," and an underestimation of the personal and social importance of the concept of "psychical reality."

Recalling that Wilde's contempt for "reality" was not escapism but a political positioning—a deliberate repudiation of an oppressive normativity—illuminates the value of "psychical reality" to social practices of countersignification. Wilde's and Jarman's narcissistic constructions of new psychopolitical identities constitute forms of psychical reality that differ most radically from the Freudian conception in that they are self-consciously deployed and inter-subjectively realized. Unlike the pathogenic "psychical realities" of Freud's clinical examples, these fantasies are irreducibly public, working toward the imagining of communities rather than exhausting themselves in the private symbology of individual neurotics.

The sentence in *The Interpretation of Dreams* in which Freud first used the term "psychical reality" went through many tranformations in various editions. The one I find most relevant to the present discussion is from the 1919 edition: "If we look at unconscious wishes . . . we shall have to remember . . . that psychical reality . . . has more than one form of material existence" (620 n. 1). We see some forms of this material existence in the cultural practices and identity politics of gay men. Wilde's story and Jarman's writings and film textualize "psychical realities" as units of exchange by means of which narcissistic coun-terhistorians construct an "external" pleasure ego (Shakespeare as the lover of Willie Hughes, Caravaggio as the lover of Ranuccio Thomasino) in which each writer can at once recognize and express his sexually differenced subjectivity.

The Stakes of Sublimation

The kinds of identifications Wilde and Jarman mobilize require a deliberate disengagement from the sublimation of homosexual desire that is incessantly imposed on narcissism and its operations. We have already seen one aspect of the stakes involved in the "sublimation" of homosexuality, in the assimilation of the "ideal homosexual" as a "hom(m)osexual" of the patriarchal order. We are now prepared to discern in the politics of sublimation the antagonisms between the anaclitic and narcissistic subject types, and their respective modes of representational agency.

The two pairs (sublimated/nonsublimated; anaclitic/narcissistic) and their four individual terms can chart antagonistic relations of sexual identities and demarcate typologies of representational agency according to a subject's rela-tion to the dominant sex/gender system, sexuality, and representational prac-tice. The categories "anaclitic" and "narcissistic" specify the Oedipalized het-erosexual male and the gay male subject positions, respectively. The categories "sublimated" and "nonsublimated," at least within the argument of this book, asymmetrically traverse the polarities of sexual orientation: sublimation *typifies* the anaclitic subject and *accommodates* the "ideal homosexual." Sublimation, therefore, is intrinsic to the definition of the anaclitic subject (the "hero" of the reproductive reality principle), but the alternatives of sublimation or non-sublimation for the homosexual or gay man depend upon his intrapsychic ac-ceptance or rejection of his sexuality and his intersubjective realization or sup-pression of it.

The sublimated homosexual and the nonsublimated gay male are the politically polarized modalities of sexual subjectivity for the narcissistic subject
type. In terms of representational subjectivity and agency, the sublimated homosexual corresponds to the encrypted subjects of the Neo-platonic euphemistic tradition, and the nonsublimated gay male corresponds to the iconoclastic
subjects of the scandalous epistemophilic break.[45]

As early as "On Narcissism" (1914), where the term first appears, the ego
ideal has been implicated in a conception of homosexual sublimation as a form
of psychosocial group formation and maintenance. In my reading of Freud's
essay in chapter 1, I noted that the infant's sense of itself as a perfected being,
the "ideal ego," does not withstand the demands of socialization, and that the
internalization of role models and other external expectations the child encounters forms the ego ideal, that which the subject wishes to become, in an attempt
to regain the ideal ego. The ego ideal comes into being "from the critical influence of [the child's] parents . . . to whom were added, as time went on, those
who trained and taught him . . . —his fellow men—and public opinion. . . . In
this way large amounts of libido of an essentially homosexual kind are drawn
into the formation of the narcissistic ego ideal and find outlet and satisfaction
in maintaining it" ("On Narcissism" 96).

The homosexual investment in an internalized ego ideal can also be directed into politically accommodating hero worship, the "social side" of the
ego ideal which for Freud "opens up an important avenue for the understanding
of group psychology." The ego ideal can be externalized as "the common ideal
of a family, a class or a nation," which "binds not only a person's narcissistic
libido, but also a considerable amount of his homosexual libido. . . . The want
of satisfaction which arises from the non-fulfillment of this ideal liberates homosexual libido, and this is tranformed into a sense of guilt (social anxiety)"
(ibid. 101–102). Sublimation of homosexual desire is encouraged as a social pal-
liative for the otherwise disruptive subject. This passage, however, indicates that
the manipulation of homosexual desire (its arousal and frustration) is also a
means of interpellation, indoctrination, or neutralization of the potentially un-
cooperative ("nonsublimated") subject.

The narcissistic operations responsible for the ideal ego and the ego ideal
suffer much more oppressive conceptual recontainment in *Group Psychology and
the Analysis of the Ego* (1921) and *The Ego and the Id* (1923). In *Group Psychology*,
Freud defines "identification" as the most primitive emotional bond the child
experiences, which "plays a part in the early history of the Oedipus complex,"
predictably offering as his principal example the male child's relation to his
father: "A little boy will exhibit a special interest in his father; he would like to
grow like him and be like him. . . . He takes his father as his ideal. This behavior
has nothing to do with a passive or feminine attitude towards his father. . . . It

is on the contrary very masculine. It fits very well with the Oedipus complex, for which it helps to prepare the way" (*Group Psychology* 105).

In *The Ego and the Id* the original identification with the father in *Group Psychology* is transfigured into an internal fascism. In the "origin of the ego ideal" Freud now discerns a male "individual's first and most important identification, his identification with the father in his own personal prehistory. This is not in the first instance the consequence . . . of an object-cathexis; it is a direct and immediate identification and takes place earlier than any object-cathexis" (*The Ego and the Id* 21). This ego ideal is in fact the superego, the agency of conscience and the intrapsychic representative of the Law, an internalized paternal authority that is fully installed by the dissolution of the Oedipus complex in the heterosexual male subject (the anaclitic subject). Unlike the weaker ego ideals of "On Narcissism" that could "demand" but not "enforce" sublimation of sexual instincts ("On Narcissism" 94–95), the superego is virtually the intrapsychic personification of absolute sublimation: "The super-ego arises from an identification with the father. . . . Every such identification is in the nature of a desexualization or a sublimation" (*The Ego and the Id* 44).[46]

Because this ego ideal is "the heir to the Oedipus complex" (ibid. 36), the subject is not allowed the degree of identification that would subvert the absolute authority of the Oedipal father. The superego/ego ideal's "relation to the ego cannot be exhausted by the precept: 'You ought to be like this (like your father).' It also comprises the prohibition: 'You may not be like your father—that is, you may not do all that he does; some things are his prerogative' " (34–35). The inner impossibility of full identification with one's super-ego is reversed in the Oedipal son's external life when he imperfectly "fills his father's shoes" by assuming the same role in the next generation. "By becoming a father in turn, the former child hands the Oedipus complex down to his own descendants like the torch of civilization, and takes his place in the great lineage of Humanity" (Hocquenghem 93).

This repetition of failed imitations generates the ideal father, simply by virtue of the repetition itself.[47] Such practices vindicate Althusser's idea that ideology is material, and that faith is a result of specific practices such as going to church or kneeling to pray (Althusser, "Ideology and Ideological" 166–69). The internally flawed representations of the father in the psychical structures and familial functions of the Oedipal male produce the God to whom they submit. Other "absolutes" are generated and insulated from critical inquiry from this process as well: "The ego ideal answers to everything that is expected of the higher nature of man. As a substitute for the longing for the father, it contains the germ from which all religions have evolved" (Freud, *The Ego and the Id* 36).

Established as a self-evident essence through an analogy to the superego,

the "higher nature of man" also generates its own manifestations equally in-
sulated from critical inquiry, among them the Truth of the historians and the
Author of the canonical literary scholar. In Freud's *Leonardo* biography, the
Truth (the "secret" of Leonardo, his "self") and the transcendent Author
("Leonardo the Genius") coalesce in a single figure. Ironically, Leonardo, as
Freud renders him, should be a model rebel against this paternal lineage of
embodied authority and transcendental Truth. Freud insisted that Leonardo,
who "escaped being intimidated by his father during his earliest childhood, and
has in his researches cast away the fetters of authority," could not believe in
dogmatic religion, since "a personal God is . . . nothing other than an exalted
father" (*Leonardo and a Memory* 122). Leonardo's blasphemy, however, is recuperated by the Freudian narrator's insistence on the sublimation that supports
both Leonardo's empiricism and the mystique of the superego. Leonardo's
scientific disregard for authority "presupposed the existence of infantile sexual
researches uninhibited by his father, and was a prolongation of them with *the
sexual element excluded*" (122–23; emphasis mine). Just as Leonardo's demysti-
fying skepticism is attenuated by the value system of the narrative that presents
him, Freud's radical theories of meaning are recontained by the "Truth"-based
agenda of the historical method he utilized.

Leonardo's science could not dissipate the superego because that science
already obeyed the Law of the Father in the sublimation it accomplishes and
whose accomplishment it is. If Leonardo's desexualized scientific effort could
not kill the "Author," Barthes's orgasm-inspired (*jouissance*) playful intervention can: "To give a text an Author is to impose a limit on that text, to furnish
it with a final signified, to close the writing. . . . Refusing to assign a 'secret',
an ultimate meaning, to the text . . . liberates what may be called an anti-theological activity, an activity that is truly revolutionary since to refuse to fix meaning, is, in the end, to refuse God and his hypostases—reason, science, law"
(Barthes, "Death of the Author," 147). The desublimation effected by the narcissistic subject, therefore, can liberate the identificatory processes and demystify the theological appurtenances of Truth.

The doubled transcendence of Truth and Author in Freud's Leonardo
should also figure the "Shakespeare" of Wilde's "W. H." and the "Caravaggio"
of Jarman's writings and film, but they do not. In both cases the narrators took
identification—not faithfulness—as a motivating principle of the portraits they
fashioned. These counterhistorical meditations are informed and conditioned
by a narcissistic aim and object: a practice of self-portraiture based on the "I
desire" instead of the "I am," enacted through a proleptic identificatory relation to a belated and composite cultural ideal ego whose confirmation grounds
the unlimited semiosis of bivalent and multivalent identifications (ego ideals).
Caravaggio, "Willie Hughes," the names in Wilde's excursus, and even Wilde
himself become fantasy figures for subsequent revivification and ongoing coun-

tercultural traditions. They are textual instances of an identificatory semiosis which takes place between the gay male subject and an earlier figure through which that subject seeks an ego ideal, a pleasure ego with which he will identify, and through which (as image) he will identify himself to others, and offer his "self" for other identifications. This kind of identificatory semiosis, as well as the reenvisioning of the social subject that such semiosis enables, is dependent upon and productive of "psychical realities."

The anaclitic subject's polymorphous perversities are domesticated and subordinated under the genital organization in the service of reproduction. By the same token, his narcissistic operations of identifications and internalizations are stabilized, unified, and sublimated in the installation of the superego as the culmination of these processes. Contrarily, the nonsublimated, narcissistic subject's identifications involve ego ideals whose artificiality, transience, specificity, contingency, and multidirectionality of address inhibit a uniform progression or coherent teleological structure that would culminate in a patriarchal superego.

The compulsive and compulsory vindication of an already accepted social truth in the motivation and teleology of the scientist/historian typified by the *Leonardo* narrator, and the disenchantment from such truth and disregard for its parameters evidenced in the narcissistic pleasure-principled investigations of Wilde and Jarman, reflect the divisions in group identifications and fantasy operations described by Felix Guattari. Guattari distinguishes between "dependent groups" and "subject groups," according to each group's type of group fantasy, "established institutions and transitional objects," respectively. The "established institutions" that define the dependent group maintain a self-justifying mythic knowledge about themselves that inhibits interrogation: the Church does not question the nature of its God, nor the dominant class the nature or justice of its monopoly on power ("The Group and the Person" 38–39).

The members of such groups evince the suspension of a critical faculty regarding the contingency of the object the investment in which unites its members through the identification this common cathexis provides. Freud explicates this structural dynamic in *Group Psychology*, using as his primary examples of the libidinal structures of artificial groups, the Church and the Army (93–99). Each of these organizations inculcates a sense of eternality in the abstraction of the group that allows members to commit psychological and literal self-sacrifice for the group in the certainty of participating in that eternality. "What does it matter if I die, says the general, since the Army is immortal?" (Deleuze and Guattari, 62).

Guattari's "subject groups," on the other hand, are revolutionary formations that continually interrogate themselves, their identifications, and their modes of being. Their transitional fantasies are constantly subject to transformation, redefinition, and practical reassessment ("The Group and the Person"

38–41). The group fantasies of dependent groups encourage identification with static myths and commodification of identities in a false eternity of the group, whereas the transitional fantasies of the subject groups encourage a perpetual revolutionary "taking account of desire" (42–43).

The immutability of the Truth and the certainty of the self are the hypnotic residue of the transcendence of the patriarchal superego that subjectivates the dependent groups of "positively" Oedipalized anaclitic male subjects. Contrarily, the very irreverence to the figures with whom Wilde and Jarman identify, and their disbelief in the "transcendence" or essentiality of the "identities" they fashion through those figures, are precisely what enables their desiring and unauthorized identifications. The disenchantment from the Truth and the guarantee of transcendence means that these deviant strategists assume identities they know are artificial and evanescent. This assumption of an identity and recognition of its transience is where the negating affirmation and the intersubjective narcissism of the gay male subject coincide most legibly and poignantly. This revolutionary acceptance of contingency and finitude allows gay men to fashion their transitional fantasies as pleasure egos for self and other, without reifying those fantasies or inhibiting the ongoing identificatory transformations.

3

Imagining It Otherwise

Alternative Sexualities in
the Fictions of Samuel R. Delany

I was so ravished and full of wonder I had an impulse to tell the people in my
neighborhood about my orgasm as though it were a flying saucer.

—Robert Glück, "Denny Smith"

A T THE CLOSE of the previous chapter, I juxtaposed the Oedipal Truth resulting from Freud's psychohistorical analysis of Leonardo to the anti-
Oedipal fantasies fashioned in Wilde's and Jarman's counterhistorical dream
work. The acts of deliberate fantasizing that Wilde and Jarman organize as
signifying practices of disobedience to the "real world" suggest affinities with
radical uses of science fiction. Even the term "science fiction" itself conjoins
two realms of signification that are mutually exclusive. The cognitive and moral
dissonance the conjunction of "science" and "fiction" incites evinces an evaluation derived from the opposition of the reality principle to the pleasure principle that structured and conditioned the predominant modes of marginalization of homosexuality we examined in the first two chapters. The adaptation
of science fiction to deviant strategies of representational practice resonates,
moreover, with the histories of gay male oppression and resistance. The choice
of a noncanonical genre such as SF as the preferred form of expression is itself
a rejection of the values of the dominant society, similar to the rejection of high
cultural seriousness foundational to gay camp sensibility; in its displacement of
the "real world" with counterfactual and usually "impossible" alternatives, SF
recalls the deliberate and spectacular refusals of Jean Genet, the Cockettes, and
others to acknowledge "official reality" as a categorical moral imperative.[1] In
both his practice and his theory of science fiction, Samuel R. Delany reiterates,
extends, and contemporizes the political and culturally vital refusal in Oscar
Wilde's flamboyant preference for art and artifice over the "actual." Furthermore, Delany's work demonstrates the capacity of SF to accommodate complexes of contradiction, in his use of the medium to address the questions of

multiple oppressions—questions that constitute his lived experience as a black, gay, profeminist, dyslexic, paraliterary writer.

Science Fiction as Deviant Strategy

The turning point in the intergalactic war in Samuel R. Delany's *Babel-17* is a linguistic breakthrough, the exploitation of which enacts certain counter-discursive practices of disenfranchised populations. Once the Alliance's Rydra Wong had mastered the Invader's language ("Babel-17"), Wong "use[d] its precepts to change it and thereby convert it from an Invader weapon to an Alliance weapon," analogous to the cultural practices of Delany and other black writers who "have mastered the language and turned it against its formulators in protest, one of the many facets of warfare" (Weedman 158). Wong's actions reflect what W. E. B. Du Bois called the "double consciousness" of the black writer who "has an advantage having lived it. He [*sic*] has first-hand knowledge of the struggles and the triumphs of living and thinking in two diametrically opposed worlds, mastering both in order to survive physically and mentally" (159).[2] I would also read into this episode Foucault's "reverse discourse," the prototypical instance of which was the incipient consolidation of a "homosexual" subcultural identity, effected by appropriating the vocabulary of the pathologizing and criminalizing discourses of the late nineteenth century (Foucault, *History I* 100–101).[3]

Babel-17 as a novel, in fact, is itself an example of the practice Wong's tactics allegorize: the use of the "language" of SF to undo the most conservative tendencies which have accrued to the genre. The novel is modeled on the "space opera," which, as the name implies, often transposes the traditional western ("horse opera") pulp onto outer space. Like a western, the stereotypical space opera's dramatic resolution is "reassuring: . . . moral categories are easily defined. . . . Action taken quickly and boldly will bring a favorable solution to any problem, and . . . a morally superior creature will win any conflict with ones less palatable. . . . [These messages] are encoded within the structure of the work. . . . A space opera, by the very nature of its real communication, cannot be genuinely extrapolative or thought provoking. It must soothe, not ruffle" (Hardesty 68). Delany overcomes the constraints of the form by allowing the elements constituting the space opera themselves to figure his theoretical speculations (linguistics, semiotics, and communication theory) that ground the novel (ibid. 64).

There is a strange interpretative knot here, however. Even if Hardesty is accurate in both his generalization of the typical space opera and his assessment of Delany's counterstrategy, his statement may reinforce certain presumptions about SF that Delany specifically opposes. A sophisticated critical appreciation of SF and a practical awareness of the form's expressive possibilities require that we "keep narrative/aesthetic forms (space opera . . . parallel-world stories, social-alternative tales, etc.) distinct from aesthetic quality" and keep "these two areas of judgement . . . separate from a third, the value systems that control the text." Conflation of these areas of judgment results in "the assumption of unilateral cross-category associations ('all space operas necessarily express only one value system')" (Delany, "Three Letters" 199–200), which is precisely what Hardesty does in an otherwise sophisticated reading of *Babel-17*.[4]

Like many other innovative SF texts, *Babel-17* is an attack not on SF but on the self-fulfilling conception of science fiction as an endemically uncritical entertainment. Delany's novel challenges the habituated acceptance of SF's "imaginative strengths" and its "political conservatism" as "inextricable aspects" of the genre, underlying the reading public's resignation to SF's social and aesthetic inertia (Steiner, "Trouble" 97–98).[5] *Babel-17* does not invalidate the genre it reinhabits *tout court* but, on the contrary, by its own example disengages the form from the socially repressive messages with which it had come to be identified. If Delany, as Hardesty avers, radicalizes the space opera by *synthesizing* his conceptual motifs with the structural components, this serves to *dissolve* the connection between the intellectual pleasures and politically conservative heritage of science fiction, a connection which, ironically, Hardesty inadvertently reinstates.[6] Delany's transformative uses of SF are neither iconoclastic nor revolutionary, but rather reflect a respectful and emphatic attention to the genre's specific sociocultural histories, its distinctive modalities of signification, and the underutilized potentials thereof.

Science fiction offers unique modes of conceptual, rhetorical, and didactic expression, in its independence from mimetic faithfulness to the world as it is. The cultural survival and political direction of an oppressed group depend to some extent on that group's ability to envision an alternative reality. At times science fiction is the "web of possibilities" for foreseeing social configurations not yet achieved—even if solely by virtue of the inclusion of people of color or women characters in positions other than what has been "the case" (Delany, "Shadows" 81, 91–92).

Drawing on his personal history as an adolescent reader, Delany illustrates this potential of science fiction with Robert A. Heinlein's *Starship Troopers*, a novel generally cited as a paradigmatic example of U.S. science fiction at its most "hopelessly chauvinistic" ("The Necessity of Tomorrows" 29) and warmongering ("Shadows" 80). But these "adult" reassessments of the novel cannot detract from the importance of the young Delany's original thrill when he first came to the passage, nearly "two-thirds through the book," in which "our young hero, having survived the first 200 pages of dangers . . . looks in the mirror . . . [and] makes a passing mention of the nearly chocolate brown hue of his face" ("The Necessity of Tomorrows" 30). The casual and late inclusion of the hero's race in the novel as one detail among others indicates a society in which racial inequities have been resolved (ibid. 30–31; "Shadows" 80). Delany underscores the importance of this image by citing Suzanne K. Langer's "proposition that this initial experience of the image, a vision of something not yet real, is the impetus for all human progress, scientific, social, or aesthetic. If you don't see it, you can't work for it" ("The Necessity of Tomorrows" 31). In this glimpse in the mirror, Heinlein provided an image of a nonracist society that might guide those readers who wished to make such a possibility a reality.[7]

Delany writes of the strategic necessity of such visions in his fiction as well. When the young wanderer Pryn asks Madame Keyne about the Warrior Women of the Western Crevasse, Madame Keyne replies: "The Warrior Women of the Western Crevasse do not exist. Nor have they ever existed. They only grew up in stories because women like you—and me—from time to time wished they existed, because men like my father and brother were terrified they might. I think we use them as a kind of model. A model for thinking" (*Neveryóna 180*).[8] In telling his life story, Gorgik the Liberator describes the epiphany that prompted his political awakening while he was still a slave as nothing "more significant than a chance configuration of fog on a morning meadow that lets us recognize, momentarily, the shape of some imagined dragon, so that, ever afterwards in imagination, we are able to ride her where we wish" (Delany, "Game of Time and Pain" 56).

Besides its usefulness in focusing a proleptic identity politics for the non-represented subject, Joanna Russ also values SF for the expansive influence its postulated alternatives can have on the reader. Russ considers SF a conducive medium

> for any kind of radical thought. Because it is about things that have not happened and do not happen. . . . It's very fruitful if you want to present the concerns of any marginal group, because you are doing it in a world where things are different. I was talking to an ex-Mormon, and she said it was science fiction that had gotten her out of the ethos she had been born into, and she said it was not the characters but the landscapes. . . . Those landscapes made her understand that *things could be different.* In many social encounters and in many discussions, I've had a terrible time because the one thing my opponents do not have is the sense that things could be different. (Delany and Russ, 29)[9]

The visionary capacity of SF can also productively disorient a reader into an empathetic intuition of an alienated perspective on commonly accepted social institutions and beliefs. Consider the following passage, for example, from Algis Budrys's *Rogue Moon*, a work decidedly *not* about sexual marginality (precisely the opposite, in fact). A U.S. space mission discovered an alien structure on the moon, the encounter with which none of their teleported explorers long survived. In preparing a "daredevil" for another attempt, the scientist in charge briefs him on some of the rules operative within the environment they had been able to extrapolate from the previous failures:

> It is . . . fatal to kneel on one knee while facing lunar north. It is fatal to raise the left hand above the shoulder height while in any position whatsoever. It is fatal past a certain point to wear armor whose air hoses loop over the shoulders. It is fatal past another point to wear armor whose air tanks feed directly into the suit without the use of hoses at all. It is crippling to wear armor whose dimensions vary greatly from the ones we are using now. It is fatal to use the hand motions required to write the English word "yes," with either the left or right hand. (Budrys 89)

The utter senselessness of these restrictions and the absolute necessity to memorize and adhere to them will remind many gay men of the codes of masculinity whose infractions or lapses in the analogously alien and hostile environment of the homophobic high school or gymnasium could also prove fatal.[10] Edmund White's narrator in *A Boy's Own Story* articulates the observation (in both senses of the word) of these rules:

> A popular quiz for masculinity in those days asked three questions, all of which I flunked: (1) look at your nails (a girl extends her fingers, a boy cups his in his upturned palm); (2) look up (a girl lifts just her eyes, a boy throws back his whole head); (3) light a match (a girl strikes away from her body, a boy toward). . . . But there were less esoteric signs as well. A man crosses his legs by resting an ankle on his knee; a sissy drapes one leg over the other. A man never gushes; men are either silent or loud. I didn't know how to swear: I always said the final *g* in fucking and I didn't know where in the sentence to place the damn or hell. (White 9)

In a speech to the 1968 SF Convention, Joanna Russ addressed a specific lineage of visionary failure in SF, which she introduced by synopsizing a story she happened on while reading an SF magazine in her school cafeteria.[11] Dealing with "homosexuality on Mars," the story was based on the premise that "men who are isolated for a long time without women will attempt to get their sexual satisfaction from each other." Despite the sensational topic, it was a restrained and ("typically American") sex-free story in which one man made a sexual overture to another and was murdered. The shock for Russ came with the illustration:

> It was a picture of the murderer—this one guy who had killed the man who had made advances to him. Out of horror and disgust, you see. And the story made the point that such exaggerated horror was a product of unconscious, latent homosexuality. Well, apparently the artist had taken alarm even at *latent, unconscious* homosexuality, and had decided that by God, he was going to show you that this character was no effeminate sissy—he was a *man*—so

what he did was put layer on layer of muscles on this character, and give him beetling eyebrows and a snarl. . . . He would've made an adult gorilla look fragile. ("Alien Monsters" 134–35)

A student nearby, unaware of the context, looked at the picture and re-marked, " 'Oh, that's an alien.' " Russ concurs: "He was absolutely right. In the anxiety to show you a real he-man, the artist who did the picture had cre-ated a megalith, a monster, an armored tank, something that had only the faint-est resemblance to a human being" (135). The picture is not symptomatic simply of an individual illustrator's psychological insecurity, but of a socio-aesthetic inertia in the field of (American) SF in general, that such a figure could still be generated and circulated without reaction. It attests to the tenacious hold "this Paleolithic illusion, this freak, this myth of what a real man is" continues to have on the popular imagination. Russ also notes that among the other peculiar features of this figure is that the "he-man" cannot really experience pleasure, since his invulnerability precludes it. "Pleasure involves a kind of let-ting-go, a kind of loss of self, and he can't afford this" (140). This recalls the distinctions between the anaclitic and narcissistic male bodies I introduced in chapter 1: Russ's "he-man" is another incarnation of Theweleit's armored fas-cist body.

Thomas A. Disch challenges the masculine unconscious of SF by rereading a very particular "he-man," in fact the hero of Heinlein's *Starship Troopers*, a novel he finds "embarrassing" not so much for its authoritarian politics as for "its naiveté, its seeming unawareness of what it is really about. . . . *Starship Troopers* [is] . . . a veritable treasury of unconscious revelations. The hero is a homosexual of a very identifiable breed. By his own self-caressing descriptions one recognizes the swaggering leather boy in his most flamboyant form. There is even a skull-and-crossbones earring in his left ear" (Disch, "Embarrassments" 150). One of the reasons Disch raises these issues speaks to Russ's concerns about identifying masculinity and power. In Heinlein, Disch sees an insidious confusion of sexual identity, masculinity, and power, which "make the politics of the book more dangerous by infusing them with the energies of repressed sexual desires." In other words, the narrative not only denies its own sexual displacements but encourages similar modes of disavowal: "perhaps you're not attracted to an infantryman's life but his uniform. A friend of mine has assured me he knew several enlistments directly inspired by a reading of *Starship Troop-ers*. How much simpler it would have been for those lads just to go and have their ears pierced" (ibid. 154–55).

An apparent contradiction in Delany's theory of the image will serve to contextualize the discrepancies between Disch's and Delany's responses to Heinlein's infamous protagonist. In his reminiscence of his first reading of *Starship Troopers*, Delany concludes his paraphrase of Langer's observations on the politics of the image with the formula, "Image first. Then explanation" ("The Necessity of Tomorrows" 31). In a later essay, however, he asserts that "images do not exist without interpretation" (*Return to Nevèrÿon* Appendix A, 366). I read the second statement as not a *refutation* but a *qualification* of the first. I interpret it to mean that any image, discursively recognized as such, *necessarily occurs within an interpretation*, however implicit. The theory of representation to be read out of Delany's texts that can not only accommodate both of the above statements on the image but also allow their dialectical transformations reflects an eidectic-hermeneutic discretion, an eccentric and eclectic sense of responsibility to the contexts of intelligibility in which images are circulated.[12] This interpretative discretion facilitates nuanced appreciations as different kinds of recognition, Delany's recognition of Heinlein's hero *as a black man*, and Disch's recognition of the same hero *as a homosexual*. This is an important step in theorizing the differences in the cultural politics of representation and counterrepresentation for and of racially marginalized and sexually marginalized subjects.

In Delany's Nevèrÿon sword-and-sorcery tales, the civilized people are dark-skinned, and the barbarians are blond and blue-eyed. This reversal opens up the question of race "as structure, rather than as content; the reader sees a set of relationships . . . a set of positions anyone might fill, regardless of color— rather than a collection of objects, dark-skinned folks and light-skinned folks, each with an assigned value" (McCaffery and Gregory 86). While this strategy is particularly effective in terms of racial politics, a similarly imagined reversal of sexual politics that valorized male homosexuality over heterosexuality would only extend the tradition of phallocentric exclusionism that, in chapter 1, we traced from the classical Athenians to various post-Renaissance Neo-Platonisms. Even that superficial overview of the masculinist lineage of Western culture explains why representations of male homoerotism are not necessarily subversive, given (especially white) male privilege, generalized misogyny, and masculine self-preoccupation. Heinlein's text, in fact, clearly demonstrates that certain modes of "male homosexuality" are so compatible with certain expressions of hypermasculinity and so deeply interlaced with phallocratic power fantasies that the contexts of its representation itself may render it invisible. The obliviousness of Heinlein and his readers to this subtext—and, indeed, the enthusiastic identification such a "homosexual" can elicit as "he-man"—is not only a symptom of the internal contradictions of male dominant ideology, but a cautionary tale for gay men and people who wish to recognize gay men in representation.[13]

The atavistic defensive fantasies operative within certain traditions of U.S. science fiction that continue to offer the male reader the "he-man" as a monstrous ego ideal are a serious impediment to the realization of the genre's intellectual and aesthetic potentials. Such a masculine ideal admits only an either/or conception of power, which forecloses the exploration of the nature and transformations of power that is otherwise one of the genre's principal areas of speculative exploration (Russ, "Alien Monsters" 137–38). The narrative logic of *Starship Troopers* is itself an unself-conscious sublimation of homoeroticism into a heroic ethos; the "male identity" it presents marks a stabilizing disavowal of its own constitutive contradictions. These uninterrogated processes undermine "a central purpose of art, in conjunction with criticism, to expand the realm of conscious choice and enlarge the domain of the ego" (Disch, "Embarrassments" 155).

Delany achieves a consistent disidentification with the male dominance of both Russ's alien homophobe and Heinlein's heroic hom(m)osexual, through a critical understanding of the distances between the kinds of fictive worlds he writes and the "world-that-is-the-case," and the differences between his chosen genres and the fictional forms sanctioned as "literature."[14] Delany's politically differentiated typologies are based on an opposition of his fantastic fictions (science fiction and sword-and-sorcery) to the faithful reproduction of the "real" world in mundane fiction, and a contrastive extrapolation of the operative priorities of the paraliterary and the literary. In classifying SF as "paraliterature," Delany effectively affirms the general belief that "SF is not literature," but refuses its devalorizing connotation. He does not merely acknowledge SF's exteriority to institutional legitimation, but specifies what that exteriority means for *both* SF *and* literature.[15] Delany conceives of SF and literature "not as two different sets of labeled texts, but as two different sets of values, two different ways of response, two different ways of reading" (Delany, "Science Fiction and 'Literature' " 64). These responses and ways of reading are determined by the effects the irreal world of the SF text has on the focus of the narrative discourse and the lattitude of interpretation.

Paraliterary Dialogues: Theory

Because the SF text does not "represent" the given world but "misrepresents [it] in a readable (but not decodable) way" (Delany, "*Dichtung*" 189), the tension between the two frames a dialogic relation between the text and contemporary life that mundane fiction cannot sustain, since the latter depends on the preunderstood "real world" as its representational support. The kinds of fiction to which Delany is primarily committed, therefore, do not reflect a desire to *escape* reality as much as a desire to *confront* the given reality from a non-coopted distance. Science fiction is no more "going off to speculate on the future" than sword-and-sorcery is "going off to speculate on the past. Each represents a purely artificial convention; in sword and sorcery the past becomes your convention to establish a dialogue with the present" (McCaffery and Gregory 87).[16]

Disch's analysis of *Starship Troopers* makes it clear that such a critical dialogue is not an inevitable feature of science fiction. This novel is in fact only one example of the "inherent tendency" of SF "to reinforce commonly accepted prejudices." The writer can overcome this tendency by entering "the fictively constructed world ['the object']" thoroughly, treating it "autonomously rather than as merely a model of a prejudiciary situation ['a purely subject manifestation']." The writer "must explore [the fictive world] as an extensive, coherent reality—not as an intensive reflection of the real world where the most conservative ideas will drain all life out of the invention" (Delany, "Shadows" 41).[17] The specific differences in the "ways of reading" that constitute science fiction as a genre distinct from mundane fiction are also the means by which this critical distance can be realized.

Every science fiction text presents a world without the guarantees of familiarity or intelligibility that are taken for granted in reading mundane fiction. How each fictive world varies from the reader's world can be ascertained only in the process of reading; the reader's reception of the text, therefore, is an active deduction of the nature of that world, rather than a passive recognition of the world the reader already inhabits. Many incidents or descriptions in a science fiction text can be read literally that in mundane fiction could be interpreted only as metaphorical or indicative of a psychoperceptual disorder in the character. For example, the sentence "Then her world exploded" in mundane fiction would be read "as an emotionally muzzy metaphor about the inner aspects of some incident in a female character's life," but in an SF story the sentence could also mean "a planet, belonging to a woman, blew up" (ibid. 65).[18] The divergent readings of this sentence indicate that science fiction is a form of writing that prioritizes the "object" (the fictional world and its laws) over the subject (the characters' emotional states, etc.), and thereby inscribes a corresponding interpretative priority in the text for the reader.

These distinctions are not innocent. The interpretative constraints natural to mundane fiction support a more generalized epistemological prejudice: "In literature, the odder or more fantastical or surreal it is, the more it's assumed to be about mind or psychology" (Delany, "Semiology" 143). The subject orientation of mundane fiction, furthermore, is not simply one option among others, but has been for nearly a century a principal cultural value and a necessary condition for the "literary."[19] Literary genres began to be defined in terms of "the priority of the subject" in the late nineteenth century, at the same time that "the awareness of the problems of representation coupled with the critical gestures that separated paraliterature from literature" (Delany, "*Dichtung*" 188). Literature's preoccupation with the inner states of the characters, its representation of the subject as the perceptual focus, the phenomenological frame, of the object, underwrites an ideological investment in the centrality of the subject as a self-evident unity. It is through this ideological investment that "literature" serves as what Louis Althusser has termed an "Ideological State Apparatus" ("ISA"), a mode of representation that interpellates the individual as a specifically fixed subject (Althusser, "Ideology" 172–74), a process and a politics we first considered in chapter 1. I situated my discussion of Althusser's ISAs within a synopsis of the textual typologies of Roland Barthes: the "readerly" text and the text of pleasure that repetitively stabilize and reconfirm the bourgeois subject, and the "writerly" texts and the text of *jouissance* (or "bliss") that disrupt and disestablish that subject (Barthes, *Pleasure* 14–16; *S/Z* 3–5).

Barthes's opposing pairs of textual types share with Delany's generic distinctions a politics centered on the relation of representational practice to the conception of the subject. If the heterogeneous signifying systems and intertextuality of the writerly text shatter the subject into its constitutive heterogeneities and intertextualities, the object orientation of SF not only displaces the subject as the nexus of the meaning of the world or object presented, but posits the object or the world as the source of the subject's meaning or particular mode of being in a given situation. Much of SF explores how "beings with a different social organization, environment . . . and body [might] perceive things," and "how humans [might] perceive things after becoming acclimated to an alien environment" (Delany, "*Dichtung*" 188). This decentering of the subject is at once humbling and hopeful. While no longer the metaphysically privileged *cogito*, the deessentialized subject is thereby subject to transformation. No longer master, the subject is now "free and capable of change, of options, of alternatives; and change, options, and alternatives, are . . . what sf is about" (Delany, "Significance" 227).

It was the concentration on the object that gave the practice of science fiction an inadvertent subversive potential from its inception. "Because it was unconcerned with behavior at its beginnings, SF was eventually able to reflect the breakdown of Victorian behavioral concepts which, for all his advanced thinking, had strictured Wells. . . . American SF writers, freed from the strictures of the probable . . . not bound by the concept of universal human nature . . . sat contemplating marvelous objects in the theater of the mind" (Delany, "Critical Method" 126–27). *Science* reveals the multiplicity of codes constituting the environment, which will either directly or analogously reinforce critical attention to the codification and signifying operations underway within any provisionally stabilized experience.[20] *Science fiction* offers a tradition of representational formalization of a worldview in which the subject is not the cause but the effect of the system that sustains it, which is the radical message of Freud, Peirce, Benveniste, and Lacan.[21]

It becomes clearer why Delany's advocacy of science fiction often entails defending the genre from the attempts of well-meaning academics to claim it for literature. This incorporation would end the practice of "reading sf's presentation of alternate/world-workings as complex commentaries on the workings of our own world-that-is-the-case and to read them instead as yet another manifestation of the subject—perhaps another projection of the authorial subject, as we read contemporary fantasy" (Delany, "Disch" 155). In preserving the specificity of reading that constitutes science fiction as a genre, Delany also attempts "to preserve . . . time, space, and what might endure within them— a certain species of joy as it informs the word 'enjoyment,' or what Roland Barthes has marked in another language with the cognate *jouissance*" (Delany, "*Dichtung*" 191). *Jouissance* in Barthes's system is the subject's undoing, its liberation from its ideologically enjoined coherence and stolidity.[22]

Particularly from the perspective of marginalized subjects, the intrusion of literary priorities into SF is more than merely a misapplied critical apparatus. In maintaining SF's exteriority to literature, Delany preserves and cultivates SF's paraliterary independence from the "subject" and its ability to deconstruct and undermine the Cartesianism that grounds and is grounded in the identification of the literary with the hypostatization of the ego: "The discourse of sf gives us a way to construct worlds in clear and consistent dialogue with the world that is, alas, the case. Literature's unitary priorities do not. And in a world where such an 'alas' must be inserted into such a description of it, the dialectical freedom of sf has to be privileged" ("Science Fiction and 'Literature' " 78).

Paraliterary Dialogues: Practice

Delany's elaboration of the paraliterary differences of SF details the mechanisms by which SF has been able to use its "marginal status as a position to criticize the world" (Delany, "Neither the Beginning" Pt 1., 10). These differences thus schematized also serve as a blueprint for their self-conscious deployment in contemporary texts. The epistemological privilege of the margins and the critical dialogue of the fictive world with the "given world" are diegetically figured as the tensions between the exiled community of the "One-Eyes" and the City in *The Ballad of Beta-2*; the forest dwellers and the empire of Toromon in *The Fall of the Towers*; the Federation of Satellites and the Worlds in *Triton*; and the women of the Western Crevasse and Nevèrÿon in the Nevèrÿon tales.

Even within the fictional narratives themselves, however, the dialogic tensions are more complex than my list suggests.[23] In *Triton*, for example, the conflict between the Outer Satellites and the Worlds instantiates a specific metaphor for margin and center, without essentializing marginality itself as endemically "subversive" (just as "woman" and "gay" are not self-evident categories of opposition or subversive enlightenment). The "Outer Satellites" include the moons of Neptune, Jupiter, and Saturn; the Worlds include Earth, Mars, and Luna. Common sense would group Luna with the satellites. Luna's identity in the novel is produced by a political, not an astronomical, classification system. These designations are constructed around a metaphor of orbit types that need not necessarily correspond to a "scientific fact." Luna is a "world" because of its alliances, its self-conception as a centrality. Luna's "worldism" comprehends priorities of social coherence based on the oppositions of center to periphery, a phantasmatic schematization of hegemonic solipsism discernible in the macropolitics of the colonial power, the ethnocentricism of a monoculturally valorized western Europe, and the self-aggrandizement of the dominant white heterosexual male (the "centered self" Delany has exposed as just such a hoax [*Stars* "Afterword" 384]). The membership of Luna in the Federation of Worlds exposes the speciousness of such self-conceptions as "centered" (the moon is as much a satellite as Triton; moreover, because solar systems are heliocentric, Earth and Mars are as much satellites as the moons).

   Triton also complicates the margin-center antagonism, in that the *marginal* subject in the world of the story corresponds to the *hegemonic* subject in the world of the reader. The enlightened satellite society (the marginal countersystem) of Triton is seen obliquely in the novel through its least representative resident, Bron Helmstrom, formerly of Mars, a psychosocial throwback whose conceptions of masculinity and femininity are far closer to those of the he-men of *Starship Troopers* than those held by Bron's urbane polysexual and transgendered fellow citizens. This inversion of values allows Lawrence, Bron's homosexual housemate, to address (through Bron) the extratextual contemporary social order. In those scenes in which Lawrence represents, for Bron, Triton, the society and its values, Lawrence represents *Triton*, the novel, to the reader. It is not only the "radical" sexual politics Lawrence espouses that positions him as a personification of the text's dialogic critique of the "real" world, but the fact that Lawrence's lifestyle and views are representative of the fictive world and have the authority of the majority opinion in that world.[24]

   Other texts engage the reader in the dialogue with the critically fictive world by inciting expectations that are meaningfully disappointed. For example, in *Stars in My Pocket Like Grains of Sand*, the long description of the preparations for the dragon hunt resonate with the typical rhetoric of chivalry and masculinist adventurism of the classical sword-and-sorcery novels. As it turns out, however, the crossbow used is not a weapon but a projector whose harmless energy beam allows the hunter momentarily and unobtrusively to merge her or his mind with the mind of a dragon in flight (*Stars* 260–71). Other resignifications force the reader to confront certain prejudices that structure experience and its typical representations. The use of gender designations in *Stars* is at first perplexing. In this system, " 'she' is the pronoun for all sentient individuals of whatever species who have achieved the legal status of 'woman.' The ancient, dimorphic form 'he,' once used exclusively for the genderal indication of males (cf. archaic term man, pl. men), for more than a hundred-twenty years now, has been reserved for the general sexual object of 'she,' during the period of excitation, regardless of the gender of the woman referred to" (78). After this systematic definition has been provided, however, the continued difficulties it presents to the reader are enlightening. Even far into the novel, when the principle has been consistently applied that "women" refers to all sentient beings, sentences such as "In that war five million women were killed," or "In that city there must be at least four hundred thousand women," the reader is forced to confront her or his impression that the counts given are partial. Even when specifically designated as such, it is difficult for the reader to assimilate the use of "women" as a general and all-inclusive category.

These ruptural encounters between the reader's world and the fictive world in the dialogic engagement are often refigured within the diegesis as specific critical antagonisms. In *Triton* the conflicts range from the irreconcilable differences in the sexual politics of two housemates, to the war between two interplanetary federations based on their differing socioeconomic philosophies (a credit-based welfare state and a money-based class hierarchy). *Stars in My Pocket Like Grains of Sand* chronicles a struggle for ideological dominance by two diametrically opposed signifying systems.

Stars is an intergalactic saga set in a distant future, in which most of the thousands of known worlds are joined in an informational exchange network known as the Web. There are two major political affiliations vying for hegemony among the worlds, the Sygn and the Family. As their names indicate, the Sygn is the "radical" group identified with semiotics (and its concomitant acceptance of relativity, transition, and contradiction), and the Family is a "conservative" group committed to nostalgic ideals of domesticity and normative social stasis.

Perhaps the most extreme counterexample to Russ's theory of the radicalizing effects of the realization that "things could be different," the virulent conservatism of the Family and its counterempirical immunity to the pluralism of its multifold environments demonstrate the constricting influence of social kinship ties and taboos imposed upon the "practical consciousness" of the subject produced within that system. Lacan addresses this phenomenon in a way consonant with Delany's text: "The marriage tie is governed by an order of preference whose law concerning the kinship names is, like language, imperative for the group in its forms, but unconscious in its structure. . . . This is precisely where the Oedipus complex . . . may be said, in this connexion, to mark the limits that our discipline assigns to subjectivity: namely what the subject can know of his [*sic*] unconscious participation in the movement of the complex structures of marriage ties, by verifying the symbolic effects" (*Écrits* 66).

Approximately two-thirds of the novel is a first-person narrative of Marq Dyeth, a gay male human raised in a clone commune—a familial organization (a stream) that comprises both humans and Evelmi, the native inhabitants of his home planet, Velm, a Sygn planet. The Dyeths' generations are formed according to "streams" and "ripples" with no biological paternal transmission (no vertical descent), because there are no "egg-and-sperm relations" (*Stars* 125–26), unlike the more conventional (to our standards) arrangement condoned by the Family. Marq Dyeth explains the resulting sociologies in this manner:

> The father-mother-son that makes up the basic family unit, at least as the Family has described it for centuries now, represents a power structure, a structure of strong powers, mediating powers, and subordinate powers, as well as paths for power developments and power restrictions. It's also a conceptual structure as well, a model through which we see many different situations. . . . But there're power structures that can apply to nurturing groups. For instance, in the Family structure, the parents are seen to contain and enclose the children, to protect them from society. In the stream structure, the children are the connection between the parents and the society. (129)

How much the respective differences in the groups determine every aspect of life is a primary concern of the novel. One of Marq's "human" mothers, Shoshana, warns Marq that "the Family/Sygn conflict is in the process of creating a schism throughout the entire galaxy, concerning just what exactly a woman is" (194).[25] The Family's doctrine not only inhibits semiosis, but its endemically patriarchal politics are mystified by a quasitheological essentialism inculcated by that semiotic delimitation. This can be discerned in one of the contrastive comparisons between the Sygn and the Family, in terms of their divergent philosophies: "all human attempts to deal with death [fall] into two categories of injunctions: (1) Live life moment by moment as intensely as possible, even to the moment of one's dying. (2) Concentrate only on what is truly eternal—time, space, or whatever hypermedium they are inscribed in—and ignore all the illusory trivialities presented by the accident of the senses, unto birth and death itself. . . . For each adherent the other is the pit of error and sin" (136–37). The first injunction is the Sygn's, the latter the Family's. The Family's ideas of "eternity" and "transcendence" are articulated as the paternal transmission that these notions in turn sanctify.

In such a circular patriarchal theology, nonreproductive sexuality becomes associated with blasphemous treason. This idea of the "eternal" is also what allows individuals to work against their own interests and die for the interests of the rulers, believing that they will share in the eternality of the group.[26] "By becoming a father in turn, the former child hands the Oedipus complex down to his own descendants like the torch of civilisation, and takes his place in the great lineage of Humanity. The absolute need for the Oedipus complex to be reproduced—and not produced—explains why childhood conflicts with the father image are finally resolved by the son's stepping into the father's shoes"

(Hocquenghem 93). In forgoing this function, the male homosexual leaves a gap in the social network that calls for production—an alternative productivity that neither supports the illusion of a transcendental standard of truth, nor can claim any a priori support for its own ontological validation. It is this unmotivated production that the Sygn encourages and the Family condemns. The Sygn's freedom from the theology of the Family is associated with its adherence to a non-referentially based theory of signification and its rejection of biological definitions of families and gender identities. The intrications of signifying practice and sexual alterity (the homosexual *produces* meaning rather than *reproduces* father's empty eternality) illuminate the political cogency of a consciously maintained preeminence of unlimited semiosis over the reception and transmission of pregiven "truth": these are the radical priorities that the Sygn represents.

I now want to examine two instances of Delany's dialogues with the sexual politics of the "world-that-is-the-case." The first, a science fiction story, "Aye, and Gomorrah," nullifies the capacity of the phallus to function as the transcendent signifier of desire. The second, "The Tale of Old Venn," a sword-and-sorcery tale, divorces the penis from the phallus in the iconography of male dominance. The extended allusions to Freud and Lacan in these works might seem incompatible with Delany's commitment to an object-prioritized paraliterary practice.[27] We need to distinguish, however, Delany's interrogation of such conceptual traditions from a reader's adoption of Freudian theory as a critical approach to Delany's texts. Such a method would reimpose on the texts the subject as the ultimate explanatory frame of reference. Furthermore, psychoanalytic criticism underwrites one of the most common means of trivializing or recuperating SF's critical differences: the formulaic misreading as symptomatic fantasies of those elements in the plot that mark the text's dialogic distance from the "real world." Such misreadings also inevitably (either intentionally or otherwise) contribute to the institutional delegitimation of paraliterary genres, since these interpretations reflect and reinscribe the dominant presumption "that the fantastic elements [of the text] are simply the unconscious detritus of desire—rather than useful and autonomous responses (with both conscious and unconscious aspects) to a specific cultural reality" (Delany, "Significance" 226).[28] The subject-centered epistemology informing and the intellectual elitism legitimating such a critical maneuver effectively render the SF text illegible. The interpretation of the plot elements of an SF story as fantasy both aggrandizes the subject and dismisses the genre metonymically by foreclosing from consideration any extrasubjective or contestatory significance in the fantastic elements of the narrative. I hope, therefore, that my oscillating investments in psychoanalysis herein will resemble Evelmian rather than Arthurian dragon-hunting in my pursuit of Delany's meditations on sexuality and his own dialogic engagement with Freudian and Lacanian thought and their various aftermaths.

"Aye, and Gomorrah": Desire Degree Zero

"Aye, and Gomorrah" takes place in a distant future in which the extensive exploitation of outer space has necessitated the development of a large standing specialized work force known as "spacers," astronauts neutered and genetically altered at birth to be able to withstand long exposure to cosmic radiation. Sexual attraction to spacers is considered a perversion called "free-fall-sexual-displacement-complex," and those who experience such attraction are known as "frelks." A subculture of bars, clandestine meeting points, pornography, and prostitution has developed around the frelks and spacers, and the typical attitudes of spacers are analogous to certain types of heterosexual males' attitudes toward homosexuals.[29] The spacers talk obsessively and derisively about frelks, seek them out, suspect strangers, solicit money, occasionally taunt them, and most of all deny the possibility of any reciprocal need or desire.

Although "Aye" on one level is a compelling parody of the relation of generalized homophobia to the libidinal economy of repression and aggression in "straight" hustler subcultures, to read the story principally in these terms yields both the most impoverished interpretation of the text and the most ungenerous evaluation of Delany's achievement. The failure of such a reading underscores the importance, mentioned above, of distinguishing the appropriateness and scope of representational strategies of racially marginal and sexually marginal subjects. The reversal of the "civilized" and "barbarian" roles in the Nevèrÿon tales reconceives of racial identity as "structure, rather than as content . . . a set of relationships . . . a set of positions anyone might fill, regardless of color." If, however, the spacer-frelk situation is reduced to the heterosexual-homosexual ambivalence, this "set of relationships" that persists "regardless of" sexual identity contrarily would suggest that the kind of repression of male homosexuality and oppression of male homosexuals typical today is merely a particular manifestation of a necessary sociosexual dynamic. Therefore a reading of "Aye, and Gomorrah" that delimits the story's significance to the parody it includes, in effect accepts the relational redefinition of racial identity allegorized in the Nevèrÿon tales as indifferently applicable to redefinitions of sexual identities. This strategy, however, deconstructs neither heterosexism nor homophobia but in fact rearticulates their inevitability. Fortunately, "Aye" exceeds any such totalization. The allegorical allusions to the libidinal politics of sexual subcultures do not constitute the center of the story but form an integral backdrop to an ec-centric meditation on the motivations and ends of sexuality, a meditation Delany incites through a rigorous refusal to imagine (to image) an object that might stabilize or rationalize desire.

The first-person narrative concerns the frenetic r-and-r weekend of the off-duty spacer crew to which the narrator belongs. (For the sake of simplicity I will use the pronoun "he" to refer to the narrator since he was born male, although this information is not immediately advanced.) The off-duty spacer crew first sets down in Paris, near a "tearoom," a public lavatory frequented by gay men seeking sexual encounters. When one of the gay men asks the spacers to leave, fearing their rowdiness will bring the police, the narrator asks him if he is a frelk. The man says no, and adds: "You look as though you may once have been a man. But now . . . You have nothing for me now" ("Aye" 534). The narrator asks the same question of a prostitute in Matamoros, and receives a similar reply: "Sorry. But you have nothing that . . . would be useful to me. It is too bad, for you look like you were once a woman, no? And I like women, too" (535).

In Istanbul the narrator leaves the group to wander alone. He encounters a woman who claims to be a Greek tourist, but who eventually admits to being Turkish, a frelk, and interested in the narrator. She asks the narrator what sex he had been at birth, and invites him to her apartment, claiming that as a poor artist she cannot afford the "going rate" of sixty lira, and adding that she does want to pay him, in any event. The spacer accompanies her home, but he does not stay long. When their negotiations founder, the woman comments, "I want something. But . . . you are not the one who will give it to me," and asks him to leave, admitting that after he has gone she will visit her friends "and talk about . . . the beautiful one that got away" (544).

The story omits any clear description of spacer genitalia; nor does it specify the alterations in secondary sexual characteristics. Although spacers are "not even androgynous" (539), the questions the narrator is asked on three occasions indicate that his original sex cannot be deduced from his present physical appearance. Therefore, the frelk orientation does not correspond to either a gender- or a sex-based object-choice. Furthermore, the paralleled responses of the French man and Mexican woman suggest a significant alteration in the allocation of sexual identity in this future world: each of them regrets that the spacer "has nothing" for him or her now, in contrast to the spacer's (supposed) former sex as a male or a female, respectively. Taking this most literally, what is "missing" is a sex-determining genital, whether penis or vagina.[30] Thus, the standard binary governing sexual difference—plus or minus penis—has been displaced by the binary plus or minus sexual organ, with both men and women on the "plus" side of that divide. But history repeats itself: "loose, swinging meat" is not "nothing," just as the vagina is not nothing, albeit misconstrued as "nothing" in phallocentric epistemologies.

These structural contradictions in the general sexual politics of the world of the story are more interesting as they are particularized by the Turkish art student when she explains her perversion to the spacer: "I want you because you can't want me. . . . I wonder how many people there were before there were you, waiting your creation. We're necrophiles. I'm sure grave-robbing has fallen off . . . A pervert substitutes something unattainable for 'normal' love: the homosexual, a mirror, the fetishist, a shoe or a watch or a girdle. . . . Frelks substitute . . . loose, swinging meat" (541). Her comparative overview of perversions is rhetorically flawed in that the "mirror" is a metaphor, while the fetishist's objects are literal. More important (although certainly related), her statement is *completely inaccurate*: none of these "substitutes" is unattainable. On the contrary, the technical beauty of fetishism is *precisely* the *attainability* of the (substitute) object.[31] What *is* unattainable, however, is the "always already" lost original Object of desire, whose very unattainability founds desire and makes possible an infinite series of substitutions. And this is true for all desiring subjects, including the heterosexuals, who even in the unexamined terms of the artist's own definition are perverts too, since "normal love" is only a specific codification of substitutions for that lost original as well.[32]

What distinguishes frelks from other perverts is neither the loss of the true object nor the inadequacy of their substitutions, but rather the *incommunicability of their desire*. Both their desire and its object exceed symbolization: frelks are exiles from a sexual intelligibility based on the phallus as the transcendental signifier of desire. Just as they cannot metonymically transfer their desire for the lost Object (as Phallus) to the penis, they cannot metaphorically signify their object (or the object of Desire of the Other) as phallus. The art student's admission that she "wants" the spacer because he cannot want her deforms the Lacanian principle that one always desires the desire of the Other; the frelk indeed desires the desire of the spacer, but desires that desire knowing it to be nonexistent, and desiring it *for its nonexistence*.[33] Just as the penis is no longer the determinant of biological sexual difference, the phallus cannot mark the object of desire. If desire is the desire of the other, the frelk cannot represent it at all because it does not exist, and cannot become its object, because nonexistent desire has no object. As such, the frelk's sexuality exposes the enormity of desire that other perversions (including, if not especially, normative heterosexuality) usually distribute and domesticate within their signifying systems. This is one reason that, as the narrator observes when he puts his hand on his crotch, this gesture is "so much more obscene when a spacer does it" (540).

Thus the frelk's sexuality remains transparent to the foundational insatiability of desire itself: the consciousness of this structural impossibility of desire cannot be deferred, the futile and yet essential movements of this desire cannot be fixed in object signifiers such as the penis, the breast, a shoe, pain, knowledge, etc. Frelks are *unable to euphemize* the primordial lack in the subject incessantly reenacted as the awful bliss of desire's essential tragedy. The terrible lucidity of frelk sexuality begins at the body of the spacer, the site of the meta-castration which severs desire from the prosthesis of its would-be signifier and/or surrogate signified.[34] The loose, swinging meat signifies the absence of desire in the spacer, which is precisely what the frelk desires—the desire of the spacer *as irretrievably lost*. The spacer's wound as mark of metacastration does not signify the frelk's desire but that desire's double negatives.

The negation of the phallus as the transcendent signifier of desire in "Aye" entails a displacement of the "plus or minus penis" binary as the determining paradigm of sexual difference. "The Tale of Old Venn" presents a complementary challenge to phallic binarism. While the "plus or minus phallus" binary is reinstalled within a gendered difference that is conflated with sexual difference, this binary is not ultimately bound to biological sexual difference since the phallus that represents "masculine" power is divorced from any somatic support.

"The Tale of Old Venn": Power Tools without Jock Support

In her old age, the scientist, philosopher, anthropologist, and former companion of the legendary architect Belham, Venn, taught the children of her native Ulvayn islands. Among her lessons, she included the story of her years as a participant observer of the Rulvyn hill tribes, when she had married into the family of a woman named Ii, and shared a husband, Arkvid, with Ii and several other women ("Venn" 76–77).

One day while Venn was cooking, her stepdaughter Kell was teaching Venn's two-year-old son how to urinate: "she would grasp her genitals and say proudly, 'Gorgi!' and then she would pat the boy's genitals and say . . . 'Gorgi!' and he would do the same, and laugh." After urinating in front of him, Kell tried to explain to the boy that "he, less economically constructed than she, had best use his hands to guide himself" (88). To aid in instruction, Kell raised her father's apron, lifted up his penis, and shouted "Gorgi!" which action the boy repeated. Then Kell went over to Venn as Venn was putting on her apron and said, "Bye-bye, gorgi," which is what she had also been saying for the boy's benefit whenever any male was dressing or putting on a penis sheath (88–89).

Just then Arkvid called his son over to give him what he had been carving. " 'Bye, bye, gorgi.' My son waved at my vagina and turned to his father." Arkvid gave his son a rult, "a special, wooden carving that Rulvyn fathers make and give to their infant sons" which they wear on their chests. Rults are not given to girls, who are not to touch them, refer to them, or see what is inscribed on the back. When Kell attempted to look at it, Arkvid blocked her view, which angered and upset her (88–89). Realizing that the object was the same thing that her father wore on his chest, Kell refused to play with her little brother. Holding a clay pot top on her chest, Kell pretended to have her own rult, a game that made her father uneasy, since girls pretending to wear a rult was considered obscene.

Several nights later, while the adults were still around the table after supper, Arkvid offered his thoughts on the differences between the sexes that this incident had brought to mind. "The little girl sees that her brother and her father have rults . . . and she is jealous and envious of the rult—as she does not possess one. It is right that she should be jealous, for the rult is strong, full of powerful magic." Although the initial jealousy is seemingly forgotten, "the little girl will put this jealousy down in the dark places below memory where things eat and gnaw at one all through life, in silence, without saying their names." He speculated that women overcame this jealousy through pregnancy, that they imagined that the fetus was their own rult growing inside them, a fantasy particularly fulfilled by a male child. A woman's open defiance of or disrespect for men Arkivd attributed to a more pronounced rult jealousy (92). When Ydit remarked that Arkvid's description did not fit her experience, he replied that the jealousy functions at so deep a level, one might not be aware of it. Acia, the other wife, remained silent.

Venn, however, spoke up, calling Arkvid's notion "ridiculous" and observed that if "you carried on about your . . . gorgi . . . the way you carry on about your rult, you'd have the little girls jealous of that in a minute." Arkvid found Venn's suggestion "truly ridiculous," asking, "Why would a little girl be jealous of a little boy's gorgi when she has a perfectly good gorgi of her own, and more compactly built at that?" He then diagnosed Venn's objections as "deep-down rult-jealousy" (93). Venn reminded him that she was a foreigner, and two years previously she " 'had never even *seen* a rult,' " which Arkvid dismissed by invoking the universal significance of the rult that transcended even "the rult itself," namely: "the power, strength, and magic that the rult embodies" (93–94). After Arkvid had left for the Men's House, Venn diagnosed Arkvid's notion of "rult-jealousy" as a symptom of "his own overevaluation of the rult" (95).

The broad and rather blatant parodies of certain Freudian traditions lend a humor to the text that detracts from neither its significance nor its concision. Delany's caricatures of "penis envy" and phallocentrism disarm their rhetoric and provide a means of strategically disengaging from the "real life" history of these myths. Moreover, the very obviousness of the models for Delany's parable makes Arkvid's inability to conceive of a possible analogy between rult and penis all the more incredible—which induces the reader to confront the difficulty of separating the two in "real life" because of the effective naturalization of their conflation in our prevalent discursive environments.[35]

In "Aye, and Gomorrah," the shift in sexual difference from a male-female opposition to sexed-neutered opposition replaces the phallocentric binary of plus/minus penis with plus/minus sex organ, thereby granting equal ontological status to male and female sex organs.[36] The plus/minus rult binary of the

Rulvyn gender system parodies but reiterates the masculinism of the more typical phallic binary it displaces. This binary, however, can neither naturalize nor
mythologize its iconic revelation of a masculine essence through appeals to the
male body. Just as the frelk's sexuality obviates a metonymic relation between
the penis and the Phallus as object of desire, the way the rult is imagined in
the Rulvyn culture suppresses a metaphoric identification between Phallus and
penis as signifier of dominance. The frelk's sexuality exposes the transrational
nullity of desire itself; the rult system remains transparent to its own production
of gendered subjects it entitles or excludes, that is to say, subjects whose gender
identities are constituted as such by that entitlement or that exclusion.[37]

The key differences in phallic politics and representational strategies of
male dominance touched on here are brought out in an interesting way in
Joanna Russ's comparative survey of eleven SF stories dealing with either violent gender role reversals or civil wars between the sexes (ten by men, one by
James Tiptree, Jr. [Alice Sheldon]). Russ contextualizes her findings through
the work of the anthropologist Joan Bamberger on the narratives of certain
indigenous peoples of the Amazon detailing male victory over matriarchies.
These narratives center upon "the secret objects belonging to men (masks,
trumpets) [which] . . . are badges of authority, permitting one sex to dominate
the other. However begun, the myths inevitably end with the men in power.
Either the men have taken from the women the symbols of authority or have
installed themselves as the rightful owners of the ceremony. . . . In no versions
do women win" (Bamberger, qtd. Russ, "Amor" 2). Russ adds: "The men's
Sacred Objects—the badge of authority and means of domination over others—are stolen or contaminated by women, who then become dominant over
men. . . . Women lose because they abuse this power or are immoral whereupon
the men seize or reclaim the Sacred Objects, sometimes with supernatural aid"
(ibid.).

The male SF writers whose work Russ analyzes depart most profoundly
from their Amazonian counterparts by making "biology itself the guardian of
the Sacred Object: they install the Sacred Object on their own persons. All the
stories . . . (except Tiptree's) use as their Sacred Objects the male genitalia; possession thereof guarantees victory in the battle of the sexes. This victory is
therefore a victory of nature, and so the battle may be won without intelligence,
character, humanity, humility, foresight . . . or even responsibility" (3). In the
texts of the male SF writers, the triumph of the men is "so natural . . . that
most of the stories cannot offer a plausible explanation of how the women
could have rebelled in the first place" (ibid.). Venn's tale, on the other hand,
provides plausible explanations, both for the scientist's reckless suppression of
meaning in his proclamation of the Truth, and for the storyteller's commitment to the "unrealistic" vision in her responsibility to rebel.

Metaparaliterary Dialogues

Some of Delany's texts begin at the level of a paraliterary dialogue with
the "world-that-is-the-case" but develop a metaparaliterary dialogue with specific principles operating to produce that world's normative system of meanings. The sexuality and politics of Gorgik the Liberator figure a metadiscursive
dialogue with the sexual politics surrounding the mutually defining antagonisms of the narcissistic and anaclitic subject types as we have delineated them
in the two previous chapters, in particular the opposition between the sexual
and the useful. One of the tales, "The Game of Time and Pain," engages a
metaparaliterary dialogue to the second degree: the paraliterary dialogue with
the sexual politics of the world-that-is-the-case is embedded within a metaparaliterary dialogue with the sexual politics of the practice of the narrative
representation of that world, which in turn is embedded within a meta-meta-
paraliterary dialogue with the sexual politics of contemporary narratology.

Sexualizing Resignifications

Of the major characters in the Nevèrÿon tales, Gorgik the Liberator perhaps most vividly embodies a coherent style of representational agency. A former slave, Gorgik led several military campaigns against the institution of slavery. Even after his manumission Gorgik continued to wear an iron collar, both
as a sign of solidarity with those still in slavery and as an insignia of his sexuality, expressed principally with other men in master-slave fantasies. In the Old
Market in the major port city of Kolhari (where the young Gorgik spent his
last free days of childhood), the collar is commonly worn on the Bridge of Lost
Desire by both clients and prostitutes to indicate such predelictions and the
willingness to cater to them.

Early in his military campaign, Gorgik bought the young Prince Sarg, a
southern barbarian nobleman who had been captured and enslaved. While still
in the position of Sarg's "owner," Gorgik introduced him to male-male sexuality ("The Tale of Small Sarg" 143). The two became lovers, and Sarg tolerated
Gorgik's need for one of them to wear the collar as slave and one to play the
role as master, although he claimed not to share Gorgik's erotic excitement
from this game (Delany, *Neveryóna* 181). These sexual games also provided the
models for their strategies of infiltration and sabotage. Gorgik and Sarg took
turns posing as a slaver selling the other into the household of a slaveowner.
Once inside, the "slave" would foment unrest and prepare for the "master's"
attack (ibid. 178–79).

Regardless of the roles played or who was wearing the collar, Gorgik asserts
that they are "both free men. For the boy the collar is symbolic—of our mutual
affection. . . . For myself, it is sexual—a necessary part in the pattern that allows
both action and orgasm to manifest themselves within the single circle of de-

sire. For neither of us is its meaning social, save that it shocks, offends, or de-
ceives. . . . As one word uttered in three different situations may mean three
entirely different things, so the collar worn in three different situations may
mean three different things. They are not the same: sex, affection, and society"
(Delany, "Tale of Dragons and Dreamers" 238–39).

By drawing out the parallels between the S/M reenactments of scenes of
domination and the strategic impersonations of master and slave in the service
of the revolution, we can discern where a new sexual politics of signification
emerges from the complementary failures of sexual signification in the two
stories we examined above. The transvaluation of the slave collar catalyzes the
fluidity of sexual meaning—so devastating to the frelks—with Arkvid's tauto-
logical overevaluation of power symbology. The overdetermined collar is essentially a sexualized rult—and it is precisely this sexualization which liberates the
collar's signifying potential from the politics of the rult's meaning, just as gay
male desire can sexualize the penis in ways that liberate that organ from the
transcendence of the Phallus.[38] The use of sadomasochism to sexualize the collar also speaks to Freud's hesitation in the *Three Essays* to classify sadism as a
"perversion," because of the useful role sadistic impulses in the male played in
executing copulation independent of consent (*Three Essays* 157–58, 159 n. 2).[39]
The utter absence of empathy in Freud's remark is one of the features that in
his later writings disqualify this type of "sadism" as "sexual,"[40] another irony
that figures in the reversibility of roles in Gorgik's sex games.

Gorgik realizes his "perversions" through a kind of theater that resignifies
the social through the sexual, a practice that intensively accesses and articulates
the relations of desire to signification that were only negatively elaborated in
the frelk's metacastration fetish. Such resignifying practices also exceed the
kind of self-mystifying power politics that the rult-fixation of the Rulvyn men
typifies. Gorgik's power politics are externalized and ritualized through a microsocial libidinal economy, rather than sublimated into the legislative homeo-
stasis of a male-centered gender identity system.[41]

Perverting the Master Narrative

A specific mise-en-scène of Gorgik's resignifying sociosexual theatrics
structures an elaborate demystification of phallic regimes of intelligibility in
"The Game of Time and Pain." This tale takes place after slavery has been
officially abolished in the empire and Gorgik has become a respected public
figure. "Game" derives its title from an incident in "The Tale of Dragons and
Dreamers," set in the first period of Gorgik's "outlaw" career. In this tale,
Gorgik is being held captive by the Suzeraine, who, suspecting Gorgik of con-
spiracies with the Southern Court of Lord Aldimir, is torturing Gorgik to ex-
pedite the interrogation. The Suzeraine tells Gorgik that he calls his manner

of torture "the game of time and pain" ("Tale of Dragons and Dreamers" 230). Neither this incident nor the source of the title is mentioned in "Game of Time and Pain," but this hidden relation of the two stories highlights their remove from each other, schematically redescribing the absolute distinction maintained in each story and in the ethics of this type of sadomasochistic practice, between "real" torture (as in "The Tale of Dragons and Dreamers") and sex games with superficially similar power dynamics (as in "Game of Time and Pain"). Neither tale, however, glosses over the intimate ways concrete social situations including violence inform the fantasy structures of sexual expression. Through thematic and metaphoric manipulations of the structural dynamics of an S/M session, "The Game of Time and Pain" achieves a metadiegetic meditation on the interanimation of sexuality, narrative, and power.

Resting overnight in an abandoned castle on his way to the funeral of Lord Krodar, Gorgik discovers Udrog, an adolescent barbarian, asleep in front of a roaring fireplace. Udrog offers himself to Gorgik: "I like to do it with strong men, big men. You ever fuck real rough?" and suggests that they might find a broken slave collar. Gorgik provides one he keeps with him, and Udrog readily agrees to be Gorgik's slave: "Gorgik closed the collar around [Udrog's] neck— 'You're my slave,' Gorgik said. 'You do what *I* say now. . . . What I want you to do is be quiet.' 'What are you going to do?' the boy asked. 'Tell you a story' " (14–15).[42] The randy boy protests, being far more interested in fucking than listening, but he reluctantly acquiesces, assuming this ritual to be one of Gorgik's "kinks" preliminary to "real" sex.

Between Gorgik's declaration and the beginning of his tale is interposed a narrative synopsis of Udrog's life, from his childhood to events shortly before the encounter with Gorgik. This account includes plausible "reasons" for Udrog's sexual tastes. Orphaned at seven, he drifted through several variously abusive domestic situations. In one of them, the older children took him to the woods, where they played games "in which they tied each other up and pretended to beat each other and cuffed each other, games that now and again had an overtly sexual side. . . . But reducing to play what once had been true torture gave them . . . the power over the mists of pain that was all memory had left . . . of childhood" ("Game" 25). These children's games from Udrog's case history, and Gorgik's sexual scenarios after emancipation illustrate ways in which the vicissistudes of the sexual drives that "lean on," for representational form, memories of abuse—of being rendered the unwilling *object of the aggression* of an Other—can facilitate the means by which that individual perversely becomes *the subject of signification*. In fact, of all the Nevèrÿon tales, it is only in "Game" that Gorgik acts as the narrating subject of his own life story.

Gorgik tells Udrog of his days as a slave, his freedom, and his campaigns against slave owners, but he focuses on one incident while he was still enslaved that enabled him to reconceive social justice once he had been freed. While working in the Faltha Mountain obsidian mines, one of the slaves was seriously injured in a wrestling match with a lord in which the slave had been forced to participate. One of the more humane lords arranged for Gorgik and two other slaves to watch over the injured man; he temporarily removed their collars, and instructed them to report to him immediately if there were any changes. When the injured slave's condition worsened, Gorgik went to summon the lord. Opening the tent flap, he found the lord naked, fastening an iron collar around his neck. "I recognized it as a sexual gesture with an intensity enough to stun me and make all my joints go weak. . . . my own sexual interest in the collar was as precocious . . . as yours." The lord was also stunned when he first saw Gorgik watching him: "We were both naked. We were both male. I had seen him; and he knew I had seen him. Now he saw; and from what he saw he knew of me just what I knew of him. . . . I could not have denied my reaction to him any more than he could have denied his to the iron" ("Game" 66).

Finally recomposing himself, the lord reestablished his "mastery": "He came over to me, raised the iron, and closed it about my throat. The lock snapped to. And just as I had recognized the sexual in his placing of it about his own neck, I knew that, though lust still reeled in his body and still staggered in mine, this gesture was as empty of the sexual as it is possible for a human gesture to be" (67). It was too late, however, to negate the effects on Gorgik of his discovery:

> I had known that the masters of Nevèrÿon could unlock the collar from my neck or lock it on again. What I had not known was that they could place it on their own necks and remove it. . . . I would not be content till I had seized this freedom and power for myself, even though I knew I had to seize the former for every slave in Nevèrÿon—before I could truly hold the latter. . . . I wanted . . . the power to remove the collar from the necks of the oppressed, including my own. But I knew, at least for me, that the power to remove the collar was wholly involved with the freedom to place it there when I wished. (69–70, 72)

The real fascination of "Game" is not merely the content of Gorgik's tale but the relations of narrative content to narrative situation, of that intradiegetic narrative situation to the extradiegetic situation of reader and text, and the paraliterary dialogue between the textual operations and contemporary theories of narrative, semiotics, and sexuality.

Many critics consider narrative progression coextensive with desire, in both the development of the plot and the engagement of the reader's interest. Peter Brooks sees plot as the nexus between the desire represented in the text and the reader's desire the text manipulates: "We can . . . conceive of the reading of plot as a form of desire that carries us forward, onward, through the text. Narratives both tell of desire—typically present some story of desire—and. . . .

make use of desire as a dynamic of signification" (Brooks 37).[43] Narratologies of this type rely on the logic of the quest, a progression from a lack to a fulfillment, whose sequential representation incites the reader's "passion for meaning."

The act of reading for pleasure indeed makes an easy analogy with sexuality, in the ambivalent relations between appetite and satisfaction that characterize them both. Both experiences are typically cognized as a pursuit of a goal, a pursuit pleasurable in itself, but ultimately a means to an object the desire for which initiated and motivates the process. The attainment of the goal (Freud's "end pleasure") extinguishes the pleasure of the approach (Freud's "forepleasure"). The analogy is supported by a conception of desire defined solely by the sexual telos of the anaclitic (or "positively" Oedipalized heterosexual male) subject.[44] The masculinist bias of this erotics of narratology is not always merely implicit:

> The archetype of all fiction is the sexual act . . . what connects fiction . . . with sex is the fundamental orgastic rhythm of tumescence and detumescence, of tension and resolution, of intensification to the point of climax and consummation. In the sophisticated practice of sex, much of the art consists of delaying climax within the framework of desire in order to prolong the pleasurable act itself. (Scholes, *Fabulation* 26–27; qtd. de Lauretis, *Alice* 108)

In this system, narrative and dominant male sexual experience become parallel and mutually vindicating teleologies of coherence. The narrative, like the "mature" (read: "male heterosexual") genital sexuality regimented by the reality principle, is pleasurable in itself, but is subordinated to the greater pleasure of the culmination to which it is driven. Delimited by a normative male heterosexual epistemology, the operations of narrative desire are streamlined in a unidirectional linear progression toward the goal, and the imperative to attain that goal eclipses the lateral pleasures of the approach. Narrative progression thus reiterates the reproductive genitality of the phallic stage, and the monocular pragmatics of the reality principle.

But the implications of this go beyond the phallic morphology of the principal metaphoric obsessions. Narrative is a process of knowledge production and transmission ("to narrate" and "to know" have a common etymology). The narrator is the powerful one (the one supposed to know); the narratee is the supplicant, who seeks the narrator's knowledge, the perfection of which is the "whole story." The sexual metaphor imposed on this narrative drive significantly alters the conception of narrative as an organized empirical *askesis* we observed in Freud's *Leonardo da Vinci* monograph. In Freud's model, the primacy of the goal over the process was maintained by the reality principle. At the time (1911), as I have already had frequent occasion to observe, Freud's conceptual apparatus included several mutually opposing binaries; the opposition of the reality principle to the pleasure principle was read as a correlatively arranged parallel binary of the self-preservative instincts and the sexual drives.[45] For this reason, the ideal subject of the narrative was a seeker who sublimated his sexuality in his tenacious scientific curiosity.

The emphasis on a "narrative desire," on the other hand, amounts to a shift from a de Vincian to a Baconian scientist-subject. Francis Bacon conceived of science as the means by which the "masculine" rational mind and the "feminine" corporality of nature were joined in a "holy and legal wedlock" (qtd. Keller 36). This marriage was to result in the enslavement of "nature" to "man," and the scientific mastery of nature has been since Bacon frequently envisioned as a sexual domination.[46] Such a goal-conditioned sexual pragmatism is reminiscent of Freud's more ominous speculative asides on a biohistorical "sadism"—a response to "the need for overcoming the resistance of the sexual object by means other than the process of wooing" (*Three Essays* 157–58).[47] The narratee as a post-Baconian scientist resexualizes this will-to-know and associates it with mastery over the object thus violated.[48]

"The Game of Time and Pain" parodies and plays off such associations without affirming them. The heteropatriarchal conceptions of narrative as a signifying practice confirming the acquisition and dispensation of knowledge as a sexual teleology of phallic mastery form the horizon against which the text's subversive plurivocity exfoliates. Although "Game" inscribes the reader in the position of the naked, collared, unwilling listener, the affective dissonance between the reader and Udrog precludes complete identification. While the premise of the narrative encourages anticipation of a sex scene between Gorgik and Udrog at the conclusion of Gorgik's tale, the reader nevertheless maintains a pleasure in the text that Udrog does not experience at all. The half-promised liaison, however, potentially stimulates a "prurient" voyeurism in the reader, which literally sexualizes both the reader's motivation to read the story to the conclusion, and the nature of the final reward. The object of the reading is doubled: the "what happened" of Gorgik's story, and the sexual encounter to take place after the story's conclusion. Udrog's impatient listening imbues the narrative presentation with a sexual expectation that parodies and displaces the (sexualized) narrative object and aim. This also allows Udrog's repeated attempts to hasten the narrator's progress, to mark (and incite) the sexual drives of the reader in the textual surface.

The intradiegetic narrative situation models a typical reader-fictive text relation in several aspects. A few days previous to this encounter, Udrog had shared a bonfire and a meal with a thief who had claimed to be Gorgik. Later that evening Udrog witnessed the thief being murdered by bandits, and when he subsequently heard of the state funeral for a great lord (actually Lord Krodar), he decided the thief had indeed been Gorgik. Now in the castle, Udrog listened to the man's tale without accusing him of lying—certainly out of self-defense, but also to ingratiate the tale teller in hopes of achieving his sexual aim at the tale's conclusion.[49] As narratee, therefore, Udrog displays a "suspension of disbelief" comparable to that of a modern reader of fiction, for whom such a practice also facilitates the pleasure to be derived from the "encounter" with the narrator. Of course, the reader's is a voluntary "suspension of disbelief"; Udrog's is merely a pretended credulity. The former is a self-conscious manipulation of the nondifferentiation in the primary processes (of the pleasure principle) between an imagined and a real object, which enables the reader to enjoy the fiction. Udrog's feigned belief is part of his tactical willingness to listen to the tale (for him the antithesis of and impediment to pleasure), which he endures as a means of obtaining greater gratification in the future: in other words, the reality principle. The object of the reader's suspension of disbelief is the pleasure *of* the narrative; for Udrog it is the pleasure *after* the narrative. This difference is a key element in the dialogic tension between the text and the theories it *legibly misrepresents*.

Udrog's situation in some ways makes more sense than the reader's, in that the central paradox of sexual teleology has been resolved: Udrog wants the story to end in order for pleasure to begin; the libidinous reader replays desire's conundrum of pleasure's insistent progression to its extinction. For Udrog, hearing the story provides no pleasure at all—in fact, he refers to it as a "kind of torture" he didn't "have in mind" (74). Let us consider the scene of "real torture" that gave this tale its name, the episode in "Tale of Dragons and Dreamers" in which the Suzeraine, while interrogating Gorgik in a dungeon, explained to him the "rules of the game [of time and pain]." Announcing his intention to inflict "little pains" that could "go on for days," the Suzeraine admitted that "the infliction of these little torments gives me far more pleasure than would your revealing the information that is their occasion. So if you want to get back at me, to thwart me in some way, to cut short my real pleasure in all of this, perhaps you had best tell me" (230).

There are at least three distinct libidinal economies structuring the relations among desire, pleasure, and knowledge in the narrative operations. The "implied reader" of "Game" takes pleasure in the story as it unfolds, but that pleasure incites the reader's desire to discover the "whole story," the revelation that will satisfy that desire but end the pleasure that stimulated and sustained it. Udrog's progression through the narrative is motivated by a belief in a pleasure to be granted at the story's conclusion. Both the reader and Udrog proceed through the narrative for the conclusion, but for the former the conclusion is the end pleasure and the end of pleasure—particularly the end of the subsidiary pleasures of the narrative itself (the forepleasure); for the latter the conclusion marks the beginning of pleasure (including, if not especially, forepleasures).

The Suzeraine seeks knowledge from Gorgik, and motivates Gorgik's narrative by inflicting pain (unpleasure). But the act of inflicting pain, the process of soliciting knowledge (the narrative) itself, is also pleasurable to the Suze-raine. If Gorgik were to divulge the knowledge that the Suzeraine seeks, he would also end the Suzeraine's pleasure. Both the reader and Udrog consider the conclusion of the narrative to be a greater pleasure than the process (Udrog, representing a perverse parody of the reality principle, finds no pleasure in the narrative process at all). The Suzeraine is perverse in finding greater pleasure in the process (the forepleasure) than the goal.[50] In the Suzeraine's situation, *Gorgik gives pleasure by withholding the narrative*: in Udrog's case he *withholds pleasure by presenting the narrative*; in the reader's case the narrator *both gives and withholds pleasure by presenting the narrative*, his stylistic flourishes and nar-rative digressions are (fore)pleasures of the text that also prolong its attaining a climax, its coming to its end.

Gorgik's withholding the (narrative) object in "Dragons" is an occasion for the Suzeraine's *sadistic* pleasure. In "Game," Gorgik's teasing of Udrog suggests that his withholding the (sexual) object in this case could be the oc-casion for *masochistic* pleasure: " 'You smile, waiting: for me to confirm the pleasure you, too, know can be excited by carefully planned delay to truly ter-rifying heights' " ("Game" 82). As we have seen in other dialogic inscriptions, such as Lawrence's speeches to Bron in *Triton*, Gorgik's suggestion here makes more sense as an address to the reader than to Udrog. Udrog's reception of Gorgik's narrative is radically motivated by the reality principle, which totally desexualizes the narrative's affect, abhors detours, and precludes masochistic pleasure. Such a pleasure is more feasible for the reader, given the reader's plea-sure-principled relation to the text, and the reader's diffracted identification with Udrog's figure as a (literally) masochistic surrogate.

This supposition of diffracted address is given further support by the tenor of the story of Udrog's life, interposed immediately after the scene in which the suggestion is strongest that the two men will make love after Gorgik's tale is told. It opens: "We pause before this tale within a tale within a tale—to insert another tale. We'll write awhile of Udrog" (24).[51] This conspicuously marks the interlude as a deliberate interruption and a tease, analogous to Gorgik's narra-tives that at once promise and postpone sex. The interposed story, moreover, is addressed exclusively to the reader, a correlative object that encurges the reader's empathy with Udrog's perception of narrative as an impediment to sexual satisfaction. Finally, in the logic of masochistic pleasure evoked in the oblique address to the reader, the explicit address exacerbates the sexual under-current of the pleasure of the text in foregrounding the narrative not as a *with-holding* of sexual pleasure, but as a *seduction*. In this metadiegetic seduction the deflection of the (sexual) goal is itself sexualized. The prohibition of pleasure is made pleasurable. The experience of frustration is eroticized, in a perverted narrative agenda whose erotic frustrations are games of time and pain, putting into play unmasterable forepleasures. The role of the reader is reenvisioned as fellow fantasist, displacing both Freud's desexed and Bacon's sex-criminal scientists.[52] Delany's use of S/M as a dynamic architecture of the narrator-narratee exchange, and his exposition of (sexual) sadism and masochism as implicated in the narrative processes of the social subject, reflect and amplify an articulate alienation from the gender-dichotomized stasis of the mandatory (political) sadism promulgated in the heterosexual coitus-based narratology.

Fictions Critical and Mundane

Besides its parodic meditation on the sexual politics of narrative and narrative theory, "The Game of Time and Pain" is also compelling for its portrayal of sexuality as neither the "truth" of the individual nor the essence of an interiority, but a form of social signification. In a written interview on the Nevèrÿon series, part of Delany's response to the question, "What does it mean to explicitly eroticize class relations?" began with a counterquestion:

> Is anything ever eroticized *other* than class relations—or the signs of class relations, which, simply because they are not quite the same thing, allow for the necessary *shift* in class relations themselves despite the fixes of desire? . . . Since all human signs have their class associated aspects, anything we find erotic must be an eroticizing of "class relations." . . . The question should be, rather, why is the eroticizing of certain class relationships egregious and always made explicit in an accusatory tone, while the eroticizing of certain others is always mystified and allowed to remain implicit by calling that process anything other than it is? (Delany, "Column" 545–46)

One of the power imbalances inherent within the dynamics of a desiring economy perfectly describes the narrative pact between Gorgik and Udrog: "She or he who desires, listens. She or he who is desired, speaks. . . . I might go so far as to say that to speak is to constitute oneself as a desired subject. To listen is to constitute oneself as a desiring subject" (ibid. 547). But one of Delany's most suggestive insights on these erotic class politics (and on his strategies behind Nevèrÿon) concerns those eroticized relations that are deliberately made invisible in the patriarchal social order. He offers as a "limit case . . . the well-brought-up middle-class heterosexual white woman, who declares: 'There isn't any physical type at all that I'm particularly attracted to. All I'm really interested in in a man is personality and intelligence,' " which Delany decodes to mean: "The people I find erotically acceptable are generally those in or near my own social class" (545–46).

Later in this discussion, Delany notes that although he depicted desire in the series traversing all directions of the class spectrum, there was one he "consciously attempted to downplay . . . the one on which patriarchy grounds itself:

that is the desire of women for men a microclass above their own. This is . . . the one 'sexualization of class relationships' perceived as somehow not really sexual at all. Its implicitness is its exploitability. This is the mode of desire by which most of the major, easy, and hardly ever redressable exploitations of women by men occur. . . . In the *Nevèrÿon* tales, rather than subject it to analysis or theory, I chose simply not to support it with representation" (548–49).

However, Delany does, in fact, represent such a subject and such a relation in one very frightening character in his 1974 SF novel *Dhalgren*: Mrs. Richards. Her depiction emphasizes the extraordinary and destructive charades and self-deceptions the entire family must maintain for Mrs. Richards's delusional identity to remain *psychotically intact*.[53] In drawing attention to his deliberate exclusion from Nevèrÿon of the class relations that produce a "Mrs. Richards," Delany underscores the fact that his depiction of Gorgik's sexuality not only clearly distinguishes real violence from consensual fantasy, but also distinguishes honest sexual perversions from politically repressive ideologies. In *Triton*, Lawrence makes the latter distinction in his diagnosis of Bron's "difficulty" with women: "Your problem . . . is that you are a logical pervert, looking for a woman with a mutually compatible logical perversion. . . . The mutual perversion you are looking for is very, very rare—if not nonexistent. You're looking for someone who can enjoy a certain sort of logical masochism. If it were just sexual, you'd have no trouble finding a partner at all. . . . Fortunately, your particular perversion today is extremely rare" (*Triton* 254).

Bron's counterclaim that "in one sense, women are society" (257) should be considered in the light of Delany's reading of Sade: "Sade goes to great pains to show that the idea that women are upholders of the values of society and civilization is an illusion fostered on them purely to get the better of them —so they may be raped, enslaved, and all money and economic power . . . can be stripped from them the more easily" (Delany, "The Scorpion Garden" 4). The real subversion then of the S/M in the Nevèrÿon tales is not the "positive" representation of eroticized class relations between Udrog and Gorgik, but the exposure of the normative white middle-class heterosexual couple as a covertly eroticized and deliberately pathological class imbalance.

Delany's speculations on some of the negative reactions to *Dhalgren* also suggest reasons for the general failure to discern an eroticization of class relations in the valorized forms of middle-class white women's heterosexuality (whose psychically crippling consequences *Dhalgren* so vividly exposes in the Richards family). Delany surmises that the readers who had the most difficulty with *Dhalgren* were those who "still see 'real' society as a projection of an 'idealized' sex act (which somehow involves vast amounts of male aggression inchoately coupled with total female passivity), and read all fictional accounts of sex-and/or-society as accurate, relevant, and charged with the value as they constitute themselves under the shadow of this model. Such a mistake is understandable. Precisely this model charges with sense the fiction of writers as diverse as Lawrence, Mailer, Malzberg" ("Of Sex" 40–41).[54]

Of course, such beliefs are partially the result of the reading protocols of mundane fiction that reify the text's presumed transparency to the world it represents. Delany's respecification of the object of mundane fiction is particularly useful here: "The writer of mundane fiction tells a story set against . . . a section of the given world. I say 'given world' rather than 'real world' because often the most naturalistic piece of mundane fiction is a highly conventionalized affair . . . that has far more to do with other works of fiction than with anything 'real' " ("Some Presumptuous Approaches" 49). The "pregiven world" is produced by Barthes's "already read," the network of clichés, stereotypes, and truisms that ensure the intelligibility of the readerly text and the fixity of the readerly subject's "self." The science fiction writer who recognizes the artifice of *any* "given" world, and the paraliterary writer who sees the fictionality of the readerly "self," are subject to transformations of identity and meaning not dependent upon but in alienated dialogue with the material situations of contemporary society and the "given world" through which those situations are mediated, created, and/or mystified.

These considerations also encourage shifting the focus from the opposing groups of writers or text-types (mundane/science fiction; literary/paraliterary; readerly/writerly) to two somewhat corresponding groups of readers that I shall call the compliant and the resistant reader, respectively. Many who fall in the latter category may have become "resistant" readers because their marginality makes the fictiveness of cultural beliefs abundantly clear. Daily life in the U.S. makes it impossible for most members of racial minorities to believe in the "racial equality" "our country" has achieved, even if they wanted to. The social cohesion provided by the dominant fictions (along with their status and power), however, affords the members of the ruling class the luxury of gullibility. As Disch observes, "The upper classes possess a great initial advantage in discovering while still young that the world is in essential agreement with *their* fantasies of power" ("Embarrassments" 151).

The compliant reader accepts the uniqueness of the individual, the naturalness of a monolithic sexuality, the self-evident justice in patriarchal social orders, etc. The compliant reader as dominant heterosexual subject also (necessarily) considers novels to be accurate reflections of the world as it is, rather than a cultural practice which contributes to the construction, maintenance, and naturalization of that world's fictions.[55] The sexually disenfranchised, however, cannot afford such interpretative complacency.

This may be one reason why the sexual outlaw in Delany's novels often engages a metadiscursive intervention in the unself-conscious fiction she or he confronts, in contrast to the heterosexual male character who is "realistically" living out a "pregiven" fiction. Unlike the other characters in *Triton*, Bron inhabits the kind of SF that Delany's original title for the novel (*Trouble on Triton*), parodies, the kind that operates on the principles that Tak, the gay man in *Dhalgren*, recites in a metatextual moment parallel to the metasystematic description of the obsolescent sex/gender system Lawrence summarized.[56] Such metadiscursivity is the "double consciousness" of the marginalized subject illuminated in the dialogue between a subject who believes its constitutive fictions and a subject who does not. The latter subject does not invest in the "truth" of its fictions, but in those fictions' specific meanings and potentially unlimited meaningfulness.

Delany's theoretical blueprints for and his own examples of the kind of critical fiction that the science fiction writer can achieve revalorizes the "fictive." The specific importance Delany places on the paraliterary differences of the genre at once constitutes a challenge (like Oscar Wilde's) to the dominant obfuscating obsessions with "authenticity," while providing eloquent theoretical grounding for that challenge as well as for textual practices that prioritize signification over referentiality, the production of meaning over the repetition of "Truth." It is science fiction's foundational infidelity to the "real world" that affords the fictive world the status of a critical model. As Delany observes, "If sf has any use at all, . . . it gives us images for our futures. . . . Its secondary use . . . is to provide a tool for questioning those images, exploring their distinctions, their articulations, their play of differences" ("The Necessity of Tomorrows" 31).

Affirmation of the meaningfulness of homosexuality parallels the meaningfulness of the fantastic elements of SF. If Heinlein's war stories simultaneously demonstrate that SF is not endemically radical and the depiction of homosexuality is not necessarily subversive of heteropatriarchy, Delany's critical fantasies are "useful and autonomous responses . . . to a specific cultural reality" (Delany, "Significance" 226), just as "homosexual object-choice and the fantasies that sustain it . . . are not a freestanding, innately determined possibility, nor a developmental failure, but are one of the forms that resistance takes" (Fletcher 94).

4

Graphic Specularity

The Sexual Politics of the Specular

The Dominant Scopic Regime

THE CONTEMPORARY SCOPIC regime predicated on a hierarchized gender binary of a male viewer and a woman as object of contemplation derives its metaphysical foundation from the modes of seeing geometral perspectivism affords. Renaissance optics imagined Descartes's transcendental "I" situated in the eye of an observer of a distant scene,[1] which further determined the intimate relations between the Renaissance "self" and perspectivist painting, whose principles were first formalized by Leon Battista Alberti (1404–1472). Alberti envisioned a straight line proceeding from the eye of the painter to the surface on which the image manifests itself, and from that image to the retina of the viewer, simplifying "the body of the viewer . . . into a punctual site of reception" (Bryson, *Vision* 103), which redefines the viewing subject "as a non-empirical *punctum* of observation" (110).[2] There is, however, nothing inherent in this conjunction of speculative egology and specular technology that necessarily transforms visual culture into a sexually differenced polarity.[3] Recalling my discussion in chapter 1 of other aspects of early modern European intellectual history, we may assume that the gender binaries of Neo-Platonism and Baconian philosophy of science contributed to a normative template organizing the experience of Cartesian seeing as a unidirectional encounter between an unimplicated masculine observing subject and a visually accessible feminine object.[4] We find traces of this structuring fantasy in the tendency to figure mastery as a visual disequilibrium between an invisible male observer and a feminine (or "feminized") display: the scientist at his telescope or microscope, the voyeur hidden in the dark beneath a bedroom window, the man at the stripshow or in the movie theater.

Jacques Lacan remarks the significant roles visual technologies played in establishing the "universality" of the Cartesian *cogito*: "It was at the very period when the Cartesian meditation inaugurated in all its purity the function of the subject that the dimension of optics . . . called 'geometral' or 'flat' . . . optics was developed" (*Four Fundamental* 85). Although Lacan vehemently rejects the notion of a unitary, coherent subject, his arguments against the reification of the *cogito* as viewer of a perspectivist painting reinforces the gendered dichotomy of masculine spectator and feminine spectacle that this representational tradition gratuitiously supported.

Lacan's deconstruction of Cartesian perspectivism begins from the presumption that the subject's self-certainty as *cogito* depends upon a mastery defined as a privileged position as unseen seer. Thus constituted, the *cogito* can be demythologized by considering the reversibility of the gaze in any act of seeing. The seeing subject can imagine him-or herself as that "non-empirical punctum of observation" only by denying the fact that the object viewed is also a potential punctum of observation from which the viewer is equally visible (ibid. 95–96). The supposed subject *of* the gaze is thus actually always subject to the gaze that exceeds the subject's control. If the gaze is always outside the body, the subject's access to visual perception (thus to mastery) also situates the subject as exterior to itself, placing that body in the field of visibility (and the potential mastery by the "annihilating" other) (98).

The exteriority of the gaze to the subject leads Lacan to classify the gaze as an example of an *objet a* (or *objet petit a*). An *objet petit a* is any part of the subject's body that appears to be detachable, and thus conducive to symbolizing the lack that founds the subject and motivates desire.[5] In this case, the relation of the gaze to the eye characterizes the gaze as an *objet a* (106). Its function as an *objet a* explains why the structure of the gaze is at once foundational and traumatic for the subject, since the paradigmatic *objet a* is the penis after castration anxiety has taken hold. The detachability of the penis that the threat of castration confirms, inaugurates the lack at the center of the subject as desire, and postulates the Phallus as desire's transcendental signifier (Lacan, "Meaning" 81–83).[6] The viewing subject thus traumatized seeks in the act of looking the fetish object that might compensate the lack that this apprehension of the gaze effects; the ultimate fetish object would be the gaze itself. The analogies drawn between the eye and the gaze and the penis and the phallus, therefore, underwrite a transcription of the anxiety over "being seen" into a "universal" castration complex.

Lacan finds one of his favorite illustrations of the function of the gaze and its relation to castration in a passage in *Being and Nothingness*, in which Sartre pictures himself gazing through a keyhole when a sound behind makes him realize that he is also subjected—as object—to the gaze of the other, a realization he experiences as "shame" (Sartre, *Being* 235–37). Recontextualizing Sartre's situation through the relation of the gaze to castration anxiety, Lacan translates Sartre's "shame" into "annihilation" (*Four Fundamental* 82–85). Although the tension between the gaze and the subject in both Lacan and Sartre is described as an abstraction of the phenomenological dilemma of any human subject, both descriptions are inflected by an unexamined gender dichotomy. By identifying the individual's recognition of the unmasterability of the gaze with the constitutional catastrophe of castration anxiety, Lacan reinforces the gendered dichotomy traditionally associated with the Cartesian specular economy he otherwise refutes. The decentering of the subject through the inevitable (and structurally necessary) reversibility of the gaze is by definition equally applicable to both sexes. Nevertheless, Lacan describes the trauma and resolution through metaphors based on the peculiarities of the male sexual anatomy (castration anxiety and fetishism).

Reading more broadly in Lacan's text, it becomes evident that while the apprehension of the gaze in which the subject becomes object is unambiguously threatening for men, it is part of an implicit contractual subjectivity for women. Shortly before his discussion of Sartre, Lacan imagines a "Platonic perspective" of an "all-seeing being," which, in "the phenomenal experience of contemplation . . . is to be found in the satisfaction of a woman who knows that she is being looked at, on condition that one does not show her that one knows that she knows" (ibid. 75). This aside betrays the sexual politics in his theory of the gaze, while the extended analogy therein makes explicit the clandestine exchanges of looks and occulted vectors of specularization that mark the "accomplishment" of the Freudian notion of proper "feminine" narcissism, and which establish female "stardom" as the social institution for the fetishization of the female body in classic cinema. One of the pleasures of film viewing for the male spectator replays the disavowal of castration that the female body first signified for the male child. Dominant cinema provides a means of defense from that anxiety by allowing the spectator to transform the (otherwise threatening) body of the woman on screen into the "phallus"—a process which Laura Mulvey terms "fetishistic scopophilia" ("Visual Pleasure" 18–20).

In sum, Lacan's demystification of the Cartesian subject as the viewer of a perspectivist painting depends upon (1) identifying the reversibility of the gaze with the castration complex; (2) categorizing the male subject's (in the figure of the voyeuristic Sartre) fear of being caught looking as evidence of the "annihilation" that being the object of the gaze constitutes; (3) discovering a specifically "feminine" satisfaction in being the object of the gaze while pretending not to know it. Synthesizing these statements, and considering them in the light of the male film viewer's castration crisis and its cinematic resolution, we find that Lacan's dismissal of the specular *cogito* actually authorizes "fetishistic scopophilia" for the male spectator whose apprehension of the gaze as castration anxiety requires a compensatory fetishistic spectacle to return him to the very illusion of a punctual (whole) self in the coincidence of subjective integrity and visual mastery that Lacan's analysis had been intended to dispel.

This is only one illustration of the cultural entrenchment of the sexual within the visual that makes the question of gay male intervention in sexual representation such a difficult one. This synopsis of a specular economy and its fetishistic and fetishized mastery also makes it clear how important it is to theorize the differences in the gay male subject, and to actualize those differences in practice.

Pornography as Apparatus

Not all representational strategies deployed by deviant subjects are as consistently self-conscious and explicitly defined as Delany's paraliterary dialogics or as overtly political and unambiguous in their agenda as Jarman's revisionary appropriation of Caravaggio. The uses of visual pornography, for example, present special problems in the analyses of gay male representational politics. The cultural and psychological significance of gay male pornography for its intended audience cannot be understood within normative heterosexual moralism. On the other hand, the history of oppression, exploitation, and objectification of women and minorities in pornographic visual texts makes a facile categorization of pornography as a "strategy" both insensitive and inaccurate.

Sexually explicit representations derive from radically divergent political, psychic, and social motivations, producing ultimately unpredictable significations and effects, and eliciting diametrically opposed responses. Pornography encompasses many institutional structures, economics, modes of address, and audiences, and it cannot be satisfactorily summarized in any unitary fashion; "pornographic" texts, therefore, do not denote a single readily definable strategy available for unambivalent deployment or unequivocal reception.

Because of these difficulties in defining "pornography" in terms of either a coherent intentionality or an unambiguous political positioning, I wish, preliminary to my discussions in this chapter, to offer a working conception of "pornography" in gay male cultural practices, as an apparatus. I develop the definition of "apparatus" through selective appropriation of the meanings given the term in several disciplines, in order to discuss *strategic uses* of pornography in gay male representational practices without collapsing under the rubric of "strategy" the irreducible contradictions making up pornographic traditions and institutions.

I begin with Foucault's conception of "apparatus," by which he meant a strategic formation of heterogeneous elements that arises "at a given historical moment" in response "to an urgent need" (*Power/Knowledge* 194–95). His apparatus is not entirely conscious, voluntaristic, or individually instigated. Neither its inception nor its effects can be uniformly classified as either hegemonic or subversive,[7] which suggests its relevance for a typology of practices of resistance, although for Foucault the "apparatus" almost invariably refers to efforts of the dominant institutions to neutralize power shifts and maintain a repressive status quo. While I base my understanding of "apparatus" as social formation on Foucault's usage, I emphasize its relevance to the sub- and countercultural practices of the marginal gay male and homosexual populations as shifting responses to discursive exclusion, rather than those "apparati" that re-produce normative heterosexuality and contribute to the naturalization of its enforcement.

The gay pornographic photograph meets an "urgent need" in preserving secret sexual realities of oppressed minorities, and in foregrounding the vacillating dynamics of power and resistance. The isolation reflected in J. A. Symonds's posthumously published *Memoirs*, the fate of Oscar Wilde, and the state-imposed discursive nonexistence of homosexuality attests to the necessity of materials that would express and confirm the sexualities of these men. The underground pornographic fiction which began circulating during Wilde's life and burgeoned in the 1920s in Paris served such purposes.[8] Sexually explicit photographs became part of the homosexual black-market educational lifeline networks by the turn of the century. In these photographs can be read the photographers' "strategies of cultural resistance and survival, and their sometimes inadvertent documentation of our personal and collective histories" (Waugh, "Hard to Imagine" 65).[9] Gay pornographic texts were among the first nonapologetic expressions of homosexual desire. In its role as a medium for self-understanding within a repressive social regime, pornography lends visibility an urgency in both the political and the scopophilic senses of the word. Thomas Yingling argues that, "for gay male culture, porn has historically served as a means to self-ratification through self-gratification . . . and the relation of these experiences to patriarchal privilege and pleasure is not univocal" (6).[10]

To my Foucauldian notion of "apparatus" I add the already multiple valences of the term in film theory as used in "cinematic apparatus" to denominate the technological complex, the economic institutions, and the sociological practices that make the film and its spectator possible.[11] Finally, I want to include within this conceptual amalgam the dynamic or at times dialectical intersections of technology, ideology, and consciousness inscribed in the "apparatus" as understood by Bachelard and Althusser. Visual technologies do not merely enable more "faithful" representations of already extant objects and subjects, but are integral to the production of those objects and subjects, as well as their relations.[12] The new media contributed to redefining self-knowledge as a technological investment in expression and self-understanding.[13] These media therefore also engender radical transformations both of the communities within which these materials circulated and in the subject addressed and engaged by these new representational possibilities.[14]

By "apparatus," therefore, I mean a panoply of local, historically responsive subcultural practices and institutions that often produce tangible expressions of counterdiscursively realized social identities. The long-term or broader-ranging effects of the apparatus, however, are highly unpredictable and often yield divisive or ambivalent results. Operations of the apparatus are sensitive to technological innovation as well as to the transformations in social relations, modes of representation, and the subject constructions these innovations stimulate.

Gay pornography represents a long tradition of visual texts and visual environments produced by and for gay men—which means it provides prototypes and paradigms for specifically gay male spectatorship, specularity, and visibility. Pornography also most intensively foregrounds the internal contradictions of heteropatriarchal masculinity, and both the ways in which gay male subjectivity and sexuality have been implicated in it and how they can be disengaged from it.

By introducing the term "apparatus" to replace "strategy" here, I am not begging the questions surrounding the feminist debates concerning sexual representation, nor do I mean to patronize either side of these debates. I have addressed these issues at length elsewhere.[15] In the present essay I hope my use of "apparatus" will keep open the kind of critical space that the habituated arguments in the pornography debates foreclose. The antiporn activists' equation of sexually explicit visuals with sexual acts of violence against women elicits (demands) a kind of rebuttal that also continues to oversimplify questions of representation. To offer the counterargument that a representation is not a "reality" implies an adherence to a notion of representation as a correspondence to a "represented," an object or "reality" external to the practice of representation. In my conception of the gay pornographic apparatus, I hope to avoid this *cul-de-sac*, keeping a focus on representation as a process of subject-effects in meaning. With this in mind, I will specify for gay pornographic cinema Stephen Heath's general recommendation concerning cinema that it "should be examined in its institution of relations and effects, its reply to the subject production of meanings, its representing of available terms—of grounds—of subjectivity" (Heath, "Turn" 41).

My consideration of the complex possibilities of the pornographic apparatus is framed within an understanding of the differing psychosocial formations of the gay male (or "narcissistic") subject, and the dominant heterosexual male (or "anaclitic") subject. I divide my analysis in two parts, each dealing with a different context of reception. The first part examines how pornographic film operates within the subcultural contexts of the gay male spectatorial situation within gay-specific institutions.[16] In the second part I examine how nonpornographic filmmakers have adapted the gay pornographic apparatus in comparatively more "mainstream" film to express a contestatory and specifically sexually differenced gay subjectivity. Through a comparative reading of *Law of Desire* and *Matador*, I demonstrate how Pedro Almodóvar uses the gay porn film as an emblem for the gay male subject's "specular" interruption of the heterosexual Oedipal narrative. Finally, I offer illustrations from *Law of Desire* and Derek Jarman's *Sebastiane* of how interrelations of desire and identification characterizing gay male pornographic spectatorship, when brought into "mainstream" films intended for "mixed" audiences, serve to construct the gay male viewer as a spectator epistemologically and politically distinct from the heterosexual male viewer.[17]

The Gay Subject of Pornography

The fundamental significance of the gay pornographic apparatus lies in the ways in which it allows gay men to reaffirm or actualize in specular situations the determining differences between the "narcissistic" subject and the "anaclitic" subject in their respective mythic points of origin: the response to the Oedipal crisis. We recall that the young boy in the so-called "positive" Oedipus interprets the threat of castration "correctly," and acts accordingly. He renounces his desire for his mother, recognizing that desire to be the father's prerogative, enforced by the threat of castration as punishment. He renounces his desire for his father, recognizing in his mother's "castration" the necessary condition for desiring a man. His desire for his father is transformed into identification, while his desire for his mother is not, because of her "castrated" state. In order to perfect his identification with his father, the boy, furthermore, desires other women—castrated, like his mother, with whom he also does not identify.[18]

Gay male sexuality, however, emerges as a failure or refusal to comply with Oedipal prohibitions, and is articulated in oppositional or dialectical relations to the social reinforcements of the gender and sexual constraints that maintain those prohibitions as a cultural norm. Indeed, gay men often identify with the objects of their desire. The gay man often wishes to become like the desired object, in order to be as attractive to the object as the object is to him, or as attractive to himself or to others as the object is attractive to him. These principles are exploited and disseminated in the gay-oriented marketing practices in *GQ*, *International Male*, etc., and more explicitly represented in the flyers and videos in which porn stars demonstrate (for sale) penis extension pumps and other sexually enhancing paraphernalia. The gymnast, model, or porn star becomes both the object of desire and the ego ideal for the gay consumer.

These differences in fantasy operations have corresponding differences in spectator-screen relations. In chapter 1 I briefly discussed the division of representational planes in Hollywood films as gendered differences, these differences serving as guidelines for the distribution of the modes of the male spectator's visual pleasure. The woman as iconic display represents the inert spectacle, and the male protagonist represents the motive force in the film's narrative (Mulvey, "Visual Pleasure" 17–18). The representational modes thus embodied reinforce the mutual exclusivity of desire and identification in the Oedipalized male subject as spectator. The woman's sheer exhibitionistic visuality draws the spectator's voyeuristic pleasure; the male protagonist's activity ensures that the spectator's relation to that figure is an identification with mastery that is free of desire, and that the identification with the male screen figure forecloses identification with the female object of now joint sexual and specular mastery: "The spectator identifies . . . projects his look onto that of . . . his screen surrogate, so that the power of the male protagonist as he controls events coincides with the active power of the erotic look, both giving a satisfying sense of omnipotence" (ibid. 19–20).

The paralleled tensions between spectacle and narrative and identification and desire are most literally enacted in those moments in the film when the narrative halts to permit the female figure to perform a song or dance directly to the camera. Consider, for example, Gary Cooper watching Marlene Dietrich in *Morocco* (Josef von Sternberg, 1930), or Glenn Ford watching Rita Hayworth in *Gilda* (Charles Vidor, 1946). The typical voyeur scene in gay porn is a polar opposite. For example, in *Big Guns* (William Higgins, 1987), two off-duty Navy men at a motel (Johnny Davenport and Mike Henson) wager whether Henson can seduce the young man next door (Kevin Williams). Davenport gives Henson a special Navy surveillance camera disguised as a briefcase, which will broadcast the evidence to a video monitor in their room. When Henson succeeds, the scenes oscillate among direct shots of Williams and Henson, shots of the video image on Davenport's monitor (always perfect matches in many angles, despite the camera's stationary position), shots of Davenport masturbating while watching the video, and close-ups of the red light of the hidden camera itself.

If we provisionally impose on this scene the most reductive definition of gay male sexuality (the "Hellenic" model discussed in chapter 1), a division among forms of gay male desire identified as "active" anal penetration (performed by Mike Henson) and "passive" reception (Kevin Williams), the heterosexual oppositional binarism of desire and identification remains intact: the spectator would identify with Henson and desire Williams. But even then, Davenport ruins the symmetry. As surrogate voyeur, he is also a figure of masculine identification. But unlike Ford or Cooper, by masturbating, Davenport also displays himself as erotic spectacle. The gay male viewer may indeed desire Williams as recipient of the penetrative sex and of the scopophilic gaze, identify with Henson as "ego ideal" in actively engaging the narrative, and collaterally identify with Davenport as erotically stimulated spectator. But these positionalities are neither mandated nor mutually exclusive. Nor are they distinct components of a pregiven spectatorial verification of one's sexual identity (as the Hollywood film functions for heterosexual male viewers). These positionalities are labile and mutually conditioning to the degree that such clear demarcations are ultimately not feasible: any one of the three figures is a potential locus of identification and desire simultaneously or alternatively.

(Sexual) Subject Positions in Gay Porn Films

The mirror is in the eye of the reflected.

—Pat Cadigan, *Fools*

The gay male spectator's options for identification among camera, profilmic gazing male, and object of the gaze are multiple and mobile. The fluidity of subject positions for the gay male viewer is often inscribed in the pornographic film in eroticized foregroundings of the technologies of vision. In *Big Guns*, the recording light of the hidden videocam signals the visual relay of the sexual event in Williams's room to Davenport's monitor. But the zoom-in close-ups of the pulsing red light beneath the camouflaged lens imagistically reenvision the camera as an appetite and the lens as an aperture of the sexual body (the primary erotogenic zone in voyeurism is the eye [Freud, *Three Essays* 169; and Freud, "The Psycho-analytic View"]).[19] The parallel shots of the camera and Davenport "watching" double the spectator's voyeuristic surrogates. The profilmic camera (itself a narcissistic figure) metonymically inserts into the film the fantasy object of the viewer's "primary identification" with the "original" camera that created the film that, according to Christian Metz, makes cinematic spectatorship possible and meaningful (Metz 49–50).

The movie screen is also eroticized in porn films, in both direct and metaphoric representations.[20] The swimming pools in *Plunge* (1990, no director credited) alternately serve as metaphors for the movie screen as concept and as metonymies for the actual movie screen on which the images of the pools are projected during a screening. The final scene in *Plunge* plays with the various modalities of visibility represented by the pool as metaphor and metonym for the screen, and uses this overcoded space as a site for a psychodrama that enacts and delineates onscreen a network of shifting positions for the spectator to inhabit. At the opening of the scene two very macho men are asleep on separate rafts floating on the pool. Cal Jensen, a more fey type, comes out of the house, strips to his bathing suit, and leaps into the pool, deliberately splashing the men and waking them up. They grapple with him in the pool, remove his trunks, and drag him out, putting him face down on another air mattress. One man holds Jensen's hands, pressing his crotch to Jensen's face, while the other restrains Jensen's legs. The pair talk to each other about Jensen's punishment, the beauty of his ass, and their sexual plans for him. They handle him like a sex toy, and continually tell him in detail what they are about to do to him. After they eventually carry out their plans, the second man says, "See what you get for splashing us? I think you've learned your lesson." The pair sit on the edge of the pool, leaving Jensen face down on the air mattress. Then Jensen opens his eyes, smiles wryly into the camera, and plunges into the pool, repeating the cycle.

This episode begins as a comment on the specular saturation of gay male fantasy and its representation. Consider the "scene of the crime" and the site of its solicited punishment. The swimming pool in its shape suggests the movie screen, especially shot from directly overhead as in the opening sequence. Undisturbed, the surface of the water is reflective, holding images like a mirror or the movie screen. Indeed, the two "masculine" men are floating on the surface; their figures metaphorize their own on-screen image as an on-screen image—a doubling similar to the photographed camera in *Big Guns*.[21] When Jensen jumps in, he breaks that surface, destroying its representational capacity—but he also contravenes the barrier of the screen dividing the film image from its representational support.[22] This breach transforms the visual field from a reflective surface to a translucent depth, allowing the viewer to see the capture and denuding of the transgressor.

In the punishment ritual, the three men embody the identificatory options for the gay viewer, as they enact the mobility of the desiring positions in gay male sexual encounters. The viewer can identify with the two aggressive men as a "split subject" of a desire to be actively realized on Jensen as object, or he could identify with the covert libidinal relation between the two aggressors expressed as voyeurism and exhibitionism in each man's sexual activity with Jensen in the presence of the other (they do not directly respond to each other sexually). The viewer could also identify with Jensen as desired and "abused" object. These points of identification are not necessarily easily distinguished, and they can rapidly change or merge in the course of the scene. The libidinal dynamics here also make it clear why gay male sexuality is often popularly associated with sadomasochism, even when the sexual practices in question do not fall into that category. The reversibility of the gaze, the confluence of desire and identification, and the variability of the cathexes in power and *powerlessness*, all contribute to a fluidity of sexual subject positions that heterosexuality can only roughly approximate in S/M fantasies.[23]

In a subtle expansion of Freud's initial suggestion that sexual drives lean on (anaclisis) instincts necessary for life, Jean Laplanche develops a theory of the evolution of sexuality from nonsexual instincts. Drawing on Freud's "Instincts and Their Vicissitudes," Laplanche extrapolates a model for such vicissitudes, giving three examples: sadism, masochism, and scopophilia. Laplanche finds a common origin for sadism and masochism in an originally object-directed aggression that becomes sexualized only after first being directed onto the self. To summarize his observations: (1) Sadism: The pain inflicted on others in the original heteroaggression is at first turned inward, and that experience of pain becomes a source of excitation. When it is again directed outward, it is now sexualized as sadism. The sadist also enjoys the pain of the masochist through identification with the sufferer and the excitation brought about by the pain (Laplanche, *Life and Death* 91–92). (2) Masochism: The pain inflicted on others is internalized and directed at the ego in the reflexive phase of the vicissitude. It emerges as masochism, when the person seeks another to administer the pain. The person sought would then be "the object of the drive but the subject of the action" (92–93). These transformations have a three-phase structure: (A) heteroaggression; (B) reflexive phase; (C) reemergence as a sexual drive: the "active" form as sadism, the "passive" form as masochism.[24]

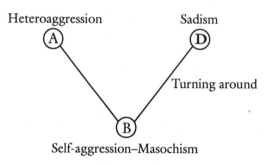

Heteroaggression   Sadism

(A)   (D)

Turning around

(B)

Self-aggression–Masochism

DIAGRAM 1

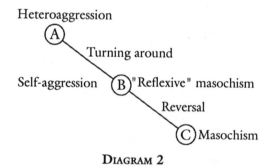

Heteroaggression

(A)

Turning around

Self-aggression   (B) "Reflexive" masochism

Reversal

(C) Masochism

DIAGRAM 2

The two "aggressive" men in *Plunge* generally represent the (structural) shift from heteroaggression to sadism. Even their verbal anticipations of the "pain" they will inflict on Jensen become "a source of excitation" (potentially for everyone—and as accessible through identification with the "victim" as through identification with the "perpetrator"). Jensen's incitement of and acceptance of the punishment represents the transformation of heteroaggression into reflexivity, and its subsequent reemergence as masochism: he sought out the agents of the aggression against him, making the men "the object of the drive but the subject of the action." The "coming together" of the two modes of sexualized transformations of heteroaggressive instincts into sadistic and masochistic drives in this scenario undermines the absolute difference of subject and object, a division the violated movie screen (represented by the pool) was meant to uphold.

Scopophilia differs from the first two transformations in its etiology, originating from the "reflexive phase" (without a prior heteroaggressive stage). The reflexive phase is *already* sexual, a primary "autoerotic" stage (*Life and Death* 93). Laplanche reproduces Freud's diagram to illustrate this:

a) Oneself looking at a sexual organ = A sexual organ being looked at by oneself

b) Oneself looking at an extraneous = An object which is oneself or part of
   object (active scopophilia)   oneself being looked at by an
                                          extraneous person (exhibitionism)

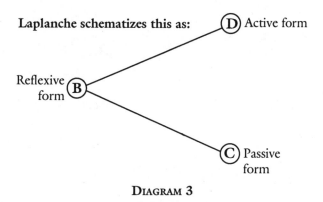

Laplanche schematizes this as: (D) Active form

Reflexive (B)
form

(C) Passive
    form

DIAGRAM 3

In this model, the active form of the drive is expressed as a need to look at an external object; the passive form of the drive is the solicitation of an external person to look at oneself (ibid. 93). Scopophilia replaces the object, exhibitionism replaces the subject of the reflexive phase. Laplanche concludes that "the transition from A to B [heteroaggression to reflexive stage] is located in the *genesis* of sexuality, whereas the subsequent transformations, starting from B, represent the *vicissitudes* of sexuality" (94).

It is important for our purposes, too, to remember that Laplanche develops this exposition from an explanation of the original *anaclisis* of the sexual drives upon biological instincts, and that aggression and the instinct for mastery typify the child's primally hostile attitude to the external world as inherently threatening, which means that the heteroaggression discussed here is part of the self-preservative instincts that become sexual (*anaclitically*) only after an intermediate *reflexive* phase. I underscore "anaclitically" and "reflexive" to emphasize the differences in psychosexual histories these transitions represent for the anaclitic heterosexual male subject and the narcissistic gay male subject, respectively. I contend that the sexuality of each of these subject types is characterized by an emblematic predominance of one of these stages in its genesis and vicissitudes. In other words, it seems that anaclitic sexual subjectivity and its modes of representation are inflected by the heterosexual male's *retention*, within his sexuality, of the self-preservative hostility in the anaclitic processes of his sexuality's initial transformations: his sexual drives [D] preserve some of the original heteroaggression [A]. Conversely, narcissistic sexual subjectivity and its modes of representation are inflected by the gay male's *extension* of the reflexive phases of those initial transformations, into the sexual drives emerging therefrom: his sexuality thereby remains organically related to his processes of identity formation.

Laplanche's diagram I above offers a schematic understanding of the desexualized aggression of the anaclitic subject, that we have already observed in various forms, from the procreatively efficient sadist Freud mentions in *Three Essays* and Thomas Disch parodies in "Planet of the Rapes,"[25] and in the sublimated investigations Freud envisioned in *Leonardo* that were also responsible for the narratives motivated by the reality principle toward an objective truth of the scientist as epistemological conqueror. The minimalized sexuality of anaclitic heterosexuality is an effect of its goal-dominated puritanism and its paranoiac defensive aggression. Recall, for example, the apotropaic erections of modern-day Perseuses; the armored homicidal body of Theweleit's "Soldier Male"; Joanna Russ's alien "He-Man" monster; or Disch's cattle-prodded ejaculatory athlete Ensign 17-J.[26] These reflections should also further contextualize my discussion of Delany's "Game of Time and Pain" in the previous chapter, in which I characterize the Scholes-Brooks heterosexed narratology as a "badly desublimated" heteroaggressive teleological pragmatism also manifested in "reproductive sadism" and Baconian philosophies of science.

The vicissitudes of the drives as schematized in Laplanche's text and fantasized in *Plunge*, furthermore, should vindicate my emphases in chapter 3 on the political value of Delany's sexualizations of oppressive scenarios and sign-systems. A gay porn film such as *Plunge* addresses the scopophilic drive of the intended gay male spectator. Scopophilia understood as the drive which begins in the reflexive, already sexual phase, resonates profoundly with the join of sexual object-choice and identificatory ego-formation processes in the narcissism we have specified for the gay male subject.[27] The viewer is solicited to identify with any of the three positions on the screen, and in fact for many viewers the real erotic charge from the final scene will stem from the multiple or vacillating identifications it elicits and confirms. The subsumption of all the roles in the pool scenario to the scopophilic drive of the intended spectator metapsychologically neutralizes their heteroaggressive, self-preservative origins, as scopophilia begins in the reflexive stage.[28]

Disharmonious Identifications

The gay male spectator accesses a network of "inappropriate" or transgressive identifications, structured by the anti-Oedipal mutuality of identification and desire. In his multiple or shifting identifications, the gay male spectator transgresses the gendered dichotomies and disrupts the Cartesian unity of self that are part of the subject effect intended in the dominant cultural representational institutions to which the anaclitic subject submits. Furthermore, the gay viewer not only identifies with figures on the screen who are betraying the sex/gender system of dominant heterosexuality, but he also identifies with the *acts* of betrayal themselves, the negating affirmations those on-screen figures commit, or the acts of negating affirmation that constitute the screen image as a representation of an *identifiable* gay male subject. The figures on screen owe their visibility to their voluntary submission to the gaze of the other and the desire of the other. In fact, the mere appearance on screen in the porn film is already an act of negating affirmation, in deliberately surrendering one's body to the desiring gaze of the other, that gaze that Lacan feared would annihilate Sartre, the reversibility of the gaze which Lacan compares to a castration trauma. The spectator's narcissistic identifications with deliberate dispersions of the male-defined whole self are engagements with the (pornographic) film that disrupt rather than harmonize with the dominant ideology.

We have already seen how the anaclitic subject perceives "castration" and what some of his defenses are (as brought forth by Mulvey). These defenses (projection of lack onto the female figure, and fetishistic scopophilia) and the "proper" identifications with the "hero" are part of the anaclitic subject's cooperation with his own ideological stabilization (his readerly response to the text of pleasure). In chapter 1 I mentioned briefly Althusser's theory of ideology and its relation to the subject. It is ideology that constitutes the subject, through the enjoining of specifically patterned misrecognitions of the "self" which confirm that individual as the subject of and to that order within which ideology functions (Althusser, "Ideology 170–71). The operation by which this is accomplished Althusser calls "interpellation," which "can be imagined" as the "everyday police (or other) hailing: 'Hey, you there!' " When the "hailed" individual turns around, he/she becomes a subject, because by turning around, the individual "has recognized that the hail was 'really' addressed to him [sic], and that 'it was really him [sic] who was hailed' " (174).

The conjunction of subjectivity and representation is very different for the anaclitic and narcissistic subjects in their respective spectatorial situations. To draw these differences out, I turn first to two Lacanian conceptions of certain fundamental contradictions within "representation," paying particular attention to how the differences in spectatorial subject processes between the dominant heterosexual male subject and the gay male subject ramify the mechanisms of interpellation peculiar to cinema.

Strictly speaking, Lacan characterizes as castration experiences the two major modes by which a subject enters intelligible intersubjective representation: visibility and language acquisition. At the beginning of this chapter we examined Lacan's demystification of the Cartesian subject as produced by geometral realistic painting. Lacan describes as "castration" the subject's discovery that "in the scopic field, the look is outside, I am looked at . . . I am a picture. It is this function which lies at the heart of the subject's institution in the visible. What fundamentally determines me in the visible is the look which is outside. It is through the look that I enter into the light, and it is from the look that I receive its effect. From which it emerges that the look is the instrument through which the light is embodied, and through which . . . I am *photo-graphed*" (*Four Fundamental* 106).

The other castration experience foundational to the subject is *aphanisis*, the fading of the subject in signification. *Aphanisis* results from two conditions of an individual's accession to subjecthood: the fact that one constitutes oneself as subject in relation to the other; and the necessity of using the language of the other in order to make one's needs and demands understood by the other (*Écrits* 269–70; *Four Fundamental* 206–208, 216–20). The use of language makes one appear as subject within the field of the other, but that act of signification also reduces the autonomous "being" of the subject to the signifier that inaugurates the subject as such. Lacanian *aphanisis* is a synthesis of Hegelian subjective dialectics with Emile Benveniste's linguistic account of subjectivity in discourse. In any subjective utterance, Benveniste distinguishes two subjects: the speaking subject, or the subject of enunciation, and the subject of speech, or the subject of the utterance. For example, if I say "Mary bought a car today," I am the speaking subject (subject of enunciation), and "Mary" is the subject of the utterance. If I say "I forgot what I was going to do," the "I" within the sentence is the subject of utterance, and the "I" who uttered the sentence is the subject of enunciation (Benveniste 218–20). In a film, the camera and the entire cinematic apparatus responsible for the film's production are the "subject of enunciation" and the characters on screen are the subjects of the utterance.

In order to assert itself as a subject, the subject of enunciation (the "real" speaking subject) must use the language of the other. By signifying itself with the "I" of the other's language, the incommensurability of the subject of enunciation and its "sign" causes a fading of the "real" subject in the very act of its discursive representation (Lacan, *Four Fundamental* 206–13). The use of "I" to designate the subject, however, both divides the being of the subject from its meaning, and also closes—"sutures"—the divide that the attempt at self-representation in the language of the other opened. "Suture" is the process by which the subject is joined into the signifying chain, allowing the signifier to stand in for the subject's absence in discourse (J.-A. Miller 26–28). The "I" as subject of the utterance substitutes for the subject of enunciation and masks its absence (Heath, *Questions* 85–86).

The concept of "suture" was adopted by film theorists to describe the technical operations specific to the cinematic apparatus that solicit the spectator as the subject of the film. The privileged example of cinematic suturing technique is the shot/reverse shot sequence In such a sequence, the first shot is matched by the second shot from the opposite 180 degree arc, of a person looking in the direction of the first shot, becoming the subject of the first perception. Thus a character in the film, a subject of the utterance, stands in for and masks the subject of enunciation (the camera), which parallels the suturing function of the "I" in discourse. This is complicated by the third term here—the spectator, whom Kaja Silverman designates the "spoken subject" (*Subject* 202–204).

That suturing which would secure the viewer as the "spoken subject" begins with the technology of realist perspective (situating the subject at a coherent spatial location within the 180 degree shot–reverse shot rule) and culminates in an interpellation within the social order. Cinematic suture is an apparatus whose coerced and coercive identifications transform the individual into the ideologically functional subject of Althusserian social theory (see Althusser, "Ideology" 158–62).

What happens when these discursive fluctuations are played out across narrative and specular registers in a specifically different psychosexual dynamic, namely the gay male homosocial spectatorial context of a porn film in a porn theater? First of all, because gay men identify with the dissolution of their "selves," it is hardly surprising that the corollaries to suture are rather anarchically polysemic. One contrasting example should suffice.

Silverman cites the opening sequence of *It's a Wonderful Life* as "an excellent example of textual hailing, which results in the smooth interpellation of the viewer."

> The opening shot of that film discloses a town-limit sign which reads: "You are now entering Bedford Falls." . . . The appeal is direct: the pronoun "you" only means something to the degree that the viewer identifies with it, recognizes him or herself in the subject of [the utterance]. The rest of the sentence organizes itself around the viewer, locating him or her in the narrative space soon to be occupied by George Bailey, who will function thereafter as the chief signifier of his or her subjectivity. By identifying with the statement

"You are now in Bedford Falls," the viewer permits his or her subjectivity to be established by the figure of George Bailey and circumscribed by the limits of small-town America. (*Subject* 49–50)

An advertising poster (and subsequently the video box) of a gay porn film from 1989 featured a medium shot of a young man without a shirt behind bars, looking seductively into the camera. Over his head the caption reads: "You're in for . . . LEWD CONDUCT!" The meaning of the sentence depends upon the referent of "you" and the grammar of "for" (purpose or consequence): (1) "You" is the character, in jail for "lewd conduct," i.e., the charge on which he was arrested; (2) "You" is the actor, in jail (as the character) in order to engage in lewd conduct for the benefit of the film viewer; (3) "You" is the viewer, and "in for" is invitational anticipation, as in the phrase "You're in for a treat," meaning "You will see lots of lewd conduct" in this film.

Potential identifications and the peculiar transgressions of audience-screen relations in the gay porno theater generate yet more meanings. The majority of men in porno theaters engage in solo or mutual masturbation and (at least until the AIDS crisis) other sexual acts as well. The "lewd conduct," therefore, occurs on both sides of the screen. Furthermore, "lewd conduct" is the most frequent charge brought against men in gay porno theaters, whether or not they were engaging in any sexual activity. This identification is then both libidinal and political. But note how the linguistic interpellation of the Capra film rigidified the subject through the insistent univocity of its meaning. "You're in for lewd conduct" is a grammatical sentence that could also be a sentence imposed by the Law on either the on-screen or viewing subject for the transgressions through which each achieved his subjectivity.

Ecstatic Enunciation: Aphanisis

The self seems deep because it can use two vanishing points.

—Robert Glück, "Denny Smith"

The recursive reciprocities involved in intersubjective narcissism at least double the work involved in analyzing the cinematic representation and production of the gay male subject, since the subject has to be accounted for in its expressions as both spectator *and spectacle.* Identifications can also form around the transgressions of masculinity in the on-screen male's deliberate self-objectification, his deliberate surrender to the annihilation of the gaze. Embracing the specular mode of annihilation to assert one's "identity" as object of the other's gaze suggests a subject type inconceivable within anaclitic subject politics: the narcissistic exhibitionist, expressed as a subject spectacle or *intentional* spectacle.

I use "intentional" in the ordinary sense of "deliberate," but the category "intentional spectacle" is also an inversion of the phenomenological concept of the "intentional consciousness," that consciousness that posits or *intends* its objects or contents. The narcissistic exhibitionist effectively inverts intentionality in constituting himself as subject by positing his body as image-object in the consciousness of the other. Through the deliberate presentation of his body to the desiring gaze of the other, the narcissistic gay exhibitionist constitutes himself to himself as a desirable object for the other. Through the desire of the other, the narcissistic exhibitionist re-en-visions himself as an anachronistic ideal ego (a postsymbolic reversion to the mirror stage) while temporalizing that process, bifurcating the interchange as an act of self-exposure and the re-cognition of himself as figure of the other's desire (thus projecting himself as an ego ideal as well, recuperated as the image accomplished within the other's desiring gaze). This process radically recontextualizes Lacan's contention that "in exhibitionism what is intended by the subject is realized in the other" (*Four Fundamental* 183).

The gay male exhibitionist (the subject spectacle or intentional spectacle) complicates the dialectic between self and other through his sexual difference as "bearer of the look" in both senses of the verb: his right as male to "bear" or wield the desiring look, and his transgressive desire as deviant to "bear" or sustain the desiring look of the other.[29] In his display to the gaze of the other, the intentional spectacle succeeds in obtaining a self-image at the cost of his male-gendered ontology. He is confirmed as desired object in the gaze that annihilates his being-as-subject. The seemingly paradoxical dynamics of gay narcissistic exhibitionism in effect merely specifies a more generally prevalent contradiction structuring any subject's attempt at self-constituting representation. Benveniste's characterization of the basic motivation of discourse could be a description of our exhibitionist: "The subject addresses the other in order to constitute himself in his own eyes" (Benveniste 67).

The gay pornographic apparatus transforms the two Lacanian castrations of specular self-objectification and aphanitic self-exposition into representations of negating affirmations of the gay male subject. These affirmations "come together" in the on-screen pornographic subject, particularly the subject of the erotic confession genre. In these films, the would-be subject addresses the other through both linguistic and visual appeal (note the bivalence of this noun), displaying his body to the viewer and his secrets to a listener, the "other" represented by the camera or an off-screen interlocutor, respectively. The "erotic confessions" genre often represents the other-dependence of the subject in both the specular and narrative registers: the visual exhibitionism of the subject is integrated with the diegetic self-exposure of telling his life. Jean-Daniel Cadinot's *All of Me* is an excellent example of these double exposures.

All of Me is a portrait of the porn actor/model Pierre Buisson. The sound-track consists of actual taped phone conversations between Cadinot and Buisson prior to and (at least one) shortly after their first photo session. In these con-

versations Buisson recounts three key sexual experiences that essentially led him
to consider working in porn. The visual track features Buisson posing on an
overstuffed leather sofa; Cadinot is represented by a man whose face is obscured
by a still camera, incessantly taking snapshots (the clicks of the shutter punc-
tuate the interview). This scene is interwoven with reenactments of the three
stories Buisson tells on the soundtrack. At the conclusion of the third story's
depiction, the scene returns to the couch and Cadinot asks Buisson to masturbate to orgasm. Buisson complies, after which Cadinot asks Buisson if he would
like to make a film of his experiences, to which Buisson enthusiastically agrees.
The narrative concludes with the narrator's detumescence, and the film concludes with the moment of its own inception.

The site of Buisson's apparent self-production as star is a leather couch (like
those typically associated with the psychoanalytic session) on which he "exposes
himself" (his key sexual secrets) and "exposes himself" (fondling and manipulating his genitals and buttocks for multiple and maximum visibility to the camera). The couch's numerous deep upholstery holes look like anuses themselves,
and their repetition suggest the repetition of the sex scenes, as well as the repeated exposures for the camera, and disclosures for the microphone.[30] Furthermore, the buttons within these holes are literally the *point de caption*, Lacan's
domestic metaphor for that which stops the sliding of the signifier (*Écrits* 154).
The restaged interview between Cadinot and Buisson (like a "construction in
analysis") mimics an analytic session, and the film fixes the images to the stories
recounted (the specular to the narrative), just as the upholstery buttons hold
the couch's shape in patterns that visually echo the erotogenic zone most intensively under spectral contemplation.[31]

In the confluence of oral autobiography and nude posing, *All of Me* initially
articulates a sexually differenced subject as an intentional spectacle, and exposes
itself as a deviant representational practice in showcasing a spectacle that does
not *impede* the narrative, but—quite the contrary—*generates* it.[32] Although
Pierre is the subject of the utterance of the film, within its presentation, the
"Pierre" on the couch telling his life story is an embedded subject of enunciation, and the "Pierres" who appear in the enactments of the stories he tells are
(doubly embedded) subjects of utterance.

The perverse convergence of spectacle and narrative in the figure of Pierre,
however, does not consolidate an "identity" but in fact structures the radical
destabilizations of any identity provisionally presented. Because the visualizations of these stories entail varied and richly detailed settings and direct interpersonal encounters, the "Pierres" that are the subjects of these utterances are
not subordinated to the "Pierre" on the couch, their putative "master narrator,"
whose utterance they inhabit. These stories therefore proliferate "Pierres" that
at least rival—if not surpass—the ontological vitality of the supposed subject
of enunciation. *All of Me* never attempts to reintegrate the subject's fragmen-

tations, nor does it conceive of a subject as a psychological reality prior to its representations.

The synthesis of narrative and spectacle constituting "Pierre" is also undermined by the conspicuously unrelated sound and image tracks. While Buisson is posing for the still shots, his silences and speaking never correspond to his voice narrating his "story."[33] The only synchronously recorded sound-image cluster in the film is the clicking of "Cadinot's" still camera. This cluster is topographically multivalent. Within the film's fantasy, each click signifies the "captation" of Buisson's image. The moments in which the "subject" is transformed into pure image are the only points in which the divergent representational planes of the scene are bound in a tentative mimetic synchronicity: the very sound that signals the reduction of a "real" subject to an image is also the sole instance of the imaging processes presenting themselves as "real." This deliberate cognitive dissonance inscribes within the film (both metonymically and metaphorically) the priority of representation over the subject that representation makes possible. This principle, thematically and metadiscursively expressed by the camera's *synched* sound, is enacted in the *unsynched* speaking voice of "Pierre," a voice whose very discontinuity enables a vertiginous union of subject of enunciation and subjects of utterance.

When the opening situation of the film marks Pierre on the couch as the embedded subject of enunciation, the aphanisis he experiences in signifying himself in the language of the other is cinematically figured in the separation of the speaking (subject) voice from the on-screen body from which it should emanate, and the relativization of his "being" in the proliferation of "Pierres" as subjects of his specularized narratives. The alienated voice describes a middle distance between the first "Pierre" and each narrated "Pierre." The unfixed voice becomes a common soundtrack for both sequences of "Pierres." This diffractory collocation of three disparate signifying chains reconciles the narrative with the specular, and the embedded subject of enunciation with the subjects of utterance, but only technically, that is to say, only on the level of filmic discourse, not on the level of mimetic realism (Pierre's voice and body are not rejoined, for example). The heterogeneous coherence of the film therefore is accomplished without suturing the divisions between the subject of enunciation and the subject of the utterance.

The formation of the subject ("Pierre") in the signifying operations occurs on the side of the cinematic apparatus (the camera, the editing, the interviewer), while the film as a whole also records the (on-screen) subject's aphanisis. While such fading of the subject in the act of signifying itself, according to Lacan, happens whenever a subject speaks, Cadinot's film foregrounds the paradox with a perverse literality—both in the dynamics of confession elicitation and in the filming of Buisson's orgasms. These orgasms are actual moments of the introceptively experienced annihilation that exceeds both the aphanisis of signification and the denegation of the subject as object of the gaze. In Cadinot's film the epiphanic instances of sexual ecstases become visible anagogically through the image of the filmed body that incarnates those ecstases and is in turn en-visioned in the film as a corporealized instance of the subject that necessarily stands outside itself and disarticulates its posited identity through its own self-presentations—whether linguistic or phenomenological, whether in its voluntary telling itself in the language of its interlocutor (aphanisis) or in its exhibitionist submission to the annihilating gaze.[34]

However rudimentary, the majority of porn films are fictional narratives. Such films produce the subject-as-aphanisis by exploiting dynamic contradictions significantly different from those typical of the "erotic confession." Before discussing these differences I want to introduce and define terms basic to a consistent analysis of levels of narrative discourse and cinematic presentation, divisions corresponding to my larger categories of "narrative" and "specular." The narratological terms are derived from *diegesis*, meaning "telling." "Intradiegetic" is anything which occurs within the main narrative. "Extradiegetic" designates the narrative level immediately above the main narrative level, the level from which the main narrative is generated. By "metadiegetic," I mean any element or discursive maneuver which focuses attention on the production of the narrative itself.[35]

The nonanalogous differences in the modes of representation in verbal and filmic narratives require some classifications peculiar to film and photography. The "profilmic" is anything that appears on screen, and "extrafilmic" is anything (or any situation, circumstance, etc.) that does not appear on screen. In the film *Dick Tracy*, the image of the central male is intradiegetically "Dick Tracy" and extradiegetically Warren Beatty, but the profilmic image is not bound exclusively to either identity. At least theoretically, in a documentary, the people appear as themselves, in real situations—which means a maximal identification of the intradiegetic and extradiegetic and the profilmic and the extrafilmic. In Beatty's cameos in *Truth or Dare*, the same profilmic "figure" that appeared in *Dick Tracy* now signifies Beatty's extradiegetic, extrafilmic identity.

In the most naive viewing of a conventional narrative film, the "profilmic" and the "intradiegetic" are effectively identical: what appears on screen is what exists in the story. But if an actor steps out of character to address the camera directly as him- or herself, the actor as imaged presence is still profilmic, but his/her identity is "extradiegetic," his/her relation to the film metadiegetic.[36] When a famous actor appears as him/herself in a fictional film, the equation of extradiegetic and intradiegetic identities is qualified by the differences between the extrafilmic world and the intradiegetic world and events: even when the profilmic figure represents the extrafilmic identity (the "real" person), what that "real" person does in the fictional narrative of the film (intradiegetically and profilmically) is not real.

Pornographic film effects uniquely different relations among the diegetic and visual levels of representation, and between the "real" and the fictional. In a porn film, for example, whether or not the actor appears as himself, the sex acts he performs are real.[37] No matter how complex the plot or character involvement in which a sexual event is embedded, the extradiegetic actor experiences the same real orgasm as the intradiegetic character, and that coincidence (or internal division?) is realized in the profilmic image of the ejaculation. The ejaculation ecstatically marks the incommensurability of the intradiegetic fiction of the narrative and the extradiegetic (specular) "reality" of the sex acts. Sex in the porn film is en-visioned not as "significance" but as evidence. The sexual acts are not reducible to plot elements; the significance of sex is not exhausted by the "meaning" it supposedly holds for the characters who "had" it. The imagistic exorbitance of on-screen sex metaphorizes its transgressive facticity through which it exceeds the intradiegetic (narrative) stabilizations of its presentation to become an extradiegetic (specular) address to the viewer.

There is an enacted aphanisis in *The Boys of Venice* (William Higgins, 1980) that directly engages the viewer's relation to the screen in its metatextual reflections on the heterogeneous registers of representation constituting a fictional narrative film. *The Boys of Venice* is a loosely connected series of vignettes involving Eric Ryan and his friends in Venice Beach. Scott Taylor plays a photographer named "Scott Taylor," who appears in several of the episodes. In one scene, however, the narrative pauses and Ryan's voiceover announces, "Here is my friend Scott Taylor at work in his photography studio." Taylor's full name had been mentioned twice before this scene, which indicates a significance in the coincidence of character's and actor's name. In this discussion of this scene, I will distinguish three "phenotypes" of the profilmic figure: Scott Taylor (without quotation marks) will designate the extradiegetic actor, "Scott Taylor" the intradiegetic character, and [Scott Taylor] any identity either underlying both of the first two, or in some way constituted by the interrelations between them.

In his studio "Taylor" sets up an arsenal of still cameras and lighting, and masturbates to a disco beat within the crossfire of motorized cameras and automatic strobe flashes. "Taylor's" studio in this scene is a site for private sexual play and for the production of a visual record of that play as a means of self-representation as a sexual object. The interfusion of sexuality and its representations are articulated in the tensions among the scene's psychosomatic, technological, and diegetic constituents. The shots of [Taylor's] penis as he masturbates are intercut with close-ups of the cameras as they fire and rewind, and with medium-to-close shots of the light umbrellas as the flashes ricochet off them. As [Taylor] approaches orgasm, these syncopated cuts become tighter and more frenetic, the cameras "shoot" more rapidly, and the flashes increase in frequency and in effect on the image. The diegetic constituents of the scene are those elements that situate the sequence within the larger narrative discourse and circumscribe [Scott Taylor] as a nonidentical subject whose intra- and extradiegetic "identities" are asymptotically inscribed across the representational topography of the film.

Within the context of the "story," the intradiegetic "Taylor" masturbates for personal satisfaction; his use of the cameras to record his arousal, to cause his arousal, or both, marks him as a narcissistic exhibitionist, but it does not necessarily imply that he posed to produce pictures of himself for public consumption. The extradiegetic Taylor, however, *is* a professional porn model and masturbates in this scene to arouse others. "Taylor" directs his performance (for his own pleasure) at the profilmic, intradiegetic still cameras; Taylor directs his performance (for the pleasure of others) at the extrafilmic, extradiegetic movie camera. Although the profilmic [Scott Taylor] comprehends both of the other two, the profilmic acts [Scott Taylor] performs have differing topographical valences depending upon which [Taylor] is the focus. "Scott Taylor's" posing for the still cameras is an intradiegetic act, an event within the fictional narrative. Scott Taylor's posing for the still cameras is a metadiegetic act, one which calls attention to the relation of the exhibitionistic narcissistic subject and the pornographic apparatus in which he "realizes himself." "Scott Taylor's" intradiegetic pose for the still cameras thus signifies Scott Taylor's metadiegetic gesture that posits a difference between the film and reality, while the pornographic genre which it represents elides that difference (Taylor is "really doing it").

The scene structurally calls attention to the difference between self and image while Taylor's performance deliberately collapses them. Taylor transforms the passive identification of self with specular image in the mirror stage into an active and transitive projection of that conflation, forcing his profilmic image into the specular apparatus. Of course, the image inscriptions within the still cameras are inaccessible to the viewer, creating a specular embedding (analogous to narrative embedding), a *mise-en-abîme* of a vanishing point.[38] The "Scott Taylor" ideal ego Taylor thereby achieves on screen represents a self-inscription in a system of imagistic relays of the present absence of the object represented. While the intradiegetic "Taylor" is being photographed, the extradiegetic Taylor is being, in Lacan's terminology, *photo-graphed*: each moment of intradiegetic inscription obliterates Taylor's profilmic image for the viewer (the subject of the [filmic] utterance). The cameras' flashes wipe out the picture, which also serves as a metaphor for the momentary obliteration of the self in orgasm (reminiscent of William S. Burroughs's catch phrase, "the flashbulbs of orgasm"). Taylor enacts the aphanisis or fading of the subject as the infinite regress of representations into their technologies. But each flash that destroys his profilmic image also connotes another reproduction of his ideal ego (the photograph), both intradiegetically (when the photographer "Taylor" develops them—an impossible future) and extradiegetically (when *The Boys of Venice* is screened—the viewer's actual present moment of viewing). This makes a remarkable allegorical illustration of the relation between the negating affirmations of gay male subjectivity and the deconstructive strategies of its representation. That orgasmic flash is the cinematic inscription of the deviant identificatory complexes (the intersubjective narcissism) through which both the intentional spectacle Taylor/"Taylor"/[Taylor] and his spectator at once affirm a gay subject and assume representational agency.

The dynamisms between and among the viewer and the screen and film and its genre unstably integrate the topographically divergent actions of the diegetically disparate subjects. Within the viewing situation the intradiegetic and extradiegetic "subjects" converge in a single profilmic image, which also subsumes "signification" and "referent" in an open-ended "psychical reality" emerging from the relation of the film viewer to the film fantasy.[39] The vacillating conjunctions of the heterogeneous subjects of the film's utterance are effected by the overdetermined profilmic image and by the hermeneutic fantasies of the spectator. The profilmic image embodies and enfigures the decussation of these ontologically irreconcilable "subjects," instantiating the co-incidence of both [Scott Taylors] as a catachresis—a represented subject that is conceivable only as a (metadiscursively contradicted) representation; but it is precisely as a representation that the screen image offers the viewer a range of psychical realities as phantasmatic possibilities for articulating subject positions within the spectatorial situation, especially because the viewer's drives themselves are, fundamentally, representations.[40] As such, the catachrestic multiple subject can be considered the "ideal" realization of the narcissistic exhibitionist as intentional subject (whether or not these sexual drives are fully operative within the fantasy scenarios of either "Taylor" or Taylor). [Scott Taylor] is a direct visualization of gay sexual drives in the reflexive moment of the scopophilic vacillations of exhibitionism and voyeurism (as Laplanche's diagram 3 above demarcates it), which stimulates the viewers' narcissistic quasipolitical confirmation of perverse sexual subject types and marginal communal identities.

Screening the Subject

Wallace Potts's film *Le Beau Mec* (1976) presents itself as a first-person narrative, a film autobiography of French hustler turned Paris stripper Karl Forest. Forest is credited as scriptwriter, but most of his monologues in the film are voiceovers edited from interviews with a soft-spoken interrogator (presumably Potts). Forest tells of growing up in rural France, his teen years as a juvenile delinquent, technical school, military life, and hustling in Marseilles after the army. His hustling led him to Paris, and eventually into his career as a sex entertainer. The presentation of autobiographical narrative in a film offers peculiar variations on the divisions between the "subject of enunciation" and the "subject of utterance," further complicated in *Le Beau Mec* by the narcissistic exhibitionism inscribed within Forest's screen persona. *Le Beau Mec* also articulates enunciative positions and diegetic levels differerently from the films considered so far. Although the on-screen Buisson played out an embedded "subject of enunication" in the contiguity of his image on the couch to his voice on the soundtrack telling his story (and the juxtaposition of this image and the images of Buisson in the visualizations of those stories), this "subject of enunciation" is clearly subordinated within the cinematic apparatus (the "true" subject of enunciation). Because Karl Forest is depicted as the "author" of the text of *Le Beau Mec*, and the creator of his public persona, his images more insistently figure a metonym for the "subject of enunciation" than either Buisson's hypotactic speaking subjects in *All of Me*, or Scott Taylor's diegetically split subject in *The Boys of Venice*.

The title sequence of the film features Forest performing in a nightclub. In this routine he wears a World War I helmet, overcoat, and whip. After stripping he rides what appears to be a giant phallus, which the stagelights eventually reveal to be a cannon. The first actual scene is set in a forest with his voiceover narrative of a childhood memory, beginning: "I was born near abandoned forts." He and his friends played soldier in these forts, often with real guns that had been left behind by the French resistance who had hidden there during the war. He continues: "You know what happens when a boy finds a gun—he wants to show it off to his buddies. We'd end up playing games." A hand-held camera pans through a forest path to a clearing where Karl and another man make love, their soldiers' uniforms strewn about the ground. Forest's narrative did not indicate that "playing soldier" included any sexual experimentation.[41] As this scene concludes, Karl states on the soundtrack that when he actually was a soldier as an adult, he "never did anything with my buddies in the army. I was a commander—of 40 men, I couldn't afford to get a reputation." This erotic idyll in the woods, therefore, restages a childhood game in its retrospective sexualization, and the processes by which personal histories become the fantasy scenarios for adult sexuality.[42] As such, the scene is an interesting illustration of the mechanisms of fantasy. But in terms of the narrative project of the film, the scene is both mimetically discoherent (adults playing children) and historically fallacious.

On the soundtrack of another sequence, Karl summarizes the major events and stages in his adolescence and young adulthood, particularly his problems with the authorities. The visual track is composed of interlocking tableaux that illustrate the incidents in Karl's narrative. When Karl describes his trouble with the law as being "screwed by the police," it is represented by an actor in a police uniform and helmet handcuffing Karl over a school desk and literally "screwing" him. The visual literalization of the dead metaphor in Karl's figure of speech recalls the tendency in dreams to translate abstract concepts into pictorial language, one of the most frequent means by which the dream work manages what Freud called the "considerations of representability" (*Interpretation of Dreams* 5: 339–40). Forest discusses his dreams in the only scene in the film in which he speaks on camera (in synchronized sound): "In my dreams I always have a rifle or a pistol or a machine gun. I spray bullets everywhere. I don't know if it's sexual." After a few parodies of pop-Freudian dream interpretation, he says, "I see a film at night and I'm in that film, I'm the actor," which incites laughter from behind the camera. It is here where the real questions the film poses begin to emerge. More than the divisions between reality and fantasy, the film plays on the relations of fantasy and subject, as it elaborates the differences between fantasy as ego construction and fantasy as a mode of address.

The profilmic image of Forest in *Le Beau Mec* at any point in the film is a variable cross-section of two different modalities of the subject and two different types of fantasy. The film as "sign" posits as its "referent" an extrafilmic Karl Forest who is an agency of the cinematic subject of enunciation; the "signification" of the filmic sign is the "Karl Forest" produced by the film. Each of these subjects is identified with a particular kind of fantasy: the extradiegetic subject-of-enunciation Karl Forest with the private fantasy of the individual, and the intradiegetic subject-of-utterance "Karl Forest" with the "publicly produced fantasy" of a film.[43] In the private, psychoanalytically defined fantasy, the subject does not appear as a monadic entity within a world or scenario distinct from that subject, but rather the subject is that which pervades the mechanisms and movements of the entire presentation. The subject "does not pursue the object or its sign; one appears oneself caught up in the sequence of images. One forms no representation of the desired object, but is oneself represented as participating in the scene although . . . one cannot be assigned any fixed place in it . . . As a result, the subject, although always present in the fantasy, may be so in a desubjectivized form, that is to say, in the very syntax of the sequence in question" (Laplanche and Pontalis, "Fantasy" 26–27). While this describes a plausible relation of the extrafilmic subject-of-enunciation Karl to the film,[44] such a relation only contingently figures in the film in which he commodifies himself as a fantasy for others. Karl as subject-of-enunciation becomes a desubjectivized thematic structuration of the film fantasy; "Karl Forest" as "subject of utterance" of the film is realized in an intense localization of subject processes as "star" (similar to the ideal ego). The subject produced in the extrafilmic Karl's relation to the film he makes, therefore, is disseminated throughout the film-as-private-fantasy; but the cinematic apparatus itself causes that dispersed subject to recoalesce as the "Karl" of the film—that is, as the narrative image in the film-as-public-fantasy. The "narrative image" is "a kind of static portrait in which [the film] comes together. . . . The consistency . . . of this image . . . is . . . the film's currency, that on which it can be bought and sold" (Heath, *Questions* 133).[45]

Le Beau Mec divides the subject phantasmatics into three registers: (1) the relation of the subject-of-enunciation "Karl Forest" to the fantasy of the film itself; (2) the relation of the subject-of-utterance "Karl Forest" to the film that articulates it; (3) the subject positions inscribed within the film for the spectator. The various scenes in the films based on memories or sexualized metaphors of memories enmesh themselves into a persona which the narrating "I" gives his name—"Karl Forest," just as Forest in his dream sees a film and becomes an actor in it. While Forest as "star" of the film may be a product of the cinematic apparatus, and Forest as the "narrative image" an aggregate of heterogeneous imagistic configurations, his "desubjectivization" cannot be preserved in the screening of the film as a record of that psychic operation pertaining to the extrafilmic Forest, because, apart from the reasons just mentioned, the implicit subject of the film's fantasy in this situation would be the viewer, not the already absent actor. In other words, the desubjectivization of Forest's (putative) private fantasy informing this project is translated into a fantasy scenario for the viewer to occupy. But instead of being dispersed across all the elements and the "syntax" of the fantasy/film, the viewer is afforded multiple and shifting subject positions therein: his subjectivity, therefore, however mobile, is never as diffuse as that of the subject of a private fantasy. Therefore, in the overlapping disjunctions between the psychoanalytic fantasy and the public fantasy, and the on-screen subject and the viewing subject, the "Karl Forest" as subject of utterance of the film will variously function as a punctual, imagistic concentration of the subject productivity of the signifying operations of the cinematic apparatus (which includes the spectatorial situation); the iconic trace of the exhibitionist subject who elicits/requires the desiring look of the other; the object of scopophilia; and a possible vehicle for identification for the gay male spectator who invests his subjectivity therein.

As much as Karl's persona and career are parts of other people's fantasies, he seems strangely reluctant to assert his own. At the beginning of the film, he claims that when masturbating he does not fantasize. During a long pan of a sex shop beginning with porn magazines and moving to sex toys, bondage paraphernalia, and S/M accoutrements, Karl discusses his sexual openness in terms of his willingness to do anything with a client, but his steadfast refusal to act on his own fantasies: "I can do anything I have no hangups. Yeah, I do fistfucking—both ways. I give and take it. . . . I've got a ton of fantasies but fantasies are like playing with fire—because a lot of times when you act them out sometimes you're disappointed. I don't think it's a good idea to act out your fantasies. I think you should keep them to yourself. You know in the beginning . . . if you act out your fantasies . . . it escalates." The extrafilmic Forest, the professional sex performer, the Forest most closely identified with the subject of enunciation, would not include his own fantasies in the film, because the project of the film for that "Karl Forest" is the definitive totalization of his "self" as a fantasy ideal for others. The subject as absolutely desired object cannot appear as a desiring subject. Forest as intentional spectacle performs himself, stages his "self" in the mirrors the gaze of the other provides.

Mirrored Stages

A sequence in a mirrored gymnasium is prefaced with a shot of Karl naked, face down on his bed, presumably asleep. The black sheets accentuate the sculptural quality of his body, as his voiceover on the soundtrack says: "I go to the gym two hours every day to do these exercises that shape me aesthetically." The first image in the gymnasium is a medium full-length shot of Karl wearing only a jock strap, lying on his back on a bench, lifting weights. The camera pans slowly, revealing this image to have been Karl's reflection in one of the mirrored walls. As the camera completes its turn to the "real" Karl, it also includes in the frame a young man in a corner behind Karl, in street clothes, staring at him. In the next shot in this sequence, Forest stands in front of a mirror watching himself lift weights, but we see this first through the reflection in the opposing mirrored wall, in which the young man is watching Karl. When the young man turns toward Karl "himself," he also turns toward the camera, thereby doubling the image of his face, as he directs this doubled en-visaged gaze from Karl's reflection to Karl's physical presence (or, from the viewer's perspective, from Karl's reflected image to his "real" image).

When the camera frames Karl in a "natural" shot before the mirror, his voiceover states: "I keep myself physically prepared, I work out for myself. It's not narcissistic because I don't like how I am. I want to get better and better." While the image track of his looking at himself in the mirror rehearses the ideal ego of the mirror stage, the sound track (denying the narcissism of the image track) connotes the ego ideal of the form he wishes to become, and is working toward becoming. While the image, as would be expected, represents the pleasure principle, Karl's statement mimics the reality principle. The co-occurrence of these psychically dissonant sound and image tracks merges a representation of the mythic past of original narcissistic subject constitution (the Imaginary) with the projection of a future attainment of a new identificatory model (the Symbolic). In the gymnasium, the mirrors aid Karl in constructing his body within both of these registers (self-recognition and the diagnostics of weight training). But that process also is carried out within the gaze of the young man in the gym, not working out, and not even dressed as if he had intended to. His sole purpose is to sustain Karl's body as object of desire within his field of vision.[46]

Karl leaves the gym alone, and, standing in front of it, he makes eye contact with a hustler across the street. After several meaningful glances, Karl abruptly refuses the hustler's advances. The next scene inexplicably finds the young man from the gym in Karl's apartment, staring patiently as Karl undresses. Karl's deflected seduction of the hustler reenacts another mythic moment in the origin of the subject, although this reenactment disfigures that moment's specular deflection, in a way that produces a very suggestive analogy between this episode and the archaic narcissistic structure it parodies. In the mirror stage, the child sees not only itself but also the ego ideal, "that being that he [*sic*] first saw appearing in the form of the parent holding him up before the mirror. By clinging to the reference point of him who looks at him in a mirror, the subject sees appearing, not his ego ideal, but his ideal ego, that point at which he desires to gratify himself in himself" (Lacan, *Four Fundamental* 256–57).

Karl could not have afforded the phantasmatic cost of sex with another hustler, because there always would have been the question of who was the "customer," who was the desiring partner. By choosing instead the young man at the mirror, Karl preserved his identity as the exclusive object of desire. In Karl's seeing himself through the young man's gaze at him reflected in the mirror, Karl's ideal ego is himself as embodied fantasy he projects onto his admirer, his specular support. I will return to this scene in the next section.

The Off-Screen Subject

In the imaginary dynamics of film spectatorship, the screen is structured as the divide that joins the on-screen subject-as-image and the off-screen subject-as-spectator. The on-screen subject construction of *Le Beau Mec* implicates the spectator both in its construction and through the subject positions made available to the viewer within the conjoining spectacle. Forest has *deliberately* become the "picture" instead of the "geometral point" of ordinary perceptually defined subjecthood. Lacan offers three triangles diagramming the major relations of subject and object in the visual field, as part of his critique of the Cartesian guarantees of a unitary self schematized in perspectivist painting. The first triangle represents the situation as commonly imagined:

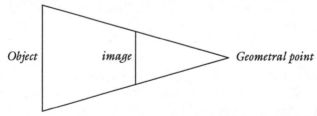

The subject as geometral point is at the apex of the triangle, the object the opposing base. A vertical line bisecting the triangle is marked "image," the form in which the object appears to the subject: The potential for undermining the certitude of this subject lies in the reversibility of the terms in any act of vision. The fact that the subject can see the object is due to the light reflected off the object, which light envelops the subject as well, making the subject visible to others:

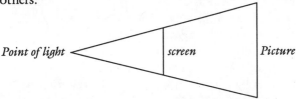

The "photo-graphed" subject experiences this reversal as a traumatic discovery of lack, the perilous determinate point of desire. In *Le Beau Mec*, Forest's subjectivity is constituted by being photo-graphed. And *The Boys of Venice* records a literal photography session that "pictures" the annihilation of the subject in this photo-graphic process.

Lacan represents the simultaneity of the two schema, "functioning of the scopic register," by superimposing the two triangles:

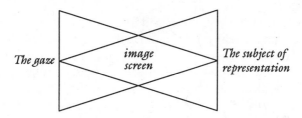

The absolute coincidence of the object and the point of light constitutes the gaze, and that of the geometral point and the picture the "subject of representation."[47] The two converge in the image/screen. The viewing subject becomes a picture in response to the gaze: "From the moment that this gaze appears, the subject tries to adapt himself to it, he becomes that punctiform object, that point of vanishing being with which the subject confuses his own failure" (Lacan, *Four Fundamental* 83). Forest's "failure" is his stardom, a deliberate aphanisis as the assertion of the subject spectacle in the film, which makes the Lacanian screen and its function quite literal, because Forest is not "entirely caught up in this imaginary capture. He maps himself in it. . . . In so far as he isolates the function of the screen and plays with it . . . the screen is here the locus of mediation" (ibid. 107).

Forest's successful "play" with his image on the screen extends the semiosis of narcissistic subject-production in the audience. Forest has made himself "the picture," that is, the film (films are colloquially "pictures"), but that picture questions the identity of the viewing subject, because "in as much as the picture enters into a relation to desire, the place of a central screen is always marked, which is precisely that by which, in front of the picture, I am elided as subject of the geometral plane" (ibid. 108). However, precisely because that picture ("Karl") has deliberately entered a relation to desire (as intentional spectacle), and because desire and identification are mutually conditioning drives for the gay male spectator, the elision of subject of the geometral plane here is not a source of castration anxiety, but a spectatorial position correlative to the screen actor's ("Karl" as picture) assertion of his subjectivity in/as his aphanisis.

The convergence of the image and the screen also marks a specifically gay male spectatorial situation. Through a desiring identification with the intentional spectacle, the gay male viewer assumes the position of the geometral point of triangle 1 (in his *desire* for the on-screen figure), and consciously affirms his concomitant assumption of the position of "picture" of triangle 2 (in his *identification with* the on-screen figure). In his desiring identifications with the aphanitic subjects of the cinema, the gay male spectator is erotically invested in the simultaneous assumption of these positions relative to the gaze, which then places the spectator in a metacinematic identification with the screen figure, since both occupy the position of the "subject of representation" of triangle 3.[48]

This peculiar geometry is inscribed in the film as well. Instead of suturing the viewer as spoken subject of the filmic discourse, *Le Beau Mec* actually as a film *identifies with* the viewer. These identifications are achieved in at least three ways: metaphorically, spatially, and metacinematically. The first "identification" is related to the avoidance of or indifference to suture. Because aphanisis does not have the inevitable association with castration anxiety in the construction of the narcissistic subject (as it does for the anaclitic subject), the spectator is not dependent upon forms of suture typically provided in mainstream film to ensure a stable subject position. In fact, the modes of identification available to the gay male spectator are more frequently directed to the aphanisis on screen rather than its disavowal.[49] The destabilizations of the sexual subject of representation are also figured in *Le Beau Mec* through visual tricks (other manipulations of the screen) that interfere with the viewer's ability to ascertain a consistent spatial position relative to the scene. Heath notes that the "work of classical continuity" of the film is "to contain [off-screen space], to regularize its fluctuation in a constant movement of reappropriation. . . . The join is conventional . . . and demands that the off-screen space recaptured must be 'called for.' . . . [It] must arrive as an 'answer,' 'fulfillment of promise,' . . . (and not as difference or contradiction)—[it] must be narrativized. . . . One of the narrative acts of a film is the creation of space" (Heath, *Questions* 45–46). Such a narrativization of space also fixes the spectator as spoken subject of the film within a coherent spatial orientation within the profilmic world—something which *Le Beau Mec* scrupulously refuses to do.

A scene representing Forest's hustler past opens with an exterior shot of a neon "Hotel" sign above a window, which turns out to be a window to the room in which Karl is entertaining a john. In the next shot, the neon "Hotel" letters are emblazoned across the image of the client going down on Forest. Because it is shot from within the room, the superimposition must be a reflection, but if so, the "Hotel" should be backwards, which it is not. None of the shots in this sequence allow a reconstruction of the point of view that could naturalize this image. In a reprise shot later in this sequence, however, "Hotel" is indeed backwards—but this "correction" only confirms the previous derangement of vision, it does not explain it.

We have already examined the use of mirrors in the gymnasium scene. When Forest takes the young man home, mirrors are again employed, but quite differently. Karl's bedroom walls are jet black, matching his sheets. The scene begins with the young man standing at the bed in medium shot. When Karl lays him down, the scene is filmed in the reflection of a long wall mirror, and framed to include one end of the bed and rumpled blankets, which allows the careful viewer to recognize the scene as a reflection in a mirror. The scene is then reframed so that the mirror is a long central strip across the absolute blackness of the wall. This makes the mirror a perfect double of a movie screen. Without any exterior point of reference, moreover, the relation of the image of the pair making love to the blackness of the wall makes it impossible to tell if this scene is shot through an opening in the wall, or is a reflection in the mirror. This ambiguity dis-places the viewer: if it is a mirror, the viewer is situated in front of it, looking at it from the direction of the bed (and thus in the same room), but if it is an opening, the viewer is *behind it*, in another room. The imaginary space of the spectator in relation to the screen figures is thus indeterminable.

A new sequence begins with a cut to a shot of the bed that includes two walls in the frame, revealing both of them to have long mirrors directed at the bed. The scene shifts abruptly from the ethereally decontextualized epiphany to a kaleidoscopic exposure of the vicissitudes of vision, whose scandal is transferred to the sex scene triply revealed (in the direct shot of the couple and the reflections in both mirrors). When the scene returns to the shot from the single mirror, the spectator can now "locate" himself, but this shot now also represents the ability of the cinematic apparatus to dislodge the spectator from a perceptually intelligible subject position. The differences in intended affects of these tricks and a typology of viewer responses structure within the film's "appearance" an active recognition of the specific differences characterizing the gay male spectator's subjective processes. The serial disorientations the film imposes can result in the viewer's sense of a loss of control over his viewing position, which can easily translate into a loss of a sense of "self" within the spectatorial situation. This is, of course, the response of an anaclitic subject.

For the narcissistic subject, the same "loss of control" can mean freedom of vantage point; the instability of the spectatorial position is also the simultaneity of possible or potential perspectival positions. The film's usurping strategies are not an aggression against the (gay male) spectator but an empathetic acknowledgment of his narcissistic divagations. The disorientations therefore are intended not as traumas to the subject's certainty but as opportunities for the subject's anarchies. These "tricks" signify the identification between the cinematic apparatus and the gay male viewer in terms of the multiplicity of identificatory positions open to him as a gay male spectatorial (or sexual) subject. The playful disruption of perspectival unity does not serve to frustrate the viewer but rather to align the filmic discourse with the subject processes it engages.

The spatial identification is accomplished through another manipulation of mirrors. In this scene Karl is lying on a couch, facing toward the camera, but looking off screen and downward. Behind him a television can be seen, broadcasting a costume drama. The physical ensemble of the scene and the patterns of the previous scenes lead one to surmise that the TV is actually a reflection of the one Karl is watching, in a mirror too clean to see. Eventually, Karl raises one of his legs far enough that it casts a reflection behind it, confirming these suspicions. Note the jigsaw trajectories of the directions of looks and the specular logic of their representational contexts: Forest is looking off screen, *forward* (toward the audience), but what he is watching is a conventional narrative movie on TV, which the spectator will see as *behind* Karl. This is the obverse of the spectator's position within the visual apparatus. Forest is looking in front of himself, at an image that apparently exists behind him. The spectator is looking forward at an image, whose source is *actually behind* him/her (the projector). The "meanings" of this scene are of course derived through critical interpretation; the simple concrete situation of the scene also demands deduction and synthesis of earlier patterns. Most films would have naturalized Karl's intent stare off screen with a reverse shot from his position to reveal what he was looking at, but none is offered here. Of course, such a reverse shot is the paradigmatic technique of cinematic suture; any possible suture is fractured in the mirror image of the object of Forest's look. The only thing that allows the viewer to see the mirror as a mirror, and thereby to know what it is Forest is watching, is his leg, raised slightly, causing a partial reflection behind him. Thus it is his body (a part of it, a fetish object, an *objet a*) reduplicated (screen image, reflection) that solves the visual riddle and *reorientates the spectator as disoriented* in relation to the profilmic space as organized on screen. In this enigmatic resolution, the scene offers in tableau a mirror image of the spectator's relation to the screen and the source of the image before him.

The metacinematic moment of identification in the TV scene's reference to the spectator's relation to the projector is extended and reelaborated in the sex club scene, one of the most intimate and multileveled identifications enacted, as it also images the spectator's imaginary conceptions of vision and his scopophilic drive. The scene is shot with a hand-held camera and a single hand-held spotlight lamp, in a totally dark basement. The spotlight's movements are at first extremely erratic and aleatory, and the blackness is so complete that nothing is visible unless the lamp's light hits it. At times only the light itself is visible. The camera's pans and the light's wanderings syncopate a random choreography of the acts of making something visible, which heightens the sense of effort involved in seeing. Gradually there is a sustained pan of the single spotlight roving across old stucco walls and wooden planks. Some of the planks are numbered, and the sporadic coincidence of the spot and the camera reveals these planks to be rudimentary doors. At this point the soundtrack includes heavy breathing from a distance. Eventually the camera follows the spot through an open door. Once inside the promiscuous apparatus illuminates various body parts of quite a few people in sexual activity. The eccentrically framed and fragmentary samplings eventually include Forest's head and shoulders, which also inaugurates the increasing synchronization of camera work and lighting and progressively longer and more cognitively intelligible shots of men fucking, always centered on or gravitating to Forest. Even at this point, however, the ecstatic pointlessness of the orgy and the restrained technology preclude any sense of narrative structure or coherent movement within the scene toward closure. It finally ends when the camera turns toward the spotlight lamp itself, and the close-up obliterates the picture.

Lacan observes that a light whose brilliance calls attention to itself obscures the object it would otherwise reveal, and therefore requires a screen placed between it and the object for it to appear (*Four Fundamental* 107–108). The spotlight in the dark on the screen which will make the orgiasts visible replicates the light from the projector in the theater that is making the film visible. The searching, roving motion of the beam of light (looking for the men having sex—which is what the viewer is doing, too) and the function of a screen that will allow the "object to emerge" also foreground the imaginary structures of vision operative within the spectator's unconscious or semiconscious perception of his situation: "All vision consists of a double movement: projective (the 'sweeping' searchlight) and introjective: consciousness as a sensitive recording surface (as a screen). . . . During the performance the spectator is the searchlight . . . duplicating the projector, which itself duplicates the camera, and he [*sic*] is also the sensitive surface duplicating the screen, which itself duplicates the filmstrip" (Metz 50–51).[50] When the film has as its only object the light searching for the sources of the voices of men obviously having sex, the light simultaneously functions as an incitement and a figure of the spectator's scopophilic drive; a metadiegetic exposition of the conditions of the film's visibility (the searchlight being the only light in this scene); and a metacinematic thematization of the spectator's internalization of projector and screen in the act of viewing. When the camera turns from the bodies to the actual lamp of the spotlight, the light's intensity destroys the picture: an iconically Oedipal moment—the film's seeking the source of its visibility (and thus the source of its being) results in blindness.

The final scene begins with another voiceover statement contradicted by the mirrored images of the visual track. Karl states: "I use my fantasies as little as possible. Sometimes I find it doesn't depend on me as much as the other person's imagination. I try not to count on mine too much," yet on screen we see him enter his apartment in black leather pants, and slowly strip and masturbate in front of a mirror that occupies an entire wall (forming another plane subtending the screen). The last lines of the voiceover occur before he finishes disrobing: "I'm 27 years old today—I wonder if I'm not saturated. I ask myself if sexually—" at which point the voiceover breaks off abruptly, replaced by a synthesizer score.[51] During his strip and masturbation, his reflection is always in focus. When both Karl and his reflection are in frame, either they are both in focus or only his reflection is. If there is only one image framed, it is always the mirror image. These reflections are shot from a variety of angles, some of which make the body before the mirror look as if it is someone else.

As he approaches orgasm, he leans against the mirror, rippling the reflection, and leaning his head too close to the camera light, which also ruins the picture. During his orgasm there are repeated close-ups of his face and its reflection and his ejaculating penis and its reflection. The ecstasis is imagistically doubled, just as the mirror doubles for the screen and the reflections mirror the representational capacity of the film. Forest asserts himself in the moment of this self-dissolution in orgasm, but he emblazons that moment onto the mirror and onto the screen. His embrace of the gaze of the other—not as an annihilation of his subjecthood but *as its condition*—distinguishes his subject production from Sartre's existential dread and Lacan's Hegelian fastidiousness. Karl's narcissistic exhibitionist practice of self-articulation chiasmically integrates the rupture such articulation entails as a process essential to the subject thus realized. His image in the mirror and his image on the screen are traces of his agency in this construction: like the *literal* construction of his body image through the mirror in the gymnasium, the image he imposes on the movie screen is also an *act* of subject construction. Forest knows himself to be the object of the gaze—but this results in neither Sartrean shame nor Freudian paranoia, because he is en-acting what Lacan perceives to be the subject's ability "to locate himself within" the "imaginary captivation" of the gaze of the other "to the extent that he isolates the function of the screen and plays off it" (*Four Fundamental* 107).

Karl's sexual climax in the mirror coincides with the narrative/specular culmination of his cinematic self-representation as a perverse conflation of his ideal ego (the mirror stage, the Imaginary) and his ego ideal (the narrative image, the Symbolic) in his projected/introjected gaze of the other. That the join of these egos "comes" in front of a mirror reminds us that one of the functions of the imago "is to establish a relation between the organism and its reality—or, as they say, between the *Innenwelt* and *Umwelt*" (Lacan, *Écrits* 4), which would account for the visual sign of the deliberate incorporation of the soundtrack into the plane of the specular. Moreover, since the "conception of the mirror stage" and "the light it sheds on the formation of the *I* . . . leads us to oppose any philosophy directly issuing from the *Cogito*" (ibid. 1), the film's visual disorienting of the spectator's position can be explained in that the abandonment of the *cogito* would also obviate the need for the film to provide imaginary assurance of the subject's mastery as the geometral point of perspectivist painting. Portrayed as both the subject of enunciation (as "author" of the film) and the subject of utterance (as star of the film), Karl's screen figure marks a join between self and image that is a strange, projective reverse of the mirror stage: the self is recognized as the image, but this time *the image is not elsewhere*; instead the two are collapsed within the same point of light (the point of light which is both picture and gaze on the screen). This is similar to the join of intradiegetic and extradiegetic [Scott Taylors] in *The Boys of Venice*. Forest's and Taylor's specularized embodiments therefore enact a split between ego and subject that the typical sutures (of ordinary language or cinematic conventions) obscure. This too is complicated in *Le Beau Mec* because of the diffracted status of Forest's image as "narrative image" of the film but not subject of his fantasy, while metonymically embodying the syntax of that fantasy. Perhaps the aphanisis rendered iconically in *The Boys of Venice* and in the mirror scene of *Le Beau Mec* also constitutes a point of ecstatic identification for the spectator that exhausts itself neither in the interpellative harmonics of the Althusserian imaginary, nor in the Lacanian fatalistic acknowledgment of the gaze that legislates the fetishistic politics of disavowal crucial to the phallocentric fantasies of specular mastery.

The Specular and the Narrative in Gay Male Pornographic Film

The specular and the narrative often seem diametrically opposed in a porn film: the plot of the film stops at the spectacle of the sex acts whose unmotivated visual excess overpowers the linearity of meaningful acts the narrative is meant to organize. The specular undermining of the narrative is abetted by the film's construction: the blocking, lighting, camera angles, editing, and choreography of bodies accentuate the visibility of each act, at the expense of any naturalistic illusion characterizing a more holistically contextualized reality. The sex scenes also transgress the boundaries of genre (fiction, documentary); semiotic categories (symbolic [narrative], iconic [visual record]); and ontologies (real, false). Real sex within the porn film constitutes a semiological trauma the narrative sustains and the film memorializes.

In many porn films, however, more intricate relations obtain between the narrative and specular modes, particularly in the genre known as "erotic confession." In *A Matter of Size* (Matt Sterling, 1984), Bill Henson and Eric Stryker tell each other their recent wet dreams. The dreams are shown without overlaid narrative, and simply replace the verbal description that initially frames them. *Giants* (David Winter, 1987) has a nonpresent master narrator who tells the story of a party thrown by his friend Jeff Converse, where he persuades his "straight" college buddies to play a game in which each has to "confess" to a gay sexual experience—it can be made up but it has to be "convincing." As each man begins his story, the scene shifts to an enactment of that story, and the narrative is taken over by the master narrator, who describes every action in detail as it happens, so that each scene has parallel narrative and specular versions of the same sexual event. The ambiguity of the "truth" of the confession (in the plot of the film, its narrative register) is problematized by seeing it happening (in the film's specular register). The specular rendition of the "confessions" meta-diegetically resolves the suspense (did he or didn't he?) operative within the narrative.[52] Both of these films, moreover, highlight the peculiar ontological status of actors in porn in that in both of the frame stories, the characters may never have had the experience they relate (the dreams in *Matter* and the possible bluffs in *Giants*), but the actors who portray those characters actually perform the acts in the film's en-visioning of their narratives.

The elicitations of verbal testimony of sexual behavior are often implicated in the tendency of pornography to reflect on its own mechanisms of fantasy production. There are films which focus on virtually every aspect of the industry: the filming (*Closed Set* [Joe Gage, 1980]; *Closed Set II* [Joe Gage, 1984]; *Casting Couch* [William Richhe, 1990]); the editing (*Freeze Frame* [ND, 1985]; *Rough Cut* [Steve Scott, 1980]); the creation of the porn star (*The Bigger They Come* [Scott Masters, 1987]; *The Next Valentino* [Jim West, 1988]); the fetishization of established porn stars' celebrity (*On the Rocks* [Stryker Productions, 1988]; *Truth Dare or Damian* [Vivid, 1990]); the video store and video booths (*Flexx* [Chi Chi Larue, 1989]; *Head Trips* [Al Parker, 1984]); and the porn theater (*The Back Row* [Doug Richards, 1973]; *Bijou* [Wakefield Poole, 1977]). There are two films that dramatically illustrate the confluence of confession elicitation and the self-reflexive nature of the porn film: Jean-Daniel Cadinot's *All of Me* (1983), which we have already considered, and Jim West's *The Next Valentino*.

The Next Valentino stars Kevin Glover as an out-of-work "legitimate" actor who decides to try porn. This is highly overdetermined in that Glover actually is a traditionally trained actor who does appear in more "legitimate" vehicles as well. His acting ability is one of his trademarks in porn, and the contrast between his polished method acting techniques and the often deadpan performances of the other models prevents his acting from simply merging into a larger gestalt of naturalistic illusion. Instead his acting becomes conspicuous, and the films seem to be a documentary of someone "really acting," just as they are a record of someone "really having sex." This contradiction is fully exploited in *The Next Valentino*. For his screen test, the director (Butch Taylor) tells the actor to masturbate while relating a hot sexual encounter. Glover tells a story about having sex in a public restroom with a trucker and being threatened by a police officer, who then engages in a three-way. Glover's rendition of the story is highly theatrical, and the camera work and editing are a baroque mosaic of black and white and color, tape and film, pans and close-ups, fragmenting the body and establishing clear distinctions between the visual and the narrative modes.

As in *All of Me*, this scene ends with Glover orgasming and landing his first job—a glory hole scene in a construction-worker film featuring "real-life" porn stars Eric Manchester and Steve Hammond. This is both humorous and interesting in terms of performance semiotics. Glover is conspicuously acting (but a role based on his actual life) the part of a nervous and starstruck ingenue, and established porn stars Manchester and Hammond play themselves unconvincingly, since they do not have Glover's command of the "professional" acting techniques of "being oneself."[53] We see the introductions, setup, rehearsals, missed cues, retakes, and the actual sex. The real sex is bracketed and diffracted across different registers of representation: Glover the actor playing "Thad" the newcomer, Manchester and Hammond playing themselves playing construction workers, "directed" by fellow porn star Butch Taylor. The film concludes with Thad's big break—starring as "himself" in a film based on the story he told during his screen test, the filming of which we also get to see. As in the other erotic confession films, the narrative is visually actualized, but not flawlessly as in the fantasy zone of the dream sequences in *A Matter of Size*, or in the visualizations of the stories in *Giants*, but blatantly behind the scenes, transparent to its own performative and technological construction.

Another, more direct elicitation of the "truth" of sex occurs within the act of directing a pornographic performance for the camera. That truth is then produced, a truth irreducibly an effect of that elicitation (and therefore not "truth" in the strictest sense of the term, as a preexistent reality, subject to discovery).[54] The screen tests of would-be performers are paradigmatic for this kind of truth production. William Higgins also plays with the notion of "behind the scenes" and the incorporation of the origins of "porn stars" into a cinematic record retroactively, by releasing compilations of his real screen tests of young men, most of whom went on to appear in "real" films (*Screen Test* [1987]; *Screen Test No. 2* [1988]). In these tests a voice instructs a young man to sit down on the bed, stand up, slowly undress, and eventually masturbate to orgasm, precisely what happens in the beginning of Pedro Almodóvar's *Law of Desire*, a film pivotal in my theorization of gay male cinematic subjects outside of—but partially developed from—the specialized situations of the pornographic apparatus.

The Gay Subject of Cinema

The Postpornographic Apparatus in the films of Pedro Almodóvar

In turning to "legitimate" cinema, I will argue that Pedro Almodóvar uses the apparatus of gay male pornography in his film *Law of Desire* (1986) to develop a cinematic representation of gay male subjectivity. In reading this film against *Matador* (also 1986), I will also show how Almodóvar's deployment of pornography as a metonym for gay male sexuality figures within the interaction of the narrative and specular modes of representation as technologies of subjectivity and as contrasting emblems for homosexuality and heterosexuality, respectively. Finally I will extrapolate a "gay male spectator" from the opposition of the two films, paying particular attention to how Almodóvar advances such a spectatorial model in his recontextualization of its "illicit" and subcultural origins within mainstream cinema and a largely heterosexual audience.

Specular Tricks: *Law of Desire*

My comparison above of Almodóvar's visual transgressions in *Law of Desire* with Higgins's *Screen Test* must be qualified by the differences between Almodóvar's film and the pornographic traditions to which he is indebted. Although *Law of Desire* features gay characters, it is not a film exclusively (or even primarily) for gay men; although the film evokes gay pornographic film and quotes its conventions, *Law* itself is not gay porn. This internal dissonance and the larger audience the film addresses institute two important suprastructural differences between *Law of Desire* and gay male pornography:

1. The relations between the narrative and the specular are played out as tensions between the first scene and the rest of the film, and as specularized modes of resistance to the master narrative of the Oedipal development of compulsory heterosexuality.

2. The gay male spectator the film posits will be ineluctably politicized, and will emerge as a contestatory subject position *vis-à-vis* the "general" audience.

The film opens with a young man walking into a sparsely furnished bedroom. Taking directions from an off-screen male voice, he strips to his underwear and kisses his image in a full-length mirror. He is then told to rub his genitals against his reflection until he becomes excited, after which, still following directions, he lies on the bed and continues to stimulate himself, removes his underwear, and eventually masturbates on his knees until orgasm. After the young man climaxes, a man puts money on the stand next to him.

The boy counts it and lays it down again. The director's voiceover says, "Freeze it and 'The End,' " when the scene changes to a hand marking a film reel, which then changes to a close-up of the money on the nightstand and the large red letters "Fin." This, then, was the final scene of a film-within-a-film.[55] Suddenly, a red-haired woman appears walking away from the "Fin" image (leaving the theater where that film had just been screened), and seeing a man in the lobby, she embraces him, as a young man walks past them. This scene is also frozen, and the words "*Law of Desire*, a Film by Pedro Almodóvar" write themselves across the scene (in spite of the fact that the "official" credits were already shown before the first scene). The frozen scene outside (and within) the theater (the lobby with the doors open, still exposing the false movie on the inner screen) is also a complex of both neutralized and inverted syntagms of "appearance" and "reality" that can be understood only retrospectively: the pair embracing are not lovers, but brother and sister; the brother is not heterosexual (as it appears in his embrace of the woman) but homosexual; the man walking by (Antonio Banderas) is not an incidental figure (Barthes's "effect of the real") but a key figure in the love triangle and murder intrigue that will ensue.

These inversions contain further inversions: the man (Eusebio Poncelas) embracing the woman (Carmen Maura) is the "real" (intradiegetic) director of the film whose final scene opened the main film; the woman is "actually" a transsexual (the siblings are brothers). The "sister's" story is a travesty of the Oedipus: as a young boy she had an affair with her father; when the mother discovered this, the father and child fled to Algeria, where the boy had a sex-change operation, only to be abandoned by the father subsequently. In other words, the boy child's desire for the father is punished by the mother by exile and real castration. The inversion of the Oedipus obviates phallic narrative closure just as the alterity of sexual orientations and the reversals of gender codes disestablishes the mutually exclusive divisions of artifice and reality. Within the context of the discovery of the film's inaugurating tricks, it is important to reread the economy of desire in the first scene, and the traversal of the representations of that desire across disjunctive planes of reality (noncongruent ontological levels).

At the beginning of the opening scene, the director's voice tells the young man, "Don't look at me. Remember you are alone." When the man kisses his reflection, the voice instructs him, "Do it again. Pretend you are kissing me and you like it." The repeated "fuck me" is taken over by a man standing next to the director with his own microphone. In fact, we first see the director when the actor initially hesitates to say the line. As the actor continues to masturbate, the director says, "Imagine that I'm fucking you and you like it. I only want you to enjoy." The sexually aroused responses now come from both the actor and the man next to the director, although it is difficult to tell whether the second man is actually aroused or merely adding sound effects. When the actor says, "I'm coming," the director responds, "I am too." Although both the director and the second man then make sounds of sexual satisfaction into the mikes, accompanying the "actual" orgasm of the actor, the director remains cool and businesslike, foregrounding the "false" nature of the entire enterprise. The porous boundaries of the real and the false are thematized throughout the scene (typical of actual gay porn), here spanning the intra- and metadiegetic levels.

The fact that it is a movie set makes the scene directed "really" false. The actor is not alone, but is told to pretend that he is. The pressure toward reality is based on the specificities of the male body. He must become "really" aroused in order to complete the scene, a scene which is "false" but will contain a core of sexual reality for the fantasies of subsequent viewers. In order to facilitate the real of sexual arousal, the director suggests fantasies to the actor: "Pretend you are kissing me and you like it"; "Imagine that I'm fucking you"; "Can you feel me inside you?" These fantasies have "real" effects, and indeed suggest a reality outside of the film situation: the actor must have an "off-screen" sexual attraction to the director in order for the fantasies to work—but in this case such a relationship would occur within the narrative of the film that comprehends this scene.

Within the doubly embedded masturbation sequence (a film within a film), a psychic drama is enacted. The man at the mirror joins his introceptively experienced anatomical "self" with the externality of his image, and invests this image with a significant libidinal charge, at the urging of the voice. When he masturbates, he gives way to the raptures of the primary processes, allowing fantasies to stimulate him sexually and to lead him to full satisfaction in the absence of any "real" object. Yet even here, psychic functions of different levels are operative simultaneously. Although the actor is using fantasy—thing presentation—to drive him to satisfaction (primary process, pleasure principle), his fantasy is prompted and guided by the voice—that is, word presentation—from the realm of the secondary processes and the reality principle. The clear distinctions between pleasure and reality principles are blurred: the ultimate aim of the actor's performance is money—certainly the reality principle at work, but here it does not entail deferred satisfaction; in fact, the autoerotic satisfaction within the pleasure principle coincides perfectly with the financial satisfaction of the reality principle: libidinal and literal economies intersect (as they do in *All of Me* and *The Last Valentino*).

The distinctions between reality and fantasy are also subverted. The actual anatomical cause of his orgasm is his manual manipulation of his "real" penis, yet the apparent psychic cause of his orgasm is the absent penis that penetrated him in fantasy. This too, however, is subject to question: we only surmise the actor's fantasy through what the director tells him to imagine. The actor tells us nothing. This is the reverse of a psychoanalytic session. The voice of authority provides the fantasy; the auditor responds sexually but discloses nothing discursively.

Locating the scene within the cinematic event, these aporia undergo further bracketing. Although the actor's orgasm is portrayed as the "real" result of an imaginary tension between the actor's actual penis and the phantasmatic penis invoked by the director, the truth of this scene is that neither penis is there—both are productions of fantasy. When the intradiegetic actor faces his image in the mirror, the visual doubling resonates with the narrative doubling, producing a metacinematic commentary on the artifice of the film's production. Both images of the young man are just that: two-dimensional specular configurations of a "real" body that is nowhere present; the fictional actor's embrace of his ego-imago in the mirror becomes the split emblem of the film embracing itself as film: the reduplicated, fascinated/fascinating image of the body confirms the resistance of the autotelic spectacle to narrativization. The autoerotic body produces nothing, nor does it reveal any secrets. In an early paper on the ego, Lacan describes the "inertia" in the ego "as the resistance to the dialectic process of analysis. The patient is held spellbound by his ego, to the exact degree that it causes his distress, and reveals its nonsensical function" ("Some Reflections" 12). In his classic paper on the mirror stage, Lacan notes that the "conception of the mirror stage" and "the light it sheds on the formation of the *I* . . . leads us to oppose any philosophy directly issuing from the *Cogito*" (*Écrits* 1). The image-ego, the self-pleasuring image (the masturbating actor as a metonym for the film itself), in its "nonsensical function" resists analysis—it refuses to tell its story (it doesn't have one; the spectator is seduced into supplying it). The thematic presumption of the narcissistic constitution of the I (and the film) forecloses the possibility of Cartesian certainty, the position necessary for the phallic coherence of narrative. The metadiegetic reflection of the film upon itself, parallel to the vision of the actor in the mirror, inhibits the generation of a master narrator (a privileged viewing subject or omniscient incorporeal storyteller) as it exposes the contingencies and ambivalences within the narrative compulsion toward a univocal truth—a monolithic reality prior to and independent of subjective and intersubjective compromises.

The first scene is a specular event that does not resolve itself in a naturalizing narrative, and does not contribute to the narrative of the film as a whole. The resistance of the first scene to incorporation into the narrative whole of the film is parallel to a kind of resistance the gay male sexual subject offers the teleology of the master plot of the male child's journey into patriarchally defined heterosexuality. Gay sexuality, like the first scene, is a specular subversion of the Oedipal narrative. Besides the narrative arrest at the mirror stage that serves as a subliminal structuring fantasy within one tradition of homosexual pathologization, I have also noted in chapter 1 that the polycentricity of the gay male erotic body maps co-occurrent erotogenic possibilities that seem to correspond to the oral, anal, and phallic stages through which the anaclitic subject passes.[56]

The contrast between the specular and the narrative, with each mode designated as gay and heterosexual, respectively, can be seen by comparing *Law of Desire* with Almodóvar's *Matador* (1986; U.S. release, 1987). In fact, the resistant relation between the specularity of the first scene of *Law* and the narrativity of the film thereafter finds a parallel relation between *Law* and *Matador* as entire films. The two films lend themselves to comparison, having been made the same year, with essentially the same principal actors. Both films open with scenes of masturbation; the major plots of both films are set in motion by murder (although *Law* contains far more detours and lateral plots than the murder-centered plot of *Matador*). In both films the murderers are heterosexual (although the murderer in *Law of Desire* is sexually involved with a man, he states that he "normally doesn't sleep with men" and is obviously both inexperienced and overwhelmed by his own desires). Although only *Law* is an overtly gay film, *Matador* can be seen as a gay-oriented parody of conventional male heterosexuality; both films therefore appeal to a gay male spectator as an arbiter of their intelligibility.

Heterosexuality Can Be Murder: *Matador*

Matador begins with a shot of a woman being simultaneously strangled and drowned in a bathroom sink, filmed upward from the bottom of the sink as her head is plunged into the water. This shot is followed by a close-up of a man's face, heavily perspiring and showing signs of physical exertion. The next shot is of a man opening a straight razor, placing the drowned woman's corpse in a bathtub, and slashing her wrist. The subsequent scenes are of increasingly gory murders of women and discoveries of mutilated female corpses, alternating with various shots of the same male spectator, who is masturbating facing a television. One shot is filmed from behind the man's chair, his feet framing the television screen where the butchering continues, his panting mixing with the screams from the video and the music of the soundtrack.

In the gay *Law of Desire* the masturbation occurs on the site of cinematic production, for the pleasure both of the figure being filmed and of the specular network comprising the director, technical assistant, and spectator. The corresponding scene in the (heterosexual) *Matador* is in a private home in front of a television (site of passive visual consumption) where a solitary man masturbates while watching video excerpts of slasher movies. In *Law* the masturbating actor is the bodily center of a nexus of intermeshing and mutually disseminating desires (voyeurism and exhibitionism, fantasy narratives, memory play) and indeterminately recursive avenues of pleasure, emanating from the production of a film. It is creative, and intersubjectively narcissistic. In *Matador* the mas-

turbating man is simply viewing excerpts of already made films, lacerated segments of films metaphorizing the dismemberments depicted therein. The relationship of (profilmic) viewer to scene in *Matador* is necrophilic, parasitic,
autistic, and fundamentally homicidal to women—in other words, the paradigm of hegemonically valorized male heterosexuality.[57]

The masturbator is Diego Montes (Nacho Martinez), a celebrated toreador
until a bull-inflicted leg injury ended his career prematurely, relegating him to
running a school for would-be bullfighters. The next scene is actually two interlocking sequences: the matador lecturing his students on the "art of killing"
the bull in the ring, and a beautiful woman (Assumpta Serna) picking up a man
on the street, taking him to a hotel room, and killing him by plunging a ra-
pier-like hairpin through the back of his neck during sex. Her actions are described metaphorically by the phases of the kill the matador elaborates in the
lecture, and her deadly sex act is intercut with the students' practice sessions
using bulls' horns and horned carts. After the lesson, the matador speaks with
Angel (Antonio Banderas), one of the students who seemed upset by the descriptions of killing. During their conversation, the matador discovers with
surprise that Angel has never had sex with a woman (an assertion in symmetrical opposition to Banderas's character in *Law*, when he tells the director that
he doesn't sleep with men). To encourage him, the matador tells him, "Chicks
are just like bulls, you've got to hem them in first and just take them." The
gender confusion within this simile is generated from the phallic stage in compulsory heterosexuality, at which point "there is only one sexual organ." In
other words, women are a negative form of men, and both are defined in relation to the deadly penetrative power of the phallus. Sex amounts to closing in
for the kill. Both of these statements had been realized in the murder scene
previous to the conversation.

The relationship between the heterosexuality parodied in *Matador* and the
narrativity it eventuates is sexually thematized early in the plot. At the end of
his encounter with Diego, Angel feels both his heterosexuality challenged and
his unresolved homoerotic attraction to Diego only ambivalently acknowledged; he responds by trying (unsuccessfully) to rape Diego's fiancée (Eva
Cobo). Unable to win the affection of his *maestro*, Angel attempted to compensate for his loss metonymically, by sexually assaulting the woman his teacher
desired. This is the logic of a narrative chain; Angel's crime illustrates the violence committed upon women within the sequences such narrative logic legislates.[58] Overcome with guilt, Angel confesses to several murders that he did not
commit: two male victims of the hairpin killer, and two missing women.

The lawyer who agrees to defend the boy is the murderer herself, and therefore knows him to be innocent. The other person who is convinced of the boy's
innocence is a police detective played by Eusebio Poncelas, who played the gay
director in *Law*. Here Poncelas's character's sexual orientation is not made ex-

plicit, but in his surveillance of the bullfighting school, as he watches the
would-be matadors in training, the camera moves in for obsessive close-ups of
the students' crotches in their tight toreador pants.[59] The detective's desire to
know the truth, to see "it," is here imbricated with the desire to see *It*—the
phallus, the pillar of the masculinist order. In changing roles from the overtly
gay director in *Law* to a detective in *Matador*, the actor enfigures the sublimation of erotic desire into epistemophilia, as advanced by Freud in his account
of da Vinci's "homosexual nature" transforming itself into his "love of knowledge" (*Leonardo and a Memory* 79–80).

During the course of the investigation, the murderous lawyer, Maria,
meets the matador, and the two of them prove to be suicidal/homicidal soul-
mates, devoted to a vehemently phallic and death-oriented sexuality. Maria is
profoundly male-identified in all aspects of her persona: in her profession, she
represents the Law (the monolithic and repressive law of the father, not the
chaotic and subversive "law of desire"); in her cultural identity, she idolizes the
matador to the point of enshrining his accouterments—his cloak and dagger,
etc.; in her sexuality, she adheres to a definition of sex based on penetration
and mastery, which expresses itself in a transitive negativity through which the
satiation of desire is externalized as the literal destruction of the object of desire, by murdering the partner through impalement. In their first encounter,
when Maria notices Diego following her, she takes refuge in a movie theater,
and when he finds her, she chooses the men's lavatory in which to hide. More
than betraying her ambivalence regarding her wish to elude her pursuer, the
choice of lavatory affirms her male identification through her willful "failure"
of what, in Lacan's scheme, is one of the most fundamental, sexually determined means by which the signifier is fixed: the choice of one of two doors,
marked "ladies" and "gentlemen," respectively (*Écrits* 150–51).

Near the end of the film, we discover that the lawyer and the matador are
perfectly symmetrical sexual partners: the matador had been killing young
women and burying them on the grounds of the school. Both are serial killers,
and both are invested in penetrative acts of murder to compensate for perceived
deficiencies in their psychosexual integrity: the lawyer's "real lack" of a penis,
and the matador's symbolic castration by the bull that curtailed his career.
Ironically, it is the institution of phallocentric compulsory heterosexuality that
induces the sense of loss and predicates the lethal narrative project of an impossible restoration.

Law of Desire and *Matador* can be distinguished in their divergent emblems
of specific orientation toward the "real" both represented and thematized
within each film: in *Law of Desire*, the pornographic film, in *Matador*, the murder mystery. While the first scene of *Law of Desire* is not technically pornographic (we do not actually see the actor masturbate, nor is his erection ever
visible), its reliance on the image and dynamics of the pornographic scene allow

us to typify the film in this manner. In the murder mystery, all actions remain on the level of fiction, in the realm of the Symbolic. The narrative is set in motion by an act whose perpetrator is unknown. The sequence of events and interpretations which are instigated by that act are structured teleologically as the discovery of the identity of the perpetrator. This is the exact reverse of the pornographic film: in visual pornography, the act is real, and is far more important than the identity of its agents, and the coincidence of act and image that pornography requires ruptures the isomorphism of any naturalistic fictional film in which it occurs; in the murder mystery, the central act is not real, the identity of the agent is primary, and the occurrence of the act founds the narrative and determines its signifying processes. The murder mystery dramatizes the progress from signifier to signified (deduction of clues), as it dramatizes the eschatology of the phallogocentric sign toward a univocal Truth, through the detective's ordeal of discovery (is it merely coincidental that English slang for "detective" is "dick"?). The culmination of the murder narrative is the uncovering of the identity of the murderer, a reconstruction of a past event that seeks to enact Justice (the Law of the Father) as an imperfect restitution of the lost object (the murder victim). The manifold tragedy of the narrative is predicated upon the contradiction that the discovery of the truth will end the narrative impulse (the contradiction informing quest literature that the attainment of the goal brings about the end of the action, and that sexual satisfaction will obliterate the desire that sought it) and that its fulfillment cannot restore the loss that had occasioned it. The archetypical subject of such a tragically structured murder mystery narrative is Oedipus, a detective whose catastrophic discoveries install the Law of the Father as absolute. The act of deduction in the murder mystery, moreover, rehearses the intellectual activity necessary to determine the father of a child, a necessity Freud uses to assert the primacy of the concept of fatherhood and the establishment of a nonrepresentable, unitary Father-God as a watershed in the evolution of civilization (*Moses and Monotheism* 112–14).

The murderer is the reverse side of the same authoritarian identity, whose act of destruction assumes a godlike privilege over life that the act of begetting a child is perceived to be within the patriarchal logic that inaugurates the metaphysics of fatherhood. The ironic distance at which the gay male spectator views the heterosexual liaisons in *Matador* finds a corresponding ironic distanciation internal to the film itself, in the broad parodies of heterosexual behavior, and in metadiegetic intrusions into the otherwise linear progression of the narrative. It turns out that Angel is plagued with psychic visions of murders, and that two of the murders he had "confessed" to (two women whose bodies had not been recovered) had actually been committed by Diego. We see them through Angel's mind's eye: the first woman Diego strangles and then rapes, and the second woman he drowns in the bathtub and then rapes. The second woman is almost identical to the drowned woman in the slasher video in the opening sequence. Thus, we have a violation of the levels of the ontological status of figures in the film, similar (but reversed) to that in the opening scene of *Law*. Both the supernatural origin of this revelation and its visual representation highlight the fictionality of the narrative that the typical narrative is meant to conceal.

An even more remarkable metadiegetic—even metacritical—intervention into the narrative occurs when Maria flees into the movie theater. The film playing is *Duel in the Sun* (King Vidor, 1946), and Diego enters the theater and stands next to Maria just in time to view the last scene, in which Pearl (Jennifer Jones) and Lewt (Gregory Peck) have shot each other, and die happily in each other's arms. This not only foreshadows the murder-suicide pact that Maria and Diego will soon enter into, but this is the very film which prompted Laura Mulvey to reconsider the possibilities for the female spectator she had formulated in "Visual Pleasure." In Pearl, Mulvey sees the figure of the oscillation between "masculine" and "feminine" phases of the libido, here split between the two brothers, Lewt and Jesse, who "represent different sides of her desire and aspiration" (Mulvey, "Afterthoughts" 35). Although this split allows an innovative illumination in mainstream cinema of the "female spectator as she temporarily accepts 'masculinisation' in memory of her 'active' phase," the radical potential here is not realized, and Pearl's " 'tomboy' pleasures, her sexuality, are not fully accepted by Lewt, except in death" (37).[60]

The vacillations between passive and active in the female spectator of *Duel* are frustrated by the necessary sacrifice of the female figure who embodies them, just as the sexual autonomy of Maria in *Matador* is contained within a phallocentric economy which channels it into a homicidal and suicidal compulsion. The critical difference between the two films, however, is that *Duel* was produced, distributed, and traditionally received within the discursive parameters of an uncontested ideology of sexual difference and an absolutely unquestioned heterosexual presumption. In *Matador* all heterosexual liaisons are always already bracketed as contingent concatenations of power differentials, and the heterosexual appeals to universality are exposed as internally contradicted hoaxes that victimize both those outside of this ideology and those who perpetrate and perpetuate it. This message, as thematized in *Matador*, addresses the gay male spectator whose specifically embodied knowledge of the hoax of heterosexuality and his own countervailing erotic capacities allow him to read it.

Pornographic Tropes in Mainstream Venues: Constructing the Gay Male Spectator

In positing the "gay male spectator," we must also account for the dialectic activated between the contradictory identifications arising during the viewing of a film: the identification with the desiring (and organizing) gaze of the camera and its male surrogate within the film, and the erotic identification with the male object of desire—in other words, the dialectic between the culturally enjoined position of the male spectator as subject of the gaze (the involuntary patrimony imposed upon the gay male by the very order that would erase him), and the culturally proscribed identification with an objectified male body (the incommensurability of his socially mandated gender role and his "antisocial" sexual orientation). The specificity of the gay male spectatorial situation can be most clearly illustrated in its divergence from the model of heterosexual male spectatorship developed by Laura Mulvey.

Mulvey's heterosexual male viewer's visual pleasures are divided into two opposing categories, which in turn represent two mutually exclusive drives. His scopophilia (directed at the female image), a function of the sexual drives, "arises from pleasure in using another person as an object of sexual stimulation through sight" and "implies a separation of the erotic identity of the subject from the object on the screen." His identification with the active male protagonist, motivated by "the spectator's fascination with and recognition of his like," is a function of the ego drives (Mulvey, "Visual Pleasure" 16–17). Because of these separations, and because the heterosexual male cannot "bear the burden of objectification," figures of desire and identification never coincide.

The gay male spectator, on the other hand, regularly identifies with the figure he sexually objectifies. In other words, he experiences a coalescence of drives that are radically dichotomized in his heterosexual male counterpart. For the gay male spectator, the pleasure of looking at the male object of desire potentially merges with an erotic identification with that object; scopophilia and identification become interanimating components of a specifically ego-erotic subjectivity. Of course, the process of identification, even for the gay male spectator, still involves the network of "looks" that make up the cinematic experience: "1) the camera looks . . . at someone, something, the profilmic; 2) the spectator looks . . . at—or on—the film; 3) each of the characters in the film looks . . . at other characters, things, the intradiegetic" (Heath, *Questions* 119). Like the heterosexual male spectator, the gay male will also identify with the camera at times (the position of mastery) and at others with a surrogate male character, whose look orders the spectacle within the film. Here, however, the parallels between the process of identification of the gay male spectator and the heterosexual end. The relay of looks proliferate for the gay male spectator in ways not imaginable in the standard account. The gay male spectator's options for identification among camera, profilmic gazing male, and object of the gaze are multiple and mobile.

In order to distinguish the gay male spectator from the hegemonically constructed heterosexual spectator, I return once more to the anaclitic/narcissistic opposition. Freud introduced the term "anaclisis" (*Anlehnung*) in the *Three*

Essays, to denote the relations between sexual drives and biologically necessary instincts, such as hunger. Although the sexual drives and desires are modeled on these instincts, they soon become independent of them (the pleasure derived from sucking becomes independent of the nourishment received from the mother's breast, for example). Anaclisis becomes somewhat more complicated than its genealogical use here when Freud distinguishes two types of love object, the anaclitic, which is other-directed, based on the child's original relationship with the mother (and therefore consonant with self-preservative instincts), and the narcissistic, which is based on the subject's relationship with him/herself (Freud, "On Narcissism" 90–94). In my adaptation of these terms, I would like to suggest that in the association with the earlier meaning of anaclisis above with heterosexual male object-choice, the self-preservative instincts are no longer merely the models for sexual drives, but a socially inscribed self-preservative impulse continues to be thematized within them. In Oedipalized, compulsory heterosexuality, therefore, anaclitic scopophilia would serve the heterosexual male film spectator in at least two ways: (1) the gazing on the body of a woman who cannot return the gaze installs a subject position as a form of mastery in its unidirectional epistemological privilege engendered as male; and (2) the focus upon the female figure as the embodiment of "lack" protects the male from his own castration anxieties (Silverman, *Subject* 223).

The perceived need for "self-preservation" in the face of sexual difference and the deployment of scopophilia as a defense against such a threat are both predicated upon the kind of male subjectivity produced within heteropatriarchy, and the power of scopophilic gazing to effect such a defense is dependent upon the mutual exclusivity of the scopophilic and identificatory drives in the male subject. For the gay male spectator, the on-screen object of scopophilic pleasure and identification are often the same. Even when they are different (in a voyeur scene, for example), the spectator's identification with the voyeuristic surrogate is qualified by that surrogate's also offering himself up as sexual spectacle—masturbating for the camera (Davenport in the *Big Guns* scene discussed above, for example). Furthermore, recalling that one of the other elements in my composite definition of the pornographic apparatus is its response to "an urgent need," the visible signs of gay sexuality confirm the gay male viewer by valorizing the forms his desire takes: scopophilic pleasure here is reinforced not by a mastery drive but by a political as well as erotic identification with his like on the screen. Hence, the narcissistic scopophilia here also underwrites an act of spectatorship that parallels the process by which narcissism establishes the ego itself.[61]

The sexual politics of identification specific to the gay male spectator derive in part from the discrepancies between the act of self-identification as gay and the external imposition on the gay male of a "homosexual" diagnosis, constituted as an object for negative identification in the society at large. Simon Watney reminds us that there are two modes of "identification" described in the psychoanalytic literature, "the transitive one of identifying the self in relation to the *difference* of the other, and the reflexive one of identifying the self in a relation of *resemblance* to the other" ("Spectacle" 78). Therefore, when the male body as a male-desired object and the incarnation of a male-desiring subject appears on the screen in *Law of Desire*, the processes of identification triggered in the viewers divide the audience radically, in a mutually reinforcing yet antagonistic manner: the heterosexual males identify transitively ("that's not me!"); the gay males identify reflexively. The (hegemonically conceived) heterosexual male would be further traumatized by the deliberate display of the male body as object of pleasure, which violates both the epistemological exclusionism that confirms male subjectivity, and the ideology Laura Mulvey discerns in the "active/passive heterosexual division of labor," which determines dominant narrative structures, because this ideology makes it impossible for "the male figure . . . to bear the burden of sexual objectification," thereby making "man . . . reluctant to gaze on his exhibitionist like" ("Visual Pleasure" 20).

Speaking of bodies, the somatic parameters of the desiring subject—and its capacities for pleasure—escalate the degrees of possible spectator-screen identification beyond anything conceivable within the confines of passive viewing. The tangibility of these degrees of identification is particularly clear with the example of male masturbation films—the genre the opening scene of *Law of Desire* quotes. Because many men in gay male movie theaters engage in sexual activity either singly or together, the coincidence of erotic affect between screen and spectator is infinitely more concrete than in conventional cinematic situations. Almodóvar's choice of a masturbation scene, rather than two gay men making love, ensures maximal identification between both screen/spectator pleasure and activity. Since the AIDS crisis particularly, there has been a marked increase in both solo male masturbation films and videos, and the limitation of sexual practices to masturbation within the audiences. Masturbation as a microsocial act, and one whose aim is both self-gratification and the sexual stimulation of others, makes autoeroticism intersubjective, and transfigures the masturbating man in the opening scene of *Law* into an embodiment of being-for-itself-for-others: a combination unforeseen in Sartre's phenomenology, and certainly one disallowed in Lacan's championing of Sartre's abstraction of "love" in Lacan's seminar on intersubjectivity and object relations.[62]

Almodóvar is not the only filmmaker who has adapted the gay pornographic apparatus for the representation of gay subjectivity and the construction of a gay male spectator. To suggest the variety of possible strategies and, more important, to clarify the larger implications of Almodóvar's practice, I will close this chapter with a brief look at the very different inscription of a gay male spectator in Derek Jarman's *Sebastiane* (1975), his meditation on the martyrdom of St. Sebastian. *Sebastiane* fully exploits the implicit homoeroti-

cism in the standard iconography of the martyr,[63] contextualizing it in the deca-
dence of Diocletian's Roman Empire. The sexual excess is foregrounded from
the opening scene of an orgiastic party (thoroughly researched by a Benedic-
tine historian [Jarman, *Dancing Ledge* 158]) to the all-male gladiator island
camp, to which Sebastiane is exiled. Almost every scene is replete with copious
and deliriously gratuitous male nudity, including one lovemaking scene between
two of the soldiers in a rock pool that the cast themselves considered crossing
the line into actual pornography (ibid. 150).

Within this highly sexual visual saturation, Sebastiane accepts torture and
finally death rather than submit to the advances of the gladiator captain in
charge of the men on the island camp. Jarman only nominally cites Christianity
as a motivation for Sebastiane's refusal. Sebastiane's rebuffs of the captain instigate punishment that in itself is pleasurable to Sebastiane—as preliminary
ecstases toward Apollo, just as the "martyrdom" is an exhibitionistic climax of
union with his annihilating desire. Sebastiane's rapture at his sufferings becomes increasingly more apparent with each scene of punishment, and after his
vision of Apollo, his monologues betray his sexual anticipation of union with
the sun god.

The deliberately eroticized spectacle of Sebastiane's ordeal (contextualized
in a maximally sexualized narrative and visual environment) restructures the
viewer-screen relationship within a sadomasochistic logic that implicates both
gay male spectatorship and Jarman's appropriation of history. Sebastiane's martyrdom clearly exemplifies what Theodor Reik characterizes as the "demonstra-
tive" aspect of "social masochism," which Silverman incisively specifies as
"Christian masochism" (Reik 312–14; Silverman, "Masochism" 43–46). The
martyr's exhibitionism coincides with the gay male's voluntary rendering of
himself as object of the desiring gaze, one of the gay male's chief transgressions
of male voyeuristic privilege. If, however, Sebastiane occupies the position of
masochist as the central spectacle, the filmmaker and, by identification with the
cinematic apparatus, the viewer are positioned as sadists.[64] The sadist position
in the specular register translates into the narrative register as a specific modality
of the subject's relation to history. Jarman's manipulation of the images and
legend of Sebastian rearticulates "sadism" as a restorative historical project—
energized by a sexual identity-in-process as it was in Wilde's narrator's quest
for Willie Hughes, Jarman's for Caravaggio, or Isaac Julien's for Langston
Hughes (*Looking for Langston*, 1989). To explain the relations between sadism
and historical intervention inscribed within the film's representational strategies, I turn first to Judith Butler's very suggestive essay on Freud's conception
of repetition and its relation to sadism, an essay that was instrumental in my
formulation of the argument I will advance presently.

Extrapolating the sexualized, repetitively self-preservative notions of sadism from Freud's *Beyond the Pleasure Principle*, Butler surveys Freud's defini-

tions of repetition, noting that his earlier conception of "repetition as mastery" entailed a "fantasized return to the past for purposes of repairing an injury there incurred" and "an effort to rewrite or reconstruct a history that remains painful in contemporary experience" (Butler, "Pleasures" 264). Certainly the history of Christianity is a painful one for gay men, as Jarman's later film *The Garden* (1990) clearly demonstrates. Neither that film nor *Sebastiane* is utopian, or even literally attempting to find "gay people in history." Rather, these films, as well as *Edward II* (1992), address the contemporary political and social situations of gay men, using these figures as dialogic foci and the deliberate ahistoricity of their presentation as a gesture of defiant expropriation.[65] Jarman sees the received versions of the past as part of the legacy of hatred and sexual anxiety responsible for the murderous homophobia of the present. His reclamations of these historical texts and images are expressions of his "sadism"—if we can understand sadism as "a repetition of an urge to self-preservation, of a primary encounter with an external world as an endangering . . . field of objects" (Butler, "Pleasures" 263). That his films are also erotically as well as politically gratifying to the gay male viewer "is a sign of [this sadism's] admixture of sexual instincts and also underscores the pleasurable experience of gaining mastery over a situation in which one originally felt oneself to be the victim" (ibid.).[66] *Sebastiane* engages two conflicting senses of time: the historiographical and the psychoanalytic, the former which sees the past as separate from the present, and the latter which sees the past as coexistent with the present (de Certeau 2–5). Jarman achieves this ditemporality through his sadistic "contemporary victory over the past" (Butler, "Pleasures" 263). Within this sadistic dynamic, the scopophilic pleasures focalized in Sebastiane's intentional spectacle (and metonymically the desirous identification with the historical personae Jarman's films elicit) are elevated to a revenge against "History."

But the visual pleasures for the gay male viewer of Sebastiane's martyrdom are specifically overdetermined. The sadist enjoys the pain inflicted on the object "masochistically . . . through his identification of himself with the suffering object . . . it is not the pain itself which is enjoyed, but the accompanying sexual excitation" (Freud, "Instincts" 129). The identificatory logic of the sadist's pleasure combines with the narcissistic interfusion of desire and identification in gay male spectatorial subjectivity to produce a doubled erotic identification that allows the gay male viewer to identify with the subject of enunciation (the cinematic apparatus—the sadistic position as sexualized revenge against history) and the subject of the utterance (the figure of Sebastiane on screen) in a way that does not result in the spectator becoming, in Silverman's terminology, the "spoken subject" of the film—that stabilized social position the cinematic experience is meant to effect through the suturing of the viewer (Silverman, *Subject* 198–99).

While very different in dynamics and affect, the transmutation of suture into doubled erotic identifications Jarman achieves in *Sebastiane* resonates with the various deflections and defigurations of suturing operations we observed in the pornographic films above. These instances indicate that at its most radical, the gay pornographic apparatus and the texts that draw from its representational conventions differ from the Althusserian apparatus primarily because the narcissistic identifications solicited by the gay pornographic apparatus are neither stabilizing nor reassuring but resistant and deviant. These narcissistic identifications interrupt the interpellative process rather than foster it.[67]

Considering the identifications inscribed in *Sebastiane* illuminates certain aspects of the differences between the anaclitic and narcissistic spectators of the first scene of *Law of Desire*. The gay viewer's dual identification with the camera and the young man in the first scene concretizes both sexual satisfaction and the means through which it is attained, as a vital part of gay male subjectivity. In other words, sexual drives are at least ego-syntonic (if not constitutive of the ego) in the political imaginary of the gay male spectator. Outside of the porno theater, Almodóvar's film confirms the ego drives and sexual drives and desire and identification as mutually reinforcing constituents of the gay male spectator overtly against the horizon of the dominant male spectator for whom these pairs are mutually exclusive binary oppositions. Such a confirmation outside of the porno theater highlights the sexual difference of the gay male spectator not only as a psychosexual subject, but also as a political agency.

In introducing gay sexuality and the perceptual and epistemological positions it informs into the usually anodyne social practice of commercial cinema spectatorship, Almodóvar and Jarman enable the process of gay male subjectivity and its articulations to take on the legitimizing ethos of an identity politics that does not abandon the anarchic and excessive energies of its transgressive pleasures.

5

Scandalous Narratives

A T THE TURN of the century, when the word "homosexual" was coined, even personal recognition of homosexual desire placed the individual outside of social networks, rendering the subject an internal exile within the realization of his/her secret.[1] E. M. Forster's Maurice represents a man who became aware of his "difference" in a time when its disclosure would mean ostracism and imprisonment. "By pleasuring the body Maurice had confirmed . . . his spirit in its perversion, and cut himself off from the congregation of normal man" (*Maurice* 214). The enforced secrecy at this time (Forster himself permitted his novel to be published only posthumously, nearly sixty years after its initial composition) does not allow Maurice's discovery of his difference from "normal man" to foster an alternative social subject. The transgressions of taboos are disseminated and adjudicated through the structures of "scandal" which serves to punish the transgressors and consolidate the nontransgressive community as a "we." The Oscar Wilde trial was only the most infamous in a series of terroristic scandals in Britain which served these regulatory functions, examples of Victor Turner's "social dramas" which bring to communal attention "certain contested aspects of social behavior and through the conflict allow individuals 'to take sides in terms of deeply entrenched moral imperatives and constraints, often against their own personal preferences' " (Ed Cohen, "Legislating" 192). In the social imaginary of Wilde's, Symonds's, and Forster's Britain, "the homosexual" was an abstract medico-legal category; homosexuality was represented in the social symbolic in narratives of "gossip" or newspaper articles whose lacunae were the zero-morphs of the "unspeakable crime" they named in their failure to name, they signified in their refusal to signify.

Scandal was a social narrative (or a threatened social narrative) that served as a repressive prophylactic discursive potential in its supression of homosexuality, subtending the dominant heterosexual solidarity effected through the transitive identification with homosexuality as a "not us" in Simon Watney's analysis of the homophobic deployment of the "homosexual body."[2] In post-Stonewall cultural activism, we find another possibility of a communal force in the identification of the subjects with the scandal itself. Gay male narrative, in its localization of a specific range of male experience and its appeal to its own community, operates within and against the social logic of scandal, deriving the possibilities of countercultural identifications from a dialectical embrace of those specters conjured and sublimed in these institutions of heterosexual aversion. Robert Glück writes of his interest in "scandal's defining of boundaries . . . what is inside and what is outside" as "one way a community organizes itself, tells itself its story about what is forbidden and expected." Glück's expropriation of scandal as a mode of expression instead of a means of suppression allows him to contest the "community tenet that homosexuality does not exist verbally" (Glück, *Elements* 15). Similar strategic rearticulations of "scandal" are discernible in the work of virtually all the writers associated with "New Narrative," writers "loosely united behind our distrust of established mechanisms of narrative fiction" (Cooper, "Sex Writing").[3]

The "New Narrative" developed from the San Francisco–based writers' workshops Robert Glück conducted through Small Press Traffic in the late 1970s and early 1980s. The writers most closely identified with "New Narrative" are Glück, Bruce Boone, Dodie Bellamy, Kevin Killian, Dennis Cooper, Camille Roy, Sam D'Allesandro, and Michael Amnasan, not all of whom are gay, and many of whom came to writing with established relations to either poetry or the visual arts. Bruce Boone coined the term "New Narrative," while he and Glück initially formulated the principles that could describe the intellectual and creative tendencies evolving within Glück's workshops. Their theorizing was framed by two major considerations: the effects of the writers' nonnarrative artistic practices on their narrative form, and a response to the L=A=N=G=U=A=G=E poets, the most influential school of writers in San Francisco at that time. Boone and Glück shared the L=A=N=G=U=A=G=E poets' suspicion of the master narratives of the dominant society, but instead of "deconstructing" stories into their linguistic components, they wanted to recontextualize storytelling in terms of its countercultural potential.[4]

Like Samuel R. Delany, the New Narrative writers are interested in the dynamic tension between the two columns of social life and desire that constitutes the subject (Delany, *Motion* 29–31, 60–71 and passim; "Column"). The subject in New Narrative writing is a psychosomatic materiality that is historically realized but not reified, a multiply articulated and articulate intertext whose own signifying practices shift the terms of its identities. New Narrative strategies often traverse and trespass the psychical and generic boundaries of cultural pleasure and bliss. It is in these unauthorized territorial divides that the New Narrative writers typically inscribe their scandalous subjectivities. Glück and Killian, for example, frequently model texts on the peculiarities of pornographic film and photography to structure the transgressive interplay of the real and the fictional, extradiegetic and intradiegetic, and the specular and the narrative.

It may be that the pornographic apparatus in actual practice and in metaphoric or literal appropriations into other cultural forms (such as narrative) constitutes the most intimate and adaptable means for the representation and exposition of the peculiarly photogenic trajectories of desire and identification in gay male sexual subjectivity. In his short story "Workload," Robert Glück demonstrates the value of the pornographic apparatus as a structuring device for gay male subject processes. This is a first-person account of masturbating while looking at a photonovella about "three horny clerks," Larry, J. T., and Sean. At first Sean merely looks on as Larry fucks J. T. This situation models the intradiegetic reader-text relation on traditional film spectatorship structures. The narrator identifies with Sean as surrogate voyeur, whose "tilted gaze" he compares to "a peephole in a pillow book" (253). The narrator's erotic attention is directed to J. T., the object of Sean's look and Larry's penetration. When Sean joins in, the scene loses its interior distance, and the narrator's attraction to J. T. merges with a steadily increasing identification with him.

> It's J. T.'s excitement and I need to borrow as much of it as I can. I need to witness his excitement and I need to be him, the one whose excitement is witnessed. His image provides access to both sides of the sexual proposition. The lack of that circuitry is masturbation's drawback; jacking off resolves tension but it exacerbates the imagination's need to witness and be witnessed. The only recourse is to trick myself into believing my body is an object by dramatizing masturbation, with mirrors, with contraptions say, to provide the effect of a keyhole or proscenium arch, a window, so to speak, a photo, in other words. (254)

The narrator's shift in identification from Sean to J. T. does not indicate a conscious rejection of the "mastery" the voyeuristic position of his identification with Sean had afforded him, because within the intersubjectively narcissistic functions of the vicissitudes of the scopophilic drives, voyeurism does not retain the heteroaggressive/defensive meanings it holds for the anaclitic subject.[5] In fact, the advantages of the latter identifications made explicit in the above-quoted passage indicate some of the reasons for the different psychical and political inflections of voyeurism in this context. The narrator (a narcissistic exhibitionist) uses J. T. as part of his fantasy operations of a self-specularization anathema to anaclitic subjects exemplified by Sartre's peeping tom. The image of J. T. provides a focal point in the narrator's phantasmatic positioning of himself within the visual technology of the intentional spectacle—"mirrors" and "contraptions" that restage the narrating subject in an internalized "keyhole or proscenium arch," a "window" or "a photo." The specular modes of representation provide the circuitry for the narrator's fantasy neccessary to confirm his own position as (sexually objectifiable) sexual subject.[6]

The identification with J. T. intensifies as the narrator imagines J. T.'s feelings looking at the very photonovella in which he appears. Instead of identifying with the "profilmic" surrogate voyeur, the narrator reimagines his profilmic object of desire (J. T.) as that object's extrafilmic self, who becomes a fellow spectator of his own objected image. The narrator therefore identifies with a J. T. that exists within the exhibitionist's fantasy of "seeing oneself seeing oneself" (pace Lacan). The narrator "watches" J. T. assess the photos of his own ass. "He sees his ass and mentally nods in recognition as though a secret has been divulged. . . . A reality based on glamour and distance impresses him, he's excited by the photo and this is erotic for me; he wants to be alone with it to scrutinize and love as he loves something nameless inside himself" (255).[7] One of the phrases embedded in the last sentence reveals intrications and interanimations of desire and identifications that are quintessential to a gay male sexual subject: "*he's excited* by the photo [*of himself*] and this is erotic *for me*." The narrator imagines the object of his desire sexually aroused by an image of himself, and his sexual excitement (and its cause) is erotic for the narrator.

In "Sex Story," Glück interrupts his initial narrative of a sexual experience with his ex-lover Brian with a section of a porn novel, *Fresh from the Farm*, by Billy Farout. While in "Workload" Glück uses the apparatus of visual pornography to articulate intrapsychic processes of the sexual subject, in "Sex Story" he uses porn pulp fiction as a means to relate his subject position as writer to the larger social contexts and to the emergent community he represents. Through pornographic representational traditions, Glück expresses a subject resistant to the abstraction of "universalism" imposed by modernist reading protocols. Of course, in embracing his particularity, Glück also seeks to avoid a reified subject position of the psychologically unique individual, the fully interior "I." He therefore needs a representational mode that can bracket or quote recognizable types without faithfully reproducing them. Both satire and caricature serve these purposes, but "are often used more effectively by conservatives who believe in their community . . . than by those of us who want to change society structurally, people who were not located in an expressive community until very recently" (Glück, "Caricature" 19). Pornography is particularly suited for this, both because of its historical centrality to "our" community and because of its similarity, noted by Dennis Cooper, to contemporary art, in the tendency of pornography to forgo "the traditional notion of subject, relying instead on a display of purely aesthetic components" (Cooper, "Square One" 82).

Pornography therefore represses the psychological depth models Glück also means to avoid.

> In its social typology, pornography shows character systems in a pure form. The characters have little or no psychology, they act as a function of the plot. . . . Yet pornography is transgressive. It sets up these character systems in order to tear them down. . . . Types go hand in hand with narrative. Even the mention of a type, the cowboy, the detective, the travelling salesman . . . carries

with it a narrative. . . . Narrative pleasure derives from the accuracy and imaginative use of given material, like the medieval concept of *matière*. Only in this case, the *matière* will be the lives of members of the community, the life of the community itself. . . . In this light we can see the personal histories and journals of movement writers as extensions of this idea of type, where the writer offers him/herself as an example of the community, at the same time retaining a separate individuality. From my point of view, this is the happiest solution to the over-psychologized I. ("Caricature" 20–21)

Kevin Killian's texts, generally speaking, bear a more elliptical relation to traditional pornographic genres than Glück's or Cooper's, in that he rarely "quotes" from actual porn texts or films. His texts do, however, contain the same degree of explicit sexual material, but usually in more idiosyncratic contexts than provided by the scripting structures porn represents. Nevertheless, Killian is concerned with the way popular media contour and confirm subjectivity, and in that he shares a postmodernity with Glück and Cooper, but his personae are more liable to understand their selves via David Bowie or Hayley Mills than Jeff Hunter or Billy Farout. Even so, Killian is a principal example of the adaptation of "porn character systems," and some of what Glück writes about porn is readily applicable to Killian's work: "The brilliance of this writing lies in its juggling of systems. . . . This kind of pastiche generates a great energy. But all these systems have quotation marks around them embracing and disclaiming at the same time" (ibid. 24).

The localization of male bodies and specifications of desires in New Narrative writings also reflect affinities with the antitheological severance of the penis from the phallus in gay male porn films. As I have written elsewhere, pornography can aid in "disengag[ing] gay male sexuality from the phallocentrism of dominant culture by clearly differentiating the *political and social over-estimation* of the penis-as-phallus in heterosexual phallocracies, from the *erotic investment* in the penis among gay men," in that "gay male porn demystifies the penis by situating it within the supersaturation of its communal visibility" and its outrageous availability. The porn film makes public record of the "real scandal" of gay male sexuality: "the playful use of the penis among men resolves the contradictions within phallocentric logic that must remain unresolved for the myth of phallic primacy to remain operative. In other words, if penises become 'toys for boys' they are thus at once affirmed (and delimited) within lived experience and jettisoned from the transcendence of the ever non-present phallus" (Jackson, "Explicit" 147). In less utopian (and more sophisticated) engagements with the contradictions of gay male sexuality within phallocentric ideology and its aftermaths, Dennis Cooper and Robert Glück use—in very different ways—visual pornography to explore how melancholia generates desire and conditions both private and public fantasies.

Gay male narrative, then, can be a practice through which the gay male subject actively (even if only implicitly) disengages his sexuality from the phallocratic libidinal economy; in other words, the gay male narrator can write from an embodied subject position, whose relation to male bodies affirms the male body as one of two possible sexual morphologies, and whose desiring relation to other male bodies does not ineluctably provide an avenue through which the penis becomes theologized as phallus.[8] Such a narrator at once relinquishes the transcendence of the phallus and the unmarked position of absolute truth, through the ongoing acknowledgment of the specificity of his body, his desire, and their epistemological consequences and possibilities.

Death Drives across Pornotopia: Dennis Cooper on the Extremities of Being

You go not till I set you up a glass
Where you may see the inmost part of you.

—*Hamlet* 3.5.19–20

Perhaps our true sexual act consists in this:
in verifying to the point of giddiness
the useless objectivity of things.

—Jean Baudrillard

Like Jean Genet and William S. Burroughs before him, Dennis Cooper writes consistently within predominantly male homosexual contexts, but his subject is rarely "homosexuality" per se. Moreover, the sexual practices thematized in Cooper's work are not part of an identity politics, but are rather subordinated to an investigation into the interior of the body, a movement of objectification and obsessive violation of the body's contours, a peering inside the costume of the person to his real location. Of the generally accepted erotogenic zones, the penis receives far less attention than the anus and the mouth: orifices, ruptures between the surface of "personality" and the murky labyrinths within, apertures into the more tenebrous realities of the organism.

Cooper's concerns, however, are decidedly inflected and nuanced by the sexual orientation of his male characters. The violence in his writings can be articulated "as a kind of studying the self" without participating in or extending the history of male violence against women that complicates similar themes in heterosexual literature and film (Meyer 64). Furthermore, the AIDS epidemic is often a nonexplicit horizon of Cooper's writing—a terrible historical accident that imposes an unanticipated literalness upon the risks to the body and the self that sex constitutes in much of his work.⁹ As he writes in "Dear Secret Diary": "When I'm fucking someone and he accidentally falls off the bed I like to pretend he's about to be shot for trying to defect. Or I did before AIDS ruined death" (5). The present essay is an attempt at a critical account of Cooper's meditations on sexuality and death in his major works, and how their dynamics not only delimit but also inform human experience.

The Melancholia of Desire: "Square One" and "A Herd"

Cooper's early work celebrates the boys who were the targets of his youthful sexual obsessions (*Tiger Beat, Idols*). From *Tenderness of the Wolves* on, however, there is a shift to an exploration of the vagaries of desire itself—its nature and its location in and among the bodies of both its subject and its objects. Cooper's meditations on the enigma of desire are perhaps most densely encapsulated in "Square One," a highly personal essay on pornographic film as both a rehearsal of that mystery and a clue to its intractable solution. Here Cooper demonstrates how fantasy and memory condition sexual experience and give reality its lie. "Square One" has three foci: Jeff Hunter, "star of half a dozen videos and films . . . [whose] physical makeup fits my master plan for the 'ideal sex partner,' a guy I've refined from my 15 or more years of fucking and fantasizing" (83); George M., a "long-lost friend and Jeff lookalike . . . the most focused part of what I'd fashioned into a sex life in '71" (85); and "Ron, Rod, or Rob," someone Cooper "had sex with in a dark hall behind the screen" (89).¹⁰

Cooper retraces the history of his interest in Jeff Hunter from his first viewing of *Pacific Coast Highway* to finding Jeff accidentally several years later, burned out and being fistfucked in a porno magazine. In reflecting on his attraction to Jeff, Cooper realizes that it stems from Jeff's resemblance to Cooper's "long-lost friend," George. At the point of this recognition, the narrative scene alternates between a porn theater where a Jeff Hunter film is playing and memories of seducing George as a teenager. Cooper attempts to extricate memory from fantasy through a real sexual encounter in the theater:

> I just had sex in a dark hall behind the screen. I stretched out on a filthy mattress with someone named Ron, Rod, or Rob. . . . I don't know who I expected to fuck but it wasn't a poorly lit man whose name I couldn't catch. . . .
> I felt like saying, "You're sweet," but it didn't suit the occasion. So I said, "Bye, Ro-," muffling the last consonant to be safe.
> When I was with Ro- I thought of someone else. First Jeff reared his jaded head. I grabbed Ro's ears, shoved my cock up his ass until George's face came up for breath. ("Square One" 89–90)

"Real sex" seems to obfuscate the mechanisms of desire more than it illuminates them. In fact, the real experience on "the filthy mattress" gained its significance parasitically from the fantasy and the memories that circumscribed it. The relation between Jeff and George is clearer, but no more consoling:

> They're distinct. George is the beauty. Jeff's the statue erected of him in a
> public place, so he'll remain aloft. . . . Jeff's just the shadow that falls across
> us when we're at certain points in our lives. By now we know what we've
> missed and become depressed. I'm a man brushing tears, imaginary or not,
> from my face. (86)

The despair comes from a network of intersecting dead ends: a fantasy/film image that is unfathomable because it has no depth; a memory whose essence is the sense of loss it shapes; and a genital event that can neither correspond to the power nor fulfill the promise of either of the former.

The alternation in the narrative between the Jeff Hunter film and the memories of George figures the vacillation in the modalities of the narrator's desire between mourning and melancholia, with a decided emphasis on the latter. George is the object of Cooper's mourning, Jeff of his melancholia. Mourning is the process of reconciling oneself to the loss (usually the death) of a loved one (Freud, "Mourning" 243–44). Melancholia may be triggered by a similar loss, but often with more tenuous relations to external circumstances. Often the loved one "has not actually died, but has been lost as an object of love," as when one is "jilted" (ibid. 244). Cooper's relation to Jeff maintains the logic of melancholia, but reverses its symptom: rather than the object not really being absent, here the object is not really present. Introducing Jeff into his fantasies creates an attainment that is a form of loss, which at once ameliorates and reiterates the real loss of George.

Melancholia can also arise when the subject is not conscious of whom he/she has lost, or when the subject knows whose loss he/she is mourning but cannot understand what it is in that person that the subject has lost by losing that person (ibid. 243–44). Much of this applies to Cooper's object relations to both Jeff and George, even when George was present. In fact, the conditioning factors of melancholia describe some of the pervasive features of desire as Cooper elaborates them throughout his works. What Cooper lost in George is that which one needs from the object of desire, but Cooper characterizes his sexual relationship with George with the same melancholic inability to ascertain what that is and for what loss its attainment will compensate. The porn image as object of desire in Cooper's psychosexual system is not merely compensatory but paradigmatic. The on-screen vision of Jeff Hunter does not merely refigure the memory of George but perfects George's absence. Pierre Buisson, the French porn star (of *All of Me*, discussed in the previous chapter), incorporated as a character in Cooper's novel *Frisk*, reflects on the mysterious qualities of sexual motivations from the perspective of the "object" of melancholic desire: "The way men deal with me is like I'm a kind of costume that someone else, someone they've known or made up, is wearing" (67). Recalling a client who had been sexually enthralled with him, Pierre said his lovemaking was "like if I was where someone had buried some sort of treasure or antidote to something malignant in him" (87).

The riddle that is incessantly posed to the desiring subject is the nature of the attraction, and the relation of the body desired to the person desired, a riddle whose frustration is most dramatically expressed in "Square One" when Cooper admits, "It was [George] I imagined my cock entering each night, not just his flimsy ass, though that's the first thing I opened when I got the chance" (85). The plots and themes in Cooper's texts often involve the same operative paradox: the persistence of obsessive metaphysical gestures within a radically demystified world, gestures expressing a longing for that X which seems to inhere within a human object of desire that is nevertheless not coextensive with the physical body in which that desire is given shape and through which the desire is brought under control. A desire to know that X, that essence of the person, is overliteralized in acts of mutilation and murder. As Cooper continues to learn nothing of his own desire in reviewing memories of sex with George, he muses, "If I'd sliced into George I'd have been covered with blood at least. There'd be evidence, if no answer" (ibid. 88).

Cooper's earliest sustained prose exploration of the relations among sexual desire, the transcendence of beauty, and horror is the story "A Herd," which chronicles several weeks in the life of Ray Sexton, a serial killer of teenage boys. Sexton begins his ritual as a voyeur, the images of the boys framed in their bedroom windows analogous to the movie screen in porno theaters:

> When a boy was undressing in his room . . . he was relaxed. And if he was watched through a window, cut in three parts by the partly closed shades, by a viewer who had nothing gentle or worthy to do, it was very much like that boy was performing a striptease. . . . Everything was seen and judged from the window. . . .
> The man outside mulled an aesthetic to fit the occasion and fashioned rewards from these limits. ("A Herd" 53)

The visions of boys seen through the windows are an accidental and intermediate instantiation of those commodified images of desire that porn perpetuates, as do other, more pervasive media, such as the fanzines of teen idols who configure Sexton's obsessions: "[Teen magazine] stars were Ray's angels, freed from the limits of IQs and coordination, whose distant looks had a cloudy, quaalude effect." Sexton transforms the compromise "aesthetic" of voyeuristic/consumer passivity into an active and destructively creative one through the slaughter of the boys he desires. The "star" quality that originally attracted him to his victims appears sporadically in their faces during the ordeals he inflicts: "An idol's look would appear. . . . Then what Ray had done took on meaning" (56).

Sexton's practices suggest a kind of dark Platonism, a search for absolute beauty by destroying the individual accidents of its corporealizations. Diotima rhetorically asks Socrates a question to which Sexton provides a horrifying answer: "How would it be . . . if someone could see the Beautiful itself, pure, clear, unmixed—not infected with human flesh and color, and a lot of other mortal nonsense—if he were able to know the divinely Beautiful itself, in its unique form?" (*Symposium* 211E). Whatever and wherever a boy is once Sexton is finished with him, he is not "the thing on the table." Diotima's prescribed ascent to the Beautiful requires serial experiences of the physical beauty of boys, leading to increasing generalization and abstraction. Sexton liberated the ideal from the boys' bodies, and kept it within him, checking his memory of each victim with the newspaper photographs after the bodies had been found: "Ray looked at the face of a boy in the newspaper. The young man had put his lips close to a camera and pouted. The camera had focused, flashed. The face had slid through a hole in its side, unfogging slowly" (73).

The essence of a person becomes something which radiates from the body, as a numinous simulacrum of the face that had held it captive. This version of the ideal gives it a shape intelligible to its worshippers, transforming the boys at times into idols who look down from incomprehensible distances—at once fully accessible and absolutely unattainable (like Jeff Hunter's image on the movie screen). This is also the principle of Cooper's volume of poetry *Idols*, panegyrics to boys in high school he loved or longed for, and to teenybopper heartthrobs of the 1970s. In the prose poem "Teen Idols" Cooper reflects on the pop-culture processes of mass-market image cathexis:

> Teen idols are the best boys on the block. . . . Always romantic, they sign their photos "I think of you and you're beautiful" and then "love always" and then their first names. They know how to please us, to keep us hanging on. (*Idols 58*)

Note the similarity of this description to Sexton's of a boy called Jay: "Ray wished he could hand this boy his photo to autograph. The boy would write, 'loved you, kissed me, I'm yours . . . let's fade away' then his first name" ("Herd" 73). Sexton made Jay a celebrity, an "idol," by negating his existence, reducing it to the fleeting fame of a news photo—a photo of "someone who didn't exist." Sexton's action is complemented by Craig in the title story of Cooper's collection *He Cried*, who made enlargements of the news photos of a serial killer's victims: "He tacks it next to the others, across his bedroom wall. Ten corpses stare through the grain like hallucinations he used to worry he'd never come down from" (*He Cried* 30).

If Sexton represents a homicidal extension of the idealism of the *Symposium*, the porn theater in "Square One" is a site for a psychoanalytic inversion of the epistemology of the *Republic*. In Book VII, Socrates likens the unenlightened to people chained in a cave, forced to look only forward at the wall. Behind them is a flame, and between the flame and the prisoners, people walk continually, holding up puppets and images of animals and other objects. The only knowledge of objects those restrained have is of the shadows of the puppets projected onto the wall of the cave; such "knowledge"—*eikasia*, the acceptance of images as reality—is the only option for these unhappy prisoners (514 a-c). The men in Cooper's porno theater have consciously induced a state of *eikasia* in themselves.[11]

In Plato's allegory, there are at least two more levels of reality beyond that of the shadow play. The unshackled prisoner could turn from the shadow of the bull image on the wall to see the real bull image casting the shadow. The freed prisoner could be led out of the cave to see a real bull. No parallel options exist for Cooper's moviegoers. If the need for the real incited a revolution in the porn audience, the Platonic paradigm could not provide a basis for any reasonable or satisfactory action (in fact, all actions arising from such a need would destroy the possibility of the type of satisfaction obtained by viewing the film): "The screen hangs between paying customers and our ideal lovers. If we charged, ripped it down, we'd find a wall of unsupported brick" ("Square One" 88).

Cooper's theater does not possess the escape exits of Plato's cave, because its patrons retain the pessimism and frustration caused by idealism, but have discarded the faith in any metaphysical system that would support the epistemological teleology of Plato's allegory. The transition from shadow, to icon, to real object parallels the transition Socrates urges us to make when he condemns art in *Republic* X: from an artificial representation (a painting of a bed) to a tangible object (an actual bed) to the intelligible object (the Form of 'bed'). The images on the movie screen hold no guarantee of an accession to higher forms of objects of which they are emanations. The ontological saturation of the film image itself is an ontology by default, due to a technology that can only reproduce a reality that no longer exists by the time of its re-presentation.

Unlike Plato's cave dwellers, the porno spectators actually know the difference between image and reality, but have consciously repudiated this knowledge, in order to maintain a fantasy that feeds their desire. In fact, the men in the audience suspend their disbelief precisely because *they know that the referent of the image does not exist*. The suspension of disbelief in film spectatorship is often compared with the "split belief" of the subject's defensive disavowal of castration.[12] But this contradictory belief can also reflect aberrations in the mourning process. When the subject's resistance to the reality of the object's loss is particularly great, the subject may reject "reality" and retain the object

in a "hallucinatory wishful psychosis" (Freud, "Mourning" 244–45). Hallucination nullifies the distinction between a presentation in consciousness and a
perception (*Interpretation of Dreams* 5: 565–66); such states appear to be regres-
sions to an earlier phase in which the child imagined objects of satisfaction not
really present (ibid. 544–46), a habit gradually overcome by the adaptation to
"reality testing" ("Formulations" 219–21). Hallucinations are not actually
brought about by a regression, but rather by the ego's withdrawal of cathexis
in external reality ("A Metapsychological Supplement" 231). Dreams represent
a nonpathological form of this renunciation (232); film viewing is a culturally
sanctioned and controlled version of this deliberate withdrawal from reality
testing. The realism of a film concretely produces an analogous experience to
the identification of ideation and perception.

   If the structural dynamic of spectatorial belief resembles a refusal to complete the work of mourning, the spectator's cathexis in the screen image enacts
melancholia in its epistemological and ontological contradictions. Claiming
possession of the desired object through its image is also acknowledging the
impossibility of that possession. The image is object-as-nonexistence. The spectacle of the porn image is no longer a subject but a memorial to the abnegation
of subjectivity (the *subject's* deliberate becoming-object of the gaze); but it is
also a sign of that *object's* absence as well. Guy Debord writes that "the spectacle
is *affirmation* of appearance and affirmation of all human life . . . as mere appearance. But the critique which reaches the truth of the spectacle exposes it
as the visible *negation* of life, as a negation of life which *has become visible*" (10).
Cooper's texts are one such critique of the "truth of the spectacle." In exposing
that spectacle as the "visible negation of life," Cooper also lays the groundwork
for reconceiving representation as a concrete cultural elaboration of the death
drive. In his increasingly psychomythic narratives in which his characters embody and enact this representational tragedy, Cooper delineates the death drive
as a force whose symbolization "allows for an intuition of the unconscious,
even though it is already at the level of discursive thought: a theoretical exi-
gency, the refracted derivative of desire" (Laplanche, *Life and Death* 109).

   The inevitable temporal and spatial disjunction between the scene of filming and the scene of projection gives any film a potentially elegiac aura: even
in mainstream cinema, the film often shows stars no longer young or long dead,
times and places no longer possible to experience as they are depicted. The
mortality of the depicted real that the film image both denies and demonstrates
is magnified to its most nightmarish extreme in gay male porn. Since the onset
of the AIDS pandemic, there is a macabre likelihood that a significant number
of the cast members of any gay porno film are dead. The porn actor, who, like
any film actor, gives himself up to the camera, allowing the cinematic apparatus
to produce an image of him that will bracket (and thus negate) his biosocial
individual particularity, may also be participating in his actual (extrafilmic)

obliteration. The acts engaged in in the films also suggest the actual occasion of the infection: porn videos made since 1980 that feature unprotected anal sex may be delayed-reaction snuff films. Therefore, the general paradoxes of the cinematic situation (the viewer's deliberate ascription of reality to flickering images; the cognitively full representation of a nonpresent world) become intensely imbued with death in the gay male porn that Cooper discusses. The films hybridize the qualities of the pop star posters, in the glamorization of male beauty, and the news photos of the murdered boys in "A Herd" and "He Cried," in the funereal quality of these images. In both cases physical attractiveness is an indirect cause of death. (*Eidolon*, from which "idol" is derived, means both a representation of a god and a phantom of a dead person.)

The other major form of disavowal operative within the split belief of film spectatorship is the fetish. Because Cooper writes outside of heterosexual presumption, he returns "fetish" to a pre-Freudian meaning, independent of the castration complex and male fears of sexual difference. Instead the fixation on representation in lieu of referent becomes akin to a more traditional religious meaning of fetish: "An inanimate object worshipped by savages on account of its supposed inherent magical powers, or as being animated by a spirit. A fetish differs from an *idol* in that it is worshipped in its own character, not as the image, symbol, or occasional residence of a deity" (*OED*; see also Pietz).

Cooper's search for an absolute that would at least *justify* the vehemence of human need (most viscerally expressed in sexuality), if not *satisfy* it, recalls earlier attempts to rediscover the numinous in the phenomenal, as a response to a loss of faith. In his concentration on the physical beauty of men, Cooper betrays a nostalgia for certain patterns of Western transcendence. Equating in *Safe* the "truth" of Mark's body to a skeleton is a virtually medieval gesture both in its iconography and in its repudiation of the flesh. In "Teen Idols" he posits the teen stars as entities "behind" their photos. In "Square One" Cooper ventures behind the screen to have "real" sex with Ro-. Reality is behind the veil, but it is a disconsolate discovery, and one that leaves the ineffability of the screen images intact. It is interesting too that instead of following Plato's cavemen out into the sun, Cooper goes further into the theater, to find that the "real" is banal, and tolerable only when punctuated and screened over by the images of irrecoverably lost objects.

Although in this scenario the belief in the reality of images seems to borrow its pathos from the traces of idealism in a postidealist world, the involvement with nonreal figures acquires additional meaning from a psychoanalytic discovery not to be found in premodern thought: Freudian "psychical reality," the legitimation of unconscious fantasy, and hence phantasmatic representations (Laplanche and Pontalis, "Fantasy" 8–9). The psychical realities (unconscious wishes) that find shape most vividly in dreams allow the embodiments of the fantasies (porn stars, strippers, hustlers, movie stars, and rock musicians) to be replaced as primary objects by the visual records of their allure: these are fantasies whose gratification no longer presupposes even potential physical contact with the bioenergetic entities the icons memorialize: "There are magazines to present them endlessly, in love and lonely. . . . The boys lounge suggestively each moment of their lives. Pictures prove that. In some ways these photos are the idols, not the boys behind them" (*Idols* 58).

Visual images become an end in themselves, because of the recognized unattainability of the stars who had posed for them, and because of the perfection possible within these representations that life cannot offer.[13] While pornography aids in concretizing and confirming fantasies through its maximalization of the visible, it is also predicated upon the impossibility of the "total fulfillment" it depicts. Furthermore, the transparency of pornography to its object exposes the secrets of the body, but not the mysteries of the body's fascination for the viewer. Desired bodies can be documented, but what makes those bodies desirable cannot be so easily accounted for. The frustration involved in desire arises from the contradictory ontological status that physical beauty is assigned. Beauty is both immediately accessible and ultimately indefinable, at once apodeictic and arcane. Beauty and sexual allure take on transcendent roles within the pornographic film, at once manifest as the visible surfaces of the bodies, but also functioning to hypostatize the significance of those bodies beyond the very physical limitations that the film insistently exposes:

> Beauty . . . [is] the deity panning for gold in these wasted stars' used up bodies. It creates dreams out of people the cat wouldn't drag in, aiming our cocks at, averting our minds from "the ditch of what each one means," as Bob Dylan whined. . . . ("Square One" 92)[14]

Although the director, as high priest of the fetish religion, controls the basic structure and sequence of the images in the film, there is something inherent in the body, those images depict something before which the director "is as powerless as the trained dog running alongside a herd of cattle, each of whom could crush him with a misstep. He is merely the right man at the right place, right time" ("Square One" [*Soup*] 71). The reality of the porn film ("they're *really* doing it") is still a delayed, posthumous, one—those "real people" "really doing" it are no longer there: in fact, they perform in a nonexistent space, one Cooper finds essentially morbid: "I have faith that the man who composed [the scene] has managed an accurate portrait of what it would be like to stand in a place far beyond mine, one I compare to death" (ibid. 72). But the plane in which fantasy and reality, desire and satisfaction coincide is limited to the movie screen, and has no correlate in "real life"; there can be no change of venue, and all attempts to construct a materialist compromise, a spatialization of the ideal, result in a despondent parody (the hall behind the porno screen in "Square

One"), in paralyzing hallucinatory refuges (George's Disneyland in *Closer*), in psychotic parodies of childhood whimsy (Gary's playroom in *Frisk*), or in sheer life-denying chambers of horror (Ray's crawl space in "Herd").

Robert Glück has called Dennis Cooper a "religious writer" who, "like Poe," uses "the horror genre . . . to test the boundaries of life, generate feelings of wonder and awe" ("Running"). Glück's observation also indicates the affinity both writers have for the work of Georges Bataille, who viewed sexuality and religion as two manifestations of a "disequilibrium in which the being consciously calls his [*sic*] own existence in question" (*Erotism* 31). Glück's interest in "the sublime" and Cooper's definition of "God" are both unquestionably Bataillean in character. Glück describes the "sublime" as "nothing, . . . a catastrophe, a violent orgasm . . . anything that expresses a void which our communities have filled with religions and monsters in order to understand the absence of ground" ("Truth's Mirror" 41–42). Cooper first distinguishes his conception of "God" from the ordinary Christian one, which he dismisses as "that simple and rickety projection into which our ideas about death tend to focus when we get lazy" ("Smoke Screen" 1). He lists the probable locations of his more awesome and seductive "God" in "sleep, hallucinations, daydreams, orgasms, comas, one's own body, others' bodies, the dark, the sun," and suggests that not only is it aligned with death, but is a powerful temptation toward death, drawing the living out of the boundaries of life. God is a "Siren" and is disruptive of life in ways that inform sexual desire and aesthetic inspiration: "When we want to see God we might as well get specific—seduce someone, make art, commit suicide, masturbate" (ibid. 2).

The means by which Glück and Cooper depict sexual access to "the sublime" or "God," respectively, differ in ways that reflect each writer's schematics of the relations between sexual ecstasis and intersubjectivity. Although Glück's narrator "Bob" in *Jack the Modernist* is the penetrated spectacle for the involved onlookers in the baths, the orgasm he achieves is his own, through the others but not with them. And sexual culmination is as much an evocative negativity for Glück as it is for Cooper: "I felt a soldier's fidelity to the orgasm . . . singled out from all the orgasms in the flux. . . . The spasms that were not me overtook and became me along with a sense of dread. I felt like a tooth being pulled. . . . I relinquished the firm barrier that separated us—no, that separated me from nothing" (*Jack* 55–56).

In Cooper's system, the subject of desire is never the object of desire; the unidirectionality of desire is modeled on the relation of the spectator to the screen, which also figures both the subject's melancholia and his fetishistic awe of the object.[15] Desire is further schematized throughout Cooper's individual works in oppositions between subject meaning (meaning as an intentional act) and object meaning (meaning as effect/affect). "Subject meaning," what the subject intentionally means by what it does/desires, is one of the themes of Cooper's "Poem for George Miles" (the "George M." of "Square One"), which is an elegy for both the object of desire and the quality of that desire. The lyric voice is a twenty-nine-year-old "I" looking back at a poem written for George when that "I" was nineteen (the nostalgia and the temporal discontinuities of the speaking subject are reminiscent of Beckett's "Krapp's Last Tape"):

> When I first sharpened a
> pencil in purpling language
> and drew my first poem
> from its raveling depths
> it "poured my heart out"
> as thoroughly as I would,
> make that could, at 19 . . .
> The poem is now cleaned
> out of power, as bed is
> once sunlight has entered.
> I see its mathematics: lines
> built as an ornate frame
> around a skeletal feeling
> that's faded from sight.
> Who knows what I meant? (*He Cried* 24)

On object meaning, any number of illustrations could be selected, for example, Cooper's musings on Jeff Hunter:

> It's not Jeff who moves me, like I said. He's the part I can relate to. It's as though some concept way over my head has taken human form so we can communicate. . . . It's as if Jeff is moaning "This is as much as you'll grasp," and not, "Fuck me," continuously. ("Square One" 84)

In his prose, the object of desire (the object meaning) often proves impermeable to revelation while it remains the focal point of the narrative. The narrative itself becomes the flux of desire and is what gets revealed (the subject meaning), illuminated in contrast to the opacity of its object. This is the dynamic of Cooper's first full-length novel, *Safe*, a triptych, three separate views of the same enigmatic young man, Mark Lewis. The meaning and nature of the desired object's power are as resistant to explication as Mark is ultimately rejecting of the love of his three suitors in these narratives. At times the subjectivity of the viewer becomes "entangled" (a word Cooper likes) with the object, in the attempt to excavate the secret of the object's power. In the "My Mark" section of *Safe*, the first-person narrator, "Dennis," deconstructs a photograph of Mark in which intentional and affective meanings coalesce over

Mark's absence (or the absence which Mark embodies) and the enigma of Mark's erotic power:

> A head that has power over me. A globe lightly covered by pale flesh, curly black hair, and small, dark eyes whose intensity's too deeply meant to describe or remember the color of, seemingly smeared and spiraling.
>
> I fill a head with what I need to believe about it. It's a mirage created by beauty built flush to a quasi-emotion that I'm reading in at the moment of impact: its eyes on mine, mine glancing off for a second, then burrowing in. (62)

What Mark reveals to his lovers, his beauty—as captured in the narrator Dennis's photo of Mark's face—is also what conceals his "true self" from them. The fascination Mark held for Rob, Dennis, and Doug drew them to him but ultimately kept him a secret. Dennis's truths are always finally elegiac, his meanings trivial when compared to the inarticulate radiance of the desired object. "My Mark" is both exploration and resignation:

> What's left behind is Mark's beauty, safe, in a sense, from the blatant front lighting of my true emotion, though it creeps in. I'm moving stealthily closer, I think, to the heart of the matter, where Mark's body acts as a guide to what he has been feeling. That's his, like great art is the century's it was created in, though still alive in the words of a man who speaks well of him. (*Safe* 58)

Postmetaphysical Sacrifice: Closer

Cooper's characters have a resentful fascination with the body's limitations, without the option of cyberspace (as in William Gibson); they act on a suspicion of the body's truth, without the promise of a supraphysical plane (as in writings of religious mystics and in ghost stories). The characters in Cooper's fiction often either embody or act out a paradox central to any sexual desire and practice, no matter how refined and urbane. Roland Barthes comments on the irony in the great care he lavishes on his appearance to arouse his lover to engage in acts of passion that will ruin that very highly groomed self which had been designed to incite its own destruction. This observation on the contradictory nature of the "toilet" he performs on himself in preparation for the "encounter" leads him to investigate the etymology of the word "toilet," where he discovers two obscure meanings:

> "the preparations given to the prisoner condemned to death before he is led to the scaffold"; . . . "the transparent and oily membrane used by butchers to cover certain cuts of meats." As if, at the end of every toilet, inscribed within the excitation it provokes, there were always the slaughtered, embalmed, var-

nished body, prettified in the manner of a victim. In dressing myself, I embellish that which, by desire, will be spoiled. (Barthes, *A Lover's Discourse* 127)

In *Safe* Rob discusses Ray Sexton with his lover, "equating the shambles Sexton left high school gymnasts in to the flushed, dripping wet mess Mark becomes in his arms" (20). The contradictory impulses of self-assertion and self-abnegation that cofunction in sexual desire also subtend the parallels of violence and sexual intercourse in the (usually unwelcome) threat that violence constitutes to the physical integrity of the body and the (often sought after) threat to the ego boundaries in sexual union. These parallels, as well as the similarities between orgasm and death as annihilations of the discrete self, inform the sense of erotic horror that permeates Cooper's work.

Just as the movie screen concretizes a heaven that evacuates all metaphysical longing, the mass media problematize the structure of the psycho-physical self, particularly in terms of the relations between the external and internal "person." The boys in Cooper's work live in a media-ocracy in which the ultimate significance of a person is flattened out into a form of celebrity (as in Warhol), absolutely exteriorizing the self through a radical identification between the "self" and its public persona (the "Sean Cassidy" and "John F. Kennedy, Jr." poems in *Idols*, for example). The real boys experience contradictions between external self and internal life that never disturb the blissful sheen of their cult heroes' posters. Furthermore, the literalization of space described in "Square One" and "A Herd" is paralleled here in the pervasive interest the characters take in the difference between the beauty of the visible body and the awful "truth" of the internal organs. "Interiority" loses its mystical and psychological meanings of soul and mind, and is transposed onto viscera. Jeff Hunter's "heart" cannot even nostalgically suggest a center of human emotions, as it is simply "a lump of confusing blue tissue two feet up his asshole" ("Square One" 89). This dualism renders the human fundamentally inexplicable. The beauty, personality, and actions of the boys are a veneer whose interior reality is simply a complex of body parts that would be disgusting to most people, and meaningful only to medical specialists.

Closer concerns a half-dozen wealthy gay high school students in a suburb of Los Angeles, all of whom are sexually obsessed with one another, and in particular with George Miles. The boys are divided into subjects and objects of desire, the subjects being at least relatively articulate, and the objects either dazedly incommunicative, like George, or immersed in a fantasy world, like David, who believes he is a rock star. The key actors in the novel each have a specialty that involves a particular manipulation of the body: John is an artist who sketches the boys, Alex is an aspiring filmmaker who documents some of the sexual activity central to the plot, and Steve is an entrepreneur who fills his converted garage nightclub with bodies and sets them dancing. These would represent the positive creative urges, matched by the negative creative urges of the two adults in the novel, Philippe, who dreams of mutilating and murdering young men, and Tom, who actually does.

The body in *Closer* is repeatedly demythologized. John conceives of his drawings as a means to disable the beauty of his subjects, to "reveal the dark underside, or whatever it's called, of people you wouldn't think were particularly screwed up" (5).[16] Even sex does not allow the body to elude the sense of its grisly facticity. When John has sex with George, he wonders at the fact that "George's skin felt so great. That was the weirdest part, feeling how warm and familiar George was and at the same time realizing the kid was just skin wrapped around some grotesque-looking stuff" (7).

David's biologist father decorated the walls of their house with pictures of semidissected adolescents. At dinner David cuts his quiche "into eight thousand pieces," trying to keep his eyes averted from a poster above his father's head of a boy roughly David's age, whose "back is turned and where his ass used to be there's this thing that looks half like drawn curtains and half like what's left of a cow once it gets to the butcher's shop" (28). Such brutal reality may be one of the factors that had driven David into his rock star delusion and his obsession with his own beauty that he admits "helps me believe in myself and not worry that I'm just a bunch of blue tubes inside a skin wrapper" (22).[17]

Both of these sentiments suggest the incorporation of an ego that is as entirely surface as the posters and movies that have formed it. Such an ego bears a striking resemblance to Didier Anzieu's notion of the "skin ego," which is part of his adjustments of Freudian psychoanalytic models to empirical changes in predominant pathologies. When Freud was practicing, the majority of patients were suffering from "straightforward neuroses," but in Anzieu's own practice he notes a significant increase in "borderline cases" between "neurosis and psychosis" in which the patient suffers

> from an absence of borders or limits . . . uncertain of the frontiers between the psychical and bodily Egos, between the reality Ego and the ideal Ego . . . unable to differentiate erogenous zones, [the patient] confuses pleasant experiences with painful ones, and cannot distinguish between drives, which leads him [*sic*] to experience the manifestation of a drive not as desire but as violence. The patient . . . experiences a diffuse sense of ill-being . . . of watching the functioning of his body and mind from outside, of being a spectator of something which is and at the same time is not his [*sic*] own existence. (*Skin Ego* 7)

These borderline states lead to a profound sense of emptiness in attempts at meaning that produce, instead of an ego-object relation an ego-abject relation (Kristeva, "Within the Microcosm" 43–44; and Barzilai 295). "Abjection" is the dread of that which was once part of the body but was expelled as "unclean" or "disgusting." These abjects, however, continue to threaten the integrity of the subject with a chaotic dissolution of the boundaries of inside and outside (Kristeva, *Powers* 3–4). The precarious balance between the skin ego and the viscera in John and David's psychic structures should be clear from the above passages. The balance is displaced as the narrative progresses.

Within this wasteland of self-preempted youths, George becomes deeply involved with Philippe, an older French man with bizarre tastes. Their sex involves necrophilic fantasies, beatings, and coprophagia. Eventually Philippe introduces George to Tom, another older man, who examines George matter-of-factly and brutally, forcing a hand down his throat and up his anus. After a particularly violent threesome, Tom drives George home, and tells him if he ever considers suicide, to call him. George makes note of that invitation, and its ambivalence. He then goes into his room to examine his ass, to see if he can understand what these men find so attractive about it. Here George attempts to assimilate the inexplicable pleasure of the Other into his assessment of his own value as a person. He mistakes Philippe's and Tom's objectification of him as a confirmation of him as a subject (it is exactly the opposite).[18] This is the same error that Henry makes in *Frisk* when he describes a recent sexual experience and his interpretation of it: "Last weekend I slept with two . . . guys. . . . They kept calling me 'that.' One would ask, 'What does that taste like?' and 'What's the temperature inside of that?' . . . It made me realize I'm important to certain people" (7).

The boys' need to reduce thought to neurological quiescence through excessive drug use, and their compulsive fashioning and delimiting of the self to fit the desire of the Other, are expressions of the death drive that takes George to Tom's house after George's mother's death. As he writes in his diary before leaving for Tom's: "It's like a party or something to say my goodbye to the person I am" (*Closer* 98). George did not realize how true that might have become: Tom novocained him and began "chopping him down" in his basement. When Tom asked him if he had "any last words," George intoned the words of the Disneyland ride, "Dead . . . men . . . tell . . . no . . . tales," which brought on the tears that literally saved his life: disgusted at this display of emotion, Tom threw him out of the house (99–100).

The importance of Disneyland to George cannot be dismissed as a *deus ex machina*. It locates the kind of pervasive vacuum in which George lives and which he particularizes in both his self-apprehension and his willingness to subject himself to dehumanization.[19] George becomes a (necessarily) inarticulate embodiment of the postmodern environment that engendered him. For Baudrillard, Disneyland is "a perfect model of all the entangled orders of simulation. To begin with it is a play of illusions and phantasms: Pirates, the Frontier, Future World, etc." (*Simulations* 23–24).[20]

George becomes as much a simulation of a person as the automated denizens of the Disney pavilions, or the inexhaustibly available images of the porn stars. Alex describes George's "hyperreal" state best when he compares George's looks to "the real boy that Pinocchio was forced to become" (*Closer* 62). When Philippe sees George fall on the street, he reacts in a way that explains why he can use George as he does: "When Philippe pictured George's expression approaching the ground, he saw pretend pain, the look that would creep over dolls' faces when children left them alone in the dark" (105). George's beauty taken to be an unreal perfection of reality suggests Baudrillard's "automaton," particularly in the kind of deadly curiosity George arouses in his adult admirers: the automaton is "an interrogation upon nature, the mystery of the existence or non-existence of the soul, the dilemma of appearance and being. It is like God: what's underneath it all, what's inside, what's in the back of it?" (*Simulations* 93). These are precisely the questions that Tom and Philippe (and before them Ray Sexton, and after them the "Dennis" of *Frisk*) attempt to answer.

Philippe's melancholia reverses the disavowal of the hallucinating mourner and the average moviegoer: he looks at a real person (George) and disavows his reality. George and Philippe share a disorder that is necessary for hallucinations, and that is analogically enacted in film spectatorship: the failure to distinguish consistently between what is internal and what is external to the ego.[21] Philippe and Tom sought the secret of George through literal invasions and excavations of George's body. George (like the other boys) confused his inner self with his "innards," in a detour of abjection, which according to Kristeva is an attempt to individuate the self by demarcating the divisions of inside and outside (*Powers* 60–61).

Even when more successfully accomplished than in George's case, abjection leaves a residue of the contingency of identity in the materiality of its biological components—that which can be expelled or incorporated, but which signifies the morass into which the subject can re-devolve (ibid. 9–11; 70–71). The vehemence with which George was handled and literally reduced to bodily secretions/excretions in his encounter with Philippe and Tom actually galvanized his need for these men. The materials they forced from his body made him realize that his interior offered no support for an articulatable self. Furthermore, these "abjects" attest to the "precariousness of the subject's grasp of its own identity," foreboding the return to "the chaos from which it is formed." George's dependence on the adults' objectifying lust to fortify his exteriorized ego against this anxiety is a will-toward-death as subject, but it is also a defense against the abjection he experiences at their hands, since this abjection itself is "one of the few avowals of the death drive, an undoing of the processes constituting the subject" (Grosz, "Language" 74). The dissonance between the scatological horrors of George's sex life and the ethereality of mass-media ego ideals only perpetuates the cycle, since abjection itself constitutes a dual acknowledgment of the necessity and impossibility of the subject's "desire to transcend corporeality," in which the subject rejects yet affirms "the defiling, impure, uncontrollable materiality of [its] embodied existence" (ibid. 72).[22] Neither George nor Philippe understands what Glück calls the "disjunction between self and body" ("Truth's" 41–42). The sublimations of this disjunction Cooper's characters effect inaugurate the melancholy mystery of desire and its often tragic resolutions.

The central obsessions of the novel are figured most graphically in Philippe's memories of a snuff film made by one of the members of his circle:

> He'd picked up the hitchhiker, coerced him home, got him drunk, numbed his body with Novocaine, led him into a basement, started the film rolling, mutilated his ass, asked if he'd like to say any last words, to which the boy had said, "Please don't." Then he killed him.
>
> The only sound in the room was the clicking projector. Sometimes the clicks and the stabs matched for a few seconds. . . . Then the boy made a very bland face. "Is he dead?" someone asked. "No," the man answered. "Not yet. Watch." . . .
>
> . . . At what seemed a haphazard point, everyone in the room heard a brief, curt announcement. "Now," it said. . . .
>
> The film ended. It flapped like a bat. People redid their pants. (*Closer* 108–109)

Like the more innocuous porno audience in "Square One," these men share a fascination with what the images reveal and what mysteries they mark but mask. The boundaries among living individuals and between the living and the dead are concatenated in this awful ritual, which recalls Bataille's explanation of sacrifice in a less self-conscious historical period of human evolution: "The victim dies and the spectators share in what his death reveals. This is what religious historians call the sacramental element" (*Erotism* 82). Note the striking similarity in tone and theme in Glück's description of spectator sex in the baths:

> Men stood around, serious, watching us. . . . Others tended me respectfully because the one who is fucked induces awe by his extreme exposure. . . . Their collective mind said *he's doing it* which my finite mind repeated. Although they masturbated themselves to obtain immediate knowledge of my excitement, *it was as spectators that they solemnly shared in what my pleasure revealed.* (*Jack* 54–55, second emphasis added)

Each of the above passages concerns the communal witnessing of an event that makes intensely present an extreme boundary of human being: death and orgasm, each an incontrovertible "now" which absolutely interrupts the continuity of consciousness. The mediation of film makes the situation in *Closer* significantly different. The temporal and spatial divisions between the viewers and the center of attention structure the nonreciprocity of subject-object relations (the object cannot return their look). The boy's murder forecloses the possibility of a full knowledge of what is seen: the onlookers in the baths or in the audience can experience orgasm but not death. The spectatorial situation exemplifies the intersubjective limits of these men's desire; conversely, the transitive negativity of their desire (sexuality as annihilation of the object) informs a theory of representation that is practically an occult reverence for representation as an endlessly iterable expression of this outwardly directed death drive. The snuff film implicates representation, because the filming and screening of the murder are integral aspects of the crime.[23] The film incites a religious awe as a memorial of the point at which the person ceases to be. This, however, is only a peculiar variation on the logic of filmic practice, since any film or photograph is also a record of the absolutely lost, a testament to the absence of the object it represents. Film and photography are thus perfect techniques for realizing and preserving the de-entification of the living person. Film/photography becomes the postmodern version of the functions Bataille discerns in the cave paintings of Lascaux: "The cave drawings must have been intended to depict that instant when the animal appeared and killing, at once inevitable and reprehensible, laid bare life's mysterious ambiguity" (*Erotism* 74).

The corpse, in its hideous resemblance to the living person now gone, is an obscene subversion of personhood (Kristeva, *Powers* 9–10; Blanchot 256; Gallop 45); the photographic or filmic image is an attempt to retain what is already gone, which is informed with the death that the corpse literally embodies.[24] Sexual fantasies, either those "within" the person or those expressed in pornographic media, instigate a coalescence of the simulacrum of the corpse with the retention of the lost object. Bazin suggested that "the plastic arts" might owe their real impulse to the "practice of embalming the dead" (II, 9). Art historians tell us that realistic human portraiture began with death masks (Aries 257–58).[25] Cooper's work insistently exposes the relation between representation and death—the negation of the real in the image; the self-alienation within desire; the internal negation of the referent of the metaphor—all based on the resemblance of the corpse to the person who has died. The trajectories among representation and reality, life and death, desire and its ends, are dramatized in Cooper's work as passion plays in a childlike world where childhood has always already been invaded by the negativity of adult sexuality (Ferenzci, "The Confusion of Tongues" 156–57). The sacrificial quality of sex, in which the object becomes an opacity of negation and the subject disincorporates itself within the image of the desired object, finds an ancestral model in the cave painting of a man with an erect penis before a dying bison, a paradoxical image which (in Bataille's assessment) asserts the "essential and paradoxical accord between death and eroticism," a truth that "remains veiled to the extent that the human mind hides from itself" (*Tears* 53). This is a truth or an awe-filled intuition of the truth that Dennis Cooper explores, most recently emblematized in the entranced gaze at the fake snuff photo in the opening section of *Frisk*, in which the plaster-of-paris wound on a boy's supposedly shot-open anus takes on the forbidden fascination of death and sexuality itself—an uncanny sight that lures one into the abyss, something which, in Cooper's words, is "too out-of-focus to actually explore with one's eyes, but too mysterious not to want to try" (4).

Shocks of Recognition: Robert Glück's Scandalous Narratives

> To merely record what happened requires an imaginative
> effort similar to falling in love.
>
> —Robert Glück, *Jack the Modernist*

Local Phallic Melancholia

At one point in Samuel R. Delany's "Tale of Plagues and Carnivals," the narrator digresses from the diegesis, speculating that if "mid-twentieth century orthodox Freudian were to present" Nevèrÿon's gay Pheron "with the theory of penis envy and 'sublimation' he would probably have said: 'The only thing is I envy them too. And I've got one. Nor is it small. And heaven knows, I don't sublimate. I go right for it' " (256). Pheron's rejoinder evinces a more unambiguously antiphallic irreverence toward the penis than many of the gay porn films that document the behavior Pheron boasts of. Pheron's apostasy dispels the phallus but inversely revivifies the mystery of desire whose object is now bereft of a master narrative that would warrant such awe or devotion. The secular challenges the meanings of desire and its objects pose are central concerns in the narratives of Robert Glück.

Jack the Modernist is a first-person narrative reconstruction of a relationship between a writer, Bob, and an actor-director, Jack. The lucid paradoxes of Bob's desire often suggest nuanced narrative expositions of some of the implications of Pheron's "penis envy." In the novel Glück localizes gay sexuality in ways that disengage the penis from the socially enforced slippage between the male member and the transcendental signifier, but in his specifications of the narrator's desire, Glück synthesizes the demystification of the penis in gay porn with the melancholia of desiring representation epitomized in Cooper's work.

The demystification of the penis clarifies the object of desire as irreducibly in excess of any real object. *Jack the Modernist* offers an agnostic meditation on this excess and on the anarchic pull toward the gap left by any of the object's substitutive manifestations, in the passage in which Bob compares his physical desire for Jack's penis to a yearning "to touch it like the neck of the Winged

Victory—a shower of blue sparks" (29). The Winged Victory has been headless since its original discovery. In wanting to touch the neck, Bob wants to touch the edge between being and nonbeing, between the tangible and the ineffable, between the manifest and its mystery. The statue itself is an icon from a lost cult, an artifact whose deglossed otherness allows it to signify only its meaningfulness but not its meaning. Having senselessly survived the mythic time of its intelligibility, the statue now inspires awe based on the oblivion of the context that could justify it. Jack's penis evokes a similar *mysterium tremendum* in Bob, and harks back to an equally fabulous past of the desiring subject's prelapsarian wholeness, a primordial union with the lost object that would reveal the meaning of this surrogate's urgency. The blue sparks Bob imagines his touch will ignite are both real and mystical—delight, color, physical thrill, a warning, a punishment—and certainly the sparks that burned the Wicked Witch of the West when she attempted to take Dorothy's ruby slippers—a specifically gay canonical exemplum of the impossible object of desire.

Although Bob's erotic investment in a real and available penis as tangible object of desire may withdraw psychic participation from the dominant misidentification of penis and phallus, it does not rationalize desire or achieve a consistent control over its operations. "Pleasure is close to awe, I bowed my head. He 'let me' take his cock. . . . (Jack's cock: on which so many emotions hung their hats) . . . "I stopped a moment and looked at it—an elegance completely trustful of itself, erect and shiny. It equaled the intensity I was able to feel. I don't have a language to describe that intensity so I lack the thought. . . . What did I want from this flesh peninsula that made me so urgent? Sucking, stroking—a hopelessly inadequate language. . . . The concept of pleasure didn't touch the engagement and physical call" (*Jack* 28–29). The narrator literalizes the penis, he does not "dephallicize" it. But the "transcendence" of this phallus is rigorously localized. Jack's cock for Bob becomes a concrete absolute; the profundity of the sexual encounter to Bob's sense of his meaning as a subject is condensed in the physical contact with Jack's penis, with "the sheer exhilaration I feel each time of finding and having what pertains to me, what I pertain to" (28).

The "exhilaration" Glück's narrator feels regarding the "pertinence" of Jack's penis should be considered in the light of Pheron's riddle of "having" one and yet "going for one too." The key word here is "having"—particularly within this detailed "overestimation" of Jack's penis, "having" suggests the Lacanian model of heterosexual relations. We recall that in Lacan's schema, the man "has" the phallus and the woman "is" the phallus, but the man "has" the phallus only through the woman's recognition of his penis as the phallus she "lacks." But as a sexually differenced subject, Bob *has* the phallus while he seeks it. Although the libidinal interchange between Bob and Jack is conditioned by a phallic signifier which begs comparison with Lacan's heterosexual paradigm, in Glück's scenario the fantasies attached to the penis/phallus are contained within the relationship of the two men, and the metaphors remain within this microcosmic circulation—they do not participate in the occultation of this local "phallic signifier" as a socially generalizable *transcendental* signifier. In fact, it is clearer here that the penis is *not* the phallus than it is in the heterosexual contract.[26] By so assiduously re-playing the phallic signifier within a relationship between two partners who both "have" the phallus, Glück in this regard vindicates Lacan (perhaps more than he might have wished to be vindicated), clearly distinguishing the signifier of desire from the male member.

Glück's initial reimagining of the penis as localized phallus within a specifically circumscribed sexual dynamic between two sexually differenced gay male subjects nevertheless situates those subjects within the Lacanian phallically mediated model of sexual relations. This ostensibly imposes on that desiring subject the logic of castration as (phallically defined) sexual difference. Bob thereby occupies the "woman's" position in the Lacanian dynamic, which in turn implies the narrator's acknowledgment of his own castration. I find this model conceptually inadequate for a real critical appreciation of Glück's work, but for the moment I shall keep the question of castration and related metaphors based on sexual morphology in consideration, as I introduce the ways in which Glück rearticulates the relations among lack, desire, and signifying practice, beyond the constraints of our phallocentric epistemological legacy.

In the story "Denny Smith," another first-person narrator "Bob" describes in infinitesimal detail the moment in the De Young Museum Garden Cafe that Denny, his lover of four years, ended their relationship. The narrative is interrupted with a pseudoallegorical tale in which Denny and Bob are represented by "Mr. Pitch and Mr. Catch," respectively. The names "Pitch" and "Catch" are derived from gay male slang for the penetrative and recipient roles in anal sex. The identification of this narrating Bob with the recipient partner in intercourse seems to support the "feminine" identity the Lacanian sexual relations model imposes on the Bob of *Jack the Modernist*. Moreover, "Denny Smith," like *Jack the Modernist*, is a recollective assessment of a past relationship from the perspective of the "abandoned" partner. The hypostases of Jack's penis in the novel and Bob's allegorical self-designation as "Mr. Catch" in the story each define the desiring narrator/subject in terms of a sexual lack that the narrator recognizes and expresses as a demand addressed to the imagined plenitude of an already absent lover.

There is a complex metaphor intricately written into "Denny Smith" which at first appears to supplement and corroborate the thematic legitimacy of the parallel "castrations" the above critical anatomy of the two narrators insistently advances. I shall argue, however, that this digression in "Denny" actually illuminates some of the more sophisticated and productive differences between Glück's conceptions of sexual identity and those we have just considered. The passage in question describes "Mr. Catch's" obsessive need for sex as a means of reconsolidating his sense of self. For "Mr. Catch" sex provides a restorative union that also threatens to reveal the rupture in the subject it both compensates and causes. Even "Mr. Catch" allows this suspicion to graze his figurative mind: "Then he comes quickly and easily. . . . But does this sex keep the world from slipping away or is it an image of that disjunction?" (503). Sex here represents the suturing effect of the signifier "I" that inaugurates and conceals the fading of being, or aphanisis, in the subject that accedes to signification.

In Oedipal terms, Catch's receptive sexuality is a mark of castration; this association in turn supports Lacan's characterization of aphanisis as a primordial "castration." My examination in chapter 4 of the way aphanisis is figured and functions within the specular economies of the gay male pornographic apparatus, however, did not support this characterization. In the pornographic cinematic situation, aphanisis did not become the visible stigma of castration, but the envisioning process of the negating affirmation of the gay male subject as ecstatic image. In turning to the narrative register of deviant representational strategies, I will show how in Glück's and Killian's texts, the narrator accepts and exploits the fading of being in signification (Lacan's aphanisis) the lack-of-being within desire (Lacan's "castration") in developing a narrative mode of expression that also expresses the narrating "I" as an effect of its signifying processes. Glück's desiring subjects are not acknowledging castration, but a lack foundational to desire independent of biological sexual morphology. This "lack" is what makes sexuality possible (for everyone) instead of what makes social subordination inevitable (for women). Although abstractly a common dynamic in sexual subjectivity, "lack" will be configured differently in different sociosexual populations. Here I am concerned with the configuration of that "lack" within and among the sexually differenced subjects of Glück's deviant narratives.

One of the principal double articulations of Glück's sexually differenced narrators illuminates another hidden implication of Pheron's confession of "penis envy": "The only thing is I envy them too. And I've got one. . . . And heaven knows, I don't sublimate. I go right for it." ("Tale of Plagues" 188). The sexually differenced subject who "has" yet seeks the "phallus" does not act out a castration fantasy, but rather a melancholia. When two sexually differenced subjects have the phallus yet desire as if they lack it, that performative desiring lack structures itself as a melancholic relation between subject and object. Because Bob's possession of his own penis does not obviate a desire for Jack's specific penis as locally transcendent Phallus, the desire is inherently melancholic, even before the end of their relationship. As in my discussion of Dennis Cooper, I base my understanding of melancholia on Freud's "Mourning and Melancholia," adapting it here to include the range of phantasmatic operations the subject engages, in response to a loss of object that the subject did not actually sustain.[27] Glück's desiring melancholia paradoxically emerges from the intense introspective observation of the individual's concrete histories of sexual *satisfaction*. Such melancholia is also characterized by the subject's conscious realization that the loss is a fantasy. This split belief is the reverse of Freudian fetishism. The fetishist unconsciously says, "I know the (woman's) penis is not there, but still . . . " Glück's melancholic narrator consciously says, "I know I have the penis/phallus but still . . . " Such consciousness of the irreality of the loss one seeks to redress distinguishes this local phallic melancholia from the strictly pathological forms. In fact, this melancholia is not necessarily even an "unpleasant" condition, but rather an awareness thematized within the subject's sexuality of the constitutive contradictions of desire and its articulations specific to phallocentric societies.

Narrative Aphanisis

Local phallic melancholia supports a representational interface between the psychosexual constitution and the signifying practices of the deviant subject, in that the negating affirmation of the sexual subject becomes an aphanitic self-exposition of a narrating subject informed throughout with a consciousness of its own fictionality.[28] Glück's melancholic narrators accept the experience of lack that motivates sexuality, and the lack-in-being that structures their acts of self-signification. They express this radical acceptance (which is in itself this melancholia) in narrative articulations that transvalue both "lacks." In *Jack*, Bob's narration acknowledges his desire as a lack-in-being; but in so doing, he posits *himself as a lack-in-being*, since the narrative that "presents" him realizes him as an effect of the signifying chain.

Glück's narrators reflect an idiosyncratically conscious practice of aphanisis. The narrating personae are coextensive with the askesis of *writing oneself out* (in both senses of the phrase). The subject is realized intradiegetically as a first-person narrator/character constituted by the loss of the real that even lovemaking is based on and reenacts, and metadiegetically through the highly reflective transposition of this subject into language, a system whose signifiers connote the absence of the referents they posit: "Prolonged scrutiny can become an expenditure of self. . . . I've come to experience the unreeling of interiority and sexual disclosure as such a loss, and also part of a historical trajectory. It's a writing activity that privileges the aggression of naming . . . an ongoing colonization of self into one's own language" (Glück, "Fame" 6). The meta- and intradiegetic levels of representation often converge in the "boyfriend orientation" of the work, through which the boyfriend functions as "a disjunction to project into, a longing for unity, and the medium through which form itself is contemplated as a mystery" (Glück, qtd. Jackson, "Robert" 165).

In their elegiac moments, Glück's narrators display one aspect of Freud's melancholia that is not a significant feature of Cooper's: "an extraordinary diminution of self-regard, an impoverishment of his ego on a grand scale. In mourning it is the world which has become poor and empty; in melancholia it is the ego itself" (Freud, "Mourning" 246). Glück frequently describes the lost object of desire in terms of how its aftermath conditions the narrator's "self," a withdrawal which does not so much deplete that self as expose the lack founding it: "Rejection coincides too well with a tired romantic song of who I really am, some cancelled trip, some mix-up of modes of transportation, stone steps descending into a lake" ("Denny Smith" 505). Glück's stories of past relationships, lost lovers, or broken promises concatenate the vagaries of the self as a continually renewable sense of abandonment. The intense attention the narrating persona gives the processes of its own figuration circumscribes the narrator's deferral to the desired object as a gravitational center of greater ontological density, as something more real that provides the substantial texture of the narrator's emotive-affective relation to the world. After Jack leaves Bob, the narrator engages in a long inventory of possible ego-imagos of "Bob" gleaned from porn magazines and personal ads. He interrupts this list to address the absent Jack: "Jack, to be frank with you, I find that the more wicked of us is not myself. Nasty hypocrite. . . . If I believed in my existence as I believe in yours" (*Jack* 113).[29]

Ecstatic Subjects

Belief is a formation of the subject's apprehension of the dynamic vacuity of self that structures the relation between "castration" and "Phallus" and (narrative) aphanisis and (specular) fantasy object. But for Glück, belief is more important in its dissipation than its fervor: it is most vital as a prelude to doubt. One of Glück's most wonderful "real" characters, Margery Kempe (c. 1373–c. 1440), dated Jesus. Her union with Jesus nearly made her a saint; Jesus' abandonment of Margery made her the first English autobiographer.[30] Like Margery, the Bobs of *Jack* and "Denny Smith" are also abandoned. But, as the latter Bob observes, "abandoned" has two meanings "lonely and wild" ("Denny Smith" 506). The dual aspects of abandonment constitute the postbelief awe of sexuality for the subject jilted into autodeconstructive self-representation. The "lack" within the would-be saint and sometime lover is not a defect to be repaired but a capacity for tangible ecstasy to be realized. This lack attains its shattering confirmation in the concrete sublime, as detailed in Bob's sexual experience in the baths in *Jack the Modernist*:

> One man eased his cock into my ass. My asshole went from opaque to transparent as he lifted me off the floor and fucked me slowly with authority while another blew me and occasionally took my balls in his mouth while still another tongued my nipples and kissed me and many others touched my body

lightly as though they were sensual Greek breezes. . . . I relaxed backward,
releasing my ass and letting my head loll—the man fucking acknowledged
my shift with a whispered *ha* that seemed triumphant. . . . The purely physical
deepened, or rather became more incisive, more pressing, relegating any previous terms as though I were a body torn into existence. I, my identity, was
more and more my body so I/it cried out with each released breath, not to
express myself but as a by-product of physical absorption. But the spasms that
were not me overtook and became me along with a sense of dread. I felt like
a tooth being pulled. (54–55)[31]

The "sense of dread" experienced as the onset of sexual satisfaction differs
from the terror-filled associations of women with an abyss that the approach
of orgasm frequently triggers in heterosexual men, according to Montrelay.[32]
Glück acknowledges sexuality as both a disruptive force and one of communal
cohesion and personal identity (an identity affirmed through the attraction to
other men, and other men's desire for the embodied subject who desires them).
The void that threatens the integrity of the subject is sexuality and its excesses,
which, in certain gay male communities, becomes the mark of a range of identities and a means of mutually identificatory exchange. Sex does not fill the lack
but exacerbates it in the culmination of self-recognition as sexual subject, a
kind of morphological negating affirmation: "The more you get fucked, the
more you want it: eventually the pornographic hungry hole becomes merely
accurate. I was surrounded by an O sound that was at once the voice of sex
and the shape of the orifice he pounded" (*Jack* 28–29). It is this permeability,
not the phallus, which conditions both interpersonal and existential dynamics
of self and nonself in "Sex Story," in which a memory of swimming naked in
the Russian River is refigured as a sexual metaphor for the writer's relation to
the world and the act of writing that world: "I am the bottom man and this
river is the top man, lithe and muscular with two handfuls of flesh. I am a
bottom, the person who really controls is the bottom and sex is the top and I
arrange for it to take my streaming body and clear me of names and express
me and bring me to a point. This is pleasure and I'm no fool" (Glück, "Sex
Story" 31). In fact, to the Glückian narrator, literary praxis itself is founded on
a willingness for penetration, abandonment, kaleidoscopic invasion of voices,
bodies, memories, fantasies, dreams, and media messages. Glück's narrator in
"Sex Story" speculates, "It's hard to understand how a man can write well if
he doesn't like to be fucked" (33).

Fabulous Objects of Desire

Glück retailors narratives from "world literature" into allegories of desire
and its impossible object which resonate variously with their textual environment and the given communities of address. In *Jack the Modernist*, Bob tells

his writing workshop the story of Pwyll and the Maiden from the *Mabinogion*. Every day Pwyll would see a beautiful woman slowly riding by on a white horse. Each day he would send a man after her to find out her name, but no matter how fast they ran or rode, the woman got farther and farther away, although she never increased her speed. Pwyll tried pursuing her himself with no success. Finally, he shouted to her, " 'Maiden . . . for his sake whom thou lovest best, stay for me. 'I will, gladly,' said she, 'and it had been better for the horse hadst thou asked me this long since.' " The story entranced everyone, because it "seemed plucked from the center of a dream. . . . All his straining forward does not equal a small gesture of communication, although it gives that gesture a wonderful import. . . . Desire equals meaning in a cruder, simpler way than we might be comfortable believing" (25–27).

As his realization of the impending end of his relationship with Jack grows, Bob consoles himself with the Japanese story of "Yuki-onna," the snow woman. A man married a woman named "Yuki," and, after several years of wedded bliss, the man, reminded of something by the way a light shone on his wife's face, told her an incident that had happened to him before he had met her. Caught in a blizzard, he and an older companion sought shelter in an abandoned hut. "A snow spirit named Yuki-onna entered and breathed over the older man. She approached the younger and told him she would spare him if he promised never to mention her visit. The old man was dead in the morning" (*Jack 121*). Upon hearing the story, the wife became enraged, and transformed herself into Yuki-onna. She tells her husband that she is sparing him only for the sake of the children, and melts into a puddle on the floor. The husband in Glück's version blames himself not so much for a broken covenant with the supernatural as for an insufficiency in his storytelling technique—not a moral but a stylistic failure: " 'Well, I told it badly. . . . I should have made more of the weather the night the old man died, modulated the tempo, added a metaphor or two. . . . And I didn't describe Yuki-onna . . . bringing through the storm the absolute silence of a mirror, the silence of an object standing midair, completely out of context, alienating. I could only describe her figure by the break in space it created" (121).

In both stories, the object of desire is wholly Other. In each case its transcendent essence was contained—at least temporarily—by an earthly, intelligible form; at other times both women were characterized as utterly unattainable. The reality of the Yuki-onna exceeded the husband's ability to describe it—it could be connoted only by a lacuna in the discourse, a diffractory representation that merely marked the incommensurability of language to desire, an ecstatic signifying failure.

The Yuki-onna story serves as an allegory for desire in general, and in Glück's contexts also as an allegory of the subversive effects of gay male sexuality on the heteropatriarchal fantasy of the transcendence of the phallus. Yuki-

onna is the Phallus, the ultimate object of desire and the transcendental signifier in the dominant order. Gay male desire for penises *as* penises, and their
representations of them *as* penises, is the blasphemy of the husband who tells
the truth about the "god," a discursive act "intolerable to this divinity who
exists above or below articulation." The divergent effects of the husband's story
also support this analogy: "The story partializes her; for him it makes her actual" (121). She vanishes, violated by the shock of recognition of herself in her
husband's narrative.

The Pwynn fable, on the other hand, deals with the internally distancing
structuration of the have-have melancholia of gay male sexuality, conditioning
both pornographic representation and intersubjective sexual experiences. For
Dennis Cooper, the image of the porn star Jeff Hunter is a hierophany: "It's
not Jeff who moves me. . . . He's the part I can relate to. It's as though some
concept way over my head has taken human form so we can communicate, like
aliens did in B films" ("Square One" 84). Sexual acts also exceed the facticity
of pleasurable friction and involuntary muscle spasm: "We fuck intensely in order to assuage a longing for happiness predicated on a beautiful turn of the
head, good forearms, nice basket, nice ass, a dark Russian smile, a blond smile,
a glower—longing based on distance; distance is compelling and these encounters are the erotics of distance" (Glück, *Jack* 123). The erotics of distance are
embedded in the Pwynn fable, but further extended into pornographic representation, in that the object is both there and not there, a distance as insurmountable as either of the uncanny personifications in Glück's stories. Narrative focuses on the *impossibility* of attaining the object of desire, the specular
deals with its enigmatic *possibility*. This returns us to the sexual identity politics
in the relations established between the specular and narrative modes of representation, which we shall consider here with particular attention to the deviant
strategies for narrative articulations of these tensions and narrative interventions therein.

The Body of the Text

Our contrastive models of the anaclitic and narcissistic subjects have been
developed in dialogue with the evaluative syntagms prominent in Freud's theories of normal sexual maturation from roughly 1910 to 1915. The significance
of Freud's conception of the self-preservative instincts as antipathetic to sexual
instincts lies in its imbrication with several other hierarchized binary oppositions: pleasure principle/reality principle; pleasure ego/reality ego; anaclitic ob-
ject-choice/narcissistic object-choice, etc. Many of the drives and other psychical processes that are diametrically opposed in the anaclitic subject are mutually
reinforcing in the narcissistic subject (self-preservative and sexual drives; ego-
libido and object-libido; scopophilia and identification, for example). These an-

tagonisms ramify the connotational overdeterminations of representational modes themselves in the respective cultural practices and articulations of sexual subjects.

Freud's system transposed onto an aesthetic tendency would allow the reality principle to narrativize cognition toward a deferral-based compromise with the real, a compromise threatened by the phantasmatic and immediate satisfactions within the pleasure principle (represented most economically in the specular, the visual). We have already seen examples in Almodóvar and others of the deliberate use of specular excess as a self-consciously deviant incursion of the gay subject into the horizon of dominant representational priorities. The integration of illustrations in the text of *Jack the Modernist*—maps, movie stills, cartoons, posters, magazine covers, engravings, and photographs—enacts and deploys the opposition between the specular and the narrative within the mobile and porous totality of the work itself, a textualization of the gay male body (spatialized as the playground rather than temporalized as the narrative of patriarchal generation).

The psycho-physical effects and affects of gay male sex are also represented through visual metaphors. For example, "Bob" reflects upon the meanings of the simultaneity of anal and genital stimulation in the sexual encounter in the baths: "Getting fucked and masturbated produces an orgasm that can be read two ways, like the painting of a Victorian woman with her sensual hair piled up who gazes into the mirror of her vanity table. Then the same lights and darks reveal a different set of contours: her head becomes one eye, the reflection of her face another eye and her mirror becomes the dome of a grinning skull/woman/skull/woman/skull—I wanted my orgasm to fall between those images. That's not really a place. I know. The pious Victorian named his visual pun 'Vanity.' I rename it 'Identity' " (Glück, *Jack* 55–56).

The use of this painting is multiply significant on the levels of both content and expression. First of all, by retitling the painting *Identity*, Glück recuperates the trivial (and sexist) notion of "feminine" narcissism for a psychologically valid act of identity constitution, while intermeshing the object-libido (the tenor of the metaphor being the sexual satisfaction at the baths) and the ego-cathexis (one half of the vehicle of the metaphor being an image of a person gazing at her own reflection) and ego drives that are polarized in the Freudian account of the psychosexual dynamics of "selfhood." Secondly, the culminating point of a narrative (the orgasm at the baths) is en-figured by a visual image—the narrative is subsumed by the specular, which is an image of a specular event that in itself is simultaneously two different images, depending upon the perspective of the viewer, and hence again neutralizes linearity. This painting, moreover, is an example of anamorphosis, which, as Lacan explains in his reading of Rembrandt's *The Ambassadors*, is always a disruption of the visual mastery of the spectator in its decentering of perspectival certainty. The "annihilating" potential of this specular subversion is figured in the death's head hidden in *The Ambassadors* (*Four Fundamental* 86–89). It is interesting to note not only that the anamorphosic painting Glück incorporates into *Jack* also contains a "death's head" but that this image dominates the space (discerning the death's head in Rembrandt's painting requires concerted effort).

Vanity is reproduced in *Jack*, but—as with all the other illustrations—it appears long before it occurs in the narrative (the reproduction appears on page 13 and is not mentioned until page 55). The illustrations are always discrete interruptions of the narrative and proleptic gestures toward a spatialized temporality (the corresponding page numbers are noted in the captions), a spatialized temporality parallel to the cubist configuration of erogenous zones on the gay male body that scandalously contemporizes the three stages of the psychosexual history in the progression of the child toward masculine heterosexuality: the oral, the anal, and the phallic.[33] The specular in *Jack* is not figured as an impossible position of active, universalizing looking, a gaze appropriating the world as an exhaustively intelligible object, but rather as a field of visibility, of reflexive, self-constituting, esemplastic fantasizing of a multi-aspectual erotic body.

This painting is only the most conspicuous example in *Jack* of the deliberate evocation of the spectacle as an interruption or diversion from the linear progression of the narrative. This association allows the visuals to parallel the disruptive nature of homosexuality within the master narratives of the Oedipus (Hocquenghem 81–83) and the teleological euphemisms of reproductive sexuality (Jackson, "Kabuki Narratives" 475–77). The manipulation of the specular and the narrative metaphorically textualizes the gay male body. Glück's work also somatizes the text—realizing a musing of Barthes's: "Does the text have human form, is it a figure, an anagram of the body? Yes, but of our erotic body" (Barthes, *Pleasure* 17). The somatization of the text takes place in the sexualizing of the narrative boundaries as well: the differences between narrator and other become boundaries as interpenetrable as the men in the bathhouse orgies.

Glück's discovery of his sexuality and his fashioning of a language that could express it also illuminates the paradoxical relationship of the psychological self to the physical body, and the resistance of the body to discursive domestication. This dynamism between self and body is expressed in his writings as the incommensurability of narrative to spectacle: "I am making a big connection here between writing, coming out, and community. But learning to articulate, to be free, created a double movement, in that the secret of my sexual identity gave way . . . to the larger secrets of the self in its body, the physical thing that we are that can no more enter into the sphere of language as enter into the space created by a mirror" ("My Community" 6). The specular/imaginary is epitomized by the mirror stage, which may have implications within the dynamics of gay male subjectivity that extend into cultural articulations otherwise unintelligible if the only accepted psychosexual history of the male subject remains the teleology of male-dominant heterosexuality.

The frequency of mirror images within gay male cultural production—Jean Genet's *Funeral Rites*, Augustin Gomez-Arcos's *The Carnivorous Lamb*, and Pedro Almodóvar's film *Law of Desire*, to cite only a few—suggests interesting permutations on the mirror stage and its postsymbolic residue within the gay male social subject. Glück offers his own revision of the mirror stage:

> To show the double necessity and impossibility of narration, I want to borrow Lacan's mirror stage, the moment when a child . . . recognizes itself. . . . Lacan's model is so literal: I have a mirror, I was a baby. . . . I nudge Lacan's baby out of the way and substitute myself. I then enjoy a realization that includes the baby's lack of terms one giant second ago (nonrepresentation, his ignorance of space and difference) and also his self's moment of origin, the origin of a fiction, a Genesis story deeper than Modernist estrangement which takes language by surprise, and anterior to inner life and psychological first causes. ("Truth's Mirror" 40–41)

Glück's mirror stage is a self-conscious yet nonnostalgic fantasy replaying of an imaginary event that is essentially unrecoverable in the symbolic order initiated with the accession to language. The baby's captivation by its image is translated into the fascination with the self's bodily reality that exceeds and eludes the language that lends it meaning (a meaning the body at times deflects, diffracts, or altogether refuses). The baby's inarticulate traumatic discovery of the gap between the introceptively experienced self and the external image in the mirror becomes the model for the vertiginous asymmetries between epiphany and explanation, discrete visions and serialization, the body and its history, ecstasy and its forensics. These gaps provide the "disjunction" that Glück defines as "that sudden change of scales, the double awareness of self (narration) and anarchic body (the sublime)" ("Truth's Mirror" 41), an opposing pair that corresponds to our prinicipal representational categories, the narrative and the specular.

Undo-It-Yourself Fictions

Glück's texts are characterized by a double transgressive movement: one of scandalous "realism"—the use of real people (including himself), actual events, letters and conversations of friends and ex-lovers, etc. and one of autodeconstruction, in which the text exposes and reflects upon its own mechanisms of production, its own artifice. Because the latter is modeled on a self-conscious rehearsal of the baby's fictional origin before the mirror, Glück can synthesize the two scandals by disseminating the shock of recognition (common to the baby and the self-reflective text) among his narrating personae and the characters who find themselves in his fictions.

Glück's self-consciously staged "reflection" of his own constructedness in the postsymbolic mirror stage is itself "reflected" in the meditations within Glück's narratives on their own fictiveness. The autodeconstructive narrative, in turn, analogically valorizes deviant subject processes by patterning its mode of signification on the negating affirmation of gay male sexual expression, discursively reiterating that mode of assertion. Like the aphanitic autobiographer, the autodeconstructive narrative is modeled on subjects constituted by their disarticulations. As observed above, sexuality is both a threat to the ego boundaries of the individual and a chief means of self- and mutual identification in gay male communities. Gay male identities, in other words, are constituted by the very energies that dissolve them. (Recall *Jack*'s Bob in the baths being "torn into existence" at the point of orgasm whose approach had been dispersing his ego into spasms that "overtook and became me.")

Elements of a Coffee Service, a collection of short narrative pieces, opens with "Sanchez and Day," an account of a would-be queer-bashing Glück narrowly escaped while walking his dog, Lily. In the next story, "When Bruce Was 36 (Gossip and Scandal)," "Bob" looks at Lily and remembers an exchange with one of his students in his writing class: "I had brought some of my work to read and Margaret rustled papers throughout, writing fast, she said, to get her thoughts down. One of the stories I read is in *Elements*, the one about getting queer-baited at Sanchez and Day. The conclusion Margaret reached was that I ought to put all the poems and stories together as one chapter, smooth them out and send them to a dog grooming magazine" (10).

The last story in the book, "Violence," begins with the history of its own inspiration, during a conversation between Glück and his friend Denise. Glück had come over to borrow her typewriter to finish typing "Sex Story," one of the central pieces in *Elements*. The two of them reviewed what had gone into the collection up to this time, and what was still missing. They agreed the book was too thin at this point (under seventy pages before "Violence") and that violence was a topic yet to be addressed, hence the final story ("Violence" 70–71). The natural chronological order of "Bob's" life becomes confluent with the linear production of the texts up to the point of this metatextual, retrospective reflection on those texts, and both temporal progressions become contained within the spatializing structures of page numbers and textual arrangement. The realism of the "slices of life" is here contextualized as literary production through the transparency of the book's construction.

The conclusion of *Jack the Modernist* also exposes the fictionality that had already been imposed on the "real" of the novel's represented world. Both works thematize the necessary artificiality of the genesis of the text, parallel to the fictional genesis of the baby's self before the mirror. In one of the final chapters, Bob meets Jack at a restaurant, several months after the conclusion of their romance, to discuss the manuscript which was to become the novel at hand. During this conversation, many elements of the earlier part of the novel are exposed as fictional: the finches and sheets described in the first lovemaking scene, Jack's physical description, and even his name: "Jack wanted me to change his name. 'But Jack, none of the other characters have different names.' . . . He pondered for a moment and replied, 'I'd like you to call me Clovis.' . . . 'I think I'll call you Jack.' 'Jack? How weird. That's what everyone called my father.' 'It has the right class background and a flat A. I'd rather use your real name.' 'But I wear a moustache and a beard. The man in this story is clean shaven. I don't see how he has anything to do with me. I don't have a chenille bedspread' " (*Jack* 154–56).

In rereading the scene the two discussed (ibid. 8–10), we find that the "wrong" birds (the Cordon Blue Waxbills Bob had found in a library book [155]) are not replaced by the "correct" ones, and the chenille bedspread is still there. The name Jack, however, is also there, and one passage explains Bob's choice of the name according to the "flat A": "From an envelope I learned his name was John. Jack was a nickname. I relished it: Jack is so flat, like a flat rock or a landing strip between the flights a sentence can make" (9). Glück apparently changed the name to one that would allow the original simile in this scene to remain intact. The deliberate exposure of the book's fictions recasts as mutually enriching realms the ordinarily polarized categories of memory and fantasy, history and allegory, event and interpretation. Glück's willingness to expose the artifice of his world is what allows him his "honest fiction," a fiction that authenticates while it delimits and contextualizes the subjects it represents.

Elsewhere Glück compares the identification with one's mirror image to a viewer's identification with art ("Truth's Mirror" 43), an identification which might suspend the critical capacity essential to a fully engaged response to one's community and one's world.[34] Just as he questions his own mirror image's "inevitability" ("isn't it a writer's job to articulate and challenge that proposition?" [ibid. 41]), the ethics of Glück's aesthetic project keeps meaning an open-ended and participatory experience. At the end of a negative review of a Richard Avedon show, Glück wonders "if it's possible to be aware of the artifacted nature of the local and not be contemptuous of it?—to understand it as a construct and be moved by its depth?" (ibid. 45). In his writings on the centrality of community, he answers this in the affirmative. Within the lesbian and gay communities, the empathic responses his writings evoke reflect a "community as writer, where both the audience and the writer are responsible to their community," which "releases [Glück] from the burden of psychology and gives him access to history" ("Caricature" 27–28). In this continuum between writer and community, Glück engages in what Donna Haraway calls "a power-charged social relation of conversation," which he achieves and maintains within a specifically gay male idiom of embodiment and erotic rapport. The narrative practices that constitute *Jack the Modernist* reclaim the homosexual scandal as a gay scandal, making the subject visible as the scandal of subjectivity. Glück's writing represents the *subject as the scandal*, a scandalous subject and the narrative as the scandalous articulation of that transgressive subject-in-process.

Appearing as Oneself: Countermimetics in Kevin Killian

> Whoever you invented invented you too.
>
> —Christine Brooke-Rose, *Thru*

> Remember, you're an extra in a dream sequence.
>
> —Dialogue from Juliet Bashore's *Kamikaze Hearts*

Jack the Modernist concludes with a scene from Georges Méliès's film, *Le Mélomane* (1903), in which the director himself appears as a magician who "takes his head off and tosses it to the top of the screen where it becomes the globe of an eighth note on a musical staff. Another head appears on his neck; he removes it and tosses it up and so on." Eventually the magician undoes his spell, summoning "each head back to his shoulders where it disappears to make room for the next and the next . . . head by head, no melody, no magician" (*Jack* 165–66). It is not the filmmaker but the novelist who negates the magician here. In this join between director and narrator at the convergent conclusions of the film and the novel, Glück figures the culminating act of a self-consciously fictive subject of enunciation as an exhibitionistic disappearance.

Kevin Killian's work also exemplifies a dynamic belief in the fictionality of the self, but his narratives tend to focus on the construction of the narrator, rather than its vanishing act.[35] Killian's typical first-person narrator is constituted as an act of appearing as oneself, in both the philosophical and show business senses of that phrase.[36] Killian has literally appeared as himself (in the role of "Kevin Killian") in his own plays, such as *The House of Forks*, and his dramatic monologue *Who Is Kevin Killian?* He also performs in the work of other playwrights, filmmakers, and videographers, and his characterizations are informed with the "Kevin Killian" persona developed from playing himself.[37] The mutually implicating tensions between "self" and "character" and "reality" and "representation" discernible in the tensions among the roles Killian assumes in performance are reinscribed in the relations between the two books Killian published in 1989: *Shy*, a novel, whose first-person narrator, "Kevin Killian," is an aspiring novelist; and *Bedrooms Have Windows*, a memoir detailing how "Kevin Killian" became a writer. Each of these texts articulates the self-conscious production of an irreducibly and recursively ironic narrating subject.

If Glück's narrators dissipate themselves within writerly texts of bliss, Killian's narrators perform themselves within imitations of readerly texts of pleasure.[38] This quasi-readerly text—both the metaphor and medium for Killian's self-disclaiming narrating "I"—eventually disinvests the reader of the "I's" illusory fixity and fixations. This disillusion is also a pleasure principle (a principal pleasure and a principled pleasure) of Killian's text. It is a disenchantment that does not invalidate or demean the fascination of the narrative that had led to the deconstruction of the conditions of its possibility. Killian never punishes his reader for enjoying the nostalgia of personality. His characters (and their poignant obsolescence) are as luscious as the tropical cocktails they imbibe— and Killian's narratorial host indulges the reader's alienated nostalgia, saying, "Go ahead, have another, it won't hurt, it's not real after all." Killian's narratives entice the reader through fluctuating stages of naiveté and dis-enchantment whose wake reflects the mobile structure of a representational philosophy that productively admits both naiveté and irony as situationally valid orientations to the world, deploying and appealing to them both in its fictive articulations. I shall attempt to chart the hermeneutic choreography Killian installs in his texts in my consideration of *Shy* through its progressive disillusionments and ironizations: as a realist novel; as a modernist novel; as a postmodern novel; as a collocation of Killian's own countermimetic practices.[39]

Shy *as a Realist Novel*

In many ways, *Shy* reads like a traditional novel. The characters are complex and "believable" individuals, whose dialogue, personalities, and perspectives are rendered with acute attention to psychological nuance and sociological detail. The major structural challenge *Shy* presents lies in its paradoxical adherence to elaborate characterization and plot, while insistently breaking down the "realist" illusion these features evoke. The parody of the realist novel is so well executed, however, that even a "thematic" reading of the text does not expose its deliberate auto-undoing, as my initial observations will demonstrate.

Shy begins on the evening of June 1, 1974, when the first-person narrator, "Kevin Killian," hears his new neighbor, James Van Kuyper, take up residence in the apartment below him. Through his teen years and beyond, Kevin was in love with his best friend Mark McAndrew. Although they had experimented sexually, Kevin had to share Mark with Mark's girlfriend, Alley Culhane. Eventually Mark also attracted the interest of an older, wealthy (but married) Alder Golden, who subsequently persuaded Mark to accept an apartment from him in New York City. Kevin followed Mark to New York, and Alley went to France to study with Lacan. In 1973, while Mark was passed out on a drug overdose in a shower in Golden's wife's house, Alder stabbed him twenty-two times, wrote in lipstick on the body: "I WILL ALWAYS LOVE YOU SIN X O X O

XO SIN ANGEL," and then shot himself in the head. As the novel opens, Kevin is supporting himself as a bartender while writing his novel, *The Second Chancers*, about Mark's life and death.

James van Kuyper is a wealthy Pennsylvania socialite who was the only other person in his mother's bedroom when she "fell" from the balcony to her death. Whether or not this is the incident which triggers his action, Van Kuyper told his uncle Evelyn ("Foxy") Foxe that he needed to disappear and asked him for faked identification papers, and with his new identity as "Gunther Fielder" Kuyper moved to Kings Road, Long Island, to take a volunteer position at the Smithtown Hot Line emergency phone service.

On the train, Gunther is accosted by Paula Thiele, a drunk fourteen-year-old. After Gunther deboards while Paula is sleeping, she becomes obsessed with him and determined to find him. She enlists the aid of her friend Harry Van, a gay streetwise orphan. Harry succeeds in finding Gunther for Paula, but after meeting him becomes attracted to Gunther himself. Paula also consults Wilfred Todd, a high-school-age neighborhood snoop, whose "All Boy's Sex Club" is a clearing house and conduit for gossip. The interpersonal relations are further complicated because Alley, just returned from Europe, also works at the Hot Line, where she and Gunther begin a hostile fascination with each other. Paula finds and provides Kevin with a long letter from Foxy to Gunther, where much of Gunther's "mystery" is revealed. Harry ultimately moves into Gunther's house, and becomes involved in an S/M relationship with him. Eventually Harry runs away, and Foxy and Gunther's father appear unexpectedly at Gunther's door, forcing him into a car and back into his former life, as Kevin watches and protests from an upstairs window.

The characters each seem to be constituted by a loss that forms the empty center of each subject and the generative locus of the subject's articulations of desire and attempts toward meaning. Both Kevin and Alley are often portrayed through their mourning the death of Mark McAndrew, although the forms of that loss and their respective choices and transformations of the loss are very different. Kevin first "appears" in the story (although he is the inexplicably omniscient narrator of the entire novel) at his typewriter, working on *The Second Chancers*, his novel of Mark's life and death. "I thought this a great title for a book about a dead boy. . . . The whole world would mourn Mark, I thought" (*Shy* 7).[40] He also discusses the book and his memory of Mark almost immediately upon meeting Gunther. "Gunther and I walked quietly . . . past the honeysuckle . . . towards the beach. I tried to tell him a little bit about the book I was writing. . . . I had known a guy about my own age called Mark McAndrew, who had died a year before (1973), and I was trying to tell Gunther about him too" (18). Kevin summarized the relationship in one sentence: "I loved him but he left me for another man, then died" (20). At times it becomes clear that Mark's death is only a personally mythic structuration of the more general loss constituting the subject. When, out of sympathy for Kevin, whom Gunther had abandoned at the neighborhood bar, the heterosexual bartender gives Kevin a free drink, Kevin reflects: "He, like Gunther, must have seen how desperately I needed a friend, but had a different way of evading me. He and Gunther were alive, too, which made their ways of evading me different again than Mark McAndrew's" (20–21).

If Mark's death provides the scenario, the passion play for Kevin's interior distances, the memory of Mark embodies in its absence the desire that informs the melancholia of the subject with the inevitability of its meaningfulness, that also recasts experience as aftermath and echo. After recalling their teenaged years when, inspired by an Ann Landers column, Mark and Kevin experimented with kissing, the narrator Kevin observes: "It was only when I went to lead my own life, after he'd left mine, that I couldn't stop seeing things through the haze of sexual pleasure he'd created in me. That was really my only problem with Mark, what to do after he went away. Like people who go to Niagara Falls, and for weeks afterwards walk around with their ears ringing, the sound of cascading water pursuing them lo, even unto the desert sands?" (110–11).

Harry's losses not only define him but render him ultimately unsatisfactorily definable, particularly to himself. A mismanaged orphan, he fell through the cracks of the child welfare system, essentially bypassing education entirely. Without any memory of his parents, even ignorant of his birthdate (he estimates that he is fifteen or sixteen), and completely illiterate, his own existence is an imponderable and the world an indecipherable mystery. Harry's hard-knocks philosophy and attitudes derive from the serial abandonments of foster parents, the physical and sexual abuse in some of those homes, and a child's ability to rationalize the senseless suffering of his life. "Harry figured he had two, maybe three things going for him. He was young, and as far around as he could see, young counted for a lot. He was good looking, and looks never hurt. He was unattached—free. Didn't have a mother or a father or even a brother." When placed with a new family, he immediately noticed that neither the spouses nor the children were treated any better "than strangers on the street. . . . So all in all he had those three things going for him pretty good" (31).

One Newark foster family in particular represented for him a crystallization of parental security, its inevitable ruin, sexual confusion, and contaminated but nonetheless precious love. He had "loved [Rick and Lynette O'Malley] both so much, and they took him to the zoo sometimes and the circus one time" (35). They had been "the first adults who let him drink coffee. That meant a lot: made him feel special. . . . You feel part of things, intimate, grown up" (36). A construction worker, Rick let Harry help him finish basements, and had him work with him in their own basement in the afternoons, which included "fooling around": "Rick had a big cock and didn't mind letting Harry have a piece of the action. . . . Sometimes he'd let Harry fuck him too. These things are important to a young guy, Rick knew it, wasn't too long ago he was a kid himself you figure. . . . 'Pull the curtains,' Rick said. Then it grew darker but still you could see . . . his pants slithering down his legs. Harry felt stupid watching this, felt like running off, doing some work, blond panelling, pine oil, sawdust. . . . He wasn't sure whether or not he had his thing really in the hole, but it felt like it or something, and anyhow spread along Rick's big strong fair back, clinging to that back like a castaway on a raft, you felt so good you didn't ask questions" (35–36). Eventually Lynette must have discovered these sessions, because after a night of screaming, "The next morning the bus came at 7:00 AM to pick Harry up from the doorstep, where he'd spent the night. As he looked back over his shoulder he could see her, pretty as ever, but flat somehow, staring at him from behind the drapes in an upstairs room. Coffee cup in her hand? . . . Her face said Forgive me, I'm sorry. . . . So he tried to let them go, them whom he'd loved so much, and from now on always to look forward. . . . There's always tomorrow, like the raft the castaway clings to all the way to the distant horizon" (37).[41]

Harry's sexuality is more a habituated survival ritual than Kevin's melancholic rehearsal of the loss that inaugurates desire that in turn saturates experience with that loss. Mark, as the object of Kevin's desire, became a phenomenological frame for the posthumous world. For Harry, Lynette's face becomes that object, the infinitely retreating image of maternal love, fixed at the vanishing point of "home"—the site of familial security breached by the internal invasion of sexuality. His subsequent sexual responses are attempts to regain what his acquiescence to seduction had lost him. Harry's sexuality is a mournful ulteriority, a self-defeating pattern of repetitive attempts at refinding what he never had, and reliving the loss that sexuality meant. Some of these patterns are further confused with the pragmatism of a survivor having little other recourse: posing for Jason Summerall's pictures in return for food and clothing, and even sleeping with Kevin in order to find Gunther.[42]

Harry's desires are also enmeshed with needs to restage the missed phases of childhood, including rather savage pre-Oedipal urges at annihilating union. Harry's attraction to Gunther is the most complex and catastrophic enactment of this scenario. He first became attracted to Gunther while watching him play with a whittling knife in the Hot Line Crisis Center offices. "Cool guy. Cool knife too, like something of Charles Bronson's, long, wickedly sharp, blue sheen, black heavy handle. Under the fluorescent light its blade flickered and fenced, with a mind of its own. . . . Mesmerizing kind of. . . . The knife, its smooth flicks, must have hypnotized him. Because he couldn't remember what Gunther looked like, but he remembered the cool blade's purposeful motion— when he shut his eyes he saw it" (97–98). Gunther's sexual interest in Alley enrages Harry with jealousy that reflects both the child's demand for uncon-

ditional love and the sexual survivalist's reliance on his allure for the adult se-
ducer to effect and ensure that love: "If anything, if he had to die, or bend or
break, no matter whose ass, whose cock, he had to kiss or suck, he swore to
himself, he'd find a way to make them all fall in love with him. Love him, yes.
Or fucking recognize him, anyhow. No: love him" (102–103).

Harry pursues Gunther relentlessly, in spite of Gunther's exclusive heterosexuality, his relentless homophobia, and his increasingly brutal responses to
Harry's overtures. Somehow Harry eventually realized how to win Gunther
over. "On Gunther Fielder's doorstep Harry rehearsed his mouth to say six
words . . . 'I want you to punish me,' Harry said finally. . . . He fled in shame
to Gunther's tiny bathroom . . . the bathroom door flew open behind him. . . .
'I'm extremely bad you know.' He felt Gunther's hands snake around his waist,
to meet heavily around his navel. Here, here at last, Harry could stop. This was
the peace he'd sought so long. . . . In the medicine chest mirror their eyes met
and locked. 'I want you . . . to punish me.' . . . With a conscious abandonment
of will, Harry fell down and gave in, softly, deliberately" (184–85).

After that, Gunther kept Harry bound to the bed, and once chained him
naked to a tree in the backyard while he threw a party in the house. They
settled into a ritual of narrative demand and reprisal. Gunther would solicit an
erotic story from Harry, which would arouse Gunther into sexual activity. The
next day, Gunther would punish Harry for manipulating him that way. The sex
and the punishments, however, were not clearly distinguishable. In response to
Harry's request that Gunther get a tattoo of Harry's name, Gunther instead
began writing his name on Harry's buttocks, "performing the job very slowly,
with a sewing needle, a candle, and a bottle of Wasserman's blue ink. . . . To
make sure that the ink would never run, he had Harry sit in a handbasin filled
with water for twenty-four hours" (251). Harry encapsulates his experience of
the relationship in his suggestion to Kevin for his novel: " 'You know what you
could put, in your story, is how the character Harry ran around always looking
for a *big brother*, and he finds one, he finds Gunther Fielder who says to him,
'Yes, I will be your big brother' " (229).

The pleasure of the text at this level of reading depends upon a disregard
for the peculiarities of its narrative operations inconsistent with the reality effect they achieve. Most concretely, this amounts to ignoring the act of narration
and the differences between the narrating Kevin and the character Kevin. The
melodrama of the plot seduces the reader into accepting the text's transgressions of its own premises, into extending the suspension of disbelief to the
first-person narrator's mediation of this fictional world. Moreover, the glimpses
provided of the intersections of the characters' interior lives with their environment seduce the critic—in other words, the meaningfulness of the text is
another form of diversion and seduction on this level. The seduction of meaning occurs across the text as well as in the individual portraits, the narrator

serving as a semiotic compensation for the banality of the world presented and for the interpretative deficiencies of its inhabitants.[43]

The unwarranted depictions of Harry's, Paula's, or Gunther's interior life oddly efface the narrator's presence, sublimating it as an operation of interpretative synthesis of the fragmented attempts of the characters to make or recognize meaning. The illegibility of the Other shared by the characters in *Shy* stimulates incessant decoding and recoding of experience and memories, through whose articulation the narrator is thematized as an integrative network of associations that, while present in the world of the story, are not and could not be synthesized in this manner by any of the characters, or a naturalized "first-person" narrator. One such dissemination of the narrator can be traced through variations on the images of knives and the marks (Mark?) they leave: for example, Alley's recollection of Mark carving their initials in a tree, "in what they vaguely considered a parody of older forms of romance, forms less daring and sophisticated than their own. . . . Around the initials Alley had carved a rough heart to complete the joke. Courtship ritual. . . . She recalled vividly how she'd seized the knife from Mark's hand, to gash that heart. . . . He thought he'd put everything on the tree that needed to be said and mocked, but he'd forgotten the heart, and she'd remembered it. And she remembered it now" (95).

This image is transformed in an uncharacteristically florid sentence describing a scene between Gunther and Harry after Gunther's party: "Gunther said to Harry the same six words with which his own heart had been gashed. 'I want you to punish me' " (196). Gunther's outburst anticipates (and parodies) something Gunther reads by accident later, opening a collection of Virginia Woolf's letters at random: " 'The night you were snared, that winter at Long Barn (Gunther read), you slipped out Lord Steyne's paper knife, and I had then to make the terms plain: with this knife you will gash our hearts I said.' 1928. To V. Sackville-West. With this knife you will gash our hearts I said" (239). The words "gash" and "heart" function on several semantic levels and in more than one associational chain. When Alley "gashed" a heart, she created one—a symbolic, orthographic heart, which was an expression of love. When Alder gashed a heart, it was a real, biological heart, but Alder's action was probably also an expression of love. Alley *created* a heart by gashing it, Alder *destroyed* one by gashing it (and figuratively broke several hearts). The passage Gunther reads is an example of a metaphoric gashing of a rhetorical heart, a literary allusion that reinforces his fixation on the gashing of his own heart. The coincidence of opening the book to that letter gives it the hyperbolic significance of an oracle; its historical context also reflects several of the situations in the novel: Woolf's letter becomes another instance of intercepted correspondence, like Foxy's letter to Gunther, discovered by Paula and given to Kevin. Woolf's letter is also evidence of an illicit homosexual affair of a married person (like Alder, or as Gunther had been). But it is also pain reduced to a trope, a literary anecdote, just as the excesses of meaning in the other associations depend as much—if not more—upon cliché as they do upon psychological resonance.

When she decides to run away, Alley hastily clears out her desk at the Hot Line offices. Dropping Gunther's knife (the one that had originally hypnotized and seduced Harry) triggers another complex of images emanating from "one image, the long knife: 'I will always love you, sin angel.' Her blind, sure fingers unbuttoned her blouse and bared her breast to the flat air. She could almost . . . imagine plunging that blade into her heart. Mark took a handful of bright pills, swallowed them down, then stumbled dying into the shower. Could have done that at home. Why the shower in Alder Golden's wife's home? To create a scandal? XO XO XO XO. Hugs and kisses. Seeing such beauty flutter away, Alder Golden did take this knife (and this red lipstick) to that bent body, how garish. . . . After such daring it would be easy to imagine the knife carving the X's and O's into the translucent skin of her breast until the whole ran with blood, and the flesh started to peel away" (236–37).

The imagistic links of the knives figure writing as a form of violence and its graphic remainder as a kind of cheat. The tattoo Harry receives cheats him in several ways: its inscription is a long and painful process, which is not proof of the love he seeks by submitting to it; it is in a script he cannot read; it is not his own name (thus falsely marking him for others); it is not really Gunther's name either (it has no referent other than the pain it indexes and the false promise it memorializes). Gunther's and Harry's bond is that of a readerly coupling: the masterful author inscribes a false text on a passive recipient, a reader ignorant of the bad faith of the text's message. The relations between the pair superficially resemble one way Killian has characterized his own writing, but it is important to appreciate the differences: "My writing takes an opposite tack to modernism, the primacy of the text is no longer an issue, rather its submission and the erotic components of that submission. Every word is controlled, bent—in the direction of pleasure. I don't think you really have to be in the S/M scene personally to recognize the S/M components in reading—the writer who withholds pleasure, the reader who submits to cruelty, the suddenly increasing energy and gasp of awareness and most of all the contingency on which all of this action depends" ("Boys of Fiction" 2).[44]

This theory of narrative is not Sadeian as much as Nietzschean, particularly the Nietzsche of *The Will to Power*. The narrator does not continue the tradition learned as a passive recipient of the "already read" of dominant culture, transmitting the imposed inscription to other readers (like Harry, or Kafka's penal colonists), but rather assumes a responsibility in the active production of meanings and their flux, without affirming a Truth or a Meaning independent of the processes and instabilities of these signifying practices. It is in *The Will to Power*, moreover, that Nietzsche identifies the writerly assertion of an un-authorized subject of signification with the rejection of any notion of a transcendent or unified subject: " 'The subject' is the fiction that many similar states in us are the effect of one substratum: but it is we who first created the 'similarity' of these states: our adjusting them and making them similar is the fact, not their similarity (—which ought rather to be denied—)" (266–69). The chain of associations gleaned from the isolated characters' thoughts, that fashions the metadiegetic reflections on narrative practice and relations of subjectivity to discourse, are the operational trace of a narrator whose "existence" (as character in the narrative) is impossible, but whose function (in the text) is neccessary for these fragments to cohere as meaning.[45] Below I will demonstrate that, as Nietzsche insists, the assertion of such illicit narrative authority is in Killian intimately related to his disbelief in a self.

Shy as a Modernist Novel

The focus on the narrated events depends on suspending the question of narratorial mediation. It is also possible to read *Shy* by focusing on the narrator and his effort to construct the story around him. This change in focus also changes the presumed category of the text from realist to high modernist novel, the latter typified by a reflexivity thematized in a narrative of the text's own genesis and formation. In such a reading, the self-consciousness of the text emerges in the plot as a shift in Kevin's attention from the past (Mark McAndrew) and its novel (*The Second Chancers*) to the narrated present (summer 1974) and its novel (*Shy*). The narrator acknowledges this shift: "Now I was twenty-five. . . . I took a bartender job, I figured I'd get local color, grist for my mill, the way a man who wants to write a novel will. . . . Nothing had happened to me. Nothing except Mark, and I wasn't even keen, any more, about that memory either. I called my book *The Second Chancers*, and liked the title (kept dreaming about the movie version) but the material was beginning to bore me. . . . With this unshakable dread planted firmly in my head I turned my attention, more and more, to the man who lived below me, Gunther Fielder, and staked everything now, on finding a language to describe him" (*Shy* 111).

Even the opening chapter foreshadows this progression, when it closes with the novelist's unsuccessful attempt to catch a glimpse of the newcomer downstairs: "Disgruntled I turned back to my typewriter, but no longer could I concentrate on the dead boy's life and death. My glass was empty. For the first time, instead of refilling it, I turned it upside down on the bathroom floor and pressed my ear against it to listen" (11). Once Harry moves into Gunther's house, the glass becomes more prominent, both as a medium for eavesdropping and as an element in the plot. Even Kevin's typing changes significance: "My steady typing through all the nights Gunther and Harry had spent together had perhaps almost seduced Gunther into thinking his apartment soundproof. But all this time, I must have been eavesdropping on every yelp and cry. . . . Now that everyone . . . had left . . . I'd be listening in as though to a radio soap. I'd listened indeed, Gunther didn't know how often, to get off on the sounds of what they did and said. See, I was writing a novel, and Gunther and Harry were among its major characters. He didn't know that for sure, but he was beginning to suspect it" (194). Previously the typing was a sign of Kevin's identity as a writer and his involvement with the past and Mark. Now it is a sign of his involvement with the present and Gunther, and serves to *conceal* rather than *announce* the narrator's attention.

Much of the plot is motivated by Kevin's attempts to render from the chaotic plurality of the other characters' testimonies a coherent and linear narrative (reminiscent of the psychoanalyst). Kevin's agenda frustrates Harry's first attempts at seduction. While Harry masturbates Kevin in his car, Kevin continually interrupts the lewd story Harry tells him: " 'What was the girl doing all this time?' I asked, out of the novelist's need to keep track of all the characters. 'I don't know,' Harry said, full of the character's scorn for the novelist's niceties" (64).[46] Kevin's narratorial drive, his pursuit of the story and the "truth" of the character, is one of the reasons Harry preferred Gunther: "Harry liked me best when I didn't ask questions, but I would never stop, therefore he liked Gunther better." It was also his drive for the story that led Kevin to strike up a friendship with Wilfred Todd: "I met him on the beach, in the shadow of his clubhouse. . . . That wonderful, rose-petal complexion, coupled with his amazing aura of knowledgeability, made Wilfred Todd a kind of mirror for me I could hardly turn my eyes from. . . . With his talent for narrative I imagined he'd make a really good writer, and this alone made my rooms beautiful when they held him within their walls" (272).

The conduits of information also become key elements in the intersections between the story and the metanarrative. At one point Gunther notices the glass on Kevin's floor, which exacerbates his increasing paranoia (254). Finally, the glass fails Kevin when he needs it most, the day Foxy and Mr. van Kuyper arrive to reclaim Gunther/Jimmy: " 'Doorbell ring. All unaware, Gunther Fielder went to answer it, and when the screen door creaked open I heard the stranger's voice for the first time, addressing him with regret. 'Your father's outside in the car, Jimmy.' I couldn't make out Gunther's reply, because like a football the glass under my ear was suddenly kicked away. 'Hey!' I said, not hurt physically, but more than a little startled and offended. 'Pay attention to me,' said my guest, Wilfred Todd. 'Not to them' " (271–72). Then the two men shut themselves in the apartment. "Ordinarily this would have presented no problem for me, but Wilfred Todd—*hypocrite lecteur!*—wouldn't let me use my glass to listen in" (273). Wilfred's interference in the narrator's search for the truth is only one of numerous instances in which the earlier violations of epistemological privilege are thrown into relief by passages in which the narrator attempts to follow rules long since rendered inoperative.

The narrator frequently establishes his position within the diegesis, only to subvert it by exceeding its parameters. The first "events" in the story (Gunther's train ride and arrival [*Shy*, 4–11]) are prefaced by Kevin's reconstruction of them from Gunther's subsequent account, but that preface also highlights the impossibility of the detail Kevin's account attains: "When I met Gunther Fielder, I was twenty-five and pretty vacant. It took me quite awhile to find out even the most basic facts about him. Even from the beginning he told me lies. It was—he told me—a crowded, noisy train, the train he took out to Long Island the night he came into our lives. . . . While his account of the train ride may not have been the 'whole truth,' I know it did happen, so I'm ahead right there" (3). The scene immediately following includes the directly quoted conversation of both Paula and Gunther, Gunther's thoughts, Paula's perspectives, and specific impressions of the landscape alternately focalized through each of them. The scene ends at the point at which the novel opened—and returns to the limited perspective of the first-person narrator so easily shed, Kevin hearing the taxi door slam but missing the sight of Gunther, who has already gone inside (3, 10–11).

The accounts of the narrator's discoveries are embedded within descriptions of setting, characters' thoughts, and privileged information for which no source is given or even conceivable within the parameters of the narrative's explicit limitations. Some of the descriptions of Kevin eavesdropping include physical descriptions of the scene and the emotional states or even thoughts of the characters overheard. Scenes dealing with Gunther's suspicions of Kevin are often told in the third person from Harry's point of view.[47] Other interactions between the narrator and the narrative, however, thoroughly disrupt and delegitimate the totalization of the text as a "high modernist" self-conscious narrative, as they had its apparent realism.[48]

Echoed passages, like the associational chain outlined above, transform and extend the meanings of the repeated phrases across diegetic levels. A particularly noteworthy example occurs in the third-person Harry-focalized narrative marking the beginning of his relationship with Gunther. The scene in which Harry utters the fatal line "I want you to punish me" and collapses in Gunther's arms is followed by an oblique synopsis of the extremities of Gunther's acceptance: "Harry didn't know much, but he wanted to know love's total expression. What Gunther gave him was merely everything in the world. No little scrapes, cuts, burns or bruises were going to take away from that" (184). The conventions of free indirect discourse allow us to assume that the phrase "love's total expression" reflected words Harry actually thought. The introduction of this phrase within the context of Harry's and Gunther's relationship, and Harry's grim talent for rationalizing abuse, determine the affects and implications of the variant phrase the narrator uses twice.

The night of Gunther's party, Kevin had a long conversation with Harry while the boy was chained to the tree. Kevin remained in the yard after Gunther had taken Harry into the garage, and then, "After a while I quit the dark and went up to my apartment above Gunther's house. I began to type but no one could hear me. This was the total expression of love" (193). Shortly thereafter, Kevin heard Gunther and Harry below him: "(Meanwhile, what Gunther feared most was coming to pass. Above them, in the apartment upstairs, I lay on the floor, a water glass between my ear and the floorboards. The S/M in my novel would be authentic, all-true. In most sex novels, these scenes come off dully, ritually prosaic as the acts themselves. How different mine was going to be: how torridly evocative of the total expression of love.)" (196). The meanings which accrue to this phrase due to its initial association with Harry give Kevin's act of writing a sense of sadomasochistic sacrifice—particularly in the first instance in which the image of typing alone, with no one to hear, suggests that the sound of the typing is itself the message that deserves an addressee, rather than the content of the text typed. It also suggests that Kevin's solitary transformation of Harry's plight into a text is an act of love. The second instance clearly identifies the "total expression" of love with sadomasochistic practice, and bonds this sequence with the previous characterization of writing as S/M, extrapolated from the earlier image chain.

Of course, the theory of narrative connoted here is one which a "legitimate" first-person narrative exposition could not foster: the narrator could not have access to Harry's phrase, and these instances would not recombine within a coherent consciousness. The compensatory signifying capacities of the narrator examined above here more dramatically betray the strain they put on the integrity of the text as a whole. The meanings the narrator offers are shown to incur costs; the syntheses of meanings such a narrator achieves are coextensive with a disintegration of the "egos" presented. Although the "echoes" at first seem to unify the isolated signifying systems of the novel, the merging of voices really does the opposite, as demonstrated allegorically in a passage saturated with disparate quotes from a number of characters. But this passage is a sex scene between Kevin and Harry that re-presents the "echoes" not as a consolidation of fragments by a master(ing) subject, but as the breakdown of ego boundaries during sex, the shattering of the subject altogether: "In time, our voices grew muffled but couldn't cease; one of us gave orders, the other kept pressing, denying, refusing. . . . Our muffled voices grew confused and peremptory. . . . Harry covered his ears with a cushion. He didn't want to hear his own voice, which told him nothing. He and this sexual scenario were partners in crime. He thought, 'I've been through this scene a thousand times before,' and so did I" (210–12).

Shy *as a "Postmodern" Novel*

Modernism depends upon a depth model of the self as much as realism depends upon a monadic model. The echoed consciousnesses in the sequence cited above inform confluent violations of *Shy*'s generic masquerades. The dissolution of intrapsychic integrity marked by the shared phrase "total expression of love" is as much an affront to modernist "profundity" as it is a breach of realist integrity: Killian took the phrase from the poster of Ingmar Bergman's first English-language film, and perhaps his most colossal, schlockiest failure: *The Kiss*, starring Elliot Gould. Ironically, if Killian had included the source of this phrase in the novel, it could have provided a plausible reason for both characters to use it (since the film was released and highly publicized during the summer of 1974). Suppressing this information, however, withdraws participation in the realist project while interrupting the seriousness of the modernist. It is important to remember that the reading I am engaging at the moment is structured sequentially in a way that *Shy* is not: my shift from a realist reading to a modernist reading does not correspond to the progression or segmentation of the novel. In fact, the presentation and decentering of realism and modernism are often interimplicated. For example, the depictions of Gunther frequently pastiche both the premise motivating realist narrative that truth is something hidden awaiting (and subject to) disclosure, and the modernist preoccupation with the enigma of the self as an explorable interior distance.

In the realist mode secrecy is presented as an imminent revelation, one which will explain the character's essence with a lucidity equal to if not greater than that experienced by the character. This covers both the detective story and the "constructions in analysis" of psychotherapy. But *Shy* demonstrates that this epistemological presumption is conditioned by the classic novel Killian parodies, in a scene that Kevin impossibly "witnesses" from his typewriter: the stormy night that Harry arrives at Gunther's apartment.

> Curious, Gunther touched the flimsy, somehow greasy fabric of the cheap chintz curtains, and parted them wide. Rain washed the distant mystery lights in the colors of Turner. . . . Nearby waited his companions: a pitcher of water, a quart of Dewar's, Dickens' *Bleak House*. . . . Above he heard me, Kevin Killian, beating my typewriter like a signalling tom-tom. . . . This view of the wild night, plunging with mystery lights and phantoms, wavery branches, wasn't a view to cheer a man up. . . . *Three sharp raps at the door—then another.* Gunther started, his drink slithered in his hand. These weren't merely

words in Dickens's novel, but actual sounds he actually heard, raps at his own front door. (*Shy* 114-15; emphasis Killian's)

The sentence in italics is taken directly from the Dickens novel Gunther is reading when Harry knocks. The confusion between text and reality, language and perception is more complete in the reader than it could have been for Gunther—but this confusion is exacerbated rather than allayed by the narrator's explicit "clarification" of the distinction between a sentence in Killian's narrative and a sentence in the novel Gunther was reading (the character could not confuse an event [the knock] with a sentence describing it). The intimate relation between the Dickens novel and the mood (and plot) of the scene is virtually forced on the reader with this maneuver. Furthermore, the total atmosphere of the scene is neither an effect of nor primarily a reflection of Gunther's state of mind—or even an effect of the narrator's presentation—but rather an effect of the novel Gunther is reading, and the gothic tradition *Bleak House* metonymically represents. The entire gestalt of the brooding exile, the violent storm, the unexpected visitor, and the intrusion of dangerous sexuality into the domestic space is made possible by the gothic. The gothic is both a literary genre and a style of psychosexual expression. Harry's arrival does not call forth Gunther's "inner darkness," but merely provides the contrivance in which to enact this acculturated scenario of passion as risk.

Gunther's interior monologue on the night of Harry's appearance sets up another assault on the modes of intelligibility through which the reader's desire is typically manipulated. "Buried in the closet of the room where Harry slept and tossed, Gunther had hidden a secret, and until now he'd forgotten all about it. . . . The presence of Harry Van in the 'other room' woke him. For how could he sleep when, even now, Harry might be creeping across the room and opening the closet door there?" (121, 123). The closet slips out of the plot until practically the end of the novel (typical of mysteries), when Harry, now living with Gunther, happens upon it while housecleaning:

That's when he noticed the hole in the closet floor, something bright beneath it, glittering in oils. . . . A secret! . . . Gleaming from the open space was a small oil painting. A beautiful woman, a goddess, was leaping over a brook. Her legs were long and her white dress flew behind her, happy, and over her head in a blue sky Harry saw a string of flowers and ribbons with words written on them. He choked. Heavy tweed, brass buttons, tickled his upturned face. . . . "I can hear my own tears. Why Gunther, why?" For it must be that Gunther had hidden from him this beautiful oil painting. "Why? Why?" . . . Already the oil painting seemed to have lost some of its beauty. He'd lost something too: that beautiful faith he had in the goodness of people. (256-57)

Gunther's closeted secret, when revealed, disproves the realist presumption that a secret *can be revealed*. A individual's secret is meaningful only because it can operate on and traverse psychic topographies of signification and divergent personal and interpersonal historical contexts. Like the manifest content of a dream, the meaning of a "secret" (i.e., its secrecy) is not exhausted by its referential disclosure.

Harry's emotional integrity, which seems to be revealed for the first time in his reaction to his discovery, is also a trick, similar to the "total expression of love." Nearly the entire passage describing the painting and Harry's reaction is taken verbatim from *The Invisible Chimes*, a "Judy Bolton" mystery by Margaret Sutton. Killian changed little more than the names and the pronouns. "Judy Bolton" was a 1930s teen-detective series for adolescent girls similar to the "Nancy Drew" mysteries. This deauthenticates the emotional state of Harry represented here as much as *Bleak House* deauthenticates (by authorizing) the romance of Gunther's exile, and the gothic union of Gunther and Harry. Both segments are also metatextual variations on Killian's pattern of asserting narrative mastery only to expose it as a hoax.

Brian McHale describes the differences between modernist and postmodernist fiction as differences between ontology-based and epistemology-based aesthetics (*Postmodern Fiction* xii). *Shy* makes it clear that another framework is necessary—the semiotic. Epistemology, while qualifying the "essential" self, does not invalidate the concept. It in fact supports an autonomy of subject from object, and the modernist celebration of cognitive and cogitative plenitude as the self's bounded infinity. Semiotics (as both aesthetic and critical orientation) accepts the signifying processes that are anterior to, coeval with, and coextensive with the subject's articulation. In traditional disciplinary conceptions, epistemology can account for Mrs. Dalloway and Molly Bloom as well as Lady Dedlock or Silas Marner; it cannot, however, account for Jacques (the Fatalist), Jack (the Modernist), Gorgik (the Liberator), Gunther Fielding, Dennis Cooper's George Miles, or any of Glück's Bobs or Killian's Kevins.[49]

Grammars of the Subject

Benveniste's distinctions I introduced in chapter 4 between the subject of enunciation and the subject of the utterance are key elements in his elaboration of "subjectivity" as "the capacity of the speaker to posit himself [*sic*] as 'subject' " (Benveniste 224). He develops a radical redefinition of the linguistic concept of "person" by recategorizing the three-person pronominal system into two categories of words. The first class, which he considers "true pronouns," are the first- and second-person pronouns, "I" and "you." The second class are the third-person pronouns, "he," "she," "they," etc. "I" and "you" are peculiar in having no fixed referent. Like other words ("here," "now," "there," "then") these pronouns are shifters, meaning that the referent shifts each time it is uttered, according to the context of the utterance (the discursive instance) (ibid. 217–19). The words in Benveniste's second category all have a definite referent, meaning that "he" can also be replaced with the proper name of the specific person it designated (ibid. 221).

Benveniste also claims that the "third-person" category is not really a pronoun because it marks a "non-person." This is easier to understand if we specifically consider the "subject of enunciation" and its presence in its utterance. The first-person subject will appear in the sentence, and thus claim a subjective responsibility for it. "I believe that there are dogs in the woods." But a third-person subject of enunciation is nowhere present in the sentence: "There are dogs in the woods." This non-person can become the impersonal "voice of truth," since its absence lends the utterance a quality of timelessness and revelation (Benveniste 208, 228–29). The politics of truth games in this effect of the "non-person" of the third person is also implicated in the patriarchal hegemony on truth through the convention of using "he" as the masculine pronoun and the "universal" pronoun.

Even a superficial comparison of first-person narrated novels to third-person narrated novels makes clear the differences in the subjectivities articulated. The textual operations of *Shy* also elaborate many of Benveniste's insights on the linguistic construction of subjectivity. But the ways in which the "first person" narrator is adapted and violated in *Shy* require a narratological critical apparatus. For this, I want to reintroduce the "diegetic" terms from the previous chapter, modifying my emphases in their definitions more appropriate for analysis of narrative. I distinguish between the story and the narrative, and within the narrative differing levels of narrative discourse. The diegetic level generating the narrative is always one level above the narrative generated; this is the "extradiegetic narrative," and the narrator the "extradiegetic narrator." If within this narrative a character also tells a story, that character is an "intradiegetic narrator." The extradiegetic narrator may or may not also appear in the story she or he tells. If she or he does appear in the story, that narrator is "homodiegetic." If the narrator is not in the story, she or he is "heterodiegetic." For example, the narrator of George Eliot's *Middlemarch* is an extradiegetic-heterodiegetic narrator. "Marcel" in Proust's *Recherches des Temps Perdues* and "David Copperfield" in *David Copperfield* are extradiegetic-homodiegetic narrators. Scheherazade is an intradiegetic-heterodiegetic narrator: she is an embedded narrator (in the larger tale comprehending her situation of storytelling), but she is not in any of the stories she tells (Genette 255–62; Rimmon-Kenan 94–96).

In *Shy* "Kevin Killian" (not the author of the same name) is the extradiegetic-homodiegetic narrator, at least in general. The variations in narratorial type are one of the reasons this model will prove more capable of accounting for the distinctions than simply first and third person. (Later it will help us understand how Killian simultaneously posits and undermines the narrating subject.) It also maintains distinctions among a narrator, the narrator Kevin, and the character Kevin. These distinctions are necessary because the polytropic narrator of *Shy* exercises privileges that should be mutually exclusive: the omniscience and omnipresence of a third-person narrator, and the experiential authority of an eyewitness or the self-certainty of the diarist. The two modes of truth claims merge peculiarly in those sections in which a character other than Kevin gives his or her version of an incident that had already been related by the narrator. This is not particularly problematic when "Kevin" is also a character in the story in question.[50] In such cases, accepting the narrator's version is legitimated by the conventions of the first-person account, the readerly presumption of the narrator's sincere empiricism. But when there are major discrepancies between a character's version and the narrator's version of an event at which "Kevin" was not present, accepting the narrator's version presumes for "Kevin" an objectivity and epistemological prerogative exclusive to a third-person narrator.

One of the best illustrations of the latter begins with the chapter "Rebel Rebel," a detailed account of the evening that Paula and Harry spent with two brothers (Gary and "Popeye") they met at a bar. This occurs before Kevin has met either Paula or Harry (*Shy* 22–30). Kevin does not appear in the chapter, and the narrator is unintrusive, alternating between external description and dialogue, and interior monologue and free indirect discourse, maintaining a consistent focalization through Harry Van's perspective. This is, therefore, actually a third-person narrative. Going home with the brothers, Paula disappears with Gary into his bedroom, leaving Popeye and Harry alone. Although Popeye makes some overtures toward Harry, nothing happens between them. When Harry meets Kevin, however, the version of the story he tells is far sexier. He claims that both the brothers wanted to have sex with him, but when he refused, he suggested they have sex with each other, which they promptly did right in front of him (63). Harry's story is marked as a lie by its difference from the narrative of that evening constituting the previous chapter. But this implicit assertion of the narrator's command of the facts is qualified by the manipulation of narratorial delimitations that circumscribes the narrative presentation of Kevin's and Harry's first encounter.

After a night of barhopping with Alley, as Kevin returns to his car he says aloud, "Might as well cruise," and drives to a public sex park, where a young man meets his gaze: " 'Let's go somewhere,' he said. 'Somewhere else. You got a car?' " (60–62). While in the car, Harry begins to masturbate Kevin, and tells him the story of the libidinal brothers. Harry guides Kevin to the notorious "White House" of Jason Summerall, a wealthy man who supplies drugs and alcohol to young men who pose for him, and who engage in sex parties while he watches. Kevin and Harry spend the night there, having sex in an ornate room. Apparently having forgotten that he had already told Kevin a version of the encounter with Popeye, the next morning Harry tells an entirely different version, in which Paula is his girlfriend, and the two of them have sex in front of the brothers. This only further underscores the authenticity of the first (de facto "Kevin's") version of the original incident.[51]

The narrator's apparent possession of the "truth," however, is attenuated by a subsequent revision of the night Harry met Kevin, much later the next afternoon, when Harry wakes up in his bedroom in his foster family's house. Through his hangover, Harry reviews his "success," his self-congratulations relayed in extensive use of free indirect discourse: "What a marvelous stroke of luck it had been, last night. . . . Harry had been playing it cool, hanging out in the bars . . . nursing a beer, when out of nowhere he heard the name 'Gunther.' " Resolved to "outdo Paula at her own detective game," Harry gambled that the Maverick in the parking lot was the guy's car, and hid inside it (*Shy* 77). "Twenty minutes later, when Harry spotted the guy come out of the bar, weaving drunk like a fighter, . . . Harry knew he had it made in the shade. . . . Even if he wasn't Gunther, he would lead Harry to him. . . . The ignition key turned over, made a grinding sound. 'Might as well cruise,' the guy said" (78). When Kevin went into the woods, Harry got out of the car and pretended to have already been there. "Harry . . . got ready. He already had a hard-on, which wobbled as he entered the woods, found me there" (78). We also learn that Harry had stolen Kevin's ID, one of his chief goals in meeting and seducing him in his search for Gunther (83).

Our initial attention to two conflicting reports of one incident now reveals two pairs of subnarratives. "Rebel Rebel" and the version Harry told Kevin I will designate Popeye[1] and Popeye[2], respectively. Popeye[2] is embedded in another story which is also related twice hereafter, Kevin Meets Harry[1] (KMH) and Kevin Meets Harry[2]. They can be provisionally classified according to narrator type and "authority" as follows: Popeye[1] ("Rebel, Rebel"): third-person, true, complete; Popeye[2] (Harry's version): first-person, untrue; KMH[1]: first-person, true but incomplete; KMH[2]: third-person, true, complete. KMH[2], however, disfigures itself in a way that dramatically demonstrates the need for a more sophisticated narratological taxonomy. Although KMH[2] begins with a narrative situation identical to that of Popeye[1], when Harry's recollections arrive at the point where Kevin encounters Harry in the park, the sequence concludes with a passage taken verbatim from KMH[1]: " 'Let's go somewhere,' he said. 'Somewhere else. You got a car?' 'What's the matter, no one here?' 'Oh,' replied the kid, 'I wouldn't say that.' I waited. Finally he said, 'No one but a bunch of old fogeys. How old are you?' 'Twenty five,' I said flat out. 'I'm fifteen,' he said, adding, 'or sixteen' " (62; 78).

This conjuncture also marks the intrusion of a personal pronoun that neither the narratorial distance maintained for the previous three pages nor the focalization through Harry should allow: "Harry . . . got ready. He already had a hard-on, which wobbled as he entered the woods, found *me* there" (78; emphasis mine). When the scene in Harry's bedroom resumes, persistence of the first-person pronoun (referring to Kevin) denotes a peculiar hybrid of narrative persons. Harry retrieves an album cover from a drawer, and empties its contents onto the bed: "Across the sheets spilled a slew of I. D. cards, mine among them, filched from my wallet while I lay sleeping. He studied my name, KEVIN KIL-LIAN . . . without really reading it, since he couldn't read. . . . He put my address into his head, the way it looked, the way it felt in his heart. . . . If you had been there you would have seen him staring into space, and you would have heard him speak part of my name and part of my address over and over again, getting it slightly wrong each time—the same way each time" (*Shy* 83).

These four subnarratives therefore have four different types of narrator: Popeye[1]: Unidentified Extradiegetic-Heterodiegetic Narrator; Popeye[2]: Harry as Intradiegetic-Homodiegetic Narrator; KMH[1]: Kevin as Extradiegetic-Homodiegetic Narrator; and KMH[2]: Kevin as Extradiegetic-Hetero-Homodiegetic Narrator. The last classification marks the fact that the introduction of the first-person pronoun, while maintaining a narratorial distance and a focalization through Harry, makes the narrator both absent and present. Kevin is "present" in the story Harry recalls, but absent in the scene in which Harry recalls it. Similarly, the narrator Kevin is heterodiegetic to this spatio-temporal sequence (early afternoon in Harry's bedroom) but homodiegetic to the novel as a whole. The inclusion of the first-person pronoun does not change the baseline "person" category of the narrative, or shift the focalization from Harry to Kevin, but accentuates the violations of the epistemological restrictions the first-person narrative form imposes.

These distinctions allow for a precise appreciation of the variations within categories, accounting for the different kinds of first-person narrators—Popeye[2] and KMH[1], for example. They also aid in elaborating the various discontinuities between the narrator Kevin and the character Kevin. Long after KMH[2] (both chronologically and in terms of placement in the novel), Kevin guesses something close to the truth, which Harry denies: " 'I don't know why I picked you out in the first place,' Harry said. . . . 'It wasn't because you were drunk,' I said. . . . [But] because you'd seen me with Gunther—knew I'd lead you to him.' 'No.' . . . Harry said, 'That wasn't it, it was just a coincidence' " (210). The character Kevin, therefore, at this time still did not possess the information that the narrator Kevin had disclosed in KMH[2]. What is also important in this exchange is that the narrative logic marks Kevin's surmise as inaccurate in its imperfect approximation of KMH[2], just as that logic exposed Harry's mendacity in the incompatibility of Popeye[2] and Popeye[1]. Considering this parallel within the limits of our simpler narrative classification according to first and third person invites the following provisional formulation of truth claims: first-person narratives (like Popeye^2 and KMH^2) are inherently suspect, as they are often either fallacious or fallible; third-person narratives (like Popeye^1 and KMH^2) are capable of accurate representation of the truth. This changes our earlier definition of a "reliable" story from one told by Kevin over one told by another character, to one told by a third-person narrator over one told by a first-person narrator.

This axiom presents a problem, since the Kevin narrator freely fluctuates between first and third person. This paradox sheds more light on the metacritical complexities of the novel: the structures of narrative information in *Shy* allow us to deduce an axiom that is inapplicable to the narrative situations of the very novel whose analysis had generated it. Secondly, the axiom that the third-person narrative is definitionally more capable of accuracy and truth than a first-person narrative makes explicit one of the presumptions underlying traditional narrative practices and dominant constructions of scientific objectivity, and historical writing as "History." But the narrator's choices exploit these presumptions without confirming them. Although Popeye^1 and KMH^2 are "told" in the third person, the latter narrative exposes this objectivity as a pose of the baseline first-person (extradiegetic-homodiegetic) narrator Kevin. Popeye^1 and KMH^2 are more exhaustive than KMH^1 because they are told from the distance and through the inconceivable privileges of a third-person omniscient narrator.

Killian parodies the metaphysics inherent in the above axiom, thereby revealing the axiom's illogicality and the potential repressiveness of its deployment. The narrator operates on the prinicple that the difference between an unreliable story and a true story is the difference between *one told by someone* and *one told by no one*. When Kevin imitates no one, he imitates an authoritative narrator, a position the narrative situation of the book does not actually allow him to achieve.[52] In this light, there seem to be no real advantages to the first-person form. There would be a real advantage in first person only if *Shy* were a confessional novel or an autobiography, genres which rely on the authority of the inner self. But *Shy* is not about Kevin's psychological or emotional life. In fact, the only clues offered regarding Kevin's feelings are given obliquely through Harry's interior monologues, to which the first-person narrator should have no access.[53] If *Shy* were a third-person novel, the inner thoughts of "Kevin" would be as accessible as the thoughts and events in the lives of all the other characters in the novel, over which the narrator Kevin maintains an impossible control. In other words, Killian does not avail himself of the only privilege the first person represents (self-proximity to personal reality/inner "truth"), but constantly transgresses the limitations constituting the first-person narrator. He thus deploys the first-person narrator position for its *disadvantages*.

Speaking of strategies, at this point both the analytic advantages and the limitations of my narratorial categories should be clear. The gradations in diegetic position elude the realist/idealist sedimentations of the traditional classifications of narrative mediations in fiction, which assume an unproblematic identity among the grammatically defined "person" of the verb, the taxonomies of narratorial privilege, and the "real-life" psychologically bounded integrity of the individual. But this narratological grid is ultimately unsatisfactory because it either affirms or begs the question of the naive realist identifications of grammatical and narratological person. Although our second model certainly improves on the simple first-person/third-person dichotomy, it does not "solve" the problems of Killian's narrating subjects, but merely allows a greater specificity in describing the ways Killian's narrators transgress structural norms. Fortunately, the problems Killian's narrators present are not to be solved. Accepting the aberrant narrative situation of an impossible subject of enunciation allows us to reread the baseline narrator's relation to the text without recuperating it through either the realist or modernist travesties it commits. Does anything remain useful in the distinctions between first and third person? Perhaps the ambiguity of the terms demonstrates the fictionality of the "self," an identity dependent upon the signifying system that generates it.

Killian's "memoir" *Bedrooms Have Windows* doubly dramatizes identity as an effect of signification, in a chapter structured around a phone call Kevin received from Harry Van. First of all, Harry's appearance in *Bedrooms* intertextually violates the ontological distinction between a fictional character and a real individual (I will return to this). Secondly, Harry's monologue and Kevin's reflections on it intradiegetically suggest that, like the narratorial vacillations outlined above, the consolidation of a self as a subject of discourse is often a transitory effect of a renegotiated grammar of persons.

Harry's initial reason for calling was to confess and apologize for taking Kevin's "name in vain" (*Bedrooms* 102). The previous night Harry had slept with someone who repulsed him in the morning. When the trick expressed interest in seeing Harry again and asked for his name and phone number, Harry gave him Kevin's. Harry excused his action by saying that he had "just felt the pull," which begins a long monologue about his religious-sexual yearning, occasionally positing Jesus as its source and object, although he traces the secular effective history of his spiritual pull through the men in his past, including Gunther (ibid. 99–100).

And you can't find your father or find Jesus just by hanging out on a street corner and letting any old piece of pork take you back and you know. One night I woke up all tied up in electric cord. I loved it. I mean. You feel the pull, you follow the drill. . . . You feel it right under your balls but it's not sex, it's just a thing, you don't stop to say no, you don't say slow down. . . . You say Yes. . . . You go from New York New York to the West Coast. You see a girl that's the pull. . . . You wake up and maybe you're in bed with maybe an asshole. Rub your eyes all you want, it's still real. . . . The power of Jesus moving within one another! (101–102)

Commenting on Harry's peculiar elocutionary style, Killian writes: "I had the feeling his continual use of the second person was only a mannerism he'd perhaps picked up from . . . stand-up comedians. When he said 'you' he rarely meant 'you' he meant 'I' only a more lapidary, concise 'I' than the one he'd been saddled with. A perfect 'I' is what he meant, the 'I' of the Lord" (102). Killian's appreciation of Harry's discursive strategy illuminates an understanding of pronouns not as reified and stabilizing signifiers of a predetermined extratextual signified, but as positionalities whose unorthodox manipulations reconstitute and confabulate the subject.

This understanding of the subjective possibilities of shifters voiced by the Kevin narrator of *Bedrooms* implicates by association the shifting perspectives of the narrator in *Shy*, suggesting that they might represent gestures toward a similar exploitation of the grammatical and genre-determined categories of person as a strategy of discursive mastery. But the narrator of *Shy* only feigns the acquisition of a more potent "I" by eschewing the perspectively limited position as the character Kevin in favor of a third-person discourse whose apparent nonidentity is the sign of its mastery as subject of knowledge, a position the narrator's own situatedness renders unattainable, and, in the deliberate dissonance of the novel's fragmenting epistemologies, a position whose approximation is characterized by a transparency to its own impossibility.

In retrospect we can outline a text-reader dynamic structuring the progression of our interpretative encounter with *Shy*. The novel initially encourages "naive" readings, but each mode of reading advances to a point at which the text's signifying excesses ruin it, requiring a higher-order reading. My first and most naive reading of *Shy* as a realist novel allowed interpretation of the world of the plot and the cogency of the meanings of the characters' psychic lives, but this reading could not account for the nature of the narrator. The second "high modernist" reading admitted narratorial mediation and the act of narrating within the operations of the narrative, but this reading could not accommodate the interrelations of differing diegetic levels and their fragmentation of the temporal and epistemological coherence of the writing and narrating subjects. My third attempt, the "postmodern" reading, is the most radical, one divested of any linguistic or narratological tropes capable of stabilizing the subject.

The reader's progressive disillusionment in the narrative entails corresponding changes in the status and function of the narrator: (1) no factor—a transparent omniscience; (2) intrusive but fascinating interiority; (3) central—not as foundational support but for its internal discoherence and its decimation of both the world it presents and the selves it impersonates.

The Narrating Subject at Play

Having now dislodged the grammatically derived subject positions from the static person-ifications of the verb, and likewise having relaxed the covenant between the subject's representation and the law of genre, we are now prepared to trace the trajectories of subjectivity across the diegetic levels of *Shy*. The most significant and pervasive distinguishing mark between the two major diegetic levels in the novel for me is the different manner in which the "lack" in the subject is concretized. I have already discussed the tendency of the characters in *Shy* to define themselves in relation to a specific loss sustained by their personal histories. The subject-narrator of the baseline narrative, or the extra-diegetic Kevin narrator (EKN), on the other hand, exemplifies the Lacanian lack-in-being. In fact, the narrator literally presents "himself" as this lack-in-being, through the exposure in his narrative presentation of his "subjecthood" as an effect of the signifying processes of the text in which he "appears."

The characters articulate their constitutional lack through their sexuality, the narrator through signification—in both production and reception of meaning, since for one thing, as Lacan's clinical experience showed him, meaning does not reflect "the sexual but . . . makes up for it" (qtd. Rose, "Feminine Sexuality" 71). Unlike the characters' sexuality, the narrator's acts of signification are not a response to or a result of his "lack" but *are* his "lack." These signifying acts extend "his" mode of "being" as meaning, but the very adequacy of language to this task indicates the fundamentally symptomatic nature of the subject thus realized. The expression of the lack through signifying the self is not the result of the lack but its very (non)essence. The apparent self-representation in the narrative reflects not the ability of the subject to signify his "being," but rather the subject's total dependence on signification in order to "be" at all.[54] Thus a signifying act that expresses a self will always "mean" that self *and* the self's constitutional lack-in-being. This is a metadiscursive (or narcissistic) articulation of Lacanian aphanisis, the fading of the subject in the act of signification. Here, rather than suturing that division between being and meaning, the narcissistic subject of enunciation deliberately signifies himself and his aphanisis constituted by the same act of self-signification (the narcissistic subject of enunciation's utterance therefore is always one of negating affirmation).

Understanding these typological differences between characters and narrators enables us to schematize topographically those sequences in the text that encourage simultaneous yet incompatible readings reflecting divergent critical investments in the novel. One such sequence satisfies the requirements of intelligibilty of the realist novel, the self-consciousness of a high modernist text, and can be read through the character Kevin, the narrator Kevin, or a permutation of the two.

This sequence begins with the scene shortly after Gunther's party during which Gunther had chained Harry naked to a tree in the backyard. When Gunther found Kevin by the tree talking to Harry, he became afraid about what Kevin might do about the situation, and was deliberately insulting to him to chase him off, and then took Harry to the garage where he put him in the car. At dawn, after everyone had left, Gunther carried Harry into the spare bedroom (beneath Kevin's living room, where he was typing). Becoming suspicious of Kevin's possible eavesdropping, Gunther goes upstairs and invites himself in. Kevin greets him from his typewriter and offers him a drink. Gunther claims he wants to "apologize" for his behavior toward Kevin and that he has come up "to spend some quality time with my old friend Kevin." Kevin makes a pretense of accepting the apology and chatting, but hurries Gunther out: " 'Now, scat,' I said, 'I have to go back to my precious manuscript. It is the real *Falcon Maltese*' " (*Shy* 195). When Gunther returns to Harry's bedroom, Kevin resumes eavesdropping. Gunther then "said to Harry the same six words with which his own heart had been gashed. 'I want you to punish me.' " Harry obliges by telling him an explicit story about seeing a man and a woman having sex on a tennis court, gradually disclosing their names: Alley and Kevin (ibid. 196–97).

The section from Gunther's visit to Kevin to his return to Harry's bedroom, in both situation and exposition, can be read as either a realist narrative or a "modernist" text's elaboration of its own genesis. Either reading even accommodates metadiegetic gestures within the figural limitations of the self-referential narrative. Furthermore, the character Kevin can "embody" the EKN and his actions can allegorize the narrative situation (of practically the entire novel) without violating the constraints on the subject imposed by the commitment to an autonomous (and therefore bounded) self—a commitment equally in evidence in the realist novel and the high modernist text. Gunther's visit interrupted Kevin's work on the novel, not so much by entering Kevin's apartment but by leaving his own: Kevin could not continue writing until something else happened downstairs. On the level of realist/modernist novel, the situation is doubled: the deceptive reason for the interruption in Kevin's novel (the reason for Gunther's benefit) is that Kevin could not write while Gunther was there, but this conceals the other reason: that he could not eavesdrop while Gunther was there. But even the "secret" reason is still a "fact" that can be contained within the level of the plot.

The transition in or superimposition of levels is marked by the third aspect of Gunther's interruption: while Gunther was there, there was no one to eavesdrop on, nothing to listen to. Kevin could not continue writing until Gunther and Harry continued their interactions downstairs. In asking Gunther to leave, Kevin functions on three levels: on the level of realist/modernist plot, he maintains the conceit of having to type, and then resumes eavesdropping. But in that this dismissal sent Gunther back to Harry's bedroom, Kevin returned him to the plot. While this is dually realist/modernist narrative, the other implicit question the scene asks is: Which novel does Gunther interrupt? *The Second Chancers?* The novel of Gunther's and Harry's life, to which Kevin had secretly turned? Or the novel the reader is reading?

The scene also realistically spatializes the diegetic hierarchy of the narrative structure. By going upstairs, the character Gunther leapt a diegetic level to that of the extradiegetic narrator—we recall that the level of narration is always one level above the story narrated.[55] The spatial analogy in turn "authorizes" the character Kevin's impersonation of the extradiegetic narrator. Kevin's refusal to interact with Gunther rehearses the narrator's decision to withdraw from the world of his story in order to observe it. Kevin returns a character to the plot, the subordinate diegetic level in which subjective lack generates sexuality rather than meaning.[56] This enables Kevin to return to the acts of signification (the narrator's correlate to the character's response to lack): the pursuit of the narrative, and the covert observation of the sexual behavior of the characters in order to translate that behavior (their "lack") into meaning. Finally, the offhand reference to the *Maltese Falcon* reflects the thematic obsession with narrative as both act and object of desire.

These diverse interpretations of this section are neither antinomic nor harmonious, as they represent topologically distinct operations of meaning. Although the readings do not cancel each other out, neither do they lend themselves to a synthesis. The heterogeneous logics are neither vanquished serially in a hermeneutic teleology nor absorbed in a hierarchy of unification. The apparent alignment of these interpretations, in fact, ultimately attests to the incommensurability of the diegetic levels and their respective subjects. The sequence is multiply inscribed, in the way that Lacan describes the relation of the unconscious to consciousness as a double inscription, by which he refers to "the fact that there may be two completely different inscriptions, although they operate on and are supported by the same signifiers, which . . . occupy topographically different places. . . . These inscriptions are strictly dependent upon the site of their support. That a certain significant formation be at one level or the other is exactly what will ensure it of a different import in the chain as a whole" (qtd. Lemaire 118). Similarly, the same textual fragment of the novel here generates these different meanings on different levels. The multiply inscribed sections of *Shy* elicit and satisfy readings from several protocols (the realist novel, the modernist text, the confessional). But the very fact that they do so means that these heterogeneous legibilities foreclose any totalization of the text's signifying processes, and disrupt any stabilization of the narrating subject.

Killian's Countermimetics

The multiple legibilities of *Shy* also allow us to use the segment of the novel I just described to refocus the progressive disillusionment structuring my critical approach to *Shy* in terms of the key tendencies in Killian's overall representational strategies, which themselves consist largely of naiveté and alienation. In comparing our reading processes with the interpretative situation of the segment above, we find that just as the various readings of that segment refuse totalization without invalidating each other, the novel's self-deconstructive strategies compel increasingly ironic modes of reception without rendering the previous reading meaningless, without ever delegitimating the text's multiple deceptions. The ruining of the traditional narratives and the greater richness in the subsequently more radical forms do not detract from the meaning or the meaningfulness of those forms that were ruined—and do not demean or invalidate the interpretations derived from or even the appreciation of those forms in themselves (the most naive readings of the text).

The progressive skepticisms and the retention of the debunked readings reflect in linear fashion Killian's representational philosophy which implements these antagonisms simultaneously. Killian's texts, both prose and performance, are certainly mimetic, but he transfigures mimesis into meta- and countermimesis. The apparent first-order mimesis of *Shy* resembles that of the classic realist novel, the soap opera, the melodrama, kitsch, etc. But Killian's mimesis *is not a representation of an extratextual "real" world*, but rather a metamimesis, *a representation of a realist text* that presumes a correspondence between its signifiers and a pregiven world. The success of Killian's metamimesis is not the "believable" reproduction of an extratextual world (as in the realist text) but rather a "believable" imitation of the realist text.[57] The next order of mimesis, countermimesis, depends upon overcoming the previous success. It must ruin the accomplished reproduction, otherwise it will be recontained by the implications/politics of that first-level success. Similarly, the successful representation of a self must contain its complete ruination within its expression.

The progressive disillusionments of the reading of *Shy* have a corresponding process in the reading of the narrator, but the parallel between the reading of the text and the reading of the narrating subject does not maintain a metacritical symmetry. By this I mean that, unlike the radical reading of the narrative, the most radical realization of the subject's fictionality does indeed retroactively invalidate the realist/referential illusions of more naive apprehensions of the textual "I." Moreover, the relation of the narrating subject to signification is central to Killian's countermimetic practices. The narrator's expression

of a "self" in the text never denotes a claim to a corresponding extratextual
entity that is both origin and ultimate referent of the discourse antecedent to
and transcendent from its utterance. The signifying chain which produces the
narrator's persona, therefore, perforce constates the irreality of that persona.
The textual operations thus abjure the ontological autonomy of the self they
posit (if meaning can equal being, that "being" has neither transcendent nor
apriori reality). The "I" that signifies its own nonexistence serves as a negative
guarantee for a discourse that can deny what it predicates. The "I" is the mobile
ruin of the discourse that produces and sustains it.

Such oxymoronic discursive gestures ("An enunciation that denounces itself, a statement that renounces itself") recalls for Lacan a dream Freud described, "of a dead father returning as a ghost" who " 'did not know that he
was dead.' " This image is a Lacanian metaphor for

> the relation of the subject to the signifier—a relation that is embodied in an
> enunciation (*énonciation*) whose being trembles with the vacillation that
> comes back to it from its own statement (*énoncé*). If the figure of the dead
> father survives only by virtue of the fact that one does not tell him the truth
> of which he is unaware, what, then is to be said of the I, on which this survival
> depends? He did not know. . . . A little more and he'd have known. Oh! let's
> hope that never happens! . . . Being of non-being, that is how I as subject
> comes on the scene, conjugated with the double aporia of a true survival that
> is abolished by knowledge of itself, and by a discourse in which it is death
> that sustains existence. (Lacan, *Ecrits* 300)

Killian's narrators, however, assume the position of a dead father who knows
that he is dead.[58] The fundamental contradiction of assuming an "I" that denies
is mastery (a father that knows he is dead) is the destabilizing support of the
efflorescence of multiple, contingent, experimental subjects across disparate levels of representation, their breached boundaries marking these subjects' transgressive trajectories.

The effractions of the hetero/homo/diegetic enunciative positions in Killian's narratives correlate to the perverse cross-manipulations of the extra-
diegetic/profilmic/intradiegetic planes of the pornographic films I analyzed in
chapter 4. In both instances, the representational improprieties allow for identifications and ludic iterations of ideal ego and ego ideals that do not culminate
in the internalization of the paternal Superego. Mulvey claims that the fascination of the star system in Hollywood films works because it resonates with the
ideal ego of the mirror stage ("Visual Pleasure" 16–17). Killian's work suggests
a nearly perfect reversal: the ideal ego is merely the first discernible instance in
a series of intrapsychic and intersubjective publicity stunts that constitute the
self. Indeed, the self is the same hyperbolic imaginary process and accomplish-

ment otherwise known as "celebrity." While Killian indulges the reader's nostalgia for that intensification of phantasmatic specular fixity the stars impersonate, he does not allow this nostalgia to reify or support a coherent narrating "I." He therefore does not indulge the reader's nostalgia for her or his own "I," just as the dead father's self-consciousness of his state forecloses an essentialized "I" for the subject whose dream the father haunts.

The narrating "I" is the personification of the text's dialectical disbelief in its propositions, the discursive equivalent of Méliès's self-dis-spell-ing magician-illusion. In a similar fashion, by exercising certain representational privileges, the first-person narrator of *Shy* not only violates the psychological and epistemological integrity of the characters and undermines the referential density of the world he produces, but he also exposes "himself" as equally artifacted, as equally a contradictory productivity of the text.[59] But the reader has to recognize the impossibility and accept it, as a reader must accept certain fantastic epistemological projections in science fiction, or as the Kevin of *Bedrooms* accepts the implicit hypostasis of the subject in Harry's phantasmatic conjugation in the phone call on "the pull."

The negation of what is affirmed and the acceptance of what has been rejected are patterns in Killian's work that most fully demonstrate his debt to and multivalent elaborations of camp. Killian demonstrates that camp is a range of representational guerrilla tactics that cannot be reduced to the canonical stylistics of a self-bemused political quietism. Killian's camp informs a vengeful, split-visionary retelling of the story of popular culture as a personal and political communal history. This practice is variously realized as quasi-anthropological examinations of contemporary life similar to Barthes's *Mythologies*,[60] as loving recuperations of commodified images to express emotions those images usually serve to repress or evacuate of credibility, and as a technique of variable focalization in both fictional and expository narratives.

Killian's saga, reconstructed from the tabloids, of Victoria Principal's broken engagement corroborates Robert Glück's observation that the "love for the banal" is motivated by "the spirit of revenge" (*Jack 87*):

This week the *Enquirer* is screaming WEDDING BELLS SILENCED FOR VICTORIA AND PLASTIC SURGEON. HIS KIDS CAN'T STAND HER. Victoria leaned forward to embrace young Maryellen Glassman, who grew so upset reliable bystanders saw her shiver uncontrollably. In her anxiety the glass of soda pop she held spilled over Victoria's bare shoulders and evening gown. "It's not your fault," said Victoria, visibly angry and cold as crushed ice. "I will change outfits, that's all." "Well, I'm not going," said Maryellen, "so you can wear mine. I think I will visit my mother instead." Dr. Glassman was seen to intervene but there was little he could do to placate either daughter or girlfriend. The mention of his abandoned wife sent little tremors of guilt running up and down his spine from the fair nape of his neck to the darker pietistic cleft between his buttocks. Soon all Hollywood began to reenact this scene in any number of monkey-see monkey-do ways. Under the repeated impact of the splash the banns were broken. (Killian, "Pasiphae" 73)

Killian's deployment of figures such as Victoria Principal and Audrey Hepburn not only revitalizes camp traditions, but also illuminates some of the historical patterns of political, cultural, and emotional struggle inscribed in such representational practices. These stars and the typologically stable personae of melodrama, soap opera, and gossip columns hark back to earlier cultural stereotypes which embodied the ethos of a community. Glück traces the caricature to periods of greater communal cohesion, although modern caricature and satire often reflect the ideological quiescence of their precedent forms ("Caricature" 18–19). Because of this, "satire and caricature are often used more effectively by conservatives who believe in their community . . . than by those of us who want to change society structurally, people who were not located in an expressive community until very recently" (19).

Camp is one of the great examples of subversive retrenchments of these stereotypes, arising out of homosexual oppression as much as Killian's figures come from the fantasies of a repressive social order. From a famous Proust passage on sociosexual hypocrisy, Sue-Ellen Case rescues the insight that "the closet gave us the lie; and the lie has given us camp," and extols "the power of camp ironizing and distancing the regime of realist terror mounted by heterosexist forces" (Case, "Toward a Butch-Femme Aesthetic" 60, 61). The figures Killian uses can be saturated with contempt for the system that has produced them, or can be hieroglyphs for emotions surfacing on the screen of culture while mobilizing an internal insurrection of that culture's stasis.

The "tender" use of camp images activates the pathos that can be conveyed in these figures that for gay men have often provided "superficial expression to our deepest needs," for which we are "grateful" because "the story of our community is a story of doubt" (Glück, *Jack* 86). Killian intensifies this poignancy through his characteristic meshing of the fictional and the experiential in his short story "Santa," which closes with a real phone conversation that occurred in 1990, when Sylvia, the mother of Bill, a friend and editor of the Natalie Wood Fan Club, called Killian to tell him her son had died. Sylvia remained with him after Bill's delusionary states had driven his friends from the hospital:

At one point, she told me, he walked into the dream house from *Miracle on 34th Street* and told her, "There really is a Santa, Mom." In his last hours, he saw her, Natalie, extending her hands to him across a wide blue border, like a ribbon of cloud, murmuring his name, come to me, come to me Bill. "I'm on my way, Natalie," he said, and his mother sat nearby and her heart broke in 2 two's. "I've been waiting for you," Natalie said. "I'm coming," Bill said. Natalie smiled, her intimate, glamorous smile, and the screen dissolved the way it does in *West Side Story* when Tony first sees Maria at the big teen dance. . . . "She was his whole life," Sylvia said. "And now both of them are gone." — It certainly seems like a careless symmetry. ("Santa")[61]

The ironic narratorial distance maintained in the description of Bill's death and his mother's grief does not trivialize either (or suppress the poignancy or sympathy in the account) as much as it empowers the images in the film and the magazines to express the real emotion and compassion in a culturally legible idiom.[62]

One can see a combination of the two modes of camp pastiche (the Victoria Principal and the Natalie Wood) in the complex passage in *Shy* in which Alley, while visiting the McAndrews for the first time since she returned from Europe, recalls the morning she herself had learned of their son's murder from Kevin. It is important to remember also that this segment includes free indirect discourse and directly quoted interior monologue, both of which break the rules of a first-person narrator:

> She remembered sitting down on a bench with her breakfast, in Paris, fumbling with sticky buttery fingers at the thick Manila envelope in her lap. Haven't heard from Kevin in awhile. The strong tape tough and durable, nearly impossible to open. Trust Kevin. . . . A bundle of clippings fell out in a blur, bright in the slanting Parisian sun. The "Times" the "Post," oh, and the "Midnight Tattler" — Trust Kevin for the scoop de la scoop, I've missed my scandal. The headlines swam before her eyes: SIN ANGEL CASE . . . What could this be all about? "Are you all right?" asked a concerned stranger. "Perfectly," she replied faintly. I must look so faint. "Thank you." . . .
>
> In a flash she saw again Mark's face, but a different face: in death, white as paint, the blood drawn out from the body, and the words he'd borne in death drawn across his face and chest in lipstick: I WILL ALWAYS LOVE YOU SIN XO XO XO SIN ANGEL — the X's and O's the kisses and hugs Alder Golden had meant for him, even after he'd killed him. Twenty-two stab wounds across the body. . . . Alley remembered puzzling through the badly written article, . . . trying to figure out what it was saying: "apparently lost consciousness, his body loaded with barbiturates. The lipsticked message, written across his face and chest, reads I WILL ALWAYS LOVE YOU XO XO XO SIN ANGEL and continues to puzzle police, say inside sources. We're working on the theory that the X's and O's stand for hugs and kisses." (*Shy* 51–53)

The dramatic change in the tone and affect of these passages is part of Killian's unique refinement of camp as a narrative technique and epistemological manipulation. The ambivalent commitment to the reality of the narrative, the reliance on the garish certitude of caricature, and the cool negation of allegory take on the generic density of the novel most eloquently and explicitly in the often Dickensian arabesques of *Shy*. In *Bedrooms Have Windows*, these elements frame a false transparency, a counterfeit confessional pastiche in which the narrator is offered as origin of the text only as an effect of the text, and his "appearance" within the diegesis takes on the ontophenomenological frivolity of a celebrity's gratuitous cameo in his own bio-pic.[63]

Unauthorized Autobiography: Bedrooms Have Windows

Although Killian himself characterizes his memoir *Bedrooms Have Windows* as "an entire book about my sex life and its creation" ("Poison" 1), it is also a record of his friendship with George Grey, under whose guidance Killian had begun to write. *Bedrooms* constitutes two genealogies for the "Kevin Killian" who presents "himself" as origin and product of the textual process: writing and sexuality. Kevin's identities as sexual adventurer and writer are each presented as prodigal filiations with a lost paternal source and inspiration. The paternal influence is most literally apparent in the young Kevin's tumultuous six-year affair with Carey, an older married man fixated on his son, Nicky, who happened to be Kevin's age. But there is also a sexually transmitted patrimony figured in Kevin's relationship with George. At eighteen, Kevin went upstate to visit George for a weekend at a now-defunct college, where a blizzard trapped the two of them together for several weeks. During this time, Killian writes, George, "turned me out," that is to say, made Kevin a writer (*Bedrooms* 46). "To turn someone out" is gay slang for taking someone's virginity away, a phrase which the narrator also uses to describe Carey's initiating Kevin into sexuality.

Bedrooms is therefore both a history of Kevin's literary tutelage and proof of its success, long after George is "lost to me, like the word the stroke victim can't remember" (*Bedrooms* 79). After George married and moved to Hawaii, Kevin lost contact with him, and was unsuccessful in finding him at the time of his writing *Bedrooms* (George's mother refused to give Killian George's address). Losing George to marriage, Kevin recreates George with the skill George had taught him. The memoir closes with a story Kevin imagines of George's life in Hawaii—with George, after his wife goes to sleep, turning on a video of Kevin and watching it, trying to decipher the inaudible words Kevin was speaking. It ends with a monologue by "George' addressed directly to the reader:

> When I taught Kevin to write I knew he'd turn on me, turn my teachings inward, eventually. . . . We wrote a "book" together, *Bedrooms Have Windows*, the story of a tormented soul, its growth and development, fated collapse.

. . . Once we peered ass-deep in ivy through the slatted wooden blinds of a country cottage. Two men and a woman stood naked within. . . . It was two in the morning in our middle-class suburb, Smithtown. Kevin's eyes were bugging right out of his head. I envied him his interest in these people, whose bodies weren't svelte and whose clothes . . . showed they shopped at the Mall. (*Bedrooms* 133–34)[64]

In this passage, Kevin refashions and internalizes George as a melancholic voyeur who confirms Kevin in his fascinated scrutiny of Kevin's video image, transfixing and valorizing the voyeuristic Kevin in his own voyeuristic (but fictive) gaze. The narrating Kevin narcissistically fortifies his persona by imagining himself not only as the object of the gaze, but as an object caught looking (pace Sartre and Lacan).[65] George and Kevin's age at the time of "George's" fantasy recollection above, and the bourgeois character of the naked people Kevin watched with such fascination suggest the primal scene, the child's witnessing its parents copulating. Killian in fact has compared his understanding of sexuality to the child in the primal scene who "watches his parents have sex and doesn't know what they're doing, doesn't have a context to put it in. Well, I think I've retained a lot of the child's perspective on sex. I don't understand what it's all about" (qtd. Karr, "Triple" 36).

The primal scene is one of Freud's three primal fantasies, each of which concerns a question of origin: the primal scene, the origin of the subject; the castration fantasy, the origin of sexual difference; and the seduction fantasy, the origin of sexuality (Laplanche and Pontalis, "Fantasy" 19). All three figure in the psychosexual dynamics of Killian's narrative of his becoming a writer. George represents the primal scene, and Carey the seduction fantasy.[66] The castration fantasy is differently implicated in the functions of each of the paternal figures of the other two fantasies. Carey is the father in the Freudian conception of "castration," in that Carey's seduction imposes an acceptance of castration onto Kevin as the "precondition" of desire for the father (which the mother's castration allegedly proves) (Freud, "Dissolution" 178). George, as the source of Kevin's writing, is the father in the Lacanian notion of castration—and the deviant resignification of that notion that I have already developed in my discussions of Glück's aphanitic narrative expression of "local phallic melancholia," and of Killian's narrators' flaunting their "lack-in-being" through their self-exposure as effects of their own signifying chains.

Shy deconstructs narratorial authority through its self-canceling epistemologies; *Bedrooms* debunks the authenticity of the authorial "self" through the text's neutralization of the ontological difference between fiction and nonfiction. The unreliability of the characters as sources of information repeatedly exposed in *Shy* lends an incredulity to the narrator's reconstruction of the story. In *Bedrooms*, the narrator's skill at detailed, realistic narratives of imag-

ined futures for friends and lovers no longer in his life retroactively renders
suspect the "true stories" of Kevin's youth in the rest of the memoirs. Furthermore, *Bedrooms* complicates the determination of the narrator's "reality"
according to the narrator's relation to his or her narrative, by including in such
questions the ontological aporia of stardom and the psychical realities of mass
media. For example, in reflecting on his friend Marion's stories about her alleged friendship with Linda Blair, Killian writes: "Because I thought of Linda
as an almost entirely fictional person, Marion's lineaments became less and less
real to me, even though she was one of my roommates" (*Bedrooms* 95).

The fictive nature of any realized personality in *Bedrooms* does not emerge
from or confirm an absolute ontological opposition of being and nonbeing.
Rather, the "personalities" of *Bedrooms* are elaborated as varied gradations of
semiotic "presence" (insistence) within the diegesis. Linda Blair is obviously a
real person, but one who does not actually "exist" within the diegesis of *Bedrooms* to the same degree as celebrities who literally interact with Kevin,[67]
or even to the degree of the celebrities who figure within Kevin's narrative
fantasies (such as Bea Arthur and Betty White in Kevin's reconstruction of
George's life in Hawaii).

Within this semio-ontological gradation, the most saturated presence is, of
course, Killian himself, because of the "autobiographical contract." But such a
contract is as inapplicable to the writer-reader dynamics in the New Narrative
texts as the grammar of the verb proved an unsuitable mapping for the psychological boundaries of Killian's narrating subjects. In writing of her own work
and of Killian's, Dodie Bellamy distinguishes among three types of first-person
narrator: the autobiographical narrator, the traditional form of fictional first-
person narrator (David Copperfield, for example), and the type of first-person
possibilities opened up by New Narrative. Bellamy insists that even in New
Narrative, although "the author appears to be speaking directly . . . the author
as character is no less fictitious or less real than any other character. . . . An
illusion of confession is purposely created—it's superfluous whether or not the
content is 'true.' The 'autobiographical' first person is now about tone, a technique for creating intimacy, sometimes discomfort, in the reader" ("Incarnation" 30–31).[68]

In my discussion of the novel, I characterized the narratorial situation of
Shy as a narcissistic articulation of the subject-of-enunciation's aphanisis in self-
signification. In the generic difference of *Bedrooms Have Windows* as a memoir,
however, is inscribed the intention of the extradiegetic author, "Kevin Killian,"
to "appear as himself." To this end, the narrator's persona often emerges as the
kind of hyperbole usually associated with the stars he celebrates, but from
whose compensatory functions as prosthetic (and interpellative) ideal egos
he withholds support. These additional representational contradictions that

the narrator operationalizes thus catalyze the narrated "I," the recursively ne-gated-affirmed subject of the narcissistically aphanitic utterance, into a coun-termimetic celebrity.

As a *countermimetic* narrating subject, Killian turns his representational prowess to delegitimating the paternally figured sources of his "identity," by rewriting their truths through his fictions, an example of which we have already seen in Kevin's fictionalized account of George's life in Hawaii. This kind of revenge recalls Oscar Wilde's contempt for heteropatriarchal "authenticity" and "sincerity." Killian's text also reflects an insight into the organic relations be-tween metaphysical assumptions of the "faithful" reproduction of "reality" supporting ordinary mimetic realist practices, and the reproductively based linearity of patriarchal transmission of social dominance (father to son). In the supposedly "true" stories of Kevin's life in *Bedrooms*, Carey makes Kevin im-personate his son Nicky in a clothing store, having Kevin try on potential birth-day presents for his son. Kevin's coerced impersonation of Nicky replays on the level of the plot the father-son bond and the underlying ontological fantasy of the father as the norm (superego) from which the son is the always imperfect emanation. In the nature of the "act" of impersonation, the scene implicates ordinary mimetic realism (an extratextual Nicky to whom Kevin's performance is to correspond) with the politics of that fantasy. Contrarily, Killian ultimately exposes and rejects the patriarchal authority inscribed within that mode of re-alism, in a fictional future he writes for Carey and a new lover whose encounters parody the father-son relationship: "His ad read simply, 'Dad: I've been bad.' He . . . chose to answer Carey's only because he was the oldest one to have replied to him. . . . His real name is Tim, but . . . he took the name 'Travis' from a jeans commercial that had been big when he was 10 or 11" (*Bedrooms* 122).[69]

Before letting Carey see his "impersonation" of a Mapplethorpe photo-graph, Travis warns him that "I'm not all black and white . . . so you'll be get-ting some color values the pictures don't have" (ibid. 124). Travis's imitation of a photo, and his disclaimer which suggests he views his phenomenal reality as a technical defect, reverses the priorities of model and original; his derivation of his stage name charts a representational process that forecloses the question of the origin altogether.[70]

Although set in the period after George had already been lost to Kevin, one chapter of *Bedrooms* is written as if it were a letter addressed to George, the narrator recalling George's advice: "You told me that whenever I can't think of what to write, pretend I'm writing you a letter" (99). Within this admitted fictional premise is enclosed a radical breach of the distinctions between fiction and nonfiction: Harry Van's call to Kevin, which I cited earlier in another con-text. The strategy informing the inclusion of this anecdote is amplified in a related but even more extreme violation, also committed intertextually.

Late in the narrative of *Shy* there is an unmotivated flashback of Gunther's secret and traumatic marriage to a practicing witch named Melanie. The account of their married life and its disastrous conclusion is followed by a passage that oddly restates events of the contemporary plot as if they had not yet been related, beginning with Gunther's changing his name: "Gunther moved out to Long Island into a summerhouse, almost unattached. He took a summer job and thought about his future. Across the quiet street stood an asylum for morons and maniacs. He lived with a little boy, Harry Van, too old to be his son" (*Shy* 191). The next paragraph suggests a far more harmonious acceptance of his relation with Harry and the world in general: "Sometimes, while talking to the teenage mental patients across the fence, or to his boyfriend . . . he fell into a daydream" (ibid.).

What is completely astonishing about this passage, however, is that in his memoirs, *Bedrooms Have Windows*, Killian tells exactly the same story, but here it is about his *own* failed marriage to a witch named Michelle (*Bedrooms* 65–70). Except for the change in names and the shift from third- to first-person narrative, the portions of the two texts are virtually identical—reminiscent of the transformation of the "Judy Bolton" detective story into Harry Van's disheartening discovery. This manipulation of material and flagrant recycling is a different level of self-exposed deception from his appropriation of the Bergman film poster or the Judy Bolton novel.[71] Killian *plagiarizes himself* from one text to the other. Killian either changed his "own" experience into that of a character, writing the novel, then plagiarizing that text to reinstall it into a narrative of his life, or he inserts a fallacious incident from his novel into his memoirs. Either he is not "original" as a novelist (he borrows from his own life instead of "creating" the story), or in writing his memoirs, he makes things up.

Self-plagiarism is a deviant intertextuality that marks both texts and their respective subjects with coimplicated processes of recursive chicanery. It also completely implodes the patriarchal notions of creation *ex nihilo* and authenticity (the first because the novel might have been based on his own experience, the second because his "true life story" is taken from a fictional text). This "already read" is a travesty of the "already read" of Barthes's texts of pleasure, which demonstrates why Killian's metamimetic "texts of pleasure" are subversive rather than recuperative of the readerly subject and its representational institutions. The " 'already read" in *Bedrooms* is a passage one literally "already read" in *Shy*. The illicit congress of the novel and the memoir makes it impossible to maintain any of the regimes of coherence (of genre, subject, narrator) imitated and displaced. Thus, Killian's countermimetic "already read" undermines the interpellative process of reading altogether.

As in the misbegotten attempts at omniscient narratorial privilege in *Shy*, this plagiarism actually detracts from the coherence of the narrating subject. While replacing Gunther with Killian makes the tone of the concluding section more understandable (since Killian is comfortably gay), none of the statements there (such as "I lived with a little boy too old to be my son" [*Bedrooms* 69]) correspond to anything in the "plot" of Killian's life in the rest of the memoir.

As we found at the countermimetic culmination at the end of my multiply disillusioned readings of *Shy* through the discoherent self-plagiarism of *Bedrooms* the narrator achieves a self-deconstruction that does not allow a nostalgic retention of his prior illusions, but the stories in which he appeared and the characters of that world are neither devalued nor rendered meaningless. This camp-inspired consolation for the disillusioned reader can be reinscribed into the narrative of *Bedrooms,* to reconcile the temporally disparate emotional states of the narrated "I."

The text opens with a young Kevin exhilarated at the onset of his "secret" sexual life and romance with Carey. As a young teen on his own riding the subways in New York City, "Sealed in with the dismal frightened figures of subway America, I couldn't help but feel different and special, in that I was heading towards a love life that, I imagined, would have frightened them more, would have made them more dismal. 'Loveland' I called it, as though it were an address like Rockefeller Center. It's when you look into someone's sunglasses and try to see his eyes, or the space you feel rolling over a cliff or a ramble" (*Bedrooms* 2).

Kevin's later disillusionment is particularly apparent when, even on the night of the Stonewall riots, making love to Carey only illuminated the alienation between them and the utter mystery of another person that intimacy does not reach. The alienation is also expressed in prose so estranged from any cognitive or emotional frame of reference that only careful reading of the internal evidence surrounding the passage identifies Carey:

> The face on the pillow didn't belong to me, it squirmed and averted its eyes no matter how steady my stare, how intimate or abusive my words. I take this face as the model of the love that resists, yet endures, everything that can be put to it: all trials, sorrows, all caresses. In the morning it rises and in the summer it gets splashed with lukewarm water over a kitchen sink, in front of a mirror. It floats out of the apartment to be confronted by the headlines, black as the dark glasses through which it scans the news. (88)

The later passage, however, does not reduce the meaning of the first scene on the subway to an earlier "innocent" stage permanently "corrected." Kevin's anticipation in the opening scene is not really renounced (if anything it is vindicated) by the awe of or resignation to the lover's Otherness. Sexuality and desire are the irreversible apprehension of access to that Otherness as a capacity within the subject. Each of the above excerpts conveys that mystery and awe metonymically in the mode of the scene's presentation, because "the fragment of language evokes the melancholy pleasure of a ruin, . . . the relinquishing of meaning, the falling away and recontextualizing of human scale to include the non-human, the unshared, mysterious and unsharable . . . which is shared" (Glück, "Fame" 4).

Sex Writing the Subject

We have examined in some detail various ways Killian's texts bracket or otherwise negate their assertions. Killian's basic patterns of self-negating presentations are encapsulated in the text he wrote for a postcard promoting a writer's symposium on "Eros and Writing" he curated in 1991. It reads:

> All of us have worked very hard to prepare materials that will illustrate as vividly as we know how the links between eros and writing. First some false propositions—"Proposition #1—Writing is inscription; Proposition #2—The site of inscription is the body. Proposition #3—Inscription is desire. Proposition #4—The text is the visible sign of the mystery of desire. Visibility is contingent on the will to decode our bodies and our writing.[72]

The progressive complexity of each statement and the increasing distance between each proposition and the sole occurrence of the vitiating adjective ("false") allow the meanings and potentials for meaning in each proposition to emerge independently from their "truth" value, or their (negated) status within this text itself.

A similar agnostic semiotic indulgence structures Killian's compassionate skepticism toward the subject, its environment, and the communication between the two. Kevin does not believe his roommate Marion's stories about Linda Blair, and begins to disbelieve in "Marion," but he appreciates the meanings these stories have in Marion's act of self-fabrication.[73] There is an expressive corollary to this hermeneutic in the narrator's willingness to accommodate experience to incompatible signifying systems. Killian opens the final chapter of *Bedrooms* by summarizing the project of his memoirs and its necessary and self-consciously productive failure: "Again and again I've tried, without success, to relate my experience of the sensual world to the facts that surround me" (119). The failure stems in part from the divergence of experience and language, because language has "a separate system, an integrity of [its] own, and [it] can't be used to formulate a representation of Life" ("Sex Writing" 12). While sex writing cannot close the gap between representation and life, it can compromise it, because the practice "differs from other forms of representation in that it has some kind of chemical effect on the reader. . . . A fugue results, between the closed system of language and the complex system of molecules that holds my body together" (Killian, "Boys" 3). Sexuality can be the creative expression itself or a model for one, rather than the object or medium of representation:

"Bedrooms have windows to spy into, to comport oneself before, the way you or I might first read a book, then write one" (*Bedrooms* 78).

On the other hand, one's sexual practice may be as much a dissonant or inadequate representation of one's feelings and experience of the world as any linguistic expression of them. In describing a sadistic relationship he had conducted with another waiter, Sean, Killian wonders: "Although I knew I hated him I didn't connect it with the kind of sex we began to have on a fairly regular basis. I wonder if the kind of sex people have when they love each other feels equally disconnected, related only inconsequentially to their emotions" (*Bedrooms* 106).

Kevin's first experience with Harry Van in *Shy* suggests not only the impossibility of communication, but the wild irrelevant excess of writing:

> There I fucked him, in slow slathering strokes; first he didn't want to let me in, and my cock jumped restlessly, slapping between the cheeks of his ass. . . . Resistance makes me feverish, [I dug] . . . deep till I found a little satisfaction, and his face gleamed below me like some underwater treasure, mouthing some words I didn't bother translating, what could they have been anyhow, either yes or no, please or no thanks. In the Spanish Mission District, where I live now, there's this one movie palace where, no matter what the film is, always says "*Subtitulos*" on the marquee. That's what his words were: *subtitulos*. Fuck him anyhow. (*Shy* 69)

The *subtitulos* whose announcement is displaced with the title of the film they supposedly annotate are also, from the narrator Kevin's perspective, an unnecessary and unintelligble supplemental code that glosses what should already be intelligible (if there are *subtitulos* one can assume the film is in English and the titles in Spanish). The *subtitulos* are one more system of "words" whose extraneous "integrity" makes them unsuitable for "a representation of Life" (Killian, "Sex Writing" 5).

Narrative itself, as a "corruption of the body, of the text, of the story . . . is a faulty analogue for our experiences" (ibid. 3). The signifying excesses of the narrative can remove the subject from the lived experience the narrative was meant to substantiate. Bob of *Jack the Modernist* observed this when reading a story Jack had written about his ex-lover, "Joe-Toe": "The most foreboding aspect of the story was its total lack of pain: not in their coming together, not in their separation. . . . Alienation had become so refined it amused itself. . . . In a few paragraphs on lovemaking, Joe-Toe recedes into his own history which attracts Jack more than flesh and blood. . . . He elevates lovemaking with verities. . . . Sex concludes with a perception rather than an orgasm. . . . Joe-Toe becomes a religious principle, exiled from his own flesh" (*Jack* 94–96).

Conversely, the representational inadequacy of language can be used more profitably than its poetic autonomy. Dennis Cooper's narrative movement often describes the recoil from the desired object whose beauty refuses further conscious significance. Like Cooper's Mark or George, Harry and the others exceed the meanings Killian's narrators give their lives, because desire through them exceeds meaning. Mark McAndrew can frame Kevin's experience of the world because of Mark's absence from it. But even when present, the object of desire achieves the effects of absence, just as meaning is not reciprocal but diverted self-understanding. Harry's body fails to yield a message (from Harry), but instead the serial fragmentations of that body translate it into an ideograph of Kevin's desire. Harry's body, kinesics, and departure all "mean" Kevin's sexual attraction to Harry and the imbrication of desire and loss: "In my mind I saw Harry walking away from me forever, a walking ass exactly the width of my cock. Forever now walking away from me in my mind" (*Shy* 273).

Just as he claims the untrue as meaningful, Killian reclaims these inadequate signifying systems as at least an act of devotion—a proper, if not practical, response: just as some summer nights in 1974, regardless of the words left on the paper, the sound of Kevin's typewriter was the "total expression of love." Harry Van briefly appears in a fragmentary scene in *Bedrooms* that serves as an epiphany that mythically reconciles desire and writing. "I dropped my flashlight . . . its lighted end wavering across the dusty basement floor, pointing like a weathervane to what wasn't a man or boy, but rather a whole climate of erotic opinion. I was caught—captured—by a pair of blue eyes so vivid and so sleepy they seemed those of Loretta Lynn . . . but they belonged to a sleeping boy—a boy who sleeps with his eyes open, and his clothes open, and only his sense of identity seemed closed to me in that intolerably close room. The cave walls were slimy and covered with graffiti, big pictures of big cocks and big words, I began to see the connection. The attraction, the allure, of a language" (*Bedrooms* 85). The "allure of language" can be at best a compensation for the resistance of the desired object to interpretative stabilization. But that might be enough, and the stakes are so high. The Kevin narrator of *Shy* numbers Harry Van among those kids who are "too dumb to live, but life has loopholes through which swim or are borne like matchsticks all the dumbest kids in the world, carried by luck, good and bad, to go on suffering, with no ASPCA's to put them to sleep painlessly by gas. They're forced to live in beauty and splendor they can't understand except by translation" (*Shy* 259–60). Killian's narrators trespass on the vacant places of the dead father, to create environments in which the children can live. Not "real" lives, but fabulous lives—lived not in the (anaclitic) subservience to the Truth, but in the (narcissistic) glamour of meaning.

In Conclusions . . .

IN THE TEXTS of the first deviant strategists we examined, homosexual desire was assumed to be constitutive of the mechanics of representation, including its own representation. Oscar Wilde's narrator-researcher in "The Portrait of Mr. W. H." stipulated that the sonnets were not simply about the relationship between lover and youth, but also about playwright and actor: "To look upon him as simply the object of certain love-poems is to miss the whole meaning of the poems: for the art of which Shakespeare talks in the sonnets is not the art of the sonnets themselves . . . [but] . . . the art of the dramatist" ("Portrait" 146). Derek Jarman's reading of Caravaggio's *The Martyrdom of St. Matthew* centered on the artist's desire caught in his own gaze and in the vindication of that desire embodied in the artist's rendering of his beloved model as ravished saint.

Sexuality informs not only aesthetic expression but social discourse. Glück writes: "Society wants its stories; I want to return to society the story it has made—if unhappy, as a revenge, a critique. When orgasms appear to be produced by society there are stories about orgasms; ditto identity" (*Jack* 161). The discursive reciprocity between the social and the sexual is most vividly dramatized in Samuel R. Delany's sword-and-sorcery tales featuring Gorgik the Liberator, a former slave whose underground campaigns facilitated the abolition of slavery in the empire. The iron slave collar Gorgik continued to wear after his own manumission became a political insignia of identification with the oppressed, and an emblem of his sexual desires, the collar itself an object of intense libidinal cathexis. In their sexual encounters—together and with others—both Gorgik and his sometime lover Noyeed reenacted memories of bondage, humiliation, rape, and torture: the Master-Slave scenarios that crystalized the quintessential injustice of the institution they opposed. By conjoining, as cosignifications, Gorgik's revolutionary politics and his sadomasochistic proclivities, the slave collar enclosed a contradiction that Gorgik considered a conversation—not necessarily a friendly conversation, but a reciprocity capable of dialectical transformation: "Sex and society relate like an object and its image in a reflecting glass. One reverses the other'" ("Dragons and Dreamers" 238).

Gorgik accepted the form his desires took as "part of a price one pays for civilization." He noticed that in certain individuals, an element of "civilized life" such as fire or slavery becomes "hopelessly involved" in one of the "basic appetites" such as nutrition or sex. Just as there are "civilized" people, therefore, "who cannot eat food unless it has been held long over fire; and there are others, like me, who cannot love without some mark of possession" ("Small Sarg" 143). Gorgik's observation is most remarkable in its pertinence to contemporary "civilization" and *its* technologies, its reified economic, racial, sexual, and class power imbalances, and the polymorphously transfigured "appetites" of contemporary "civilized" subjects.

Kevin Killian showcases an example of this sexual political semiosis in *Bedrooms Have Windows*, in the romance between Travis, a nineteen-year-old unemployed actor, and Carey, a fifty-year-old married, successful businessman. They regularly had sex in Carey's apartment on afternoons his wife was not at home. A few days after attending the Robert Mapplethorpe retrospective, Travis arrived at Carey's for their regular afternoon date, wearing a black cocktail dress. Standing in Carey's bedroom, Travis said "softly but firmly: 'Undo me.' " Once unbuttoned, the dress fell to the floor, unveiling Travis's naked body, "carefully posed to accentuate the black bullwhip whose handle was firmly implanted in his anus" (128).

Travis's pose is a hieroglyph of the social, technological, and psychological elements of "civilization" that constitute the cognitive expressions of Travis's sexuality, and structure Travis's and Carey's relationship. Conversely, the stabilized inequalities of their relationship reiterate the larger power politics through and against which they each negotiate their respective social identities. This is partially expressed in the commentary on this scene that Killian's narrator introjects at the point Travis says, "Undo me." The narrator takes Travis's demand as an invitation "to a sexual deconstruction. What our bodies do, not for love or pleasure, but towards a more highly qualified social structure" (ibid.). I would modify the narrator's statement to read "What our bodies do, *even for love and pleasure* [also serve] other social structures." The phrase "sexual deconstruction" indicates that Travis's action (or its meaning) cannot be reduced to a "symptom" of social forces beyond his control or awareness. It is, rather a self-reflexive statement, calling attention to the conditions of its enunciation.

Gorgik's and Travis' fantasies and Killian's and Delany's texts are all examples of critical practices from the sexual margins. They each call attention to the ways sexuality is implicated in other discourses of social regulation, relations mystified by the ideological constructions of a "natural" sexuality. The tale-tellers at the margins of the marketplace, the Sygn artists of Velm, Cooper's boys transfixed in front of their VCRs, and his killers fixated behind their cameras all pose questions concerning the sexual subject and the contemporary technologies of the subject of representation.

We have already seen how the geometrical realism of Renaissance perspectivist painting installed a *cogito* behind the retina of the observer, thus inaugurating the history of the transcendent self with an optical illusion. The mirror and the practice of portait painting were two prinicipal innovations in the specular technologies of the early Renaissance that enabled individuals clearer visualizations of themselves, further reifying the certainty of the cogito and the authority of the "Self." The absent, unobserved viewer of a perspectivist painting complements the absence of the "Artist" (the specular version of the "Author") whose masterful vantage point was precisely this absolute distance.

Many subsequent representational practices have reinforced an image of the subject of knowledge as an unremarked, nonparticipant witness. Eighteenth-century French historiographers called for a reconceptualization of history writing based on the organizational clarity of the monocular vision of perspectivist painting (Gossman 15–16). Narrative is a technology of subjectivity that both establishes and destabilizes the subject, deploying symbolic traces of the specular that it cannot immediately represent, but which it metaphorizes as strategies of legitimation and epistemological privilege. In other words, there are sublimated forms of specularity operative in the gestures of institutionalized authority, common in both scientific explanation and (official) "historical" texts. The most universalizing strategy of narratives—from the classic realist novel to the scientific text—is what Donna Haraway calls the "god trick," the "conquering gaze from nowhere," an unexamined position from which the narrator proclaims a transhistorical and apparently perspectiveless truth. From Henry James to the most recent "expert opinion" on AIDS, one finds the voice of this unimplicated yet supernaturally privileged spectator, the spectator who "makes the unmarked category claim the power to see and not be seen, to represent while escaping representation. This gaze signifies the unmarked positions of Man and White, one of the many nasty tones of the word 'objectivity' " (Haraway 581).

At various times in their developments, both the history and the autobiography have been theorized through the specular, deployed as a metaphorical support for the phantasmatic politics of epistemological mastery these narratives were to achieve. Inspired by Renaissance perspectivist painting, scholars in eighteenth-century France introduced a historical narrative which situated "the reader, like the narrator, . . . at a distance from [the object of narration], so that it appeared to him [*sic*] as if it were situated in a framed and closed space upon which he could look out, as through a window" (Gossman 16).[1] This window structured the mastery of the disinterested historian and objective scientist, assuring the person behind the glass the position of unimplicated observer. The historian/scientist is situated at the "geometral point" in Lacan's first triangle of the gaze. An absolute division in kind between viewer and spectacle is maintained, and the "truth" of the object thus scrutinized is determined by the frame of the window.

The window also serves as a barrier against any contamination of recognition or empathy for the object on the part of the observer; this is particularly important when that object is an ethnic, racial, or sexual "other." Robert Glück envisions this literally in his story "The Purple Men," based on a rumor in the

late 1970s that scientists had painted the anuses of gay men purple to measure
the spread of parasites during sexual contact. In the laboratory, "White-coats-of
objectivity peer through one-way glass" (1). The body of the male homosexual
is the anathematized limit of corporeal and sexual integrity for the Western heterosexist order; the homosexual body is the antithesis to the ego ideal, serving
as the "non-self" of the heterosexual social imaginary, and enforced through
the social symbolic as the narrative of scandal, a kind of preemptive terrorism
that both defined the male homosexual and foreclosed any possibility of his
visible manifestation. When "the homosexual" appears as a character in a case
history—whether it be Freud's Leonardo or the far less fortunate denizens of
the medical surveillance narratives of the 1930s and 1950s (Terry, "Theorizing"),
the "otherness" of the homosexual was maintained by an absolute, scientific
distance between the narrator and the object of narratorial inquiry, a disinterested (nonidentificatory) ideal position inscribed for the reader to occupy as
well, a vantage point which kept the homosexual (a "not us") framed in the
master narrator's window, at a safe "objective" remove.[2] This is the politics of
the perspectivist narrative at work.

Glück's embodied narrator breaks that window, implicating his readers in
empathetic and intuitive responses to the profligate pleasures of localized ec-
stasies. Aaron Shurin coincidentally uses this very metaphor in discussing
Glück's narrative transgressions: "By confronting the reader, Glück not only
breaks the window of his narrative but creates and engages an audience, creates
a social registration for his writing by direct address. . . . the foregrounding of
devices and codes does not neutralize them but it can . . . reveal them not as
necessities but constructions—open to change" (Shurin 4–5).[3]

Kevin Killian reframes the window as a tranparent medium for performative exchange, a project encapsulated in the passage which gives his memoirs
their title: "Bedrooms have windows to spy into, to comport oneself before,
the way you or I might first read a book, then write one" (*Bedrooms* 78). He
conceives of his writing as a scopophilic economy, in which "the main theme
is looking and seeing. It's about voyeurism and exhibitionism, in the trope of
the reader as the voyeur and the writer as the exhibitionist" (Karr 36).[4] Such
gestures displace the scopic regime of the disembodied male gaze with responsive subject positionings within a ludic reciprocity of display and delectation
epitomized by the narcissistic exhibitionism of gay male seduction rituals. The
narcissistic subject ruins the specular mastery of the anaclitic voyeur, not only
by allowing the reversibility of the gaze but by violating the distances between
subject and object in the narcissistic subject's representational practice.

Because, as I discussed in chapters 1 and 2, the narcissistic subject's ego
ideals are often images of himself mediated through the desiring gaze of the
other (the ego ideal an image of the subject as object of the other's desire),
the subject's identifications inhibit the transformation of ego ideals into the

patriarchal superego of the Oedipalized anaclitic subject. In chapter 4 I examined how the pornographic apparatus and its peculiar indifference to or disfiguration of cinematic suture indicated how, in terms of the specular, this intersubjective narcissism does not lend itself to harmonious identifications with dominant ego ideals. In other words, I attempted to relate the psychosexual dynamics of gay male subjectivity to patterns of resistance to the ideological fixing of the subject, in particular the fixing through coercive identifications with images produced by the dominant culture industry, a process Althusser has termed "interpellation." The acquiescence to the image, the individual's misrecognition of his or her "self" therein, is that interpellation, which, we recall, Althusser likened to being hailed by the police. Interpellation is accomplished at that moment when the individual turns toward the police officer who had shouted "Hey, you there!" because the individual "has recognized that the hail was 'really' addressed to him [*sic*], and that 'it was *really* him [*sic*] who was hailed' " (Althusser, "Ideology" 174). I now turn briefly to how the intersubjective narcissistic subject resists this interpellation in terms of narrative representation.

In view of their proclivity for including themselves in their narratives, it is intriguing to read Robert Glück's and Kevin Killian's responses to other writers' texts "about" them. Glück likens the effect of Bruce Boone's description of him in *My Walk with Bob* to "an actual memory" he can't remember, similar to "a story told about me when I was a child, that I have come to remember, and even use to ascertain who I am," which makes Boone's version of Bob "a demand, the demand, in fact of any writing—which is a magic spell turning me into it" ("Fame" 2).

In a lecture on representing "real people" in narrative, Killian compares several texts in which he "appears," concluding that he cannot identify with the "Kevins" of other writers. He considers recognizing oneself in the writings of others a conventional misidentification, whose correction Killian compares to "the funny feeling you get when a stranger waves on the street, you wave back, and then you realize the stranger's not waving at you but at the little weirdo behind you in the brown fedora" ("Poison" 5).

Glück does not want to recognize himself in Boone's text, but finds himself succumbing to the "spell"; Killian cannot sustain such a self-recognition in the texts of others, but he notes this with regret. In their diametrically opposed reactions to "being written," however, the two writers share a suspicion of representation, and each addresses the politics of narrative as a mode of subject fixing. Glück's reluctant accession to Boone's affectionate portrait points to the underlying similarity between that portrait and any other fictive "version of the self" that "wants you to become it" ("Marker" 20). The seduction of Boone's narrative exerts the same kind of fascination operative in Althusser's "ideological state apparatus."[5]

Killian's professed disappointment at not recognizing himself in the other writers' texts is neither a nostalgic desire for nor an endorsement of interpellation, but rather a gesture toward an alternative account of subject construction that includes the potential for agency within that history and its expressions. The loss of the ability to misrecognize oneself in the discourse of the other indicates that the self is not necessarily perfectly "hailed" by the social order, nor exhaustively represented in the Symbolic. By denying the commutability of the "Kevins" he reads and writes, Killian refuses the notion of a self as a common denominator in-differently permeating its various iterations. His celebration of the fictionality of any representable subject is a complex and deliberately ambivalent affirmation emerging from this refusal.

Killian's counterinterpellative polygenesis of the subject informs the narrator's disruption of readerly effects of coherence reminiscent of the avoidance of suture in gay male porn films we examined in chapter 4. This is hardly surprising since the ideological function of interpellation structures the reading process of the bourgeois novel as well as the spectatorial situation of dominant cinema. For the "realist narrative" to convey its "truth," a "world without contradictions . . . appearances supported by essences," the reader must regard "the discourse of narration as the unfolding of truth," which constructs that subject "as homogeneous in ideology . . . in an imaginary position of transcendence to that system"—a subject "not questioned by the flux of the text" nor implicated in "the sliding of signifiers which disestablish social positionality." The reader becomes a "homogeneous subject, fixed in a relation of watching . . . precisely [the] relationship that becomes clear in the analysis of films" (Coward and Ellis 49–50).

For Killian, this is not a simple parallel between representational modes. Killian engages the transformative capacities of media images that Raymond Williams discerned (in television) even within their suppression in dominant popular culture, potentials for "inclusion, within the contradictions of a necessarily 'popular' medium, of historically excluded or subordinated areas of social experience, at many different levels . . . access, within the immediate signifying process to procedures of mobility, discontinuity, alternation of viewpoint, within the terms of altered social relations . . . the positive insertion . . . of a hitherto excluded or subordinated experience" (R. Williams 126). The deployment of the techniques of traditional television drama suppress their own radical possibilities; these conventions are some of the models Killian adapts to his own narrative structures. Killian often stars in his texts, or serves as celebrity walk-on mediator and occasional character, reminiscent of Loretta Young's role in her early television series—a series, in fact, to which he devoted an entire essay.[6] Killian's manipulation of these forms taps the subversive potential even of their superficiality to expose "character not as fixed forms but as processes of formation, crisis, breakdown, and re-formation" (R. Williams 125).[7]

One thing that "sickens" Glück in seeing his name in Boone's text is the way that it forces him to confront a "Bob that acts too much like himself, revealing the made-up nature of who I am" ("Fame" 4). Ironically, this is one of the principal subversive tendencies of camp, particularly in its deflation of heterosexual normativity: the exposure of the artificiality of that which is believed to be authentic (Bronski 142–44). Although camp reveals the "made-up nature of who I am," it also allows for compassionate acceptance of the self's artifice. It is Killian's use of camp, in fact, which enables him to break down and re-form the character systems of popular media, as Williams had envisioned it. Killian's camp reformulations of commodified images in turn address one of Glück's other interrogations of contemporary culture. In replaying Lacan's mirror stage by literally identifying himself in his reflection, Glück exposes the Cartesian traces (or palimpsest of Cartesian prejudices) in Lacan's notion: "Thirty-eight years later I catch sight of myself before I am prepared and the mirror returns a different kind of image. It's akin to my voice pronouncing a word incorrectly—the word becomes noise, losing meaning as it floats out of context. Instead of phonemes, I see a dying animal in the mirror . . . my self stands out, glaringly artifacted. The disjunction between matter and self engenders an instant of vertigo . . . : this animal is going to die" ("Truth's Mirror" 41).

Glück's criticism of Richard Avedon's photography returns Glück to this experience: "Behind Avedon's social critique is the more acute contempt of the artist . . . for (his) subject matter. We are invited to feel contempt for the image as I did for the self in the mirror, the contempt blocking identification" (ibid. 44). Because camp treasures the forms it burlesques and cherishes the personalities it caricatures, we find no such contempt nor any inhibitions to identification in Killian's work. During a joint interview Dodie Bellamy and Kevin Killian gave on the occasion of the premiere of Killian's play *Island of Lost Souls*, he described the work as being "about my youth on Long Island." A startled Bellamy interjected: "I can't believe he's describing it that way because the main characters are Claus and Sunny von Bulow, Jack Kerouac, Anais Nin, Yma Sumac—and Kevin plays Joey Buttafuoco as a teenager" (Linfield 31). The interviewer asked: "Is this work a pastiche of appropriated icons and personalities?" to which Killian responded: "Very much so, just as my life is" (ibid.). Killian's initial description of "Islands" indicates a dynamic understanding of the cultural construction of subjectivity and a facility with the signifying capacities of the culture's image repertoire that inform and enable Killian to use these stars as components of his autobiography. Killian's appropriation of icons in both his work and his life suggests ways in which the (countermimetically inflected) intersubjective narcissistic processes of identification and internalization condition an ironic participatory resignification of the construction of identities in a post-McCluhan media-saturated cultural Imaginary, and allows

for agency even within late capitalist consumer fetishism and pandemic commodification of all aspects of psychosocial subjective life. Furthermore, Killian's
reworking of narcissism as an unapologetic representational strategy implies a
profound dismissal of mimetic patriarchal authenticity, and represents a latter-
day revitalization (and vindication) of the pleasure principle as Freud had conceived it in "Formulations on the Two Principles of Mental Functioning."[8]

Glück traces the modern artist's contempt for his or her subject to Flaubert,
whose narratives "exposed his characters' artifacted nature, disallowing them
depth and continuity as though to punish them" ("Truth's Mirror" 44). When
Glück wonders if the postmodern artist/subject might reverse "Flaubert's scorn
by accepting an artificial self, with its own scale, depth and continuity," he
suggests as a model those "Eastern religions" that "respond to a 'made-up'
world with compassion" (ibid. 44–45). Glück's intervention recontextualizes
these aesthetic issues as ethical questions that might facilitate a dialogue
between gay male cultural practices and feminist cultural politics. Glück's genealogy is accurate: Flaubert became the "father" of "modernism" at Emma
Bovary's expense, and is credited for the avant-garde's disdain for popular culture and the identification of popular culture (the masses) with women and
"femininity" (Huyssen 188–90). The second part of Glück's question is related
to the parallel he draws between his learned contempt for his mirror image and
the artist's scorn for his subjects: the contradiction between knowing that the
self is a fiction and the need to recognize and value the particularity of one's
fictional "self."

Delany's description of this necessary contradiction returns us to specular
technologies of the subject: "The transhistoricity of the subject is, of course,
an illusion; but it is an inescapable illusion, without which there is no subject.
(It is, indeed, the ego's belief in itself.) Analogy: cinema is an illusion constituted of successive frames of light projected on a screen. But without the light
or a screen, there is no cinema—no illusion. The subject is a similar illusion,
constituted of a sequence of historical responses projected within the sentient
body. But without either history or the sentient body, there is no subject—no
illusion" (*Return*, Appendix A 376–77).

These arguments set the stage, so to speak, for a reconsideration of the
multiple legibilities of Glück's use of Méliès's film *Le Mélomane* at the conclusion of *Jack the Modernist*.

> [A] magician struts onto a stage. The image of the magician and the stage
> wavers and adjusts and wavers as though contending against that primary light
> of silent movies, but the magician is secure, exhibitionistic, preening, self-
> confident. . . . his name is Méliès although I would call him Desire . . . [He]
> takes his head off and tosses it to the top of the screen where it becomes the
> globe of an eighth note on a musical staff. Another head appears on his neck;

he removes it and tosses it up and so on. Each identical head conducts its own gabby conversation, each with its goals and urgency and point of view. . . . their grievance takes a collective form charting out a crude melody—call it "Meaning" . . . at once a made up thing and a depth in which my being is. . . . Then the process reverses itself. Méliès summons each head back to his shoulders where it disappears . . . inspiration fails along with the will to sustain a contradiction—head by head, no melody, no magician. (164–66)

Glück's choice of film is also significant. *Le Mélomane* is considered an oddity in general and in the Méliès canon. It is one of the few films that focus on the fragmentation of a *male* body. It also differs radically from many of Méliès's other films, which more expectedly feature the manipulation and caused disappearance of the female body.[9] The image of the self-dismembering magician, on the other hand, is consonant with the shattering of the subject in gay male sexuality, and an apt visual pun for the annihilation of the gaze elicited by the narcissistic exhibitionist subject. In its illuminating resonances with Killian's strategies, the multivalent functions of the film also help me to situate Killian within the general outline of gay male representational agency this book proposes. Méliès's dual identity as filmmaker and actor parallels the typical relations between narrator and character in Glück's and Killian's first-person narratives. The metaphor is greatly enhanced by Méliès's role as a magician in the film, producing all the illusions including his own image. The filmmaker thus creates an on-screen persona posited as the signifier of the "Real Self" and as the subject of the (filmic) enunciation. He concludes, however, by using the technology that produced the illusion to expose it as such and to dissipate it, a precise analogy for both Glück's and Killian's textual practices. The self-dissolving phantasm of the magician/filmmaker resolves the problem of the post-Cartesian narrator, without repressing the contradiction essential to the narrative act, as Glück describes it: "If I take the 'permanently partial' self as subject, I'm trapped (entrapping my readers) in a fiction, an ideology. . . . But if I present the self only as a construct, a nonsubject, I write from the void, a location even more improbable than the self." Glück regards these positions "as untenable, mutually exclusive, inseparable" ("Truth's Mirror" 43).

Killian also exploits the contradictions of a first-person narrator conscious of his own artifice in ways often divergent from Glück's, although their techniques share philosophies and effects. Killian's use of camp allows him a position similar to that which Glück described—a narratorial situation comprising an expression of a self (and thus an ideology his narrative itself refutes) and a radical discrediting of that self thematized in the narrative that the self supposedly produced. Like Glück's "Bob," Killian's "Kevin" serves a specific purpose: it functions as a persona from which to situate narratorial subjectivity, but is a persona whose impossibility allows the reader both to recognize the narrator and to accept it as the collocation of signifying operations of the narrative *without* believing in it.

Glück's narrators forgo the hidden keyhole of the Albertian vanishing point for the exhibitionistic vanishing act. His aphanitic elegies and abandoned rhapsodes transfer the negating affirmation of the gay male sexual subject to the resolution of the post-Cartesian narrator. Killian's narrators result from transgressive implementation of the discursive formations establishing the privileged enunciative positions these narrators ruin by their irreverent rein-habitation, a contradiction analogous to the gay male's expression of a desiring subject position that violates the laws of the sex/gender system authorizing his assertion. Like "J. T.," the porn image Glück's narrator psychically inhabits in "Workload," Killian's and Glück's subjects are "all for technique and also for the unmasking of technique" (256).

Samuel R. Delany's work also articulates the mutually implicated artifice of the subject's presentations with the essential phantasmatics of sexuality. When telling Udrog his life story in "Game of Time and Pain," Gorgik makes a claim that has an uncharacteristically Cartesian ring: "Through my chance observation at the flap of that lamp-lit tent, I gained my self, the self that seeks the truth . . . the self that tells the tales" (58). His interior monologue the next morning, however, evinces a more sophisticated disbelief in the self's predis-cursive reality:

> What am I, then? And what is this "I" that asks? Despite their separation, the questions seemed one. Yet to articulate them was to be aware of the split between them, between the mystical that asked them and the historical they asked of, between the unknowable hearing them and the determinable prompting them, so that finally he came to this most primitive proposition: only when such a split opened among the variegated responses to a variegated world *was* there any self. But, on such a morning, where do I turn to find it . . . to limit it, to seize it and secure it? Where do I look for a model, a mirror, an image of the questing self seeking self-knowledge? (128).

Like Killian and Glück, Gorgik needed a self from which to narrate his story. Selves and narrators are necessary fictions, and Delany is as careful as Glück to distinguish between the honest and the dishonest. The origins of these selves are as mythical as the archeologies of ancient cities.[10] Again reminiscent of Glück's restaging of Lacan, Delany casts a backstage light on the origin of his hero (and narrator of "Game") refracted through mirror tricks. In "Game" Gorgik traces the origin of his political awakening to his inadvertent witnessing of a naked lord putting a slave collar on his own neck as part of a sexual ritual. He compares "the gesture with which [the lord] placed the collar around his own neck, when he thought himself unseen," to "a mirror in which I saw—or in which I could anticipate—the form of my own freedom. . . . When he placed the collar again on me and locked it, he broke that mirror—but without in any way obscuring what I'd already seen in it" (ibid. 73).[11]

In "Tales of Rumor and Desire," Clodon, a slovenly, indolent thief, is befriended by a wealthy merchant, who takes Clodon to his home above his father's mortuary. There he shows Clodon a mirror. " 'Have you ever seen one of these?' Clodon had thought it was an elaborately framed window—perhaps into another room. . . . 'It's a mirror,' the man said. . . . 'Stand in front of it, and . . . it will show you something few of us more than glimpse in a forest pool or in some street puddle minutes after rain.' Moving closer, Clodon stared into the metal that, in a moment, seemed a solid surface, and, in another, something just not there. The figure inside, he only just comprehended, was he" (186–87).

The man then approached Clodon, concealing a broken slave collar in his hand.

> Clodon peered at the figure peering out. . . . When the second figure joined the first (and it was the man, Clodon saw) . . . "We'll just add this. Here." The man held something, which he lifted—and placed around Clodon's neck. A metallic clink. . . . [It was an iron slave collar with a broken lock.] In the mirror—and beside him—the man smiled. "Look. At your reflection, now. There, turn yourself left and right. And watch. . . . What do you see? . . . What is it that looks out at you? . . . Surely that's no drunken country boy. . . . Don't you see a slave? And not just any slave, but an evil one—a slave who once rose up against his master, a slave who pulled down on his careless back all punishment and retribution. . . . Can't you see him? . . . [and his] disdain for all authority, his contempt for human law. . . . We all have pieces to construct such a slave. . . . And such a slave, created of craft, artifice, and crime, may be more valuable, finally, than one formed only by the accidents of society." (187–88).

The mirror can be the screen that shows the subject bound in iron as the harmoniously interpellated citizen; or it can be the space to dissemble and disassemble those compulsory restraints and guarantees. Oscar Wilde's novel *The Picture of Dorian Gray* potentially either suspends the differences or inverts the values of the dominant binaries, "real" and "artificial," "essence" and "appearance," and "inner" and "outer." But the historical accident of Wilde's conviction as a sexual deviant and the binaries I have extrapolated as basic patterns in the general delegitimation of homosexuality since the late nineteenth century conjointly circumscribe a long tradition of ideological recontainment, reading the novel as a vindication of precisely the dualistic morality it interrogates, and completely obscuring the narcissistic insurrection inscribed in the text's preoccupations.

Returning home from mysterious "sensual" outings, Dorian "would creep upstairs to the locked room, open the door with the key that never left him now, and stand, with a mirror, in front of the portrait that Basil Hallward had painted of him, looking now at the evil and aging face on the canvas, and now at the fair young face that laughed back at him from the polished glass. The very sharpness of the contrast used to quicken his sense of pleasure. He grew more and more enamoured of his own beauty" (*Picture* 141). The plot naturalizes the contrast, and the dominant reading protocols determine the meaning of the scene as typical homosexual vanity and effeminate narcissism. Abstracting the visual technologies from the specifics of the narrative situation and the hegemonic interpretative framework, however, we can see that Wilde's character is comparing two politics of seeing: the portrait, a product of geometral perspectivism—an anaclitic, ego-bound stasis; and the mirror, an instrument of reflective vision, a narcissistic depth of field not subordinated to the vanishing point.

Dorian's mirror stage, like Karl Forest's in *Le Beau Mec*, restages the subject's recognition of self as an ideal ego, an image mediated by the gaze of the other and constituted by the other's desire. In Dorian's case his reflection is this image as captured by Hallward, the image that manifests the desire of the artist who realized it. Dorian's identification with this image is as outrageous in terms of the specular as is the Shakespearean scholar's "identification" of Willie Hughes as the addressee of the sonnets, in terms of the narrative. The identification of "Willie Hughes" also confirms an "identification with" Shakespeare as desiring poet-subject. Together the two configure the major patterns of deviant subject formation and the strategies of their representation. The graphic specularity of Dorian's mirror enshrines the desiring Other's "self-portrait" of the desired subject, which for Dorian becomes a "pleasure ego" that anticipates the counterhistorical pleasure ego ideals of the desublimated epistemophiliac. These subjects' volatilities and *jouissance* resonate with the flash at the instant of being *photo-graphed* more than the ponderous fixity of the official portrait. The portrait (generically speaking—not Dorian's, of course) has an unchanging content, and only one way of seeing it; the mirror, however, is narcissistic: its images are responsive to context and change, its surfaces are multiperspectival, and perhaps most important—the mirror allows others into the picture.

Notes

1. Calling the Questions

1. While semiotics and psychoanalysis predominate in my discussions of the subject as an effect of signification, Marxism and feminist theory ground my understanding of the ideological function of representation in constructing and fixing the subject. Feminist revisions of the social constructions of the gendered subject are invaluable to gay critical practice. We have much to learn from the political and theoretical debates within feminist and lesbian-feminist communities—but by "learning" I do not mean appropriating feminist discourse wholesale or assuming that parallel practices in lesbian and gay cultures have the same valences, motivations, and affects. The active and reflective acknowledgment of the differences between and among lesbian and gay male communities may provide a basis for new and more productive alliances. One of the most important things gay men can learn from feminist and lesbian-feminist discursive practices is *how to read and write from responsibly identified positions.* This mode of reading/writing entails an active relinquishing of the objective privilege of patriarchal scientism, in that the enunciative position of the investigator (as a gay male) will be thematically acknowledged and operative in the reading, as an ethical and critical strategy much indebted to feminist reflections on the questions of authority and the politics of "objectivity." Instead of rote applications of theoretical positions in lesbian discourse to gay male situations, we should rather read lesbian/feminist texts and critical practices in a double register—first to appreciate them within their own contexts, and secondly to engage with them dialogically, as a means to stimulate thinking through our own specificities—the somatic and cultural parameters of gay male experience.

2. If they are not "out," they potentially have full access to the very power and its mechanisms which repress them and their fellow "outsiders" who cannot "pass" (women and people of color of any sexual orientation). Gay men of color have had longer traditions of developing their own situated knowledge, due in part to their experiences of multiple oppressions and exclusions. See, for example, the writers represented in Joseph Beam's anthology *In the Life.* In his introduction, Beam himself expresses his debt to the lesbian writers of color who had inspired him to find a community of black gay writers (Beam 13). See also Samuel R. Delany's autobiography, *The Motion of Light in Water;* Hemphill and Beam, *Brother to Brother;* and Hemphill, *Ceremonies.* The situations of Hispanic gay men are beautifully celebrated in Francisco X. Alarcón's poetry collection *The Body in Flames.* Richard Fung's videos *Orientations* (Canada, 1986) and *Chinese Characters* (Canada, 1988) document the lives and the socially embattled fantasies of Chinese-Canadian gay men.

3. See Marsilio Ficino, *Commentary on the Symposium,* trans. Sears R. Jayne. University of Missouri Studies 19, no. 1 (1944); John C. Nelson; and Robb.

4. See Merchant; Keller; Harding.

5. Derek Jarman suggests this obliquely with his usual adamantine irreverence when he comments, "The *Sonnets* and the *Symposium* are a cultural condom protecting us against the virus of the yellow press. They also relocate the way we view the old photos from this fifties *Physique* magazine. Another photo of two boys giving each other a blow job records a moment of beauty. Or the photo of the two young men who have caught each other in

their arms and a flashlight which has a sweet naiveté, poignant under the damned soul from Michelangelo's last judgment" (*Modern Nature* 163).

6. See Winckelmann's letter to a young Roman nobleman on Greek conceptions of beauty as male (qtd. Pater, "Winckelmann" 191–92).

7. See: Pater, "Winckelmann" 191–92 and 214–15; "Age of Athletic Prizemen" 258–61 and 263–65; *Plato and Platonism* 241–43 and 255–56. I discuss Oscar Wilde's parodic and defensive uses of these codes in chapter 2.

8. On the bizarre racial, nationalist, and sexual politics involved in Western canonization of Mishima Yukio, see Jackson, "Phallic Imperialism."

9. The erasure of all differences here also demonstrates the need for specifically differentiated strategies among men and women, gay and lesbian writers and artists. Regardless of one's position on the ultimate efficacy of "essentialism" in certain feminist texts, its strategic deployment certainly reflects sociohistorical conditions specific to the women addressed. Parallel attempts to use "essentialism" for rearticulating masculinity would simply replay the dominant obsessions: phallocentrism is *already* male essentialism.

10. Jonathan Dollimore discerns in homophobic attitudes toward gay men an adherence to a binary opposition of "masculine" and "homosexual" that derives from a conflation of two other dominant oppositions: "masculine/feminine" and "hetero/homo" ("Homophobia" 5). This insight exposes the misogyny inherent in the loathing that gay men inspire in heterosexual men. It is ironic, however, that the dyad "masculine/homosexual"—which in the social system from which Dollimore extracts it would translate into male heterosexuality/male homosexuality—does not figure in either Frye's or Irigaray's analyses as a binary opposition. In Frye their potential antagonisms are subsumed under the commonality of male supremacism; in Irigaray they are literally synonymous.

11. I discuss Dworkin's antigay positions in "Explicit Instruction," and my review article of *Pornography and Representation in Greece and Rome.*

12. See King; Rubin, "The Leather Menace"; Rich; and Patton.

13. One of Frye's statements elaborating her second principle is perfectly corroborated in Moravia's novel and in Schwenger's commentary: "Male literature proves with convincing redundancy that straight men identify with their penises and are simultaneously alienated from them" (132).

14. In "Responsibility" (142–43) I discuss Frye's arguments in terms of the indifference to racial and ethnic differences that has characterized much of the writings of white cultural feminists and lesbian separatists.

15. On the Latin American and Chicano/Latino situations, see Alonso and Koreck 110–113; Lancaster; Almaguer.

16. By presuming an invariant equation between penetration and domination, Frye essentializes biological sexual characteristics and gendered positions of subordination, and reinforces a generalized phallocentric definition of sexual politics. This is why Frye's very welcome suggestion of the potential for a radical and politically subversive efflorescence of gay sexuality at the conclusion of her essay (145–46) seems so utopian, since none of her critical formulations, based on male heterosexuality and its phallocentric cooptation of homosexuality, would account for it.

17. Frye's reasons for objecting to men's identifying themselves as victims of "oppression" (Frye 1–16) support my arguments for the importance of a more complex definition of sexual difference as part of a more nuanced critical apparatus for evaluating the sexual politics of any given cultural formation. The differences in the political, social, and cultural histories of men and women which make it senseless for men to claim to be "oppressed" also render suspect interpretations of gay male sexuality based on male heterosexual history.

18. Heterosexual ideology obscures the fact that the perfect execution of these two positions within a relationship would inevitably result in profound dissatisfaction for each party requiring constant acting against one's own self-interests. For a man chiefly identified as subject of the "male sex drive discourse," being the object of the "have/hold discourse" should prove intolerably constrictive, just as the woman's identification with the latter subject position demands a repetitive self-sacrifice as object of the male partner's discursively authorized aggressions.

19. See Teresa de Lauretis's critique of this conclusion ("Technology" 16–17) and Sue-Ellen Case's commentary on de Lauretis's critique ("Towards a Butch-Femme Aesthetic" 55–56).

20. In another significant parallel to Frye's contemporary depiction of male hegemony, Halperin details the dependence of Greek male citizenship on sexual propriety. To accuse a fellow citizen of prostitution was a particularly powerful defense against lawsuits in Athens, because those male citizens found to have been prostitutes lost all civic rights, including the right to press lawsuits (Halperin 94–95). To be penetrated is to lose male citizenship. It is precisely the Athenian's phallically derived citizenship and the modern heterosexual male's phallically derived subject position that make the conscious "submission" to penetration an outrage against the institution of masculinity itself. See also Floyd Salas's novel in which a man who was raped was expelled from his Chicano community (Salas 37–39; Bruce-Novoa 72–73).

21. Teresa de Lauretis finds Foucault's theory of sexuality ultimately unsatisfactory because it shares with other "radical but male-centered theories" the strategy of "combat[ing] the social technology that produces sexuality and sexual oppression" by denying gender. This is unfortunate because "to deny gender, first of all, is to deny the social relations of gender that constitute and validate the sexual oppression of women; and second, to deny gender is to remain 'in ideology,' an ideology which . . . is manifestly self-serving to the male-gendered subject" ("Technology" 15). It also disenables any theory of sexual difference that could distinguish gay male sexuality and subjectivities from their heterosexual counterparts. While I share de Lauretis's criticism of Foucault for his "denial of gender," our agreement on this point is not nearly as important as are the differences in our respective agendas in which we each advance such a critique. In the essay I quoted above, de Lauretis argues for a reconceptualization of "gender" that will exceed "sexual difference," because, among other reasons, the conventional reduction of gender to "sexual difference(s) . . . constrains feminist critical thought within the conceptual frame of universal sex opposition (woman as the difference from man, both universalized; or woman as difference *tout court*, and hence equally universalized)" (ibid. 2). In her analyses of the dominant social constructions of "woman" and her formulation of feminist interventions in those constructions, de Lauretis gives theoretical and strategical priority to "gender" over sexual difference. In disarticulating gay male subjectivities from phallocentric constructions of "Man," I rely on a model of "sexual difference" that includes gender. In other words, de Lauretis and I are responding to diametrically opposed historical effects of different "universalizations." For me, "sexual difference" refers to a classification of sexual subjects by at least two terms—"sex/gender" and "sexual orientation." By "sex/gender" I mean the individual's biological sex and the attendant social ramifications of that individual's representation of his/her sex (as gender). Therefore, in my framework, de Lauretis's assertion that Foucault's denial of gender leaves him within an ideology "manifestly self-serving to the male-gendered subject" would be rewritten as "to the *heterosexual* male-gendered subject"—which is a further criticism of Foucault, who, as a *gay* man, should have known better, after all.

22. For a suggestive theoretical grounding for the formulation of the gay male identity

as a spectrum of new subject positions, see Laclau and Mouffe, *Hegemony*, particularly chapters 3 and 4. The clear distinction they make between "discourse" and Althusserian "ideology" is also very helpful ("Building a New Left: Interview with Ernesto Laclau," *Strategies* 1 [Fall 1988]: 17–19).

23. On the inability of the male to "bear the burden of objectification," see Mulvey, "Visual Pleasure" 17–18; on the ambivalence of heterosexual male objectification, see Dyer.

24. Although it is a woman who views the act, it is a man who wrote the novel (John Cleland). Perhaps the female protagonist is a necessary shield from even fictional exposure to such a scene.

25. Halperin addresses the discursivity of sexual meanings in his analyses of the "phallus" in the politics of Greek intercourse. He defines the "phallus" as "a culturally constructed signifier of social power" (166 n. 83). In cases when "the phallus and penis have the same . . . reference . . . they still do not have the same . . . meaning: 'phallus' betokens not a specific item of the male anatomy *simpliciter* but that same item taken under the description of a cultural signifier" (164 n. 67). In this system, only one partner could have a phallus and also had to have: in male-male intercourse, the passive boy was considered not to have a phallus, and in female-female "tribads," one woman was considered to have a phallus that penetrated the other (166 n. 83). Note how the specificity of Halperin's distinction between penis and phallus differs from Lacan's. Lacan's claim of their difference in defense of his conception of the phallus as transcendental signifier of desire, in fact, actually functions to stabilize the association. I discuss this in chapter 5.

26. As Claire Pajaczkowska observes: "In the oedipal structure, the threat of castration, or the father's prohibition on rivalry towards the mother, comes to be conflated with the visual instance of the gaze at the female body, a repetition that recalls the earlier moments of sight and their unconscious symbolizations as imagos, all which make the Law of the Father have meaning. But in order for psychoanalysis to serve as theory, the explanatory method cannot do what the infant does, conflate both parents to a 'phallic mother' nor can it do what the oedipal boy does in conflating them once again in another hallucination, that of the woman's body as the representation of the castration threat" (87).

27. I do not read this text literally for its ethnographic claims, but rather as Carpenter's coded but polemical declaration of the epistemological validity of his own marginality as a basis for alienated interrogation of the dominant cultural order. By citing this here I in no way mean to ascribe to the contemporary appropriations of Native American practices, such as the Burdache, for a gay male mythic identity; I completely agree with those who find such identifications racist and ethnocentric (see Gutiérrez).

28. I will explain this in detail below; I treat other aspects of this dynamic in chapters 2 and 4.

29. I discuss this in chapter 2.

30. "The Oedipus complex offered two possibilities of satisfaction, an active and a passive one. He could put himself in his father's place in a masculine fashion and have intercourse with his mother as his father did, . . . or he might want to take the place of his mother and be loved by his father. . . . But [once he accepted] the possibility of castration, his recognition that women were castrated, made an end of both possible ways of obtaining satisfaction. . . . For both of them entailed the loss of the penis—the masculine one as a resulting punishment and the feminine one as a precondition" (Freud, "Dissolution" 176).

31. I do not accept (at least not for the gay male subject), however, Freud's identification of the ego ideal and the super ego in *The Ego and the Id* (32–34).

32. Freud also claims in this essay that the failure to fuse the "sensual" and the "affectionate currents" of erotic attraction (the two components of anaclitic object-choice) is a primary cause of impotence ("On the Universal Tendency" 180).

33. See Jacqueline Rose's discussion of this in *Sexuality in the Realm of Vision* (177–78).

34. This passage also underwrites the "logic" of the use of "surrogates" of the penis against this Other, which would conceivably include knives, guns, fists, baseball bats, papal bulls, camera lenses, etc.

35. "A child's intercourse with anyone responsible for his [*sic*] care affords him an unending source of sexual excitation and satisfaction from his erotogenic zones. . . . His mother herself regards him with feelings that are derived from her own sexual life . . . she treats him as a substitute for a complete sexual object" (Freud, *Three Essays* 223).

36. See Merleau-Ponty, *Primacy* 126–30, and Grosz's discussion of this passage in *Jacques Lacan* 36–37.

37. Freud discussed this, albeit in different terminology: "The ego is ultimately derived from bodily sensations cruelly from those springing from the surface of the body. It may thus be regarded as a mental projection of the surface of the body, besides . . . representing the superficies of the mental apparatus" (*Ego* 22).

38. Parveen Adams distinguishes the "real," anatomically defined body from the "body-image," the proper object of psychoanalytic accounts of the relationship of the human subject to his/her body. Adams bases her analysis of the body as a category on the work of Paul Schilder, for whom "knowledge of the existence of the body and its perceptions are an effect of that active, constructive process that is the body image" (30).

39. Because the ego, as Elizabeth Grosz observes, "is partially a consequence of idiosyncratic and socially structured psychological relations between itself, others, and its body image" (*Jacques Lacan* 32), I cannot find fully satisfactory traditional Freudian accounts of the ego's genesis in its relative autonomy from the particulars of its sociocultural and historical situation. Merleau-Ponty describes the body "as the place where [the] appropriation [of space] occurs." The difficulty in rediscovering "the relationship between the embodied subject and its world" arises from the transformation of this subject, "by its own activity, into the intercourse between the epistemological subject and the object" (154). The dual role of the embodied subject as "epistemological subject and object" illuminates not only the phenomenological but also the political dimensions of the multiplex constitution of the subject in the imaginary of the society at large. The body in its intersubjective articulations is the site of meanings for the society which may be significantly at odds with the meanings and affects it has for the embodied subject.

40. "The fear of the feminine is investigated in a seemingly endless series of liquid images in which woman is associated with all that might threaten to deluge or flood the boundaries of the male ego. . . . The armored organization of the male self in a world that constantly threatens it with disintegration provides the key to understanding the emotional underpinnings of fascist militarism" (Rabinbach and Benjamin xvii).

41. This is written not as a confrontation but as a complement to his depiction of heterosexual male sexuality. I should also note that having no "subject position" from which to concur with or contradict Smith's exposition of male heterosexual experience, I accept his "inner witness" accounts of heterosexuality with the same deference a linguist accords to native informants of Inouit or Waray-Waray.

42. It should be stressed that this depiction of gay male sexuality is not a glorification of unsafe sexual practices. Since we are here describing the "imaginary" register, the real exchange of bodily fluids is not necessary for the erotic and ontological contours of male lovemaking to be actualized.

43. Obviously, some gay men also never assume the recipient role in anal intercourse, but because the possibility of assuming it is there, the choice not to do so is just that—a choice, and part of a general practice in a personal configuration of one's erotic parameters.

44. In his description of the behavior of L.A. police during a gay pride parade, John

Rechy writes, "The cops had blocked two streets, sealing off the parade route. It was the only gesture they could come up with to make their presence known, to reassert their hatred. . . . Sixty black-uniformed cops holding sixty wooden cocks protectively before them" (181).

45. See Foucault's analyses of the subjectivated entities of the apparatuses of power in "The Subject and Power" and *Discipline and Punish*.

46. On the flaws in Althusser's model, see Heath, "The Turn of the Subject," and Hirst. On the inadequacies of Althusser's theories in terms of feminism, see de Lauretis, "Technology." On the ideological function of cultural productions, particularly bourgeois literature, see Macherey.

47. "To give a text an Author is to impose a limit on that text, to furnish it with a final signified, to close the writing. Such a conception suits criticism very well, the latter then allotting itself the important task of discovering the Author (or its hypostases . . .) beneath the work: when the Author has been found, the text is 'explained'—victory to the critic. Hence there is no surprise in the fact that, historically, the reign of the Author has also been that of the Critic, nor again in the fact that criticism . . . is today undermined along with the Author. . . . In precisely this way literature (it would be better from now on to say writing), by refusing to assign a 'secret,' an ultimate meaning, to the text . . . liberates what may be called an anti-theological activity, an activity that is truly revolutionary since to refuse to fix meaning, is, in the end, to refuse God and his hypostases—reason, science, law" (Barthes, "Death of the Author," 147). I explicitly contextualize this passage within both negating affirmations and intersubjective narcissism in chapter 2.

48. On such criticisms against Foucault, see Haug et al. 195–97; de Lauretis, "Technology" and "Violence"; Martin; Bartky. For a criticism of the politics of both Foucault's and Barthes's poststructuralism, see Schor.

49. The correlation I give here holds true within the parameters of the argument I will advance. I should note, however, that the textual categories of "readerly" and "writerly" in Barthes's *S/Z* are complicated by his subsequent demonstration therein of the possibility to engage in "writerly" readings of "readerly" or "classic" texts.

50. The specular negotiations of subject positions in gay-erotic situations (porno cinemas, strip shows, buddy booths, sex clubs) generate fields of play with no heterosexual corollary. In one of the San Francisco clubs, for example, all patrons are nude except for shoes. The interconnected rooms feature mirrored tables and walls, and video monitors that alternate between pornographic films and live action from other rooms in the complex. The participants also include paid and unpaid bodybuilders and models. The space becomes an environmental theater in which the divisions between voyeurism and exhibitionism, spectatorship and performance, are fragmented and redistributed into a weave of nomadic reticulation of desire.

51. Our purposes here permit me to offer a definition of the "pleasure principle" that does not take into account the difficulties presented by Freud's various definitions of "pleasure." On these problems see Bersani, *The Freudian Body*; and Laplanche, *Life and Death*, chapter 6.

52. "An organization which was a slave to the pleasure principle and neglected the reality of the external world could not maintain itself very long" (Freud, "Formulations" 219–20 n. 1).

53. The association of ejaculation and life preservation parallels the apotropaic defense that the erection is imagined to be in the encounter with the "Medusa" of female genitalia, discussed above. The identification of the ejaculation with fertilization, however, perhaps helps resolve the anaclitic ambivalence regarding ecstasy we have already seen in Montrelay's analysands' fear of orgasm and in Theweleit's male soldiers' terror of the contagious chaos of pleasure.

54. In a footnote added in 1924, Freud specifically places sadism and masochism "outside the class of the remaining 'perversions' " (*Three Essays* 159 n. 3).

55. I go into this in greater detail in chapter 4.

56. Dennis Cooper has noted the ineffectiveness of the conventional gay novel: "Point is, it's kind of pointless for gay writers to just try to fit in. Why not either give up all literary pretensions and write mindless publicity for the gay lifestyle, which we could actually use, or else really work at it and try to represent the complications involved in being alive here, now, etc." (Latsky 25). The same is true in the political and aesthetic inertness in both gay and lesbian films with traditional plots, and easy appeal to "general" audiences. On this problem in terms of gay male film, see Finch. In terms of lesbian film, see de Lauretis, "Film and the Visible" 256–57. Derek Jarman's "historical" films are always alienated assaults on their traditions that deliberately resist dominant identifications. The often uncomfortable difficulty of Jarman's films was beautifully described by Howard Brookner, who stated, in Dennis Cooper's paraphrase, "The key ... was to accept the films' strange imbalances and pretensions, lags and lurches, as what naturally happens when an artist has had to wrest his material from countless years of heterosexual ownership. There were moments when the liberation was complete and the picture in focus, and moments when Jarman's struggle became the point" (Cooper, "Queer King" 37).

57. Douglas Crimp argues that the internalized homophobia and demonization of gay male sexuality in Randy Shilts's *And the Band Played On* is generated by his choice of the bourgeois novel form of his narrative (Crimp 238–46). In attempting to create female characters outside of stereotype, Samuel R. Delany discovered that the "basic templates for bourgeois fiction are themselves sexist, patriarchal, and oppressive" (Delany, "Interview" 100). Typically male characters were constructed as combinations of purposeful, habitual, and gratuitous actions, but "good women" were given only "gratuitous actions" and "bad women" only purposive. When he attempted to grant women characters all three action types, Delany discovered that "the 'natural workings' of the story seemed to conspire to exclude this diversity of action from the women" (ibid. 99–100). In her reading of several realist "lesbian" plays with tragic outcomes, Jill Dolan concludes that "the structural codes of realism operate to mark and finally purge the lesbian engima from its bourgeois, moral midst" (" 'Lesbian' Subjectivity" 44–45). Juliet Mitchell's defense of Lacan's deliberate "difficulty" could easily be an argument for the necessity of "difficult" or alternative expressive forms for gay male sexuality and subjectivity: "a challenge to ideology cannot rest on a linguistic appeal to the same ideology" (Mitchell 4).

58. My exclusion from the present study of other forms of representational practices is not meant to slight or devalue them. Indeed, among the artists whose work deserves critical attention I would like to mention the painters Jerome Caja and Brett Reichman, the mixed media artists Nayland Blake and Twistophine Daniels, the graphic artists Wayne Smith and Rex Ray, the performance artists Luis Alfaro and Joan Jett Black, and the cabaret writer/performers Justin Bond ("Dixie McCall's Patterns for Living" and "Kiki and Herb on Fire!") and David E. Johnson ("Latino Fan Club" and his terrifying masterpiece, "Gone Dollywood").

59. "Narrative" and "specular" cannot be reduced to textual narrations and visual images, nor are they usually exclusive of each other. Consider, for example, the visual narratives of cave paintings, freizes, triptychs, comic strips without speech balloons, uncaptioned photonovellas, silent films, the hula, etc. Furthermore, some forms of narrative technique are modeled on visual technology: the "birds-eye view" panoramas of Tolstoy, the increasingly mature descriptions of scenes in Flaubert (like a fisheye lens), Gertrude Stein's repetitive narratives inspired by the filmic illusion of movement. Even theories of narrative borrow visual terms to account for narrative structures: "perspective," "angle of vision," "point of view," "focalization" (Rimmon-Kenan 71).

60. On history see Scott, *Gender*, Kelly; on science see Haraway; Merchant; Harding; Keller.

61. The narrative can be disturbed through either fixation on a stage or a regression to a previous stage; both "fixation" and "regression" have been cited as possible "causes" for "homosexuality," and a prime reason for its classification as a "perversion." See Lewes 95–98. The male homosexual, furthermore, undermines the individually realized and the macrocosmic narratives of patriarchal tradition. Male homosexuality not only sabotages the individual psychic history of the healthy adult male, but also derails the lineage of succession—the communal history constituted of families passing down the patrimony of male privilege and female servitude to their descendants—whose reduplication fosters the myth of the insuperability of the masculine identity as hegemon and guarantor of social coherence. The adult male homosexual betrays both the masculine past and the masculine future—in his noncompliance with reproductive sexuality, he opts out of the system that transforms the individually realized masculine subject into the vital link in the great chain of being, the *man* of "mankind."

62. This is discussed in more detail in chapter 5.

63. According to Voloshinov, the "contradiction embedded in every ideological sign cannot emerge fully" when the dominant order succeeds in stabilizing these signs according to their most conservative meanings, which is what "is responsible for the refracting and distorting peculiarity of the ideological sign within dominant ideology" (23–24). The optimism at times encouraged by Foucault's exposition of "reverse discourse," Derridean deconstructive stategies, or the heterogeneity Althusser perceived within any ruling ideology, is often premature. Althusser admits the possibility that the same ideology which sanctions "class exploitation and domination . . . can also give rise . . . to the expression of the protest of the exploited classes," but this in turn conditions the recontainment of that protest because "that working-class protest against exploitation expresses itself within the very structure of the dominant bourgeois ideology, within its system, and in large part with its representation and terms of reference" (Althusser, "Theory, Theoretical" 30). Substituting "working-class" with "gay men" yields a concise abstraction of the gay politics Marilyn Frye critiques, and underscores the cogency of her arguments. Althusser's working class remains a prisoner of bourgeois ideology without "the help of science" ("Theory, Theoretical" 30–31). At the risk of sounding patronizing, I think that the liberatory equivalent for the gay man to Marxian science for the working class is feminist theory.

64. This is why I am skeptical of the political efficacy of a continued encoded gay semiosis as advanced by Harold Beaver: "The homosexual is beset by signs, by the urge to interpret whatever transpires . . . between himself and every chance acquaintance. He is a prodigious consumer of signs—of hidden meanings, hidden systems, hidden potentiality. Exclusion from the common code impels the frenzied quest . . . every sign becomes duplicitous, slipping back and forth across a wavering line" (104–105). Such arguments encourage a nostalgia for the secret languages necessitated by even more repressive times than the present, which implies that "coming out" or public, nonapologetic activism entails an impoverishment of signifying density, and also encourages a kind of political quietism within the clandestine semiological apostasies of an underground resigned to and mesmerized by its own disenfranchisement.

2. History and Its Desublimations

1. This essentialized "homosexuality" appeals to the humanist myth of the "individual genius" central to the traditional biographical treatments of the same figures. Such studies,

therefore, support the reification of the "Author" that the radical deviant strategies of Samuel R. Delany, Roland Barthes, and Michel Foucault demystify, for reasons we examined in the previous chapter.

2. Although I mention the film *Caravaggio*, this will not be an analysis of the film, but of the historical figure of Caravaggio as reimagined by Jarman in his writings preparatory to the film, his filmscript, and subsequent writings.

3. *Leonardo and a Memory* 117 n. 1 refers to the passage in *Three Essays* (223) dealing with a mother's erotic feelings for her child. These erotic feelings are among the multiple cathexes that I enumerate in chapter 1 which are important to the inauguration of the child's "Ideal Ego" as a narcissistic accomplishment of the mirror stage. Here Freud uses this component of this important process as a major contributing factor to male homosexuality (although his own text suggests it is an important part of the formation of the ego in general).

4. In the original German, the first passage reads: "Die Mutter, die das Kind säugt— besser: an der das Kind saugt—"; the second passage reads: "Ihr auffälligster Zug war doch, daß sie das Saugen an der Mutterbrust in ein Gesäugtwerden . . . verwandelte" (Freud, *"Eine Kindheitserinnerung"* 119, 124); The transformation is from "to suck" (active) [*saugen*] to "to suckle" [*säugen*] (active/causative) to "to be suckled" [*gesäugt werden*] (passive-causative). The first transformation drops out of Freud's analysis.

5. This obscures the fact that in most twentieth-century western European and U.S. communities the "homosexuality" of those acts depends upon the sex of the partners engaged in them rather than the role of each partner. Unlike the classical Greek model (and others) I described in chapter 1, both male partners in these sexual encounters would usually be considered "homosexual."

6. Although Freud does not offer Leonardo's disappointment in his mother's "lack" of a penis as a direct or determinate cause of Leonardo's homosexuality, his elaboration of this factor in the male child's development in this context certainly does not discourage such an inference.

7. He also accepts Merezhkovsky's conjecture that the "Catarina," whose funeral expenses are detailed without comment in Leonardo's papers, is Leonardo's natural mother (*Leonardo and a Memory* 104–105).

8. At the opening of his Dora case history, Freud characterizes his patients as people incapable of "giv[ing] an ordered account of their life" ("Fragment of an Analysis" 16–17). Steven Marcus reads this to infer that "human life is . . . a connected and coherent story, with all the details in explanatory place. . . . An illness amounts to . . . suffering from an incoherent story or an inadequate account of oneself" (Marcus 277).

9. In a more exteme example (supported by the theory of sublimation), the absence of any emotional anguish at a woman's funeral or any mention of who that woman was, other than the name Catarina, identifies her as Leonardo's mother and proves his deep feeling for her. Da Vinci's strange details of expenses in his notebooks include "Expenses of Catarina's death for her funeral." Freud assumes this means that Leonardo's mother was Catarina, and this coldness and absence of further comment proves the depth of his love for his mother: "He had succeeded in subjecting his feelings to the yoke of research and in inhibiting their free utterance; but even for him there was occasions when what had been suppressed obtained expression forcibly. The death of the mother he had once loved so dearly was one of these" (*Leonardo and a Memory* 105).

10. The young Leonardo was accused but subsequently exonerated of sexual misconduct with a male (71). As evidence of Leonardo's aversion to sexuality, Freud offers Leonardo's statement: "The act of procreation and everything connected with it is so disgusting that mankind would soon die out if it were not an old-established custom and if there were not pretty faces and sensuous natures" (qtd. *Leonardo and a Memory* 69). Given Freud's presup-

position that Leonardo was a homosexual, this remark is an expression of distaste not for sexuality in general, but for compulsory heterosexuality "in the service of procreation." Gertrude Stein made similar statements regarding the repulsiveness of childbirth, citing this as one of her reasons for leaving medical school.

11. See Foucault, *History* I, 42–44; Halperin 41–54. I do not mean to ignore the essentialists, but in the contexts of this argument, I am sure they would agree that if Leonardo had not indulged, there would be nothing to call him.

12. Sodomy was considered a sin from whose temptation no human was immune (A. Bray 15–20).

13. Several things about this monograph are important to the history of psychoanalytic attitudes to male homosexuality. This text was the first in which Freud had used the word "narcissism," and one of the earliest (although not as yet named) elaborations of the Oedipus complex, and certainly the first direct association with the Oedipus and male homosexuality.

14. Freud conjectures that a timely paternal influence might have saved Leonardo from his fate. "It seems as though the presence of a strong father would ensure that the son made the correct decision in his choice of object, namely someone of the opposite sex" (*Leonardo and a Memory* 99).

15. And also: "The development that turned him into an artist at puberty was overtaken by the process which led him to be an investigator, at first still in the service of his art, but later independently of it. . . . The research . . . now took the place of artistic creation" (132–33). The mournful affect of these passages undermines the symmetry between the oppositions already noted in chapter 1 among the binaries: art—science; pleasure principle—reality principle; homosexuality—heterosexuality that the text otherwise fosters.

16. The phantasmatic retention of the mother's phallus strengthens the association between the lost stages in the male child's psychosexual history and the archaic periods of mythographic imagination as preserved in the phallically endowed mother goddesses, such as the vulture-headed Mut.

17. See chapter 1 on this process of homosexual assimilation into phallocentric patriarchy. Freud's insistence on Leonardo's "ideal" homosexuality suited the sensibilities of the general readership, as we see in the introduction to A. A. Brill's 1947 English translation of *Leonardo*. Brill misconstrues Freud's ambivalent presentation of sublimated homosexuality as license to deny the existence of homosexuality *ex cathedra*. His supplementary examples are incoherent travesties of Freud's already infelicitous argument. Invoking the legends of David and Jonathan and Damon and Pythias as exempla of "ideal friendship[s] [in which] no sensuality played a part," Brill launches into what appears to be a compilation of anecdotal evidence of Hermann Melville's homosexuality, incongruously peppered with reassurances that "Melville led a normal psychosexual existence . . . [there was] never any intimation that he was anything but sexually normal" (Brill xxxiv–xxxv). Melville's "philanthropy," according to Brill, denotes a "higher degree of homosexuality . . . [with no] taint of the abnormal"— the same kind shared by "Marlowe, Shakespeare, Montaigne, Tennyson . . . [who] have actually been accused of pathological homosexuality, yet nothing in their lives could justify such assumptions" (xxxvi). Such "unjust accusations" stemmed from old prejudices when "any fervent expression for a person of the same sex was immediately interpreted into something abnormal. Thanks to Freud we now know differently" (xxxvi). Apparently what we "now know differently" is not that homosexuality is a valid variation in sexual development, but that it does not really exist. Brill's essay not only ignores the text it purportedly introduces, but misrepresents Freud's larger theories of sexuality and the perversions (of the *Three Essays*, for example) to make them seem to support the naive and moralistic conclusions to be drawn from the Leonardo fantasy. Brill is one of the psychotherapists who considered the

Leonardo text an important contribution to the understanding of the causes and nature of the perversion.

18. Senatspräsident Schreber's descent into antisocial delusionary states is an example of such derailment: "Some unusually intense wave of libido . . . may lead to a sexualization of the social instincts and so undo the sublimations which they had achieved in the course of their development" (Freud, "Psycho-analytic Notes" 64). Ferenczi is far more uncharitable in his depiction of the volatility of even the "ideal homosexual"; in his diagnosis of the potential threat homosexuals pose, he allows a slippage between "repression" and "sublimation" which the theory does not support: "Only a minor part of [homosexual libido] gets rescued in a sublimated form in the cultivated life of adults. . . . Insufficiently repressed homosexuality can later . . . become once more manifest" (Ferenczi, "Nosology" 296–97).

19. "Ardent priest" is Marilyn Frye's phrase. See Frye 133, and my discussion of her text in chapter 1.

20. In 1904 Freud gave a lecture on psychotherapy at a medical college, in which he illustrated the differences between hypnotic suggestion therapy and psychoanalysis by comparing them to Leonardo's contrasting definitions of painting and sculpture. "On Psychotherapy" 260–261. Freud was delighted with the publication of the Leonardo text. In the 1920s he referred to it as the only "beautiful book" he had ever written, and it was reportedly still among his favorite works at the time of his death (Jones 1: 451).

21. For very different reasons, the fellatio fantasy here is even more preposterous than the one in *Leonardo*. See, for example, Willis 49–50 and Sprengthnether 264–66. The declaration of "the truly disgusting nature of the perversion" and its "innocent" origin that Freud gives in *Leonardo* are directly borrowed from the Dora case history. See "Fragment" 50–51 and *Leonardo and a Memory* 86–87.

22. Anzieu, *Freud's Self Analysis*.

23. Schur.

24. See, for example, Rose, "Dora"; Glenn; and Gearhart 118–20.

25. This seems an extension of the kind of countertransference that Freud experienced with Dora, which he channeled into writing the case history immediately after she ended therapy (Marcus 309–10). The phantasmatic docility of the analysand affords Freud an unimpeded hermeneutical prerogative, which constitutes, after all, a countertransference. The sexual politics involved here must be considered. Freud's countertransference in Dora's case made him unable to recognize her female homosexuality; his countertransference in the Leonardo analysis ensures his recognition of Leonardo's male homosexuality. The former preserved ignorance, the latter guarantees "knowledge."

26. For example: "That was a time when my fond curiosity was directed to my mother, and when I still believed she had a genital organ like my own"; and "Through this erotic relation with my mother . . . I became a homosexual" (*Leonardo and a Memory* 98, 106). Mink attributes some of the more grandiose versions of history to the operative presumption that history is "an untold story" waiting for the historian to discover it and retell it (Mink 134–35).

27. Didier Coste employs etymology to illustrate the often ignored but crucial differences between "fact" and "event." In many European languages, including English, the word for "fact" (like *fait* and *hecho*) is derived from the past passive participle of the latin *facere* "to make"—which means "fabricated" and implies a human agent, unlike "event," which comes from the past participle of *evenire*, "to come out," implying simple occurrence without human causation. Therefore an "event" is something which merely "happened," but a "fact" is a meaning created out of that event, by someone. This distinction and the distinction between reference and signification are essential for a critical analysis of the means by which "history" becomes incontrovertible "truth" (Coste 21–22). Some historiographic definitions

of "event," however, seem to combine Coste's "event" and "fact," as attested in Mink's statement of the difficulty in determining at what points an "event" begins and ends (Mink 145–47); see also Nowell-Smith.

28. This principle is more clearly illustrated in comparisons between interpretations that admit the "homosexuality" of the object of investigation with those that refuse to accept that homosexuality by refusing to accept the evidence. We will see examples of this in our discussion of Shakespeare's sonnets below. Freud's use of historical evidence is different in that he accepts the evidence of homosexuality but denies its content.

29. The deep structure of Freud's presentation of evidence is a four-point assertion: (1) Historical document X states that da Vinci behaved sexually with other men; (2) I accept the validity of this document; (3) but da Vinci did not behave sexually with other men; (4) I offer this document as evidence of Leonardo's homosexuality.

30. For a bibliography of critical literature on the issue of the sonnets' dedicatee, see Booth 543–49.

31. For the complex and mysterious publication history of the latter, see Summers 34. When quoting the originally published version, I will cite it as "Portrait," and the longer version as *Portrait*.

32. Ironically, Lord Alfred Douglas, Wilde's former lover (and cause of Wilde's criminal prosecution), actually discovered the existence of a William Hughes in Canterbury, who had been apprenticed to John Marlowe, father of Edward, in 1593 (Gagnier 43–44).

33. For example, in his survey of actual scholars and their theories regarding the controversy, Wilde includes the contributions of a bogus "German commentator Barnstorff" ("Portrait" 146).

34. This reflects Graham's own plight with his family, and Erskine's love for Graham.

35. It turns out that Rowse's identification of the Dark Lady as Emilia Lanier was exploded almost instantly, since it depends entirely on his reading a sentence in Simon Forman's diary that says "in her youth very brave" as "in her youth very brown," this having been his only evidence for her darkness. Just as Leonardo's mother-dominated homosexuality depended upon Freud's faulty Italian, Shakespeare's heterosexuality in this case depends on Rowse's inability to read Elizabethan calligraphy. I am indebted to Stephen Orgel for bringing this to my attention.

36. The political conservatism this monolithic interpretative certainty serves is glaringly evident in Rowse's dedication of his edition of the sonnets to Ronald Reagan.

37. Ironically, Shirley Nelson Garner selects this sonnet for a bizarrely naive and literalist reading to equate what she perceives Freud and Shakespeare shared—an aversion to their own "bisexuality" which they warded off through their homophobia. She does this in an exposition of Freud's "homosexual transference" to Fliess! (Garner 88–89).

38. I am not taking sides on this debate, nor do I mean that Rowse's heterosexual interpretation is "wrong." Neither am I reducing interpretative commitment to the sexual orientation of the critic (I am not accusing Rowse of being heterosexual himself). Gregory Bredbeck's "gay identity" or his situating his work within "lesbian and gay studies" does not compromise his use of this sonnet as an illustration of his larger theory that the sonnets figure the possibility of sodomy as the impossibility to read sexual meaning with any determinacy (Bredbeck 175–80). For other contemporary "gay readings" of the sonnets, see Pequingey; and Bruce R. Smith 228–70. Rowse eventually had a change of heart, and went on to write a much sillier book entitled *Homosexuals in History* (1977). For two accounts of W. H. Auden's typically despicable hypocrisy on the question of homosexual desire in the sonnets, see Summers 224 n. 43, and Bruce R. Smith 231.

39. For two differing discussions on this incident, see Summers 37–38 and William A. Cohen, 220–21. Cohen's treatment of the story is far more text-immanent than mine, and I

recommend his intriguing analyses of the encoding processes within the language of the narrative.

40. Note the uncanny similarities between Wilde's ironic passages and Brill's "serious" discussion of Melville quoted above.

41. Explicating the sonnets in this way, the narrator has completed the kind of dream interpretation conceived of by Freud's predecessor Scherner (*Interpretation of Dreams* 4: 83–87), which "implies assigning meaning to [a dream] . . . —that is, replacing it by something which fits into the chain of our mental acts as a link having a validity and importance equal to the rest" (ibid. 96). This falls short of one of Freud's primary stipulations—that the interpretation "should not be concerned with what occurs to the *interpreter* in connection with . . . the dream, but with what occurs to the *dreamer*" (ibid. 98 n. 2, emphases Freud's). This being infeasible in either Shakespeare's or da Vinci's case, the analysts adhere to the earlier definition of dream interpretation. On dream work, see Freud, *Interpretation of Dreams* 5: 506–20; and on the distinction between dream work and interpretation see Freud, "Remarks on the Theory of Dream Interpretation" 111–12. Freud consistently breaks his own rule in his interpretations of Dora's dream. See, for example, "Fragment" 73–74, 76–77, and 95–98, 105. This seems to be one of the factors in that case which establishes the precedent of the process I am formulating as countertransference directed (or sublimated) into interpretative authority realized in a narrative act whose artistry precludes the narrator's reflections on its epistemological justifications.

42. On the "Narcissism" text, see chapter 1; on "Mourning and Melancholia," see chapter 5.

43. In response to a request from an art gallery to do an exhibition related to AIDS issues, Jarman did huge collages of front pages from sensationalist homophobic newspapers and planned "to paint on them in my own blood" until his doctors expressed concern about the "amount I would need to paint [such] huge canvases" (*San Francisco Examiner*, March 22, 1992, Edward Guthmann, p. 19).

44. And, through the depiction of the homosexual desire, the novel becomes a self-portrait for Wilde as well. See Beckson.

45. The phrase "epistemophilic break" is a play on the Bachelardian-Althusserian conception of "epistemological break" (which I discuss in chapter 4) and the Freudian conception of epistemophilia which Leonardo, according to Freud, sublimated his sexuality. I coin this phrase to refer to a conscious rejection of the sublimation of sexuality into the search for Truth (à la Freud's Leonardo); and a self-conscious acknowledgment of the responsibility to representational practices in excess of Winckelmannian Hellenism, in response to historico-cultural shifts in the parameters of the politically defensible, as Delany described the shift in acceptability of "readerly" and "writerly texts," which I discuss at the close of chapter 1. See the last section of chapter 1 for a discussion of these subject types.

46. Freud's supposition that Leonardo's scientific genius derived from his early freedom from the prohibitions of the father suggests a "negative Oedipal" variation on this equation, in that the father's absence allowed the boy a nonsublimated (sexual) intellectual license that the post-Oedipal Father-imago of the superego absolutely forecloses.

47. As Sartre observed, an "ideal" is a conceptual hallucination produced by the abstract form of anything produced in a series (*Transcendence of the Ego* 16–19).

3. Imagining It Otherwise

1. Delany situates the strategic use of science fiction within other cultural struggles besides those particular to gay men; he also notes other factors in the choice of delegitimated

forms such as SF besides deliberate defiance: "Sf grows up outside [an] established set of literary texts and I think it's always easier to appropriate the margin; it always has been for blacks and women, for anyone who is in a marginal position. . . . This is what people in a marginal social position have been doing constantly, appropriating what is marginal in the rest of cultural production" (Delany and Russ 29).

2. Mary Kay Bray points out that the term "double consciousness" comes from W. E. B. Du Bois (57). Weedman does not note this.

3. See my discussion of Foucault's concept in chapter 1.

4. It is not only space operas that posit fantastic futures while evincing structural and ideological affinities with historical fiction, "vulnerable to an unhistorical fetishism of the past . . . in which the merely aesthetic relish of costume and exoticism triumphs over the genuinely conceptual issues of historical specificity and difference (post-Tolstoyan historical novels of best seller lists)" (Freedman 187). Certain texts subliminally support reactionary political agendas: the interplanetary adventures glorified colonial expansionism as a white Euro-American manifest destiny; "invader" stories subliminally supported the cold war as well as sexual, racial, and ethnic prejudices by obsessively depicting any manifestation of Otherness as a menace to be eradicated.

5. "K. Leslie Steiner" (Delany's alter ego) sees the perpetuation of uncritical science fiction as partially the result of a reading public who has accepted "SF's imaginative strengths and its political conservatism" as "inextricable aspects" requiring the reader "to put up with" the latter to enjoy the former (Steiner, "Trouble" 97–98).

6. Of course, Hardesty has a point, similar to one Delany raised in an essay where he stated that one of the reasons that SF was essentially the only subversive writing published in the U.S. during the McCarthy era was the general realization of the limitations on how "subversive" adventure novels could actually be ("Quarks" 139).

7. Note also, from Delany's autobiography: "If I may indulge in my one piece of sf for this memoir, it is my firm suspicion, my conviction, and my hope that once the AIDS crisis is brought under control, the West will see a sexual revolution to make a laughing stock of any social movement that till now has borne the name" (*Motion* 175).

8. The strategic importance of conjuring the myth of these women in Madame Keyne's statement is supported in the narrative on several levels, first in the irony that she tells this to Pryn, who, like the reader of this novel and the other tales, has knowledge of the "actual" existence of this alternative female-dominant society. In fact, Pryn had first heard of the women of the Western Crevasse from the tale-teller Norema (in the novel's first chapter). Norema (Venn's star pupil during her girlhood in the Rulyvn islands [see the discussion later in this chapter]) had been Madame Keyne's secretary until, while on an errand for Madame Keyne in the south, she ran away with Raven, one of these fabulous warrior women ("The Tale of Potters and Dragons"); *Neveryóna* concludes with Pryn seeing one such woman sneaking into a mummer's wagon.

9. This destabilization of received belief is dramatized in the transformation of faith in a priest assigned to a mission on another planet in James Blish's *A Case of Conscience*, and wickedly satirized in the decline of the Catholic church as a result of the discovery of extraterrestrial life in Thomas A. Disch's "Concepts." See also the effect the "visitor" has on the young girl in Joanna Russ's story "The Second Inquisition."

10. Ironically, the one person capable of surviving all the rituals is the ultimate daredevil, whose entire life substantiates masculinity as a death drive. *Rogue Moon* is an indictment of two kinds of dominant emotional paralysis typical (indeed encouraged and celebrated) among men: the he-man, and the intellect-absorbed scientist.

11. Russ refers to the advantage of her own alienated perspective in this speech: "Because

I'm a woman I can [perhaps] stand outside this whole business and be somewhat more objective than if I were caught up in it, as I think a man has to be, to some degree" ("Alien Monsters" 137).

12. Furthermore, in Delany's essay he presents the image fully within and as part of an interpretation. Delany's initial surprise at encountering this image when he first read the novel also indicates that the image is already within an interpretative context: Delany's situation as a young black man in the U.S., which includes his culturally enjoined "knowledge" that heroes are white. He did a "double take" upon realizing that this hero "was not the blue-eyed, blond hero of countless RKO WWII films" ("The Necessity of Tomorrows" 30).

13. Heinlein's unwitting double agent exposes one of the ways in which the visionary extravagance of SF and the social contradictions of gay male identities recomplicate each other. The imaginative license of the genre often leads writers to premises whose multiple significations may have unanticipated and undesirable politico-cultural implications. "Mainstream" science fiction often denaturalizes the dominant fusion of "sex" and "gender"; sword-and-sorcery at times brackets sex/gender systems within an anthropological relativism, at times intentionally, at other times as an epiphenomenon of the plot—which means that a text's effects might be in serious conflict with the sexual (or other) politics of the writer. The potential destabilizing effects of science fiction interfere with the political or philosophical guarantee of the discourse. Even the most conservative sexist writer cannot ultimately insulate the univocity of the intended message from the fantasizing indeterminacy of the medium. On the other hand, the opposite is also possible, especially if the writer indulges in the exoticism of otherness without a self-interrogating consideration of the politics of its representation.

14. Delany's theoretical writings on science fiction are to a great extent structured around a sophisticated meditation on the politics of genres. My discussion of his theories above will be based on two binary oppositions that inform his arguments: mundane and speculative fiction, and literature and paraliterature. "Speculative fiction" is a term first used by Robert A. Heinlein that enjoyed considerable popularity in the late 1960s and early 1970s, and Delany himself used it at times, although he and most other science fiction writers have discontinued its use. I use it briefly here as a category that can encompass science fiction, fantasy, and sword-and-sorcery. "Mundane fiction" refers to any fiction that constitutes a representation of the given (or "real") world.

15. Delany's disidentification of SF from "literature" bears a rough structural resemblance to the "double rejection" I mentioned at the opening of this chapter: the rejection of dominant cultural values in the deliberate adoption of a noncanonical representational form, and the rejection of the authority of "official reality" in the production of fantasy worlds.

16. Both science fiction and sword-and-sorcery can facilitate dialogues with the present through differently fantasized restorative interventions. Science fiction set in the future often rereads the dominant ideologies of the present as superstitions of the past already discarded, as we see in the social philosophies of the satellite societies in Delany's novel *Triton*. Sword-and-sorcery can denaturalize contemporary beliefs by detailing the rise and spread of fictive mythic systems, providing clear analogues of how our own myths became naturalized as Truth and identified with social order and coherence. The creation myth of the women of the Western Crevasse is a vivid example of such a critical analogy ("The Tale of Potters and Dragons" 269–77). As this book was going to press, Wesleyan University Press began to publish a new, four-volume edition of the Nevèrÿon tales: *Tales of Nevèrÿon* (1993), *Neveryóna* (1993), *Flight from Nevèrÿon* (1994), and *Return to Nevèrÿon* (1994).

17. Bracketed phrases are Samuel R. Delany's handwritten additions to the text.

18. Or, a favorite gleaned from my own SF reading: " 'David, you still can't marry me.' . . . My face fell, and I grabbed it and hid it under my coat" (Sturgeon, " 'Derm Fool' " 11).

19. Delany draws on Foucault's "What Is an Author?" to make explicit the intimate relations between the metaphysics of a unified Self and the institutions of Literature. He contrasts Foucault's "four unities" with four corresponding pluralities of SF ("Science Fiction and 'Literature' " 67–69). See also Foucault, *The Order of Things*; D. A. Miller; Macherey.

20. On other destabilizations scientific perspectives can inculcate, see Delany, "Quarks" 139–40.

21. On Benveniste, see chapter 4; On Peirce and Lacan, see my *Fantastic Living*.

22. See my comparative discussion of Delany and Barthes in chapter 1. I also discuss *jouissance* in relation to Delany's textual projects in greater detail in *Fantastic Living*.

23. Metatextually, the margin-center positions are reconfigured as Appendices–Main Text, and within these, the "critical fictions" and "theoretical fictions" of the main text undergo inverted transformations to fictional critics, such as K. Leslie Steiner and Kermit for the Nevèrÿon tales, and Ashima Slade in *Triton*. Slade's "modular calculus" is a fictional theory that figures in both *Triton* and the Nevèrÿon series. All of these tactics, in turn, analogically reinforce the critical validity of the fictions in the main text.

24. See, for example, the scene in which Lawrence reminds Bron that "the difference [between men and women] is simply that women have only really been treated . . . [by society] as human beings for the last . . . sixty-five years . . . whereas men have had the luxury of such treatment for the last four thousand" (*Triton* 252–53).

25. Shoshana Felman is a critical theorist whose work Delany mentions in key places (*Neveryóna* 77 and 97, for example). See also my discussion of this critical intertextuality between Felman and Delany in *Fantastic Living*.

26. The army becomes the patriarchal family and the unchallenged transmitter of patrimony. See Deleuze and Guattari 62–64, and the discussion of this passage at the close of chapter 2.

27. Delany does in fact contrast Freud's theories with Dickens's, as object-based and subject-based, respectively (Delany, "Disch" 150).

28. Delany, "Significance" 226.

29. This perversion in turn generates variations. One of the crew claims to have beaten up a man and a woman impersonating spacers in a known frelk hangout. The idea of normally sexed individuals "queer for frelks" causes a violent and disbelieving response in the spacers ("Aye" 536).

30. Of course, the woman could be referring to other things besides the vagina: the breasts, the entire female body, the sense of a woman's identity, etc. But I would also note that the "clarity" of what the man means and the "ambiguity" of what the woman means could also reflect contemporary conditioning regarding sexual difference and "feminine sexuality." I do not have an answer to this, nor do I assume one to be found in the text; the text's richness is the confrontation it promotes with questions such as this.

31. Her statement is also rhetorically skewed in classifying the homosexual's substitute as a "mirror": first in its incongruity with the tangible objects of the other perverts, and secondly in the redundancy of the trope, given that the act of substitution itself is the operation of metaphor.

32. See Freud, *Three Essays* 210–12; Laplanche, *Life and Death*, especially 13–16. Here "we must reckon with the possibility that something in the nature of the sexual instinct itself is unfavorable to the realisation of complete satisfaction" (Freud, "On the Universal Tendency" 188–89).

33. There is also another sense in which the frelk desire is incommunicable. Without a

signifiable object, the "exchange" between the art student and the spacer is limited to demand, in the Lacanian sense that demand is always a demand for something as a proof of love. Their ability to relate soon breaks down into this pattern of dual inexplicable demands: " 'Give me something,' I said. 'Give me something—it doesn't have to be worth sixty lira. Give me something that you like, anything of yours that means something to you' " ("Aye" 541); " 'What will you give me? I want something,' I said. 'That's why I came. I'm lonely.' . . . She put her head on my knee. 'I want something. But . . . you are not the one who will give it to me.' . . . 'You're not going to pay me for it,' I countered. 'You're not, are you?' " (ibid. 543).

34. Consider also Lacan's observation that "desire is for nothing namable" (*Seminar* II: 223) and his specifically psychoanalytic formulations of this peculiarity of desire (ibid. 211–12 and 226–28).

35. This is the same principle I mentioned above by which the reader of *Stars in My Pocket* is led to confront the difficulty of allowing "women" to mean people in general.

36. In "The Tale of Old Venn" this status is lexically supported in the single term for both in the Rulvyn language, and explicitly defended even in Arkvid's otherwise chauvinistic discourse.

37. For relevant discussions on the cultural production of gender, in particular the production of gender through the rigid allocation of discursive positions within fixed power imbalances, see my discussion of the work of Wendy Holloway and the gender analyses of Catherine MacKinnon in chapter 1.

38. I discuss this in more detail in chapter 5.

39. See chapter 1 for my discussion of this in terms of Disch's parody of its implications in his short story "Planet of the Rapes."

40. I refer to Freud's "Instincts and Their Vicissitudes" and Laplanche's amplification of that text, both of which I discuss in detail in chapter 4.

41. Gorgik's subversive sexualization of signs and practices of domination is comparable to the sexualized (or "desublimated") epistemophilic counterhistories exemplified by Wilde and Jarman in chapter 2.

42. Gorgik's statement takes on a special irony if considered in the light of the vociferous and proactive readership peculiar to SF fandom.

43. See the discussion of this text and the narrative theories of de Lauretis and Winnett in chapter 1.

44. Barthes's ironic characterization of "narrative suspense" as "corporeal strip tease" succinctly describes this view of narrative while distancing the texts of *jouissance* from this libidinal economy (*Pleasure* 10).

45. See chapters 1 and 2.

46. See Keller 33–42; Rossi 10–16.

47. Even after Freud redefines eros as a life-affirming force, sadism maintains its "practicality." In *Beyond the Pleasure Principle*, Freud suggests that sadism is a death drive diverted from the ego to the object, through sexuality. At the "oral stage" of libidinal organization, "the act of obtaining erotic mastery over an object coincides with that object's destruction; . . . at the stage of genital primacy, [sadism] takes on, for the purposes of reproduction, the function of overpowering the sexual object to the extent necessary for carrying out the sexual act" (54).

48. It is a "bad" or only "partial" desublimation. See chapter 4 for a fuller discussion.

49. This situation is mirrored in the last section of the tale when the aging Vizarine Myrgot tells her tale to "Gorgik," whom she imagines to be in her carriage on the way to the funeral. The first half models the reader's relation to an absent (or fictive) narrator, the

second half models the relation between a narrating "I" and an imagined narratee. Note also that Myrgot's hallucination specifically models a relation of presence to absence peculiar to a written narrative, since a tale-teller always has an audience.

50. Such diversions from the object are a chief mark of "perversion," as I have noted in my examination in chapter 1 of Freud's warnings against the "dangers" of "forepleasure" in *Three Essays* 210–22.

51. This technique recalls a passage near the end of *Dhalgren*, another metadiegetic reference to the reader's probable relation to the narrative: "My life here more and more resembles a book whose opening chapters, whose title even, suggest mysteries to be resolved only at closing. But as one reads along, one becomes more and more suspicious that the author has lost the thread of his argument, that the questions will never be resolved" (*Dhalgren 831*).

52. Delany's text is subversive of the narrative-sexual politics it parodies in the multiplicity of the variations on narrative relations it imagines, rather than in offering any one of them (or any combination of them) as a definitive alternative to the dominant narrative norms. Like Susan Winnett's narratology I discuss in chapter 1, "Game of Time and Pain" is "ultimately more valuable for its relativizing function than as a scheme competing for authority with the Masterplot" (Winnett 508).

53. There are several scenes in which the exertions of the other family members are concentrated on allowing Mrs. Richards to pretend she is still a middle-class housewife in a contented urbane nuclear family. What is left out of this picture is the indeterminable cataclysm that has cut their city out of time and rendered the streets and apartment buildings incessantly burning territory for roving gangs. Mr. Richards pretends to go to work every day, although all conventional forms of government and business have been decimated and cognitive reality has lost its spatio-temporal coherence. Mrs. Richards's insistence on maintaining an idolatry of the family's stability also precludes her from being an effective or concerned parent. Her fantasy does not allow her to recognize her own daughter's picture or name in the paper that obsessively details her ravishment on city streets by the mythically proportioned "Black Man" George Harrison. Nor does the fantasy allow her to protect or worry about her elder son who had run away, or her younger son, possibly murdered by his own sister over a poster of George Harrison.

54. One of the most intelligent, insightful, and engaging critical responses to *Dhalgren* remains Jean Marc Gawron's introduction to the Grafton Press edition.

55. This contrast is illuminated in the ideological battle between the pro-Oedipal nuclear patriarchy of "the Family" and the polymorphously perverse semioticians of the Sygn in *Stars*: "The Family [is] trying to establish the dream of a classic past as pictured on a world that may never even have existed in order to achieve cultural stability, and . . . the Sygn [is] committed to the living interaction and difference between each woman and each world" (Delany, *Stars* 87).

56. In discussing the peculiar nature of the city of Bellona with the Kid, Tak suggests that the city itself is a real "science fiction" which "follows all the conventions. . . . First: A single man can change the course of the whole world. . . . Second: The only measure of intelligence or genius is its linear and practical applications. . . . Three: The Universe is essentially a hospitable place, full of earth-type planets where you can crash-land your spaceship and survive long enough to have an adventure" (*Dhalgren* 414–15). Bron's sex change is not a radical change of heart. He merely took Lawrence too literally—believing that there were no longer any women corresponding to his ideal of "woman," Bron became one. As Marilyn Frye writes: "It is wonderful that homosexuals and lesbians are mocked and judged for 'playing butch-femme roles' . . . for nobody goes about in full public view as thoroughly decked out in butch and femme drag as respectable heterosexuals. . . . Heterosexual critics of queers'

'role-playing' ought to look at themselves in the mirror on their way out . . . to see who's in drag. The answer is, everybody is. . . . The main difference between heterosexuals and queers is that when queers go forth in drag, they know they are engaged in theater—they are playing and they know they are playing. Heterosexuals usually are taking it all perfectly seriously, thinking they are in the real world, thinking they are the real world" (Frye 29).

4. Graphic Specularity

1. Leonardo Da Vinci makes this analogy in his writings on perspectivism. See Bryson, *Tradition* 64–65.

2. The relevant passages in Alberti are in Book I, 43–49.

3. Kaja Silverman points out that the specular binary "seer"/"seen" is socially articulated across varying power differentials and gender positions in different historical periods and cultural milieux. "Fragments of a Fashionable Discourse" 139–41.

4. Neo-Platonism divided the world into masculine "Reason" and "Spirit" and feminine "corporeality" or "materiality"; Baconian science divided the world into a masculine scientific investigative mind and a feminine, inert nature. I discuss this briefly in chapter 1.

5. "The *objet a* is something from which the subject, in order to constitute itself, has separated itself off as organ. This serves as a symbol of the lack, that is to say, of the phallus, not as such, but in so far as it is lacking. It must, therefore, be an object that is, firstly, separable and, secondly, that has some relation to the lack" (Lacan, *Four Fundamental* 104).

6. See my discussion of this in chapter 1, in the section on Freud's essay "On Narcissism."

7. Foucault, *History* I, 92–93 and *Power/Knowledge* 195.

8. On the history of gay pornographic literature, see Leyland; Preston.

9. On the history of gay photographic pornography, see Waugh, "Photography"; on the history of porn film, see Siebenband; Waugh, "Men's Pornography" and "Hard to Imagine"; and Tom de Simone's film *Erotikus* (1978).

10. On the importance of pornography for gay male culture, see also Glück, "Who Speaks"; Wojnarowicz 138–43; Cooper, "Square One"; Tucker; Blanchford; and Yingling.

11. See Baudry; Comolli; I recognize that my composite definition of "apparatus" is exploiting the collapse in English translation of two emphases in Baudry's theory he distinguishes with different terminology: *appareil de base* and *dispositif.*

12. Pierre Macherey warns against "all forms of empiricism," because "the objects of any rational investigation have no prior existence but are thought into being. The object does not pose before the interrogating eye, for thought is not the passive perception of a general disposition, as though the object should offer to share itself, like an open fruit, both displayed and concealed by a single gesture. The act of knowing is not like listening to a discourse already constituted, a mere fiction which we simply have to translate. It is rather the elaborations of a new discourse, the articulation of a silence" (Macherey 5–6).

13. Bachelard's reschematization of the history of science includes a very useful example in his illustrations of ruptural realizations of "knowledge" and "subject" in his contrastive histories of Descartes's and Huyghen's physics of light. See *Le rationalisme* 101–107; *L'activité* 21–49, 121–41; and Balibar, 233 n. 6.

14. "Any technical practice is defined by its objectives: such specified effects to be produced in such an object, in such a situation. . . . In every case, the relationship between technique and knowledge is an external relationship, without reflection, radically different from the reflected internal relationship existing between a science and its knowledges" (Althusser, *For Marx* 171 n. 7).

15. See Jackson, "Explicit Instruction," and my review article on Richland, *Pornography and Representation in Greece and Rome*.

16. Throughout this chapter, whenever I use the pronoun "he" to refer to the "film viewer" or the "spectator," I am always referring to a male spectator. Whenever my discussions include spectators of either sex, I use "she or he"; whenever I refer specifically to female subjects exclusively, I use "she."

17. I will also reconsider the pornographic "apparatus" in chapter 5 in its metaphoric uses within narrative.

18. See my initial discussion of the so-called "positive" Oedipus in chapter 1.

19. The synthesis of a key representational principle and a sexualized zone of perception in this film is a specifically "gay" metadiscursive maneuver deserving of attention. Recall also the associations of homoerotic desire and principles of representation we found in Wilde's "W. H." and Jarman's empathetic hermeneutics of Caravaggio's painting practice. See chapter 2.

20. For example, sex through windows (*Inch by Inch*; *Windows*; *Undercover*;); sex through plexiglass partitions (*A Night at Halsted's*; *Head Trips*); sex through jail cell bars (*Powertool II*; *Boys in Prison*; *Lewd Conduct*); sex between two men on opposite sides of a mirror that is the boundary between two dimensions (*Falconhead*). See also the movie screen in Dennis Cooper's essay/story "Square One," which I discuss in chapter 5.

21. They are straight-acting, straight-appearing types, resembling the type of male film protagonist who serves as the point of identification (but not desire) for the heterosexual male viewer in classic narrative film.

22. For a more metaphysically imagined situation discussed in terms of the early silent film *Uncle Josh at the Movie Picture Show*, see Mayne 31–33; see also chapter 5 for my discussion of yet another example of this in Dennis Cooper's "Square One."

23. It is hardly surprising that male masochism occupies such a central position in Kaja Silverman's preliminary reconceptualization of the heterosexual contract (afterword to *Male Subjectivity at the Margins*).

24. A and B are Laplanche's designations. My "C" collapses his C and D, but this distinction is not relevant for the purposes of the present argument. It would be possible to chart the sexualized S/M narrative games in Delany's "Game of Time and Pain" in terms structurally analogous to this transformation of heteroaggression into reflexivity.

25. See chapter 1.

26. See chapters 1 and 3.

27. The psychosexual narcissism operative in the specular dynamics between the scopophilic viewer and the pornographic (intentional) spectacle supports and is supported by a political narcissism in the validation the gay male viewer derives from recognizing himself and his sexuality on the screen. I will return to this point at the conclusion of this chapter.

28. Multiple identifications are foreclosed in conventional heterosexual pornography, because the heterosexual male spectator's scopophilia reenacts and extends the heteroaggression that originated the first two drives. His scopophilia is an anaclitic voyeurism, a sadistic defense against the threat of castration that the female other represents to him.

29. Here I am playing on a peculiarity of the voice of the verb "to bear." Mulvey draws on other senses of the word in the same paragraph, but the absolute divisions between desire and identification that structure dominant male heterosexuality also suppress the bivalence of the term. Mulvey writes that "the male figure *cannot bear* the burden of sexual objectification." A few lines later, in explaining the role the on-screen male protagonist plays in the fantasies of the male spectator to elicit identification, she continues: "The man controls the film phantasy and also emerges as the representative of power in a further sense: as the *bearer* of the look of the spectator" (Mulvey, "Visual Pleasure" 18; emphases added).

30. The close-ups of the holes in the couch upholstery perform the same kind of sexualizing emphasis as the close-ups of the videocam lens in *Big Guns*.

31. I am not arguing that this is completely intentional; it cannot, however, be dismissed as merely accidental. Cadinot displays a sophisticated awareness of contemporary French intellectual life in his films. In *Under the Sign of the Stallion* (1986), a gay porn novelist is beset by his next-door neighbor, a graduate student in comparative literature, who eagerly attempts to apply poststructural methods to the novelist's fiction.

32. In contrast to the female figure's song or dance that literally "stops the show"— suspends narrative progression with a moment of fetishistic contemplation of her body as total spectacle (Mulvey, "Visual Pleasure" 16–17).

33. When the lips of "Cadinot" are visible beneath the camera lens, they remain motionless even when his questions are heard in the voiceover.

34. "Ecstases" is the plural of *ecstasis*, not "ecstasy." By *ecstasis* I refer to concrete instances of rapture or *jouissance*; thus the plural refers to countable experiences of "ecstasy" more readily than the modern usage of "ecstasy" would permit.

35. Most of these terms were first used (at least first used most extensively) by Gérard Genette. I have streamlined their meanings, however, and in particular, my meaning of "metadiegetic" is completely different from his. (His, in fact, seems counterintuitive and unnecessarily confusing.) (See Genette 228–31.) One of the clearest and most generally useful introductions to these and other terms is Shlomith Rimmon-Kenan, *Narrative Fiction*. The importance of these terms will be more evident in my discussion of Kevin Killian in chapter 5.

36. On the George Burns and Gracie Allen television show, both characters portrayed idealized versions of their extradiegetic identities. When George would address the camera directly, or watch the events of that episode's plot unfold on his TV in his study, he was performing a metadiegetic function.

37. Although most of what I write here would apply to actresses in pornographic film, I confine myself to male actors in gay porn, because only with male bodies can the viewer be certain that pleasure was experienced and orgasm was attained.

38. This also illustrates Lacan's observation that the gaze ultimately recedes when it is looked for, a point he makes in describing the anamorphosis in paintings such as Holbein's *The Ambassadors* (*Four Fundamental* 88–89). See the discussion of this painting in chapter 5.

39. On "psychical reality" and the political implications for gay male subjectivity and representational practices, see the conclusion to chapter 2.

40. See Freud, "The Unconscious" and "Instincts and Their Vicissitudes"; and Tort.

41. Later in the film, in fact, he mentions that his first sexual experience occurred at fifteen, too old to be playing soldier.

42. What I call "retrospective sexualization" here is a form of Freud's concept of *Nachträglichkeit*, or "deferred action." See Freud, "From the History of an Infantile Neurosis" 37–38 n. 6. Laplanche and Pontalis define it as a process important to Freudian conceptions of "psychical temporality and causality" whereby "experiences, impressions, and memory-traces may be revised at a later date to fit in with fresh experiences or with the attainment of a new stage of development. They may in that event be endowed with a new meaning but also with psychical effectiveness" (*Language of Psychoanalysis* 111–13).

43. The distinctions between these types of fantasy are introduced and explored by Teresa de Lauretis in "The Subject of Fantasy." While I draw my understanding of the distinctions from this text, my use of them here is not related to de Lauretis's argument in that essay.

44. These assumptions are, of course, deduced from the referential pretensions of the fictive autobiographical narrative presented in the film, an effect of the film's rhetorical framing, so to speak. Karl as "subject of enunciation" can be presented on film only through a

preestablished convention; this "subject of enunciation," moreover, is a fictive identity presented on the level of the film's narrative discourse, and not an extrafilmic exposure to an actual "subject of enunciation" of the film.

45. The coextensive operations of dispersion and construction of the desiring/desired subject suggest an interesting near-parallel within the specular register to a similar phenomenon I examined in chapter 2 in the narrative of Wilde's "W. H.": the narrator's *analysis* of the sonnets facilitating the *construction* of "Willie Hughes."

46. The young man's position behind Karl allows his gaze to guide the viewer's between the exaggerated phallic masculinity signified by Karl's bulging jock strap in the mirror, and the "unmediated" ruination of that masculinity of his exposed buttocks. Pronger considers the jock strap the "quintessential homoerotic ritual robe" because the front pouch "enshrines the symbol of the myth of masculinity" but the straps in the back "circumscribe the buttocks and disappear at the anus . . . the place where masculinity meets its mythic undoing" (Pronger 160).

47. See Jacqueline Rose's summary of this dynamic (*Sexuality* 190–92).

48. Cf. "The self seems deep because it can use two vanishing points" (Glück, "Denny Smith" 504).

49. Indeed, the director of *Le Beau Mec* seems to have avoided common suturing techniques. The shot/reverse shots are conspicuously rare, and when they occur, the even more infrequent eye-line matches are either diegetically or metadiegetically compromised. There is a series of eye-line matches between Karl and the hustler outside of the gym, but these only set up an expectation of a sexual liaison that Karl (and thus the film) refuses. The most intense eye-line matches are between Karl and the "policeman" in the fantasy tableaux of Karl's adolescent history: an exchange occurring in an irreal world. Therefore these sequences do not coerce identification with Karl as a privileged point of view. There are other ruptures of possible suturing conventions as well. In both *Le Beau Mec* and *All of Me*, there is a voice-off which asks the questions of the first-person subject (perhaps first-person object would be more accurate). Mary Ann Doane notes that in classic cinema, the voice-off suggests the spatial fullness of the profilmic world, and that the source of the off-screen voice almost invariably is shown to fulfill this promise (Doane 39–40). We have already discussed above the circumlocution of voice-off in *All of Me*, of Cadinot's "surrogate" with the still camera and Buisson's disseverance from his voice. None of these ever fulfills such a promise; nor does the scarcely audible voice of Karl's interrogator.

50. Metz's schema here permits us to suggest a conjunction between the projective/introjective visual paths in the specator's Imaginary and the third triangle in Lacan's model of the gaze as enacted in the image-screen-spectator dynamics of *Le Beau Mec*: "There are two cones in the auditorium: one ending on the screen and starting both in the projection box and in the spectator's vision insofar as it is projective, and one starting from the screen and 'deposited' in the spectator's perception insofar as it is introjective" (Metz 51). We should furthermore recall that introjection and projection are modes of relating to the world vital to the constitution of the narcissistic ego, and that the two are particularly prominent in the constitution of the "pleasure ego" (Freud, "Instincts" 135–36).

51. At times the film displays an instability among the levels of its representational elements, similar to the difficulty the film presents of ascertaining the spatial relation of the inscribed viewer to the on-screen space. In the last scene, once Karl orgasms, the music stops, and there is a cut to a reel-to-reel tape recorder behind him with the tape running out. This contradicts the convention of the music occurring on the soundtrack—an expectation reinforced by the music interrupting his voiceover, which places the music on the same level as the voiceover, *not within the visual plane* (which indeed must also be *true*, because if the music had been playing in the scene other sounds would also be audible).

52. The hybrid nature of reality and fantasy in the intersections between the narrative and specular versions of the stories corresponds to and elaborates Freud's notion of "psychical reality." See my discussion of the term in chapter 2.

53. This paradox is important in the work of Kevin Killian as well. See chapter 5.

54. Linda Williams characterizes psychoanalysis as "a major force in the deployment of a sexuality that has intensified the body as a site of knowledge and power, making this body the major arena for the discovery of the nonexistent 'truth' of sex," but then points out that it is "the visible intensification of the body" in cinema that makes this "deployment of sexuality, and its attendant implantation of perversions" most apparent (20).

55. There is internal evidence suggesting that the embedded film is entitled *Paradigm of the Clam*. I am grateful to Ellis Hanson for pointing this out to me.

56. See chapter 1 for a more detailed discussion. Freud, *Three Essays* 197–99, especially the note added in 1924 on 199–200; and "Infantile Genital Organization" 141–45.

57. There are other scenes that could be compared between the two films of a similar nature. In *Law*, before going to bed, Juan and Pablo engage in casual sexual negotiations, Juan asking, "It's ok if we don't screw tonight, isn't it?" which can be favorably compared with the scene between the bullfighter and his supine fiancée in which he tells her to "play dead" as he begins to pounce upon her.

58. See, for example, Rubin, "Traffic"; de Lauretis, *Alice*, chapter 5; and Sprengnether.

59. Compare this with the opening scene of Almodóvar's *Labyrinth of Passion* (1982), in which the gay male and heterosexual female protagonists are each cruising a crowded avenue in Madrid, staring with delight at the crotches of the young male passersby. Here, the gaze and the concealed bodies are both playful, and have none of the ominous valance of the phallic weaponry parodied in the surveillance scene in *Matador*.

60. My only reservations about Mulvey's thesis here concern her decision not to address the racial dynamics in the film. Pearl's "choices" between a "ladylike" and a "sexual" identity stem from her marginalization as a "half-breed" (her mother was Native American). It is unclear to what degree the former path would have actually been open to her, but it is definitely the case that her ability to acknowledge and act on the "masculine/active" components of her psyche is conflated with the "savage" half of her heritage both intradiegetically and metadiegetically.

61. See chapter 1 on this process, and Freud's vacillation on this theory, which he himself introduced.

62. Lacan, *Le Séminaire II* 240–242. Ironically, Lacan prefaces his remarks on Sartre with a rather morbid anecdote concerning a joke traditionally played on amateur matadors by the spectators at certain bullfighting ceremonies.

63. See also Peri Rossi.

64. We can further appreciate the disassociation between sadism and dominant male heterosexuality by noting that the radical political position is inscribed here in the viewer-as-sadist structure, an interesting contrast with the reader-as-masochist structure of Delany's "Game of Time and Pain," which we examined in the previous chapter. Both textual experiences, however, are based on a clear distinction between violence and representational agency in the sexualized resignifying theatrics of fantasy and a radical negotiability of desiring subject positions outside of the gendered stasis of dominant heterosexual ideology.

65. For example, the subtitle of Jarman's book of the *Edward II* film: *Queer Edward II: Improved by Derek Jarman*.

66. Consider Gorgik's lover Noyeed, whose sexual acts insistently replay his rape and abuse by the slaves and guards in the obsidian mines when he was a newly captured slave in his youth—Gorgik having been one of the rapists ("Tale of Fog and Granite" 121–23).

67. "The imaginary relation is not merely of knowledge, sense and recognition—it is

love guaranteed by knowledge—a narcissism which allows the subject to fit into a harmonious relation between self and social order, but in the psychoanalytic account—the subject's narcissistic relation to the self is seen *to conflict with and disrupt* other social relations" (Copjec 60).

5. Scandalous Narratives

1. In an essay about his college days before "coming out," Robert Glück describes the isolation of the pre-scandalous, closeted self: "I had a secret. . . . The secret did not allow me to live in my group. I was alone. I had no world—just the despicable pink satellite of my body, and in outer space there is no moral life or camaraderie, just self preservation" ("Marker" 20).

2. As Simon Watney puts it: "In the register of object-choice, the homosexual body inescapably evidences a sexual diversity that it is its ideological 'function' to restrict . . . The 'homosexual body' would thus evidence a fictive collectivity of perverse sexual performances, denied any psychic reality and pushed out beyond the furthest margins of the social. This, after all, is what the category of 'the homosexual' . . . was invented to do in the first place" ("Spectacle" 78–79). For useful comparisons with the ideological uses which developed around "madness" and its representations, see Foucault, *Madness and Civilization* 13–17, 35–37, 82–84, and passim.

3. The major works from this school include Bruce Boone, *My Walk with Bob*; Kevin Killian, *Shy* and *Bedrooms Have Windows*; Dennis Cooper, *Safe, He Cried*, and *Closer*. Cooper's recent statement on "New Narrative" seems paradigmatic: "If there is such a thing as New Narrative writing, it seems to me to be less a strict movement of writers with a program or a marketing ploy, than it is a collection of writers, not all of us gay, by the way, loosely united behind our distrust of established mechanisms of narrative fiction—that is: basically outmoded devices having largely to do with plot, and used in such a laissez-faire, gratuitous style by most of the published practitioners of contemporary lit, gay and straight, young and old, male and female, new and established" (unpublished talk at the panel "Sex Writing and the New Narrative," Out/Write Conference, San Francisco, February 1990). Heterosexual writers included in this group are Kathy Acker and Michael Amnasan (Abbott 39–55).

4. The information in this paragraph is distilled from personal conversations with Robert Glück and Bruce Boone.

5. See my discussion in chapter 4.

6. This need operates on the same phantasmatic principles as the dynamics of the narcissistic exhibitionist described in chapter 4. This story bears a relation to its "heterosexual" counterpart, "Hiding in the Open," in which "Bob" masturbates to porn in a sperm bank. The former is narcissistic, the latter anaclitic. The tension between the two is parallel to the tension I described in chapter 4 between Almodóvar's films *Law of Desire* and *Matador*.

7. Compare Cooper's musing on porn star Jeff Hunter's apotheosis in the film *Kept after School*: "Never again will his face be as gripped by what's deep in his body but slipping from his possession" ("Square One" 83).

8. In his short story "Violence," Glück addresses this question by relating and then reflecting on the stakes of an argument at a Berkeley cocktail party regarding the use of "phallus" as a generic metaphor for power (*Elements* 92–93).

9. "I think in my work there's always been a sort of terror about sex. The desire for sex that you could have with someone you objectify but the terror of having to deal with a real person. . . . Sex is a really scary thing, you've got to choose your partners carefully, and what to do. . . . I always think the sex in my books is so unsexy, because they're nervous about

each other, and it's so much about just wanting to get something out of this body they're with and some idea they have about this person. [And since AIDS] it's just a general terror that's come over sex. And I think it's reinforcing that in my work" (qtd. Meyer 64).

10. "Square One" was originally published in *Soup: New Critical Perspectives*, ed. Bruce Boone, no. 4 (1985): 70–72. When I quote a passage that appears only in that version and was not included in the later version, printed in *Wrong*, it will be cited as "Square One" (*Soup*)."

11. "An audience made up of men like me has surrendered its collective will to a film-maker's. Like a cheap spaceship prop in an old sci-fi flick, a grungy theater scattered with hopeful, upturned faces seems to speed toward its destination—giant bodies composed of light" ("Square One" 83).

12. Freud, "Fetishism" and "Splitting"; Mannoni 175–80; Mulvey, "Visual Pleasure."

13. Even people with "real" sex lives often prefer the numb and numbing refuges of the world without consequences provided by pornographic media: "The life pornography pictures is ordered. . . . Doug wants to live in this one-dimensional world. . . . If someone he fucked died he'd never hear about it and if he did the word wouldn't compute or feel real to him. He'd be involved in his latest orgasm, face drawn so tight nothing else could get under" (*Safe* 84–85).

14. The Dylan quotation, from "The Gates of Eden" (*Bringing It All Back Home*), which also refers to the "object-meaning," is used again parodistically in *Closer* (5).

15. The only major symptom of melancholia as Freud describes it that is not directly evident in Cooper's narrative personae is the tendency to berate the self as morally inferior ("Mourning" 246–48). A desiring subject in Cooper's texts does, however, tend to disregard his corporeal self as a meaningful part in any sexual encounter. In other words, these subjects never wish to see themselves as objects of desire. The "Dennis" narrator of *Frisk* states that sexual reciprocation makes him "very uncomfortable," noting that his tricks "must pick up on my tastes right away, since they almost never want to explore me. They just lie back, take it from me. . . . Usually I don't notice my body. It's just there, working steadily. I wash it, feed it, jerk it off, wipe its ass, and that's all" (50).

16. John "subtracts from" his subjects by defacing their drawings (*Closer* 4). "In porn a director can only add or subtract from what exists outside his control—attractiveness" ("Square One" [*Soup*] 71).

17. Or the clue David—despite himself—in *Closer* gives the reader of the origin of his rock star delusion: "Once upon a time I was a little boy. I rode my bike constantly. I wandered everywhere, bought stuff, sang songs to myself. I stopped in a mall. This man came up to me. He was an A & R man for a big record company. He told me I was amazing. I said okay and we went back to his house. He tried to fuck me. I bled all over the place. Then he showed me the door and said, 'Thanks for being so well designed, kid' " (*Closer* 37).

18. Other characters also assess their bodies' attractiveness in the mirror, attempting to see it as others do: Mark in *Safe* (41) and Julian and Henry in *Frisk* (13, 16–17).

19. During George's first encounter with Philippe, he envisioned it as an exploration in a mineshaft in a Disneyland western fantasy geography (50). When examining his wounded anus for its "charm" to Philippe and Tom, he compares the swollen opening to the "painted mouth" of "Injun Joe's Cave," a Disneyland ride whose entrance always gave him "goose bumps" (90–91). The macabre cross-hybridization of child's play and horror in Disneyland becomes clearer when comparing the boys with the adults. George's Disneyland LSD hallu-cination is strangely similar to a vision Philippe has as he explores his own murderous feelings toward George. George's trip: "Over his head, a Milky Way of skulls snapped like turtles" (88). Philippe's vision: "Philippe lay in bed imagining George's death. . . . The world he saw rang with percussion. Skeletons snapped" (106).

20. The "Dead . . . men . . . tell . . . no . . . tales" line comes from the "Pirates of the Caribbean" ride. See also Marin on the postmodern dilemma of Disneyland.

21. A child learns this distinction through noticing that a stimulus that can be removed by motion is external (outside, perception), and one that is not effected through movement is internal (in consciousness) (Freud, "Instincts" 119–20).

22. David also acts this out in his fantasy of being skinned alive during a rock concert he stars in (*Closer* 26–27).

23. Stephen Heath discusses the relation of filmic representation to death and crime in his expansion of Cocteau's characterization of film as "death at work" through a reading of an Apollinaire story concerning the filming of a real murder (Heath, *Questions of Cinema* 114). Film inaugurates a representation organically related to death, while becoming the epitome of the depthless surface of the psychotic subject—the "skin ego" (note that in many Romance languages the word for film is related to the word for skin).

24. "The image does not, at first glance, resemble the corpse, but the cadaver's strangeness is perhaps also that of the image. What we call mortal remains escapes common categories. Something is there before us which is not really the living person, nor is it any reality at all. It is neither the same as the person who was alive, nor is it another person, nor is it anything else. . . . Death suspends the relation to place, even though the deceased rests heavily in his spot as if upon the only basis that is left him. . . . Where is it? It is not here, and yet it is not anywhere else. Nowhere? But then nowhere is here. The cadaverous presence establishes a relation between here and nowhere" (Blanchot 256).

25. I am indebted to Robert Glück for bringing this passage to my attention.

26. Jack does not attain the status of the phallus-bearer that the anaclitic male subject does within the heterosexual contract; in fact, he acquiesces to Bob's meanings of it for Bob— he gives up the signifying power that bearing the transcendental signifier would give him (the Adamic privilege of naming): "I grab his cock, unpromising, and he says in mock bewilderment, 'What's that?' As it hardens I answer for him, 'It's my appendicitis, my inchworm . . . my garden god, my minaret . . . my candle, my Bic, my unicorn, . . . my white whale, my tuning fork, my divining rod, my cobra . . . my joy stick, . . . my shark, . . . my credit card, . . . my fetish, . . . my genie, . . . my Dark Tower' " (27–28).

27. Mourning is the process of reconciling oneself to the loss (usually the death) of a loved one (Freud, "Mourning" 243–44). Melancholia may be triggered by a similar loss, but often with more tenuous relations to external circumstances. Often the loved one "has not actually died, but has been lost as an object of love," as when one is "jilted" (244). Melancholia can also arise when the subject is not conscious of whom he/she has lost, or when the subject knows whose loss he/she is mourning but cannot understand what it is in that person that the subject has lost by losing that person (244).

28. We will see a parallel exposition of writing the self as a lack-in-being in Killian, but from exactly opposite strategic emphases.

29. In their self-destabilizing expositions as polychronic subjects, Glück's narrators resemble the volatility of Heisenberg's quanta more than the certainty of Descartes's *cogito*. At one point in *Jack*, Bob interjects into the narrated time of the story of the relationship, from the present of Bob's narrating it, a rhetorical warning to Jack concerning the "present" moment (in the story) and an incipient future (from that point in the story's chronology) that had already happened (in the present of the time of narrating): "I am going to lose you and myself and our future, a portion of that loss already forms part of my present" (*Jack* 94–95).

30. In the postface to his rewriting of Margery Kemp's autobiography, Glück explains his identification with this pathetic would-be saint and egotistical mystic. "A woman famous for her tears fails to become a saint; she turns a corner in the 1430's and writes the first English

autobiography. I respond to the failure that permeates her book. . . . For twenty-five years I kept Margery in mind. . . . I couldn't approach her love for Jesus until I also loved a young man who was above me, lyrical and wealthy. . . . declines to change my life so let this story change it. What characterizes a god: his larger existence, an imperative that meaning stay with him, the mobility to retreat from the deep surrender he inspires. Love amazed me; I exulted in my luck, in our sex; L. exasperated me; I was exasperating; I was abandoned. I want to contain this rambling story in a few words. Now I am a type: a life that is distorted because of intrinsic lack. Obsessions draw their strength from the fear of death. His name still startles me so I use his initial. L. is the god of non-relation; he leaves me with the outline of failure; I am afraid to begin, afraid that my story has also ended—I am so inured to failure that I can't see it" (*Margery Kemp* 1–2).

31. The insistence on including the emotional component of visual/visceral experience in his narrative distinguishes Glück's aesthetic philosophy from that of Rechy as well as that of the "object-oriented" avant-garde: "I don't aspire to docu-drama: William Carlos Williams's factual cat steps into the flower pot. I don't know what that reportage means, severed from its context and the appearance of motive" ("Truth's Mirror" 40).

32. See chapter 1.

33. See chapter 1.

34. Glück offers one "tactic" for "binding [textual] systems to lived experience, to praxis"—a deployment of "text-metatext, where the text is the narrative, with its time span, characters and action, and the meta-text is a running deconstruction, or analysis. . . . A simple narration can put the reader on the far side of the proscenium arch. The meta-text cuts naturalistic illusion making. It includes the reader, it asks questions, asks for critical response, makes claims on the reader, elicits commitments" ("Caricature" 28).

35. While Glück clarifies the moral and epistemological distinctions between "honest" and "dishonest" fictions, Killian returns the noun to its active verbal etymology, *fingere*, "to create" or "to make."

36. As, for example, Betty Ford appearing as herself in an episode of the "Mary Tyler Moore Show," which is part of an important scene in *Shy*.

37. Killian has appeared in the videos *Coalminer's Granddaughter* (Cecilia Dougherty, 1991), *Swamp* (Abigail Childs, 1992), and *Jo-jo* (Cecilia Dougherty, 1993), and has performed in on-stage live productions of the filmscripts of Raymond Pettibone.

38. For these distinctions and their respective cultural politics, see the sections in chapter 1 on Barthes and Delany.

39. This is one reason that Killian's fiction tends to demand a much closer attention to plot than is usually considered useful or even feasible in most avant-garde or experimental mundane fiction. Killian observes: "Long ago Hollywood films beat out what we used to think of as 'literature' at its own game. Still we continue to tell each other stories" ("Sex Writing" 13).

40. The relation of the narrating Kevin to this narrated Kevin is difficult to ascertain, but assuming a symmetry between this relation and the narrator's relation to the other character's (semi-objective but with indirect and free indirect discourse, focalization, and even direct quotation, occasional fragments of interior monologue), we can assume that this is not a direct address to the reader (out of the diegetic level) but another instance of free indirect discourse.

41. Harry's version of this story to Kevin the night they met is another example of rewriting history. In this, however, he removes the sexual experience, describing it as being forced to polish the paneling in the basement, rather than attending school.

42. Other sexual poses seem to stem more from demand than from desire, as he recalls the interlude with a man in Boston when Harry was scarcely thirteen. " 'Read me some of

those books you got there. . . . Do some educating, mister.' . . . The man pulled a hard wooden chair to one side of the bed" and announces that he will read "a fairy tale" called "Cadet Capers" set in a military school (*Shy* 248–49).

43. The sign can be unintelligible because of exclusion from the code (Harry's illiteracy, for example) or because of the sign's excess of meaning. An example of the latter occurs in a metadiegetic intrusion into the plot. On Gunther's first day at the Crisis Center, he feels a sense of satisfaction at having found the number to an abortion clinic for a caller. This scene is narrated in free indirect style, shifting into narrated monologue (so that the "I" refers to Gunther), then shifts again to a direct narratorial first-person address, drawing an analogy between Gunther's deed and the novelist's project: "In a way, he had power. *Because of me a baby dies.* . . . He might almost have been the father of that fetus, yes, fucked the mother, dreamed up the baby, now dissolved it, all with a mere 'Yes, yes' as soothing and simple as cherry coke syrup. Or he might have been the novelist I thought I was. Wave a wand, and life appears; turn the page, zippo. The big O" (43). "The big O" signifies "orgasm," the "zero" of death, and resembles the O for operator (that one dialed for emergencies in classic Hollywood melodramas). The big "O" also describes the "O"-shaped wound Alder Golden left in his own head after murdering Mark, a shape that marks his attainment of the other big O of death, and the sign for "hugs" he wrote on Mark's body: "Alder Golden had gone into another room of the big Adirondack house and shot himself. Big O. Big hole in a big blonde head" (53). Note also the strange resonance with the morphological play of the orgasmic body in Glück's *Jack the Modernist*, in a passage cited above: "The more you get fucked, the more you want it: eventually the pornographic hungry hole becomes merely accurate. I was surrounded by an O sound that was at once the voice of sex and the shape of the orifice he pounded" (*Jack* 28–29).

44. Three months prior to giving the paper in which this sentence is contained, Killian gave a lecture on Sam D'Allesandro in which this same statement occurs, its only difference being the opening phrase: instead of "My writing," it reads "Sam's writing." The substitution of Sam D'Allesandro for himself in this essay parallels the "Kevin" "Gunther" substitution in the story of the marriage to the "witch" in *Shy* and *Bedrooms Have Windows*.

45. The significations such a network achieves exceed the strictly referential (since so much of the purely referential does not explain anything in the novel, or in life). The Kevin narrator of *Shy* comments on the meaningless mysteries of the purely referential, citing as an example Gunther's first mentioning the name "Melanie": "I wanted to ask who Melanie was, or had been. I only found out later, and then it was only one of a number of factors that didn't fit in no matter how they were added up" (*Shy* 3).

46. Much of Kevin's relationship with Harry revolves around the narrative, and their joint exploration of its unfolding. One of their sessions, in which Kevin reads his version of the narrative so far to Harry, is overheard by Alley, who decides to leave without telling Kevin she is running away (226–28).

47. "In the middle of the night Gunther would wake up, startled . . . and from his crib on the floor Harry could see his eyes wide and white as baseballs. 'What's the matter?' 'Sssssh!' . . . Then Harry would focus and hear what Gunther was hearing: the tap tap tap of Kevin's typewriter upstairs. Gunther whispered, 'Writing down our lives, and then what will happen!' " (253). Of course, Gunther's paranoia was coincidentally an accurate assessment of the situation: "Gunther had been in Kevin's apartment upstairs one time, and he'd spotted a glass lying on the floor, and then he came downstairs and went crazy. 'He keeps that glass there to listen through.' 'Ah, Gunther, come off it.' 'Whisper!' Gunther said, his mouth tiny, hissing like a dragonfly. 'When he's not typing his ear's to the floor' " (254).

48. To appreciate the differences between the modernist commitment to the self and

Killian's project, one need only contrast *Shy* with Gide's *The Counterfeiters* and *Bedrooms Have Windows* with Proust's *Remembrances of Things Past*.

49. I appeal to Barry Hindess and Paul Hirst's arguments against epistemology; Foucault's discursive totalities he elaborated in *The Order of Things*; and Paul Rabinow's use of Foucault to counter an epistemologically naive basis of anthropology. Rabinow 239–41; Hindess and Hirst 10–33.

50. For example, the narrator Kevin's recollections of his first sexual experience with Mark differ greatly from Mark's account, which Kevin overhears Mark telling Alder on the phone (*Shy* 166–68, 169–70).

51. It also demonstrates the unreliability of Harry as a source of information, which makes the earlier reconstruction of that incident (or any involving Harry) even more unlikely.

52. The intrusion of the "I" ruins it. Note, for example, that while both Popeye[1] and KMH[2] are essentially the same type of narrative (third-person focalized through Harry), the latter is more glaringly aberrant than the former (isolated from the rest of the book, the former reads like an ordinary third-person narrative) because of the illicit intrusion of the first-person pronoun.

53. For example, Harry's long interior monologue on LSD in the bathtub in the "White House" contains insights into the character Kevin's psychological makeup as impossible for Harry to achieve as the reproduction of this interior monologue should be for the narrator Kevin (*Shy* 161–62).

54. In Lacanian thought, the subject "does not exist before the submersion into the order of signifiers, nor outside of that order, but only within it, as represented and sustained by the sequence of signifiers of which it is in continual want if it is to remain a subject" (Richardson 61).

55. But Gunther accomplishes this without harming the realist illusion, unlike Kevin's more typical divagations.

56. Beneath Kevin's level (Kevin as the EKN), the level of the characters, Harry's narrative is not an act of signification as much as it is a sexual act.

57. See, for example, Killian's counterfeit eighteenth-century novel *Desiree*, which essentially restages the relationship of George and Kevin, and "Brother and Sister," his revision of the original Grimms brothers' version of "Hansel and Gretel"; his collaboration with Mark Ewert on a new version of the children's classic *The Secret Garden*; and the short story "A Love Like That," Killian's version of the opening scene of William Castle's slasher film *Homicidal*.

58. Compare the function of Lord Aldamir, the dead father of the Nevèrÿon series, and the discovery of his nonexistence by Raven and Noreema in "Tales of Potters and Dragons." "There is no Lord Aldamir? . . . Ours is a strange kind of information. It is far easier to argue that something nobody believes in exists than it is to argue that something everybody believes in is unreal" (195–96).

59. The irony here is that the mimetic saturation of the narrative—the richness of the realist illusion—debars the narrator's intrusion as a cognitive subject. Such intrusions mark a text that demeans its own accomplishment, by damaging the integrity of the represented world and the credibility of the narrator who had produced that representation, because a homodiegetic narrator is an entity dependent upon the cohesion of the world it inhabits. Violation of the epistemological constraints on the narrative there undermines the world and the narrative voice. Of course, the Kevin narrator's assumption of third-person privileges is motivated by the failure they will achieve. Kevin's "I" appropriates the third-person position to debunk the philosophy of scientific objectivity and monolithic Truth behind that privilege. The retention of the first-person, intradiegetic identity of "Kevin" allows the narrator to

parody the privileges of the third-person narrator but also to display "his" own inability to approximate that withdrawn certitude.

60. For example, "Hayley vs. Annette" and "Dallas vs. Dynasty."

61. As another example of Killian's breakdown of generic barriers, he includes this passage from the story as the conclusion of his lecture "The Boys of Fiction."

62. Killian also explores "noncamp" uses of popular icons in similar veins, notably the role David Bowie plays in the lives of the adolescent heroes of *Shy*, Paula Thiele and Harry Van.

63. "I sat there telling my diary the story of the novel I hoped one day to write. 'This will make me famous,' I thought. And what was fame . . . but an extension of my present being?" (*Bedrooms* 3)

64. The final phrases of "George's" text, which are also the last lines of the book, are nearly identical to the opening sentences of Killian's memoir. It begins: "I grew up in Smithtown, a suburb of New York, a town so invidious that still I speak of it in Proustian terms—or Miltonic terms, a kind of paradise I feel evicted from. Smithtown, Long Island, kind of an MGM Norman Rockwell hometown, a place so boring they gave it a boring name" (1). "George's" version reads: "We grew up in Smithtown, a suburb of New York, a town so invidious we still speak of it in Miltonic terms. Paradise we're evicted from. Smithtown, Long Island, kind of an MGM Norman Rockwell hometown, a place so boring they gave it a boring name" (134). The suppression of the adjective "Proustian" in the reprise suggests a repression or a resolution its absence marks. The circularity resembles the narrative closure of *Recherches*, and the plots of the two texts are basically the same: The "I" becomes a writer. (In both cases the narrator and the author share a first name.) "The narrative halts at the point when the hero has discovered the truth and the meaning of his life: when this 'story of a vocation' . . . comes to an end. . . . The subject of *Recherches* is indeed 'Marcel becomes a writer,' and not 'Marcel the writer.' . . . The novelistic is the quest . . . which ends at the discovery (the revelation), not at the use to which that discovery will afterward be put" (Genette 226–27).

65. Killian in fact produces his writer's persona as "star" by fusing Sartre's peeping Tom at the culminating point in Sartre's fantasy which Sartre never reaches (in Sartre's text, there is no one in the hall to see him) with the implicit "contract" between a male viewer and a woman who knows he's watching but pretends not to know, as in Lacan's *Four Fundamental*. See chapter 4.

66. Killian himself compares his writing practice to both voyeurism and exhibitionism: "The main theme [of *Bedrooms*] is looking and seeing. It's about voyeurism and exhibitionism, in the trope of the reader as the voyeur and the writer as the exhibitionist" (Karr, "Triple Play" 36). These specular positions are stages in creative apprenticeship and expression in *Bedrooms*: "Bedrooms have windows to spy into, to comport oneself before, the way you or I might first read a book, then write one" (*Bedrooms* 78).

67. For example, Ted Berrigan, whose drugs Kevin steals during a poetry reading, or Aaron Shurin, in whose kitchen Kevin meets another celebrity, with whom he has sex shortly afterward (*Bedrooms* 86–87). Killian discusses this passage and the function of "Aaron" in "Poison" (5–6).

68. None of the guarantees of identity that either language or the realist narrative offers are long operative in Killian's texts. In his short story "Spreadeagle," the first-person narrator owns a mail-order business selling celebrity autographs. The signature, supposedly the unique mark of that individual's identity, and one whose uniformity should reflect the unitary and self-identical nature of the individual, becomes a commodity transparent to its own contradictions and hypocritical conventions engendering and mystifying them: "I can forge Audrey Hepburn's signature 100 different ways, all of them accurate" ("Spreadeagle" 13). The personality is also subject to forgery, and its creation or emendation will take on the same veneers

of authenticity that realist ideology projects as natural, which the narrator demonstrates by "writing letters from Audrey": " 'Mr. Cukor introduced me to a charming man,' I wrote, all in the up-and-down bumpy hand characteristic of Audrey on vacation in Spain, 'whose Marine uniform looked snappy outside the corrida. If I weren't happily married to Mel it might have been an occasion of sin, Eileen.' I had invented a bubbly girlfriend for Audrey who always seems so forlorn and demure. These letters, aged with soot and metal oil and scented with *Je Voudrais*, will sell for $$$ to a besotted queen in San Antonio" (13).

69. Note the difference between this self-conscious political travesty of the father-son bond, and Harry's symptomatic repetition of the same in his relation with Gunther. (" 'I'm very bad you know' " [*Shy* 83].)

70. Glück's commentary on Beverley Dahlen's poetry speaks to the issues surrounding the representation of Kevin's writing self as George's "patrimony": "I think Lacan's Name-of-the-Father applies, parental authority considered as a linguistic function, and the notion of the mirrored self as other . . . —a structural irony (doubleness) that always refers to that first sharpest cruelty of names and categories: the creation of the self with its double abdication from the world and from the body" ("Allegory" 115–16). On the relation of patriarchal transmission to transcendental mimesis, see my discussion of the Sygn/Family differences in Delany's *Stars in My Pocket* and Hocquenghem in chapter 3.

71. The use of plagiarism as a strategic attack on patriarchal "authenticity" is a frequent concern of feminist writings on mostly women avant-garde writers and artists. Kathy Acker is the most celebrated of the "literary plagiarists." See Lotringer 12–13; Jacobs; and Levine.

72. This is modeled after Jack Spicer's "Fifteen False Propositions against God."

73. He surmised that Marion's "imaginary past stemmed from her affection for the TV sitcom Laverne and Shirley" since "almost everything Laverne and Shirley did had a seedier counterpart in Marion's life with Linda Blair," a "Diane Arbus" version. Marion's "lies, her frame of reference" were so consistently grim that Kevin "wanted a pattern made out of them to darken my belief: a doubting Thomas in reverse" (*Bedrooms* 95).

In Conclusions . . .

1. Ironically, the neoclassicist project of a history as lucid as a geometral painting was ruined by innovations in literary narratives that influenced historiographical practice, particularly the narrative technique initiated by Diderot in *Jacques the Fatalist* (Gossman 17–18), a title not incidentally similar to *Jack the Modernist*, a novel, whose techniques owe much to Diderot.

2. Even the desublimated scientist perverts the god trick. Delany offers the possibility of a language that would correct the unilateral phenomenology of "ordinary" English: " 'I see the table' suggests that . . . 'I' am doing something to the table, by 'seeing' it. . . . Empirically . . . we know that . . . the table is . . . doing far more to 'I' than 'I' am doing to it. . . . A language is conceivable that would reflect this. . . . 'Light reflects from table then excites my-eyes' " ("Shadows" 85). Worthy of consideration in this context also is the reversal of visual or visionary flow in Plato's rendering of the sight of the beloved in the *Phaedrus*, in which the beauty of the (male) beloved radiates as "streams of Zeus" from his body into the eyes (and thus the soul) of the lover (*Phaedrus* 252c–253a).

3. Note the similarities and differences in these transgressions with those of screen and spectator in the gay porno film as discussed in chapter 4.

4. Karr 36.

5. See also "Truth's Mirror" 43–44, where Glück refers to this effect of narrative as a "magic spell."

6. See Killian, "On Robert Creely."

7. It is interesting to compare Killian's countermimetics to Fassbinder's use of melodrama. Killian acknowledges his debt to the latter in *Bedrooms* when he writes: "In private a Fassbinder-Sirk festival runs in my head from day to night" (27).

8. Note also that representation is always under the sway of the pleasure principle. See Safouan.

9. See Linda Williams 526–27; Fischer 30–31; and Mayne 168–72.

10. Note: "But origins are always constructs, always contouring ideological agendas" (Delany, *Return*, Appendix A 369). Compare also K. L. Steiner on the nostalgia of historical reconstruction (Appendix to Delany, *Bridge of Lost Desire*, 307–308).

11. Ironically, this metaphoric mirror succeeds where the metaphoric mirror of the Turkish frelk in "Aye, and Gomorrah" fails—her inapt symbol of the homosexual's "substitute" for the "true" object of desire.

Works Cited

Abbott, Steve. *View/Askew: Postmodern Investigations*. San Francisco: Andogyne, 1989.

Acker, Kathy. *Hannibal Lecter, My Father*. New York: Semiotext(e), 1991.

Adams, Parveen. "Versions of the Body." *m/f* 11–12 (1986).

Alarcón, Francisco X. *The Body in Flames/El Cuerpo en llamas*. San Francisco: Chronicle Books, 1990.

Alberti, Leon Battista. *On Painting*. Translated by John R. Spencer. New Haven: Yale University Press, 1956.

Almaguer, Tomás. "Chicano Men: A Cartography of Homosexual Identity and Behavior." In de Lauretis, *Queer Theory*, pp. 75–100.

Alonso, Ana Maria, and Maria Teresa Koreck. "Silences: 'Hispanics' and AIDS, and Sexual Practices." *differences* 1.1 (Winter 1988): 101–124.

Althusser, Louis. *For Marx*. Translated by Ben Brewster. London: New Left, 1969.

———. "Ideology and Ideological State Apparatuses: Notes towards an Investigation." In Althusser, *Lenin and Philosophy*, pp. 127–186.

———. *Lenin and Philosophy*. Translated by Ben Brewster. London: New Left, 1977.

———. "On Theoretical Work: Difficulties and Resources." Translated by James H. Kavanaugh. In Althusser, *Philosophy and the Spontaneous Philosophy of the Scientists*, pp. 43–67.

———. *Philosophy and the Spontaneous Philosophy of the Scientists*. Edited by Gregory Elliot. London and New York: Verso, 1990.

———. "Theory, Theoretical Practice and Theoretical Formation: Ideology and Ideological Struggle." Translated by James H. Kavanaugh. In Althusser, *Philosophy and the Spontaneous Philosophy of the Scientists*, pp. 3–42.

Anzieu, Didier. *Freud's Self Analysis*. Translated by Peter Graham. London: The Hogarth Press, 1986.

———. *The Skin Ego*. Translated by Chris Turner. New Haven: Yale University Press, 1989.

Aries, Phillippe. *The Hour of Our Death*. Translated by Helen Weaver. New York: Knopf, 1981.

Bachelard, Gaston. *L'activité rational de la physique contemporaine*. Paris: Presses universitaires de Paris, 1951.

———. *Le rationalisme appliqué*. Paris: Presses universitaires de Paris, 1951.

Baker, Houston A., Jr. *Blues, Ideology, and Afro-American Literature: A Vernacular Theory*. Chicago: University of Chicago Press, 1984.

Bal, Mieke. "The Point of Narratology." *Poetics Today* 11.4 (1990): 727–753.

Balibar, Étienne. "From Bachelard to Althusser: The Concept of the 'Epistemological Break.'" *Economy and Society* 7.3 (August 1978): 207–237.

Barthes, Roland. *Camera Lucida: Reflections on Photography*. Translated by Richard Howard. New York: Hill and Wang, 1981.

————. "Death of the Author." In Barthes, *Image-Music-Text*, pp. 142–148.

————. "From Work to Text." In Harari, ed., pp. 73–81.

————. *Image-Music-Text*, Translated by Stephen Heath. New York: Hill and Wang, 1977.

————. *A Lover's Discourse*. Translated by Richard Howard. New York: Farrar, Straus and Giroux, 1977.

————. *Mythologies*. Translated by Annette Lavers. London: Cape, 1972.

————. *The Pleasure of the Text*. Translated by Richard Miller. New York: Noonday, 1975.

————. *S/Z*. Translated by Richard Miller. New York: Hill and Wang, 1974.

Bartky, Sandra Lee. "Foucault, Femininity, and the Modernization of Patriarchal Power." In Diamond and Quinby, eds., pp. 61–86.

Barzilai, Shuli. "The Borders of Language: Kristeva's Critique of Lacan." *PMLA* 106 (1991): 294–305.

Bataille, Georges. *Erotism*. Translated by Mary Dalwood. San Francisco: City Lights, 1986.

————. *The Tears of Eros*. Translated by Peter Connor. San Francisco: City Lights, 1989.

Baudrillard, Jean. *The Ecstasy of Communication*. Translated by Bernard and Caroline Schutze. New York: Semiotexte, 1988.

————. *Simulations*. Translated by Paul Foss, Paul Patton, and Philip Beitchman. New York: Semiotexte, 1983.

Baudry, Jean Louis. "The Apparatus." Translated by Jean Andrews and Bertrand Augst. *camera obscura* 1 (1976): 104–123.

————. "Ideological Effects of the Basic Apparatus." Translated by Alan Williams. *Film Quarterly* 28.2 (1973–74): 39–47.

Bazin, André. *What Is Cinema?* Translated by Hugh Gray. 2 vols. Berkeley and Los Angeles: University of California Press, 1967–71.

Beam, Joseph, ed. *In the Life: A Black Gay Anthology*. Boston: Alyson, 1986.

Beaver, Harold. "Homosexual Signs." *Critical Inquiry* 8.1 (Autumn 1981): 99–119.

Beckson, Karl. "The Autobiographical Signature in *The Picture of Dorian Gray*." *Victorian Newsletter* 69 (Spring 1986): 11–16.

Bellamy, Dodie. "Digression as Power: Dennis Cooper and the Aesthetics of Distance." *Mirage* 1 (1985): 78–87.

————. "Incarnation." In Roy and Blake, eds., pp. 30–33.

Benveniste, Emile. *Problems in General Linguistics*. Translated by Mary Elizabeth Meek. Coral Gables: University of Miami Press, 1971.

Bernheimer, Charles, and Claire Kahane, eds. *In Dora's Case*. 2nd ed. New York: Columbia University Press, 1990.

Bersani, Leo. *The Freudian Body: Psychoanalysis and Art*. New York: Columbia University Press, 1985.

————. "Is the Rectum a Grave?" In Crimp, ed., pp. 197–222.

Blanchford, Greg. "Looking at Pornography: Erotica and the Socialist Morality." In *Pink Triangles*, ed. Pam Mitchell, pp. 26–38. Boston: Alyson, 1980.

Blanchot, Maurice. *The Space of Literature*. Translated by Ann Smock. Lincoln: University of Nebraska Press, 1982.

Bleier, Ruth. "The Lab Coat: Robe of Innocence or Klansman's Sheet?" In de Lauretis, ed., *Feminist Studies/Critical Studies*, pp. 55–66.

Blish, James. *A Case of Conscience*. New York: Ballantine, 1958.

Boehm, Felix. "Beiträge zur Psychologie der Homosexualität III: Homosexualität und Oedipuskomplex." *International Journal of Psychoanalysis* 12 (1926): 66–79.

Boon. James A. "Saussure/Peirce à propos Language, Society, and Culture." *Semiotica* 27 (1979): 83–99.

Boone, Bruce. "Gay Language as Political Praxis: The Poetry of Frank O'Hara." *Social Text* 1.1. (1980): 59–63.

———. *My Walk with Bob.* San Francisco: Black Star, 1979.

Boone, Joseph A. "Of Me(n) and Feminism: Who(se) Is the Sex That Writes?" In Boone and Cadden, eds., pp. 11–25.

Boone, Joseph A., and Michael Cadden, eds. *Engendering Men: The Question of Men in Feminist Criticism.* New York and London: Routledge, 1990.

Booth, Stephen, ed. *Shakespeare's Sonnets.* New Haven: Yale University Press, 1977.

Bordo, Susan. "Anorexia Nervosa: Psychopathology as the Crystallization of Culture." *Philosophical Forum* 17.2 (Winter 1985–86): 73–104.

Bray, Alan. *Homosexuality in Renaissance England.* London: Gay Men's Press, 1982.

Bray, Mary Kay. "Rites of Reversal: Double Consciousness in Delany's *Dhalgren.*" *Black American Literature Forum* 18.2 (Summer 1984): 57–61.

Brecht, Bertholt. *Brecht on Theatre.* Edited and translated by John Willett. London: Eyre Methuen, 1964.

Bredbeck, Gregory. *Sodomy and Interpretation.* Ithaca: Cornell University Press, 1991.

Brill, A. A. "Translator's Introduction." In Freud, *Leonardo da Vinci*, trans. A. A. Brill. New York: Vintage, 1947.

Bronski, Michael. *Culture Clash.* Boston: South End, 1984.

Brooks, Peter. *Reading for the Plot: Design and Intention in Narrative.* New York: Knopf, 1984.

Brossard, Nicole. *The Aerial Letter.* Translated by Marlene Wildman. Toronto: The Women's Press, 1988.

Brown, Tony, ed. *Edward Carpenter and Late Victorian Radicalism.* London: Frank Cass, 1990.

Bruce-Novoa, Juan. "Homosexuality and the Chicano Novel." *Confluencia* 2.1 (1986): 69–77.

Bryson, Norman. *Tradition and Desire: From David to Delacroix.* Cambridge: Cambridge University Press, 1984.

———. *Vision and Painting: The Logic of the Gaze.* New Haven and London: Yale University Press, 1983.

Budrys, Algis. *Rogue Moon.* Greenwich, Conn.: Fawcett, 1960.

Burnett, Ron, ed. *Explorations in Film Theory: Selected Essays from Ciné-Tracts.* Bloomington: Indiana University Press, 1991.

Butler, Judith. *Gender Trouble.* New York: Routledge, 1990.

———. "Performative Acts and Gender Constitution." In Case, ed., pp. 270–282.

———. "The Pleasures of Repetition." In *Pleasure beyond the Pleasure Principle*, ed. Robert A. Glick and Stanley Bove, pp. 259–275. New Haven: Yale University Press, 1990.

Butters, Ronald R.; John M. Clum; and Michael Moon, eds. *Displacing Homophobia: Gay Male Perspectives on Literature and Culture.* Durham: Duke University Press, 1989.

Canary, Robert H., and Henry Kozicki, eds. *The Writing of History: Literary Form and Historical Understanding.* Madison: University of Wisconsin Press, 1978.

Carpenter, Edward A. *Selected Writings*, vol. 1: *Sex*. London: GMP, 1984.

Case, Sue-Ellen. "Toward a Butch-Femme Aesthetic." *Discourse* 11.1 (Fall–Winter 1988–89): 55–83.

Case, Sue-Ellen, ed. *Performing Feminisms: Feminist Critical Theory and Theatre*. Baltimore and London: Johns Hopkins University Press, 1990.

Chabram, Angie. "Conceptualizing Chicano Critical Discourse." In *Criticism in the Borderlands: Studies in Chicano Literature, Culture, and Ideology*, ed. Héctor Calderón and José David Saldívar, pp. 127–148. Durham: Duke University Press, 1991.

Clifford, James, and George Marcus, eds. *Writing Culture: The Poet and Politics of Ethnography*. Berkeley: University of California Press, 1985.

Cohen, Ed. "Foucauldian Necrologies: 'Gay' 'Politics'? Politically Gay." *Textual Practices* 2.1 (Spring 1988): 87–101.

———. "Legislating the Norm: From Sodomy to Gross Indecency." In Butters et al., eds., pp. 169–206.

Cohen, William A. "Willie and Wilde: Reading *The Portrait of Mr. W. H.*" In Butters et al., eds., pp. 207–234.

Comolli, Jean-Louis. "Machines of the Visible." In Teresa de Lauretis and Stephen Heath, eds., *The Cinematic Apparatus*, pp. 121–142. New York: St. Martin's, 1980.

Cooper, Dennis. *Closer*. New York: Grove Weidenfeld, 1989.

———. "Dear Secret Diary." In *Against Nature: A Group Show of Work by Homosexual Men*, ed. Richard Hawkins and Dennis Cooper, pp. 5–7. Los Angeles: L.A.C.E., 1988.

———. *Frisk*. New York: Grove Weidenfeld, 1991.

———. *He Cried*. San Francisco: Black Star, 1984.

———. "A Herd." In Cooper, *The Tenderness of the Wolves*, pp. 51–75.

———. *Idols*. Rev. ed. New York: Sea Horse, 1979.

———. "Queer King: Derek Jarman." *L.A. Weekly* (June 12, 1992): 34–38, 43,

———. *Safe*. New York: Sea Horse, 1984.

———. "Sex Writing and the New Narrative." Unpublished talk presented at the Out/Write Lesbian and Gay Writers' Conference, San Francisco, 1990.

———. "Smoke Screen." In *They See God*, pp. 1–2. New York: Pat Hearn Galleries, 1988.

———. "Square One." In *Soup: New Critical Perspectives*, ed. Brace Boone, no. 4 (1985): 70–72.

———. "Square One." In Cooper, *Wrong*, pp. 81–92.

———. *The Tenderness of the Wolves*. Trumansburg: Crossing, 1981.

———. *Wrong*. New York: Grove Weidenfeld, 1992.

Copjec, Joan. "The Orthopsychic Subject: Film Theory and the Reception of Lacan." *October* 49 (1989): 53–72.

Coste, Didier. *Narrative as Communication*. Minneapolis: University of Minnesota Press, 1989.

Coward, Rosalind, and John Ellis. *Language and Materialism: Developments in Semiology and the Theory of the Subject*. London: Routledge, 1977.

Crapanzano, Vincent. "Text, Transference, and Indexicality." *Ethos* 9.2 (1981): 122–148.

Crimp, Douglas. "How to Have Promiscuity in an Epidemic." In Crimp, ed., pp. 231–271.

Crimp, Douglas, ed. *AIDS: Cultural Analysis/Cultural Activism*. Cambridge, Mass.: MIT Press, 1988.

Davidson, Arnold I. "How to Do the History of Psychoanalysis: A Reading of Freud's *Three Essays on the Theory of Sexuality.*" *Critical Inquiry* (Winter 1987): 252–277.

de Beauvoir, Simone. *The Second Sex.* Translated by H. M. Parshley. New York: Alfred A. Knopf, 1953.

de Certeau. Michel. *Heterologies: Discourse on the Other.* Translated by Brian Massumi. Minneapolis: University of Minnesota Press, 1986.

de Lauretis, Teresa. *Alice Doesn't.* Bloomington: Indiana University Press, 1984.

———. "Film and the Visible." In *How Do I Look?* ed. Bad Object-Choices, pp. 223–264. Seattle: Bay Press, 1991.

———. "Sexual Indifference and Lesbian Representation." In Case, ed., pp. 17–39.

———. "The Subject of Fantasy." In *Feminisms and the Cinema*, ed. Laura Pietropaolo and Ada Testaferri. Bloomington: Indiana University Press. Forthcoming.

———. *Technologies of Gender.* Bloomington: Indiana University Press, 1987.

———. "The Technology of Gender." In de Lauretis, *Technologies of Gender*, pp. 1–30.

———. "The Violence of Rhetoric." In de Lauretis, *Technologies of Gender*, pp. 31–50.

de Lauretis, Teresa, ed. *Feminist Studies/Critical Studies.* Bloomington: Indiana University Press, 1986.

———. *Queer Theory: Lesbian and Gay Sexualities. differences* 3.2 (Summer 1991).

Debord, Guy. *Society of the Spectacle.* Detroit: Black and Red, 1983.

Delany, Samuel R. "About 5,750 Words." In Delany, *The Jewel-Hinged Jaw*, pp. 21–37.

———. *The American Shore.* Elizabethtown, N.Y.: Dragon, 1978.

———. "Aye, and Gomorrah." In *Dangerous Visions*, ed. Harlan Ellison, pp. 532–544. New York: Berkley.

———. *Babel-17.* New York: Ace, 1966.

———. *The Bridge of Lost Desire.* New York: Arbor, 1987.

———. "The Column at the Market's Edge." Appendix to Delany, *The Motion of Light in Water* (Paladin), pp. 555–581.

———. "Critical Method/Speculative Fiction." In Delany, *The Jewel-Hinged Jaw*, pp. 119–131.

———. *Dhalgren.* Boston: Gregg Press, 1977.

———. "*Dichtung* and Science Fiction." In Delany, *Starboard Wine*, pp. 165–196.

———. "Disch." In Delany, *Starboard Wine*, pp. 138–164.

———. *Driftglass/Starshards.* London: Grafton, 1993.

———. *Flight from Nevèrÿon.* London: Grafton, 1986.

———. "Game of Time and Pain." In Delany, *Return to Nevèrÿon*, pp. 9–158.

———. "Interview with Samuel R. Delany." In McCaffery and Gregory, eds., pp. 83–110.

———. *The Jewel-Hinged Jaw.* New York: Berkley, 1978.

———. *The Motion of Light in Water.* New York: NAL, 1988.

———. *The Motion of Light in Water.* Expanded ed. London: Paladin, 1990.

———. "The Necessity of Tomorrows." In Delany, *Starboard Wine*, pp. 23–36.

———. "Neither the Beginning nor the End of Structuralism, Post-Structuralism, Semiotics, or Deconstruction for SF Readers: An Introduction." Part 1. *The New York Review of Science Fiction* 6 (February 1989): 1, 8–12.

———. *Neveryóna.* New York: Bantam.

———. "Of Sex, Objects, Signs, Systems, Sales, SF and Other Things." In Delany, *The Straits of Messina*, pp. 33–56.

———. "Quarks." In Delany, *The Jewel-Hinged Jaw*, pp. 135–140.

———. *Return to Nevèrÿon*. London: Grafton, 1989.

———. "Science Fiction and 'Literature,' or The Conscience of the King." *Analog* 99 (May 1979): 59–78.

———. "The Scorpion Garden." In Delany, *The Straits of Messina*, pp. 1–15.

———. "The Semiology of Silence." *Science-Fiction Studies* 14.2 (July 1987): 134–164.

———. "Shadows." In Delany, *The Jewel-Hinged Jaw*, pp. 38–118.

———. "Shadows and Ash." In Delany, *Longer Views*. Middletown, Conn.: Wesleyan University Press, forthcoming.

———. "The Significance of Science Fiction." *The Michigan Quarterly Review* 20.3 (Summer 1981): 224–235.

———. *Silent Interviews*. Middletown, Conn.: Wesleyan University Press, 1994.

———. "Some Presumptuous Approaches to Science Fiction." In Delany, *Starboard Wine*, pp. 46–55.

———. *Starboard Wine*. Pleasantville, N.Y.: Dragon, 1984.

———. *Stars in My Pocket Like Grains of Sand*. New York: Bantam, 1984.

———. *The Straits of Messina*. Seattle: Serconia, 1989.

———. "The Tale of Dragons and Dreamers." In Delany, *Tales of Nevèrÿon*, pp. 211–245.

———. "The Tale of Fog and Granite." In Delany, *Flight from Nevèrÿon*, pp. 3–125.

———. "The Tale of Old Venn." In Delany, *Tales of Nevèrÿon*, pp. 57–125.

———. "The Tale of Plagues and Carnivals." In Delany, *Flight from Nevèrÿon*, pp. 238–479.

———. "The Tale of Potters and Dragons." In Samuel R. Delany, *Tales of Nevèrÿon* (Middletown, Conn.: Wesleyan University Press, 1993), pp. 161–213.

———. "The Tale of Rumor and Desire." In Delany, *Return to Nevèrÿon*, pp. 159–276.

———. "The Tale of Small Sarg." In Delany, *Tales of Nevèrÿon*.

———. *Tales of Nevèrÿon*. New York: Bantam, 1979.

——— "Three Letters to *Science Fiction Studies*." In Delany, *Starboard Wine*, pp. 198–223.

———. *Triton*. New York: Bantam, 1976.

Delany, Samuel R., and Joanna Russ. "A Dialogue: Samuel Delany and Joanna Russ on Science Fiction." *Callaloo* 27–35.

Deleuze, Gilles. and Felix Guattari. *Anti-Oedipus: Capitalism and Schizophrenia*. Translated by Robert Hurley, Mark Seem, and Helen R. Lane. Minneapolis: University of Minnesota Press, 1983.

Diamond, Irene, and Lee Quinby, eds. *Feminism and Foucault*. Boston: Northeastern University Press, 1988.

Disch, Thomas A. "Concepts." In Disch, *The Man Who Had No Idea*, pp. 68–114.

———. "The Embarassments of Science Fiction." In Nichols, ed., pp. 139–155.

———. *The Man Who Had No Idea*. New York: Bantam, 1982.

———. "Planet of the Rapes." In Disch, *The Man Who Had No Idea*, pp. 162–181.

Doane, Mary Ann. "The Voice in the Cinema: The Articulation of Body and Space." *Yale French Studies* 60 (1980): 33–50.

Dolan, Jill. "The Dynamics of Desire: Sexuality and Gender in Pornography and Performance." *Theatre Journal* 39.2 (1987): 156–171.

———. " 'Lesbian' Subjectivity in Realism: Dragging at the Margins of Structure and Ideology." In Case, ed., pp. 40–53.

Dollimore, Jonathan. "Homophobia and Sexual Difference." *Oxford Literary Review* 8.1–2 (1986): 5–12.

———. *Sexual Dissidence*. Oxford: Oxford University Press, 1991.

Dreyfus, Hubert L., and Paul Rabinow. *Michel Foucault: Beyond Structuralism and Hermeneutics*. 2nd ed. Chicago: University of Chicago Press, 1983.

Dworkin, Andrea. *Intercourse*. New York: The Free Press, 1987.

———. *Pornography: Men Possessing Women*. New York: Perigree, 1981.

Dyer, Richard. "Don't Look Now." *Screen* 23.3–4 (September–October 1982): 61–73.

Edelman, Lee. "Seeing Things: Representation, the Scene of Surveillance, and the Spectacle of Gay Male Sex." In *Inside/Out*, ed. Diana Fuss, pp. 93–116. London and New York: Routledge, 1991.

Ellmann, Richard, ed. *The Artist as Critic: The Critical Writings of Oscar Wilde*. Chicago: University of Chicago Press, 1968.

Ferenczi, Sándor. "The Confusion of Tongues between Adults and the Child." 1933. In Ferenczi, *Final Contributions to the Problems and Methods to Psycho-Analysis*. pp. 156–167.

———. *Final Contributions to Psycho-Analysis*. London: Hogarth, 1955.

———. *First Contributions to Psycho-Analysis*. London: Hogarth, 1952.

———. "The Nosology of Male Homosexuality (Homoerotism)." In Ferenczi, *First Contributions to Psycho-Analysis*, pp. 295–311.

Finch, Mark. "Business as Usual: Substitution and Sex in *Prick Up Your Ears* and Other Recent Gay-Themed Movies." In Shepherd and Wallis, eds., pp. 76–89.

Fineman, Joel. *Shakespeare's Perjur'd Eye: The Invention of Poetic Subjectivity in the Sonnets*. Berkeley: University of California Press, 1986.

Fischer, Lucy. "The Lady Vanishes: Women, Magic and the Movies." *Film Quarterly* 33.1 (Fall 1979): 30–40.

Fletcher, John. "Freud and His Uses: Psychoanalysis and Gay Theory." In Shepherd and Wallis, eds., pp. 90–118.

Forster, E. M. *Maurice*. London: Edward Arnold, 1971.

Foucault, Michel. *Discipline and Punish: The Birth of the Prison*. Translated by Alan Sheridan. New York: Vintage, 1979.

———. *The History of Sexuality*, vol. 1. Translated by R. Hurley. New York: Pantheon, 1978.

———. *Madness and Civilization*. Translated by Richard Howard. New York: Vintage, 1973.

———. *The Order of Things: An Archeology of the Human Sciences*. Translated by Robert Hurley. New York: Vintage, 1973.

———. *Power/Knowledge: Selected Interviews and Other Writings 1972–1977*. Edited by Colin Gordon. New York: Pantheon, 1980.

———. "The Subject and Power." Afterword in Dreyfus and Rabinow, pp. 208–226.

———. "What Is an Author?" In Harari, ed., pp. 141–160.

Freedman, Carl. "Science Fiction and Critical Theory." *Science Fiction Studies* 14 (1987): 180–200.

Freud, Sigmund. "Analysis of a Phobia in a Five-Year-Old Boy." 1909. *The Standard Edition* 10, pp. 3–149.

Beyond the Pleasure Principle. 1920. *The Standard Edition* 18, pp. 7–64.

———. "A Case of Paranoia Running Counter to the Psycho-analytic Theory of the Disease." 1915. *The Standard Edition* 14, pp. 263–272.

———. " 'A Child Is Being Beaten': A Contribution to the Study of the Origin of Sexual Perversions." 1919. *The Standard Edition* 17, pp. 175–204.

———. *The Complete Letters of Sigmund Freud to Wilhelm Fliess, 1887–1904*. Translated and edited by Jeffrey Moussaieff Masson. Cambridge, Mass.: Harvard University Press, 1985.

———. "The Dissolution of the Oedipus Complex." *The Standard Edition* 19, pp. 172–179.

—— 197.. *"The Dynamics of the Transference." 1912. The Standard Edition* 12, pp. 98–108.

———. "The Economic Problem of Masochism." 1924. *The Standard Edition* 19, pp. 157–170.

———. *The Ego and the Id*. 1923. *The Standard Edition* 19, pp. 12–59.

———. "Eine Kindheitserinnerung des Leonardo da Vinci." In *Bildende Kunst und Literatur*, ed. Alexander Mitscherlich, Angela Richards, and James Strachey, pp. 87–159. Frankfurt am Main: S. Fischer Verlag, 1982.

———. "Fetishism." 1927. *The Standard Edition* 21, pp. 147–157.

———. "Formulations on the Two Principles of Mental Functioning." 1911. *The Standard Edition* 12, pp. 215–226.

———. "Fragment of an Analysis of a Case of Hysteria." 1905 [1901]. *The Standard Edition* 7, pp. 3–122.

———. "From the History of an Infantile Neurosis." 1918 [1914]. *The Standard Edition* 17, pp. 7–123.

———. "The Future Prospects of Psycho-analytic Therapy." 1910. *The Standard Edition* 11, pp. 141–151.

———. "Infantile Genital Organization of the Libido." 1923. *The Standard Edition* 19, pp. 141–151.

———. "Instincts and Their Vicissitudes." 1915. *The Standard Edition* 14, pp. 111–140.

———. *The Interpretation of Dreams*. 1900. *The Standard Edition* 4–5.

———. *Introductory Lectures on Psychoanalysis*. 1916–17. *The Standard Edition* 15–16.

———. *Leonardo da Vinci: A Study in Psychosexuality*. Translated by A. A. Brill. New York: Vintage, 1947.

———. *Leonardo da Vinci and a Memory of His Childhood*. 1911. *The Standard Edition* 11, pp. 59–137.

———. "The Loss of Reality in Neurosis and Psychosis." *The Standard Edition* 19, pp. 183–224.

———. "Medusa's Head." 1940 [1922]. *The Standard Edition* 18, pp. 273–274.

———. "A Metapsychological Supplement to the Theory of Dreams." 1917. *The Standard Edition* 14, pp. 219–235.

———. *Moses and Monotheism: Three Essays*. 1939 [1934–38]. *The Standard Edition* 23, pp. 7–137.

———. "Mourning and Melancholia." 1917. *The Standard Edition* 14, pp. 239–258.

———. "On Narcissism: An Introduction." 1914. *The Standard Edition* 14, pp. 67–107.

———. "On Psychotherapy." 1905 [1904]. *The Standard Edition* 7, pp. 255–268.

———. "On the Universal Tendency to Debasement in the Sphere of Love." 1912. *The Standard Edition* 11, pp. 179–190.

———. "Psycho-analytic Notes on an Autobiographical Account of a Case of Paranoia (Dementia Paranoides)." *The Standard Edition* 12, pp. 3–82.

———. "The Psycho-analytic View of Psychogenic Disturbance of Vision." 1910. *The Standard Edition* 10, pp. 210–218.

———. "Remarks on the Theory of Dream Interpreation." *The Standard Edition* 12, pp. 109–121.

———. "Some Neurotic Mechanisms in Jealousy, Paranoia, and Homosexuality." 1922. *The Standard Edition* 23, pp. 223–232.

———. "Some Psychical Consequences of the Anatomical Distinction between the Sexes." 1925. *The Standard Edition* 19, pp. 241–258.

———. "The Splitting of the Ego in the Process of Self Defense." 1940 [1938]. *The Standard Edition* 23, pp. 271–278.

———. *The Standard Edition of the Complete Psychological Works of Sigmund Freud.* Translated and edited by James Strachey in collaboration with Anna Freud. 24 vols. London: The Hogarth Press, 1953–74.

———. *Three Essays on the Theory of Sexuality.* 1905. *The Standard Edition* 7, pp. 123–243.

———. "Transference." *The Standard Edition* 16, pp. 431–447.

———. "The Unconscious." 1915. *The Standard Edition* 14, pp. 161–215.

Frye, Marilyn. *The Politics of Reality: Essays in Feminist Theory.* Trumansburg, N.Y.: The Crossing Press, 1983.

Fung, Richard. "Looking for My Penis: The Eroticized Asian in Gay Video Porn." In *How Do I Look?* ed. Bad Object-Choices, pp. 145–160. Seattle: Bay Press, 1991.

Gagnier, Regina. IIdylls of the Marketplace: Oscar Wilde and the Victorian Public. Stanford: Stanford University Press, 1986.

Gallop, Jane. *Intersections: A Reading of Sade with Bataille, Blanchot, and Klossowski.* Lincoln: University of Nebraska Press, 1981.

Garner, Shirley Nelson. "Freud and Fliess: Homophobia and Seduction." In Hunter, ed., 86–109.

Gates, Henry Louis, Jr. "The Master's Pieces: On Canon Formation and the African-American Tradition." *The South Atlantic Quarterly* 89.1 (Winter 1990): 89–111.

Gawron, Jean Marc. "Introduction." In the Gregg Press Library Edition of *Dhalgren*, pp. v–xliii. Boston: Gregg Press, 1977.

Gay, Peter. *Freud: A Life for Our Time.* New York: Doubleday, 1988.

Gearhart, Suzanne. "The Scene of Psychoanalysis: The Unanswered Questions of Dora." *Diacritics* (Spring 1979): 114–136.

Genet, Jean. *Funeral Rites.* Translated by Bernard Frechtman. New York: Grove, 1969.

———. "Interview." *Playboy* (April 1964) : 45–49.

Genette, Gérard. *Narrative Discourse: An Essay in Method.* Translated by Jane E. Lewin. Ithaca: Cornell University Press, 1980.

Galman, Sander. "The Iconography of Disease." In Crimp, ed., pp. 87–108.

Glenn, Jules. "Freud, 'Dora,' and the Maid: A Study of Countertransference." *Journal of the American Psychoanalytic Association* 34.3 (1986): 591–606.

Glover, Edward. "The Therapeutic Effect of Inexact Interpretation." *Intern. J. of Psych.* 12 (1931): 397–411.

Glück, Robert. "Allegory." *Ironwood* 23 (1984): 112–118.

———. "Caricature." *Soup: New Critical Perspectives* 3 (1985): 18–28.

———. "Denny Smith." In *Faber Book of Gay Short Fiction*, ed. Edmund White, pp. 501–515. London: Faber, 1992.

———. *Elements of a Coffee Service.* San Francisco: Four Seasons Foundation, 1982.

———. "Fame." *Poetics Journal* 10 (1994). Forthcoming.

———. "Hiding in the Open." *Zyzzyva* 8.1 (Spring 1992): 77–81.

——. *Jack the Modernist*. New York: Gay Presses of New York, 1985.

——. *Margery Kemp*. London and New York: Serpent's Tail/High Risk, 1994.

——. "Marker." In Roy and Blake, eds., pp. 19–20.

——. "My Community." Unpublished manuscript.

——. "The Purple Men." Unpublished manuscript.

——. "Running on Emptiness." San Francisco Chronicle (June 4, 1989): 9.

——. "Sex Story." In Glück, *Elements of a Coffee Service*, pp. 19–44.

——. "Truth's Mirror Is No Mirror." *Poetics Journal* 7 (1987): 40–45.

——. "Violence." In Glück, *Elements of a Coffee Service*, pp. 70–96.

——. "Who Speaks for Us?: Being an Expert." In *Writing/Talks*, ed. Bob Perleman, pp. 1–6. Carbondale: Southern Illinois University Press, 1984.

——. "Workload." In Scholder and Silverberg, eds., pp. 253–257.

Gomez-Arcos, Agustin. *The Carnivorous Lamb*. Translated by William Rodarmor. Boston: Godine, 1984.

González, Patricia Elena, and Eliana Ortega, eds. *La sartèn por el mango*. Río Piedras, P. R.: Huracán, 1985.

Gossman, Lionel. "History and Literature." In Canary and Kozicki. eds., pp. 3–40.

Grosz, Elizabeth. *Jacques Lacan: A Feminist Introduction*. London: Routledge, 1990.

——. "Language and the Limits of the Body: Kristeva and Abjection." In *Futur*Fall: Excursions into Postmodernity*, ed. E. A. Grosz et al. Sydney: Pathfinder, 1987.

Guattari, Félix. "The Group and the Person." In Guattari, *Molecular Revolution*, pp. 24–44.

——. *Molecular Revolution: Psychiatry and Politics*. Translated by Rosemary Sheed. New York: Peregrin, 1984.

Gutiérrez, Ramón A. "Must We Deracinate Indians to Find Gay Roots?" *Out/Look* 1.4 (1989): 61–67.

Hall, Stuart. "Signification, Representation, Ideology: Althusser and the Post-Structuralist Debates." *Critical Studies in Mass Communication* 2.2 (June 1985): 91–114.

Halperin, David. M. *One Hundred Years of Homosexuality and Other Essays on Greek Love*. New York and London: Routledge, 1990.

Hamilton, Edith, and Huntington Cairns, eds. *The Collected Dialogues of Plato*. Princeton: Princeton University Press, 1961.

Harari, Josué V., ed. *Textual Strategies: Perspectives in Post-Structuralist Criticism*. Ithaca: Cornell University Press, 1979.

Haraway, Donna. "Situated Knowledges: The Science Question in Feminism and the Privilege of Partial Perspective." *Feminist Studies* 14.3 (1988): 575–599.

Hardesty, William H. III. "Semiotics, Space Opera and *Babel-17*. *Mosaic* 13.3–4 (Spring-Summer 1980): 63–69.

Harding, Sandra. *The Science Question in Feminism*. Ithaca: Cornell University Press, 1986.

Harlow, Barbara. *Resistance Literature*. New York and London: Methuen, 1987.

Haug, Frigga, et al. *Female Sexualization*. Translated by Erica Carter. London: Verso, 1987.

Heath, Stephen. "Film and System, Terms of an Analysis," Part II *Screen* 16.2 (1975): 91–113.

——. *Questions of Cinema*. Bloomington: Indiana University Press, 1981.

———. "The Turn of the Subject." In Burnett, ed., pp. 26–45.

Hemphill, Essex. *Ceremonies.* New York: Plume, 1992.

Hemphill, Essex, and Joseph Beam, eds. *Brother to Brother.* Boston: Alyson, 1991.

Henriques, Julian, et al. *Changing the Subject: Psychology, Social Regulation and Subjectivity.* London: Methuen, 1984.

Hertz, Neil. "Dora's Secrets, Freud's Techniques." In Bernheimer and Kahane, eds., pp. 221–242.

Hindess, Barry, and Paul Hirst. *Mode of Production and Social Formulation.* London: Macmillan, 1977.

Hirsch, Marianne, and Evelyn Fox Keller, eds. *Conflicts in Feminism.* New York: Routledge, 1990.

Hirst, Paul Q. "Althusser and the Theory of Ideology." *Economy and Society* 5.4 (1976): 385–412.

Hocquenghem, Guy. *Homosexual Desire.* Translated by Daniella Dangoor. London: Allison and Busby, 1978.

Holloway, Wendy. "Gender Difference and the Production of Subjectivity." In Henriques et al., pp. 227–263.

hooks, bell. *Feminist Theory: From Margin to Center.* Boston: South End Press, 1984.

Hunter, Dianne, ed. *Seduction and Theory: Readings of Gender, Representation, and Rhetoric.* Urbana and Chicago: University of Illinois Press, 1989.

Huyssen, Andreas. "Mass Culture as Woman: Modernism's Other." In Modleski, ed., pp. 188–207.

Hyde, H. Montgomery. *The Three Trials of Oscar Wilde.* New York, 1956.

Irigaray, Luce. *The Ethics of Sexual Difference.* Translated by Carolyn Burke. Ithaca: Cornell University Press, 1992.

———. *Speculum of the Other Woman.* Translated by Gillian C. Gill. Ithaca: Cornell University Press, 1985.

———. *The Sex Which Is Not One.* Translated by Catherine Porter, with Caroline Burke. Ithaca: Cornell, 1985.

———. "Women's Exile." *Ideology and Consciousness* 1 (1977): 62–76.

Jackson, Earl, Jr. "Explicit Instruction: Teaching Gay Male Sexuality in a Literature Class." In *Professions of Desire: Lesbian and Gay Literary Studies*, ed. George Haggerty and Bonnie Zimmerman; pp. 136–155. New York: MLA, 1995.

———. *Fantastic Living: The Speculative Autobiographies of Samuel R. Delany.* New York and London: Oxford University Press, forthcoming.

———. "Kabuki Narratives of Male Homoerotic Desire in Saikaku and Mishima." *Theatre Journal* 41.4 (December 1989): 459–477.

———. "Phallic Imperialism: Sexual Politics in and around Mishima Yukio." Forthcoming in *Critical Japan* 2 (Spring 1995).

———. "Responsibility of and to Differences: Theorizing Race and Ethnicity in Lesbian and Gay Studies." In Thompson and Tyagi, eds., pp. 131–161.

———. Review of *Pornography and Representation in Greece and Rome*, ed. Amy Richlin (Oxford: Oxford University Press, 1991). *Bryn Mawr Classical Review* 3.5 (1992): 387–396.

———. "Robert Glück." In *Contemporary Gay American Novelists: A Bio-bibliographical Critical Sourcebook*, ed. Emmanuel S. Nelson. pp. 161–166. Westport, Conn.: Greenwood Press, 1993.

———. "Scandalous Subjects: Robert Glück's Embodied Narratives." In de Lauretis, ed., *Queer Theory*, pp. 112–134.

Jacobs, Naomi. "Kathy Acker and the Plagiarized Self." *The Review of Contemporary Fiction* 9.3 (1989): 50–55.

Jameson, Fredric. "Imaginary and Symbolic in Lacan: Marxism, Psychoanalytic Criticism, and the Problem of the Subject." *Yale French Studies* 55/56 (1977): 338–395.

———. *The Political Unconscious: Narrative as a Socially Symbolic Act*. Ithaca: Cornell University Press, 1981.

JanMohammed, Abdul, and David Lloyd. "Introduction: Toward a Theory of Minority Discourse." *The Nature and Context of Minority Discourse*, ed. Abdul JanMohammed and David Lloyd, *Cultural Critique* 6 (Spring 1987): 5–12.

Jardine, Alice, and Paul Smith, eds. *Men in Feminism*. New York and London: Methuen, 1987.

Jarman, Derek. *Dancing Ledge*. Edited by Shaun Allen. London: Quartet Books, 1984.

———. *Derek Jarman's* Caravaggio. London: Thames and Hudson, 1986.

———. *Modern Nature: The Journals of Derek Jarman*. London: Century, 1991.

Jenkyns, Richard. *The Victorians and Ancient Greece*. Cambridge: Harvard University Press, 1980.

Jones, Ernst. *Sigmund Freud: Life and Work*. 3 vols. London: Hogarth, 1953, 1955. 1957.

Karr, John. "Triple Play: Interview with Steve Abbott, Robert Glück, and Kevin Killian." *Bay Area Reporter* (December 14, 1989): 28, 36.

Keller, Evelyn Fox. *Reflections on Gender and Science*. New Haven and London: Yale University Press, 1985.

Kelly, Joan. *Women, History, and Theory*. Chicago: University of Chicago Press, 1984.

Killian, Kevin. *Bedrooms Have Windows*. New York: Amethyst, 1989.

———. "The Boys of Fiction." Lecture given at the "Worlds without Borders" Conference, Vancouver, August 10, 1990.

———. *Brother and Sister*. Illustrations by Brett Reichman. San Francisco: Jonathan Hammer Publications, 1994.

———. *Desiree*. Berkeley: Exempli Gratia, 1986.

———. "A Love Like That." Unpublished manuscript.

———. "On Robert Creeley/On Pornography/On Loretta Young." Unpublished manuscript.

———. "Pasiphae: The Appeal of Dallas and Dynasty." *Soup: New Critical Perspectives*, ed. Bruce Boone, no. 4 (1985): 73–78.

———. "Poison." Unpublished lecture, Intersection Panel, "What's in a Name?" April 27, 1987.

———. "The Real and the Unreal: Hayley Mills vs. Annette." In Roy and Blake, eds., pp. 8–9.

———. "Santa." Unpublished manuscript.

———. "Sex Writing and the New Narrative." *Sodomite Invasion Review* (August 1990): 13.

———. *Shy*. Freedom, Calif.: Crossing, 1989.

———. "Spreadeagle." *Front* (July/August 1991): 11–13.

———. "Who Is Kevin Killian?" *Avec* 7, ed. Norma Cole (1994): 22–29.

King, Katie, "Producing Sex, Theory, and Culture: Gay/Straight Remappings in Contemporary Feminism." In Hirsch and Keller, eds., pp. 82–101.

Knight, Damon, ed. *Turning Points*. New York: Harper and Row, 1977.

Koestenbaum, Wayne. *Double Talk: The Erotics of Male Literary Collaboration*. New York and London: Routledge, 1989.

Kristeva, Julia. *Desire in Language*. Edited by Leon S. Roudiez. Translated by Thomas Gora et al. New York: Columbia University Press, 1980.

——. *The Powers of Horror: An Essay in Abjection*. Translated by Leon S. Roudiez. New York: Columbia, 1982.

——. "Within the Microcosm of 'The Talking Cure.' " Translated by Thomas Gora and Margaret Waller. In *Interpreting Lacan*, ed. Joseph H. Smith and William Kerrigan, pp. 33–48. New Haven: Yale University Press, 1983.

La Capra, Dominick. *History and Criticism*. Ithaca: Cornell University Press, 1985.

Lacan, Jacques. *Écrits*. Translated by Alan Sheridan. New York: Norton, 1977.

——. *The Four Fundamental Concepts of Psychoanalysis*. Translated by Alan Sheridan. New York: Norton, 1978.

——. "The Meaning of the Phallus." In Lacan and the école freudienne, pp. 74–85.

——. *Le Séminaire. Livre I: Les Écrits techniques de Freud*. Edited by Jacques Alain-Miller. Paris: Seuil, 1975.

——. *The Seminar of Jacques Lacan. Edited by Jacques-Alain Miller. Book II: The Ego in Freud's Theory and in the Technique of Psychoanalysis, 1954–1955*, trans. Sylvana Tomaselli. New York and London: Norton, 1988.

——. "Some Reflections on the Ego." *International Journal of Psychoanalysis* 34 (1953): 11–17.

Lacan, Jacques, and the école freudienne. *Feminine Sexuality*. Translated by Jacqueline Rose. Edited by Juliet Mitchell and Jacqueline Rose. New York and London: Pantheon, 1985.

Laclau, Ernesto, and Chantal Mouffe. *Hegemony and Socialist Strategy: Towards a Radical Democratic Politics*. Translated by Winston Moore and Paul Cammack. London and New York: Verso, 1985.

——. "Postmarxism without Apologies." *New Left Review* 166 (November–December 1987): 79–106.

Lancaster, Roger N. "Subject Honor and Object Shame: The Construction of Male Homosexuality and Stigma in Nicaragua." *Ethnology* 27.2 (1987): 111–114.

Laplanche, Jean. *Life and Death in Psychoanalysis*. Translated by Jeffrey Mehlman. Baltimore: Johns Hopkins University Press, 1976.

——. *New Foundations for Psychoanalysis*. Translated by David Macey. Oxford: Basil Blackwell, 1989.

——. "To Situate Sublimation." Translated by Richard Miller. *October* 28 (Spring 1984): 7–26.

Laplanche, Jean, and Jean-Bertrand Pontalis. "Fantasy and the Origins of Sexuality." In *Formations of Fantasy*, ed. Victor Burgin, James Donald, and Cora Kaplan, pp. 5–34. London and New York: Methuen, 1986.

——. *The Language of Psychoanalysis*. Translated by Donald Nicholson-Smith. New York: Norton, 1973.

Latsky, Eric. "Dennis Cooper Hits Home." *L.A. Weekly* (July 13–19, 1990): 20–22, 24–27.

Lemaire, Anika. *Jacques Lacan*. Translated by David Macey. London and New York: Routledge and Kegan Paul, 1979.

Levine, Sherrie. "Art in the (Re)Making." *Art News 85* (May 1986): 96–97.

Lewes, Kenneth. *The Psychoanalytic Theory of Male Homosexuality.* New York: New American Library, 1988.

Leyland, Winston. "Introduction." In Leyland, ed., pp. 5–19.

Leyland, Winston, ed. *Teleny: A Novel Attributed to Oscar Wilde.* San Francisco: Gay Sunshine, 1984.

Linfield, Elliott. "Pillars of the New Narrative: Interview with Kevin Killian and Dodie Bellamy." *Bay Area Reporter* (April 1, 1993): 31, 39.

Lotringer, Sylvère. "Devoured by Myths: Interview with Kathy Acker." In Acker, pp. 1–24.

MacCabe, Colin, ed. *The Talking Cure. London and New York: Methuen, 1981.*

Macherey. Pierre. *A Theory of Literary Production.* Translated by Geoffrey Wall. London: Routledge and Kegan Paul, 1978.

MacKinnon, Catherine. *Feminism Unmodified: Discourses on Life and Law.* Cambridge, Mass., and London: Harvard University Press, 1987.

Mannoni, Octave. *Clefs pour l'imaginaire ou l'autre scene.* Paris: Editions du Seuil, 1969.

Marcus, Steven. *Representations.* New York: Random House, 1975.

Marin, Louis. "Disneyland: A Degenerate Utopia." *Glyph* 1 (1977): 50–66.

Martin, Biddy. "Feminism, Criticism, and Foucault." *New German Critique* 27 (Fall 1982): 3–30.

Mayne, Judith. *The Woman at the Keyhole.* Bloomington: Indiana University Press, 1990.

McCaffery, Larry, and Sinda Gregory, eds. *Alive and Writing: Interviews with American Authors of the 1980s.* Urbana and Chicago: University of Illinois Press, 1989.

McHale, Brian. *Postmodern Fiction.* New York: Methuen, 1987.

———. "Unspeakable Sentences, Unnatural Acts: Linguistics and Poetics Revisited." *Poetics Today* 4.1 (1983): 17–45.

Mercer, Kobena. "Imaging the Black Man's Sex." In *Photography/Politics: Two*, ed. Pat Holland, Jo Spence, and Simon Watney, pp. 61–69. London: Methuen, 1987.

Merchant, Carolyn. *The Death of Nature: Women, Ecology, and the Scientific Revolution.* New York: Harper and Row, 1980.

Merleau-Ponty, Maurice. *The Phenomenology of Perception.* Translated by Colin Smith. London and Henley: Routledge and Kegan Paul, 1962.

———. *The Primacy of Perception.* Evanston, Ill.: Northwestern University Press, 1964.

Metz, Christian. *The Imaginary Signifier.* Translated by Celia Britton, Annwyl Williams, Ben Brewster, and Alfred Guzzetti. Bloomington: Indiana University Press, 1982.

Meyer, Richard. "Interview: Dennis Cooper." In *Cuz*, ed. Richard Meyer, pp. 52–69. New York: The Poetry Project, 1988.

Miller, D. A. *The Novel and the Police.* Berkeley: University of California Press, 1988.

Miller, Jacques-Alain. "Suture (Elements of the Logic of the Signifier)." *Screen* 18.4 (1977–78): 24–34.

Miller, Nancy K. "Arachnologies: The Woman, the Text, and the Critic." In Miller, ed., pp. 270–295.

Miller, Nancy K., ed. *The Poetics of Gender.* New York: Columbia University Press, 1986.

Mink, Louis O. "Narrative Form as a Cognitive Instrument." In Canary and Kozicki, eds., pp. 129–149.

Mitchell, Juliet. "Introduction—I." In Lacan and the école freudienne, pp. 1–26.

Modleski, Tania. "Feminism and the Power of Interpretation." In de Lauretis, ed., *Feminist Studies/Critical Studies*, pp. 121–138.
——. *Feminism without Women*. New York and London: Routledge, 1992.
Modleski, Tania, ed. *Studies in Entertainment: Critical Approaches to Mass Culture*. Bloomington and Indianapolis: Indiana University Press, 1986.
Montrelay, Michele. "L'Appareillage." *Cahiers Confrontations* 6 (printemps 1982): 33–43.
——. *L'Ombre et le nom*. Paris: Minuit, 1977.
Moss, Donald. "On a Regressive Feature of Applied Psychoanalysis: From Freud's Leonardo to Chasseguet-Smirgel's *Creativity and Perversion*." *American Imago* 49.1 (Spring 1992): 63–79.
Müller, Gunther. "Erzählzeit und erzählte Zeit." In *Morphologische Poetik*. Tübingen. 1968.
Mulvey, Laura. "Afterthoughts on 'Visual Pleasure and Narrative Cinema' Inspired by King Vidor's *Duel in the Sun* (1946)." Originally published in *Framework* 15–17 (1981): 12–15. Reprinted in Mulvey, *Visual and Other Pleasures*, pp. 29–38.
——. *Visual and Other Pleasures*. Bloomington and Indianapolis: Indiana University Press, 1989.
——. "Visual Pleasure and Narrative Cinema." *Screen* 16.3 (1975) : 6–18. Reprinted in Mulvey, *Visual and Other Pleasures*, pp. 14–26.
Nelson, Cary, and Lawrence Grossberg, eds. *Marxism and the Interpretation of Culture*. Urbana: University of Illinois Press, 1988.
Nelson, John C. *The Renaissance Theory of Love*. New York: Columbia University Press, 1958.
Nichols, Peter, ed. *Science Fiction at Large*. London: Victor Gollancz, 1976.
Nietzsche, Friedrich. *The Wall to Power*. Translated by Walter Kaufmann and R. J. Hollingdale. New York: Vintage, 1967.
Nowell-Smith, Press H. "Historical Facts." In *La Philosophie de l'histoire et la pratique historienne d'aujourd'hui*, ed. David Carr et al., pp. 317–323. Ottawa: University of Ottawa Press, 1982.
Orr, D. W. "Transference and Counter-transference: A Historical Survey." *J. Amer. Psychoanal. Assn.* 2 (1954): 621–670.
Owens, Craig. "Outlaws: Gay Men in Feminism." In Jardine and Smith, eds., pp. 219–232.
The Oxford English Dictionary. 12 vols. Oxford and London: Oxford University Press, 1933. Rev. ed. 1971.
Pajaczkowska, Claire. "The Heterosexual Presumption: A Contribution to the Debate on Pornography." *Screen* 22.1 (1981): 79–94.
Pater, Walter. "The Age of Athletic Prizemen: A Chapter in Greek Art." In *Greek Studies*, pp. 242–269. London: Macmillan, 1928.
——. *Plato and Platonism*. New York: Macmillan, 1901.
——. "Winckelmann." In *Walter Pater: Three Major Texts (The Renaissance, Appreciations, and Imaginary Portraits)*, ed. William E. Buckler, pp. 183–216. New York and London: NYU, 1986.
Patton, Cindy. *Sex and Germs: The Politics of AIDS*. Boston: South End, 1985.
Peirce, Charles Sanders. *Collected Papers*. 8 vols. Cambridge, Mass.: Harvard University Press, 1931–1958.

Pequingey, Joseph. *Such Is My Love: A Study of Shakespeare's Sonnets.* Chicago: University of Chicago Press, 1985.

Peri Rossi, Cristina. "Una fantasía gay: El martirio de san Sebastían," In *Fantasías eroticas,* pp. 99–110. Madrid: Temas de Hoy, 1991.

Pietz, William. "The Problem of the Fetish, I." *Res* 9 (1985): 5–17.

Plato. *The Symposium.* Translated by Michael Joyce. In Hamilton and Cairns, eds., pp. 526–574.

Preston, John. "How Dare You Even Think These Things?" In Scholder and Silverberg, eds., pp. 1–16.

Pronger, Brian. *The Arena of Masculinity: Sports, Homosexuality, and the Meaning of Sex.* New York: St. Martin's, 1990.

Rabinbach, Anson, and Jessica Benjamin. "Foreword." In Theweleit, vol. 2, pp. ix–xxv.

Rabinow, Paul. "Representations Are Social Facts: Modernity and Post-Modernity in Anthropology." In Clifford and Marcus, eds., pp. 234–261.

Rechy, John. *The Sexual Outlaw.* New York: Grove Press, 1977.

Reik, Theodore. *Masochism in Sex and Society.* Translated by Margaret H. Beigel and Gertrude M. Kurth. New York: Grove, 1962.

Rich, B. Ruby. "Feminism and Sexuality in the 1980's." *Feminist Studies* 12 (1986): 525–561.

Richardson, William J. "Lacan and the Subject of Psychoanalysis." In Smith and Kerrigan, eds., pp. 51–74.

Rimmon-Kenan, Shlomith. *Narrative Fiction.* New York: Methuen, 1983.

Robb, Nesca A. *Neoplatonism of the Italian Renaissance.* New York: Octagon, 1968.

Rose, Jacqueline. "Dora: Fragment of an Analysis." *m/f* 2 (1978): 5–21.

———. "Feminine Sexuality: Jacques Lacan and the *école freudienne.*" In Rose, *Sexuality in the Field of Vision,* pp. 49–81.

———. *Sexuality in the Field of Vision.* London: Verso, 1986.

Rossi, Paolo. *Francis Bacon: From Magic to Science.* Chicago: University of Chicago Press, 1968.

Rombotham, Sheila, and Jeffrey Weeks. *Socialism and the New Life: The Personal and Sexual Politics of Edward Carpenter and Havelock Ellis.* London: Pluto, 1974.

Rowse, Alfred Leslie. *Homosexuals in History: A Study of Ambivalence in Society, History, and the Arts.* New York: Macmillan, 1977.

Roy, Camille, and Nayland Blake, eds. *Dear World.* San Francisco: n.p., 1992.

Rubin, Gayle. "The Leather Menace: Comments on Politics and S/M." In *Coming to Power: Writings and Graphics on Lesbian S/M,* ed. Samois Collective, pp. 192–225. Palo Alto: Up Press, 1982.

———. "Thinking Sex: Notes for a Radical Theory of the Politics of Sexuality." In Vance, ed., pp. 267–319.

———. "The Traffic in Women: Notes on the 'Political Economy' of Sex." In *Toward an Anthropology of Women,* ed. Reyna R. Reiter, pp. 157–210. New York: Monthly Review Press, 1975.

Russ, Joanna. "Alien Monsters." In Knight, ed., pp. 132–143.

———. "Amor Vincit Foeminam: The Battle of the Sexes in Science Fiction." *Science Fiction Studies* 7 (1980): 2–15.

———. "The Second Inquisition." In Joanna Russ, *The Adventures of Alyx,* pp. 163–192. New York: Pocket, 1983.

——. "Towards an Aesthetic of Science Fiction." *Science Fiction Studies* 2.2 (1975): 112–119.

Safouan, Moustapha. "Representation and Pleasure." Translated by Ben Brewster. In MacCabe, ed., pp. 75–89.

Salas, Floyd. *Tattoo the Wicked Cross*. New York: Grove, 1967.

Sartre, Jean-Paul. *Being and Nothingness: An Essay in Ontological Phenomenology*. Translated by Hazel Barnes. New York: Washington Square Press, 1966.

——. *The Transcendence of the Ego*. Translated by Forrest Williams and Robert Kirkpatrick. New York: Noonday, 1957.

Scholder, Amy, and Ira Silverberg, eds. *High Risk*. New York: Plume, 1991.

Schor, Naomi. "Dreaming Dissymmetry: Barthes, Foucault, and Sexual Difference." In Jardine and Smith, eds., pp. 99–110.

Schur, Max. *Freud: Living and Dying*. London: The Hogarth Press, 1972.

Schwenger, Peter. "The Masculine Mode." In *Speaking of Gender*, ed. Elaine Showalter, pp. 101–112. London: Routledge, 1989.

Scott, Joan W. "The Evidence of Experience." *Critical Inquiry* 17 (Summer 1991): 773–797.

Scott, Joan Wallach. *Gender and the Politics of History*. New York: Columbia University Press, 1988.

Shakespeare, William. *Sonnets*. Edited with Introduction and Commentary by A. L. Rowse. New York: Harper and Row, 1964.

Shepherd, Simon, and Mick Wallis, eds. *Coming on Strong: Gay Politics and Culture*. London: Unwin Hyman, 1989.

Sherwood, M. *The Logic of Explanation in Psychoanalysis*. New York: Academic, 1969.

Shurin, Aaron. *Narrativity*. Los Angeles: Sun and Moon, 1990.

Siebenband, Paul Alcuin. "The Beginnings of Gay Cinema in Los Angeles: The Industry and the Audience." Ph.D. dissertation, University of Southern California, 1975.

Silverman, Kaja. "Fragments of a Fashionable Discourse." In Modleski, ed., pp. 139–152.

——. "Histoire d'O: The Story of a Disciplined and Punished Body." *enclitic* 7.2 (1983): 63–81.

——. *Male Subjectivity at the Margins*. New York: Routledge, 1992.

——. "Masochism and Male Subjectivity." *camera obscura* 17 (May 1988): 31–66.

——. *The Subject of Semiotics*. London and New York: Oxford University Press, 1983.

Smith, Bruce R. *Homosexual Desire in Shakespeare's England*. Chicago and London: Chicago University Press, 1991.

Smith, Joseph H., and William Kerrigan, eds. *Interpreting Lacan*. New Haven and London: Yale University Press, 1983.

Smith, Paul. *Discerning the Subject*. Minneapolis: University of Minnesota Press, 1989.

——. "Vas." *camera obscura* 17 (1988): 89–112.

Spicer, Jack. "Fifteen False Propositions about God." In *The Collected Books of Jack Spicer*, ed. Robin Blazer, pp. 86–94. Santa Barbara: Black Sparrow, 1980.

Sprengnether, Madelon. "Enforcing Oedipus: Freud and Dora." In Bernheimer and Kahane, eds., pp. 254–275.

Steiner, K. Leslie. "Return . . . A Preface." Appendix to Delany, *The Bridge of Lost Desire*, pp. 298–310.

——. "Some Remarks toward a Reading of *Dhalgren*." In Delany, *The Straits of Messina*, pp. 57–92.

———. "Trouble on Triton." In Delany, *The Straits of Messina*, p. 93–98.

Strategies Collective. "Building a New Left: An Interview with Ernesto Laclau." *Strategies: A Journal of Theory, Culture, and Politics* 1 (Fall 1988): 10–28.

Sturgeon, Theodore. "Derm Fool." In *Starshine*, pp. 9–25. New York: Jove, 1977.

Summers, Claude J. *Gay Fictions from Wilde to Stonewall: Studies in a Male Homosexual Literary Tradition*. New York: Continuum, 1990.

Terry, Jennifer. "Theorizing Deviant Historiography." In de Lauretis, ed., *Queer Theory*, pp. 55–74.

Theweleit, Klaus. *Male Fantasies*. 2 vols. Translated by Erica Carter and Chris Turner. Minneapolis: University of Minnesota Press, 1987–89.

Thiele, Beverly. "Coming-of-Age: Edward Carpenter on Sex and Reproduction." In Brown, ed., pp. 100–125.

Thompson, Becky W., and Sangeeta Tyagi, eds. *Beyond a Dream Deferred: Multicultural Education and the Politics of Excellence*. Minneapolis: University of Minnesota Press, 1993.

Tort, Michel. "The Freudian Concept of Representative (Repräsentanz)." *Economy and Society* 3 (1974): 18–40.

Tucker, Scott. "Radical Feminism and Gay Male Porn." In Kimmel, ed., pp. 263–276.

Vance, Carol S., ed. *Pleasure and Danger: Exploring Female Sexuality*. Boston: Routledge and Kegan Paul, 1984.

Voloshinov, V. N. *Marxism and the Philosophy of Language*. Translated by Ladislav Matejka and I. R. Titunik. Cambridge, Mass., and London: Harvard University Press, 1973.

Watney, Simon. "The Banality of Gender." *Oxford Literary Review* 8.1–2 (1986): 13–21.

———. *Policing Desire: Pornography, AIDS, and the Media*. Minneapolis: University of Minnesota Press, 1987.

———. "The Spectacle of Aids." In Crimp, ed., pp. 71–86.

Waugh, Tom. "Hard to Imagine: Gay Erotic Cinema in the Postwar Era." *CineAction!* 10 (October 1987): 65–72.

———. "Men's Pornography: Gay vs. Straight." *Jump Cut* 30 (March 1985): 30–35.

———. "Photography, Passion, and Power." *The Body Politic* (March 1984): 29–33.

Weedman, Jane. "Art and Artist Role in Delany's Works." In *Voices for the Future*, vol. 3, ed. Thomas D. Clareson and Thomas L. Wymer, pp. 151–185. Bowling Green, Ohio: Bowling Green University Press, 1984.

White, Edmund. *A Boy's Own Story*. London: Pan, 1983.

Whitford, Margaret. *Luce Irigaray: Philosophy in the Feminine*. London: Routledge, 1991.

Wilde, Oscar. *The Artist as Critic: Critical Writings of Oscar Wilde*. Edited by Richard Ellmann. Chicago: University of Chicago Press, 1982.

———. *Complete Short Fiction*. Edited by Isobel Murray. Oxford: Oxford University Press, 1979.

———. "The Critic as Artist." In Wilde, *The Artist as Critic*, pp. 340–408.

———. *The Picture of Dorian Gray*. New York: Penguin, 1988.

———. *The Portrait of W. H.* Edited by Vyvyan Holland. London: Methuen, 1921.

———. "The Portrait of W. H." In *Complete Short Fiction*, ed. Isobel Murray. Oxford: Oxford University Press, 1979.

———. "Preface to *The Picture of Dorian Gray*." In Wilde, *The Artist as Critic*, pp. 235–236.

Williams, Linda. "Film Body: An Implantation of Perversions." *Ciné-Tracts* (Winter 1981): 19–35.

Williams, Raymond. "Realism, Naturalism, and Their Alternatives." In Burnett, ed., pp. 121–126.

Willis, Sharon. "A Symptomatic Narrative." *Diacritics* (Spring 1983): 43–60.

Winkler, John J. *The Constraints of Desire: The Anthropology of Sex and Gender in Ancient Greece.* New York and London: Routledge, 1989.

Winnett, Susan. "Coming Unstrung: Women, Men, Narrative, and Principles of Pleasure." *PMLA* (May 1990): 505–518.

Wittig, Monique. "The Mark of Gender." In Miller, ed., pp. 63–73.

———. "Point of View: Universal or Particular?" *Feminist Issues* (Fall 1983): 63–69.

———. "The Straight Mind." *Feminist Issues* (Summer 1980): 103–111.

Wojnarowicz, David. *Close to the Knives.* New York: Vintage, 1991.

Yingling, Thomas. "How the Eye Is Caste: Robert Mapplethorpe and the Limits of Controversy." *Discourse* 12.2 (Spring/Summer 1989): 3–28.

Index

Earl Jackson, Jr., Associate Professor of Japanese Literature, teaches on the Literature Board of the University of California, Santa Cruz. His articles have appeared in *PMLA*, *differences*, *Harvard Journal of Asiatic Studies*, and *Theatre Journal*. His performance pieces have been staged in Minneapolis, Seattle, Tokyo, and Santa Cruz. His most recent play, *He Kisses Like a Danish Summer*, premiered in 1992, directed and designed by N. Bonnie Reese.